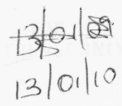

'THE LAND FOR THE PEOPLE'

'THE LAND FOR THE PEOPLE'

THE LAND QUESTION IN
INDEPENDENT IRELAND

TERENCE DOOLEY

Published by the
UNIVERSITY COLLEGE DUBLIN PRESS
PREAS CHOLÁISTE OLLSCOILE BHAILE ÁTHA CLIATH

2004

First published 2004
by University College Dublin Press
Newman House, 86 St Stephen's Green
Dublin 2, Ireland
www.ucdpress.ie

ISBN 1 904558 14 3 hb
ISBN 1 904558 15 1 pb

CIP data available from the British Library

Typeset in Ireland in Adobe Caslon and Bodoni Oldstyle
by Elaine Shiels, Bantry, County Cork
Text design by Lyn Davies
Printed in England on acid-free paper
by MPG Books Ltd, Bodmin, Cornwall

For
Conor and Áine
with my deepest affection

*

Contents

Acknowledgements

One of the pleasing aspects of completing a work such as this is the opportunity it offers to thank all of those who helped along the way. I would like to begin by thanking the National University of Ireland for honouring me with the NUI Post-Doctoral Fellowship in the Humanities, which allowed me to carry out the research upon which this book is based.

During the time I was researching and writing this book, I was fortunate to have been attached to the Department of Modern History at the NUI Maynooth. It was a great pleasure to continue my long association with the department and to once again enjoy the fellowship and unfailing courtesy of colleagues there. This is an appropriate place to express long overdue thanks to Professor Colm Lennon and Professor Jackie Hill for their inspirational teaching. Ann Donoghue and Catherine Heslin have been extremely patient and very helpful at all times. Thanks to Dr. Raymond Gillespie for allowing me to share his office at a crucial time in the completion of this work. I thoroughly enjoyed the academic stimulation provided by the postgraduate research seminars.

As always, I am particularly indebted to Professor Vincent Comerford who was one of the first to believe that this book could be written. The amount of time and energy he invested in this project and his unfailing encouragement throughout is gratefully acknowledged. I am also especially grateful to Professor Peter Hart who read an earlier draft and whose erudite comments benefited me greatly, as did his very heartening comments, which were greatly appreciated. As ever, I would like to take full responsibility for any errors that may remain herein.

For pointing me in the direction of sources and sharing their expertise and ideas with me, I would like to thank Dr Patrick Commins, Dr Enda Delaney, Dr Louise Fuller, Dr Brian Hanley, Dr Seamus Helferty, Ms Aideen Ireland, Professor David Seth Jones, Jim King, an tUasal Seamus Mac Gabhann, Dr Fearghal McGarry and Ms Ann Matthews. Ms Nellie O Cleirigh shared some valuable insights with me. Mr Jim Keenan drew the maps contained herein with his usual expertise and efficiency.

I would like to thank (in some sort of alphabetical order) the directors, governing bodies and staffs of the following: Irish Architectural Archives; National Archives, Dublin; National Library of Ireland; Library of NUI Maynooth; Monaghan County Council Offices; Records Branch of the Irish Land Commission; University College Dublin, Archives Department; Library of Trinity College, Dublin; Valuation Office, Dublin.

Thanks to all those who agreed to be interviewed but who preferred to remain anonymous. Regarding the acquisition of untenanted lands, I learned a great deal from 25 country-house families I interviewed while researching my report on *The Future for Irish Country Houses?* (2003). Their story in relation to the Land Commission deserves elucidation in its own right.

Thanks to Ms Barbara Mennell and the staff of UCD Press for guiding this work through its various stages in such a professional manner.

Around the same time that the manuscript of this book was sent to UCD Press, our beautiful daughter, Áine, was born. She has brought indescribable joy to Annette, Conor and me. Annette and Conor have been patient and supportive as ever. Conor's ability to make me laugh in the face of all adversity is a quality I hope he always carries with him in life.

As ever, thanks to my mother and father, the most spirited octogenarians one could hope to meet and, of course, to brothers, sisters, nieces, nephews and friends who help us out in so many ways.

TERENCE DOOLEY
Maynooth
December 2003

Maps

Abbreviations

ACC	Agricultural Credit Corporation
Cd/Cmd	Command Papers
CICMR	County inspector's confidential monthly report
DJ	Department of Justice
DT	Department of the Taoiseach
HC	House of Commons
ILC	Irish Land Commission
NA	National Archives of Ireland
NLI	National Library of Ireland
PRO	Public Record Office (London)
RIC	Royal Irish Constabulary
SO	Stationery Office
TCD	Trinity College, Dublin
TD	Teachta Dála (Member of Dáil Éireann)
UCD	University College Dublin
UIL	United Irish League

ONE

INTRODUCTION

Land is the most combustible subject in Ireland
KEVIN O'SHIEL
quoted in *The Irish Times*, 11 Nov. 1966

The Irish country man believes that nature intended him to be a farmer,
and there is an idea that there is enough land for all.
PATRICK HOGAN
Minister for Agriculture, quoted in *Manchester Guardian*,
10 May 1923.

I am a townsman from Tipperary but the people of my generation were reared on
questions concerning land settlement. When we were young we used to hear slogans such
as 'The land for the people and the road for the bullock'; 'We build the homes of Tipperary';
'Undo the clearances', and so on. Even the songs we were taught were all concerned with
resettlement on the lands of Ireland. The books we read – Kickham's stories, and others –
all concerned this question of land settlement and, consequently, even the people in the
towns, who stood by the people of the countryside in the old days, when we were fighting
against the tyranny of the landlord, had a great interest in this question of land settlement.
SENATOR FRANK LOUGHMAN
Seanad Debates, vol. 37, 4 May 1950, 1762.

—

I LANDOWNERSHIP AND IRISH MINDSETS

It is often difficult to appreciate or sympathise with the Irish psyche that
attaches an almost obsessive importance to the ownership of land. Historically
this attachment was largely conditioned by two factors. Firstly, the industrial
revolution of the nineteenth century failed to make any positive impact on
Ireland outside the North East. The area with which this work is concerned –
the 26 counties that now constitute the Republic of Ireland – remained predominantly un-industrialised and rural where the vast majority of the people,
ranging from landed magnates who owned tens of thousands of acres to cottiers
who rented less than half an acre, were dependent in varying degrees upon the
land for a livelihood or quite simply for survival. With the ending of the practice

I

of subdivision in the post-Famine period, access to land became more restricted while the desire (and need) for access was simultaneously intensified.

Secondly, the nineteenth century saw the consolidation of the ideology that promoted land as the basis of the nation, where landownership became indelibly related to the other great national issues of identity and independence. From the 1860s, Fenian revolutionaries were promoting the idea that a successful political revolution would result in the redistribution of Irish lands.[1] By the 1880s, prominent separatists such as John Devoy, one time Fenian and later Clan na Gael leader, clearly associated the overthrow of the landlord system with the political struggle for independence, recognising the role that the highlighting of agrarian grievances could play in the stimulation of political revolutionary activity amongst the lower strata (at least) of the agricultural classes. Most pertinently, R. V. Comerford has concluded that 'Much of the rhetoric of nationality is concerned with justifying possession of the land' and that in the Irish case:

> the myth of migratory origins sits side by side in silent contradiction to that of the indigenous people, which in turn is explicitly juxtaposed with the myth of the alien settlers. Nationality has provided, in the antinomies of native and newcomer, the most widely accepted, if not the most informative, of keys to the struggle for control of the land that has been an enduring constant of Irish life for many centuries past. As with the Magyars, the Poles and the French, so too in modern Ireland, the lords of the soil were supposed to be of different stock from the rest of the population. In the 1880s, the Irish nation was re-imagined so as to exclude them.[2]

After 1923, the great debate on who actually owned the land was effectively decided upon by an independent Irish parliament, Dáil Éireann, when it legislated for the remaining tenanted lands in the hands of landlords to be compulsorily acquired and – to relieve congestion – for the redistribution of other untenanted lands amongst farmers, 'the nation-forming class' identified by Emmet Larkin as the class for whom and by whom the Irish state was created and consolidated.[3] The importance of this should be understood. In the 1930s, George O'Brien, Professor of Political Economics in University College Dublin, contended that there was never likely to be a conflict in the Free State between members of the farming class and the nation for both were *prima facie* identical – farmers and their dependants made up the great majority of the population.[4] In the 1940s, Bishop Cornelius Lucey proclaimed: 'For the rural families are the well springs from which the towns and cities replenish themselves, and if they are drying up, then inevitably we are doomed to wither away as a nation'.[5] The inference was that towns and cities were transient whereas rural communities rooted in the soil had permanence. In the late 1950s, the Minister for Lands, Erskine Childers, was still equating the farming class with the nation.[6]

Thus the development of nationality and of nationalism in Ireland was specifically bound up with the struggle for land that continued to characterise Irish life long after independence, just as it had done for generations before. It would be difficult to exaggerate the extent to which the redistribution of lands was seen by nationalist contemporaries to be restitution for perceived historical wrongs; time and again in the Dáil public representatives associated redistribution with 'reversing Cromwell's policy'. Significantly, it was always 'Cromwell's policy', never, for example, Elizabethan policy or Williamite policy, simply because associating it with Cromwell, whose actions in Ireland had assumed mythical proportions of a barbaric nature, gave land acquisition policy a moral force that easily justified the compulsory acquisition of lands and the payment for them in virtually worthless land bonds.

The most solid indicator of the overall political importance of land issues in independent Ireland can be seen in the amount of time spent on land-related debates and questions in the Dáil from 1923 to the dissolution of the Land Commission in 1992. The debate on the 1933 Land Bill, for example, was resumed three times during the second stage alone, while that same year, the Lands estimate debate was resumed twice with lengthy contributions from over thirty speakers. Consistently, the annual vote on the Land Commission estimates attracted contributions from the majority of deputies in the Dáil who represented rural constituencies. (The point should perhaps be made that, in general, the urban-based TDs stayed aloof from such debates. In a revealing statement, J. J. Byrne (Dublin North, Cumann na nGaedheal) announced in the Dáil in 1927: 'I did not intend to take any part in this debate at all, for I always considered that the city man knows very little about land'.[7]) From 1923 to 1939, an average of 312 parliamentary questions per calendar year were tabled on land related issues (that is on the acquisition and division of lands and not on agricultural issues). This number, it should be added, does not take into consideration the fact that on numerous occasions TDs enquired about the possibility of the division of a dozen or more estates in his/her constituency which if enumerated as separate references would greatly multiply the total. In fact, on 24 July 1924, so much time was spent on the issue of land division that Major Bryan Cooper's (Dublin, Independent) only contribution to the debate was to 'remind the Dáil that there are some thirty votes yet to be discussed'.[8]

With the achievement of tenant proprietorship after a long, bitter struggle that dominated the social and much of the political life of Ireland from the 1880s, the primordial impulse to own land was arguably heightened; landownership became the only guaranteed access to social standing within the local rural community (and, indeed, was aspired to by many townspeople and professionals such as teachers and doctors who were often no more than a generation removed from landownership) and this remained very much the case until at least the 1970s, at which point the family farm economy continued to operate on a large scale throughout the country. In the interim period, the farmer who could afford to buy extra acres (or to a lesser extent rent them on a temporary basis using the conacre or eleven months' system[9]) was sure to climb the social ladder and for this reason the desire to accumulate more acres often overrode the desire to farm productively, something that became a recognised social problem by the early 1960s.[10] In 1962, Michael Moran,[11] Fianna Fáil Minister for Lands, wrote:

> It is a surprise to me that people will willingly devote money to paying for conacre or even buying new land, yet they will neglect to put money, in the form of fertilisers, into the land they already own and thus get, at probably cheaper cost, a better return than they would from the extra acres.[12]

This study begins some forty years earlier at a time when the Irish Free State was an overwhelmingly agricultural country where over half of the workforce were employed in farming, and where many of the most important manufacturing industries and wholesale and retail businesses were dependent upon agriculture.[13] In fact, in 1924, 86 per cent of total exports consisted of agricultural produce.[14]

In a society dominated to this extent by agriculture, where possession of land was so venerated, it is of little surprise that the sale of a farm of land often made headline news in provincial newspapers, and it did not have to make record prices in order to do so. At least partially responsible for this was the fact that a stigma of sorts was attached to the selling of the family farm probably emanating from the deep-rooted fear that selling would admit failure on a farmer's part, and such an admission would never do in rural Ireland.[15] To fail as a farmer, as Conrad Arensberg found in the 1930s, led to estrangement: 'it holds one up to general condemnation by the whole community'.[16] This was accentuated by the conviction that the inheritance of a family farm was a rite of passage; to turn one's back on this rite was perceived by one's peers to be almost sacrilegious. Farmers, such as the poet Patrick Kavanagh, who turned their backs on farming in the 1930s, in Kavanagh's case for the lure of the city, felt very quickly the contempt of former neighbours. Thus, when Kavanagh personified the land of Monaghan in *Stony Grey Soil*, he imagined it ridiculing his decision to abandon farming in the most vivid way: 'You sang on steaming dunghills/ A song of coward's brood'. In 1974, J. G. Esmonde (Wexford, Fine Gael) preached to his fellow deputies in the Dáil that:

There is, too, a tradition in regard to land. Land is almost as sacred to us as our religion and our national aspirations. The tendency is to hold on to land as long as one possibly can. No matter how poor the holding is the owner finds it very hard to part with it. There is always the hope that things will improve, that the holding will be improved and the farmer can better himself, perhaps by adding to the holding or in some other way. The tendency is to hold on to the family holding.[17]

Thus, as late as the 1980s only three per cent of the Republic of Ireland's estimated 12 million arable acres were changing hands per annum and 84 per cent of this was through inheritance, which meant that only a tiny proportion of land was becoming available on the open market in any given year.[18]

Other social factors were also at work. There was, for example, a widely held perception that holding on to the family farm was a form of security for old age: as long as an elderly farmer and his wife retained control of the farm, they would retain control of their home. In the 1920s and beyond, this prevalent attitude stemmed from the fear that a young daughter-in-law might marginalise the elderly farmer and/or his wife in their own home, or – worse still – force them into the county home for the elderly, an institution which was fearfully associated with the dreaded 'poorhouse' or the 'workhouse' of previous generations. Thus the elderly farmer was loath to sign over his land. In the late 1930s, Conrad Arensberg heard one young farmer complain: 'You can be a boy forever as long as the old fellow is alive'.[19] This retention of ownership by elderly farmers became another recognised social problem in the 1960s and 1970s, when the governments of the time were forced to confront the problem of aged farmers by introducing incentives to entice them to relinquish their holdings in favour of younger men who would have at least the energy (but more importantly the education and the initiative) to promote agricultural development.[20]

Traditionally, farm ownership undoubtedly enhanced marriage prospects. Again, in the late 1930s, Conrad Arensberg asserted: 'To our eyes, such a way of winning a wife seems very unromantic. It savours a little too much of hard-headed business. We should call a man a cynic who put farm and fortune ahead of personal attractions.'[21] There were many cynics in rural Ireland for whom the business of landownership took precedence over romance for, on the scale of rural status, farms were often measured by the fortunes they could provide in dowries for daughters or fortunes they could attract in dowries from the prospective wife of a farmer's son. It would make for an interesting study to establish what proportion of rural marriages from 1923 onwards were 'arranged' according to territorial considerations of farm locations. When Bull McCabe, the main protagonist in John B. Keane's *The Field* (1965) hears that his son, Tadhg, is interested in the daughter of a neighbouring farmer, he enthuses: 'Nine acres o' land! Think of it! Keep your napper screwed on and we'll be important people yet, important people, boy!'[22] Bull McCabe undoubtedly had many non-fictional counterparts.

But while it was true that to be a farmer's wife was an attractive option for most young women in the early decades of independence, regardless of the size of the farm, this gradually changed from around the 1950s when young women became more independent and looked much further afield to urban areas or to countries such as England for alternative options. Caitríona Clear has shown that while 11 per cent of the adult female population was occupied in agriculture in 1926, this had fallen to 4.2 per cent by 1961.[23] Young women were deserting the land; they were becoming more reluctant to sacrifice themselves to drudgery, which, in turn, contributed to a dramatic increase in the number of aged-bachelor-small farmers in Ireland.[24]

At the same time, young newly wed couples were becoming increasingly reluctant to share a home with their in-laws, so much so that an interdepartmental Dower House Committee was established by Eamon de Valera in 1943 to examine the possibility of the government funding second houses on a farm for either the older or the younger couple. Nothing came of the committee's proceedings but in retrospect it certainly captured the acknowledged difficulties associated with extended family life.[25]

After independence, land in Ireland continued to be responsible for what one commentator described as the 'hot flashes of anger and dispute that throw into relief deep-lying hatreds and fierce loyalties'.[26] Of course, the land question had always aroused such fierce passions in Ireland, which is heavily reflected in the historiography of agrarian agitation, the Land War and the Plan of Campaign.[27]

Irish literature of the nineteenth and twentieth centuries is not without its portrayal of such passions. From Maria Edgeworth's *Castle Rackrent* (1800) on through the works of William Carleton, Canon P. A. Sheehan, Anthony Trollope, Charles J. Kickham, Padraic Colum, Walter Macken, Michael McLaverty, John McGahern and quite a few others, attitudes to land are exposed in all their complexities.[28] Daniel Corkery has identified land, along with religion and nationalism, as one of the three great distinctive themes of Irish literature.[29] It has been said of Liam O'Flaherty's work, especially his Land War novel *Land* (1946), that it 'expresses that almost mystical feeling for land and landscape that many generations of Irish people have felt, and have not always been able to express in such a poetic way, but which has given rise to the most passionate political feelings of Ireland in the last century'.[30] The short stories of O'Flaherty, Frank O'Connor and Sean O'Faolain sometimes portray the primal magnetism of land or echo the frustration, inactivity and stagnation of Irish rural life, but perhaps nowhere are these frustrations better revealed than in Patrick Kavanagh's epic *The Great Hunger* (1942), a savage indictment of the brutalities of small farm life in the 1930s.

John B. Keane's *The Field*, the storyline of which was inspired by an actual agrarian-related murder in Kerry in the 1950s, is perhaps one of the most powerful expositions in Irish literature of the social and moral effects of land-hunger. It also powerfully evokes the emotional identification of a patriarch with his land, exemplified in Bull McCabe's highly charged speech on hearing that a field he has leased on conacre for five years (and which he regarded to be morally his) is about to be sold and used for non-agricultural purposes:

> I watched this field for forty years and my father before me watched it for forty more. I know every rib of grass and every thistle and every whitethorn bush that bounds it. . . . This is a sweet little field, this is an independent little field that wants eatin'.[31]

This emotional identification was not confined to fiction; perhaps nowhere was the intimacy of the relationship of farmers with their lands better demonstrated than in the names they often gave to their individual fields.[32]

The post-independence farming class became something of a large clique (although it is possibly foolish to suggest that that was not already the case long before 1922) with its own hierarchical social structure, and admission to it – or even to various grades within it – while highly desirable, was extremely limited. There was little room for 'outsiders' of any type. Traditionalist views could be said to have been embodied by John B. Keane in the fictional character of Bull McCabe who would not countenance speculators such as William Dee: 'I won't be wronged in my own village, in my own country by an imported landgrabber'.[33] In the Dáil in 1949, Sean Moylan,[34] former Minister for Lands, claimed: 'I know that within the parish where I have lived for the past twenty years, it would be impossible for any outsider to buy a farm in it – the bidding is so keen.'[35] Moylan was probably concealing the fact, in a diplomatic sort of way, that an outsider dare not bid for the land that locals wanted for themselves: 'no outsider need apply' was an adage as well worn in Ireland at this time as 'no Irish need apply' had been in New York in the nineteenth century. When, for example, wealthy businessman Davy Frame (a Scottish entrepreneur associated with Hammond Lane Foundry in Dublin, a firm which specialised in the demolition of big houses during the 1940s and 1950s) bought a large farm of land in County Laois in the mid-1940s, Oliver J. Flanagan (Leix–Offaly, Independent), not known for his tact, vehemently denounced him in the Dáil: 'Is it not a disgraceful state of affairs when we see huge estates . . . being allowed to be grabbed by a monster like this gentleman who comes plundering through the country as Cromwell came.'[36]

By then, it had been enshrined in article 45.2 of the constitution of 1937 that 'The state shall, in particular, direct its policy towards securing . . . that there be established on the land in economic security as many families as in the circumstances shall be practicable'. To this end, and perhaps the single most significant indicator of the importance of land issues in independent Ireland, successive governments from 1923 onwards were prepared to acquire lands compulsorily from their owners on a national scale (as opposed to a much more limited scale in both geographical and territorial terms under the pre-independence land acts) in a bid to settle the land question.

II THE LAND COMMISSION: ITS EARLY WORK, 1881–1923

It is with government policy concerning land acquisition and redistribution in independent Ireland and its implementation under the aegis of the Irish Land Commission that this book is primarily concerned. More precisely, it focuses upon the period from the introduction of the first Free State land act and the reconstitution of the Land Commission in 1923 to Ireland's entry into what was then the European Economic Community in 1973. (Chapter 6 contains a brief epilogue tracing some of the important subsequent developments in the history of the Land Commission up to the present day.) While it was initially tempting to endeavour to incorporate every aspect of the Land Commission's work, it soon became apparent that it was impracticable to do so; the scope would have been too wide and the focus consequently blurred. Historians will undoubtedly elucidate in time the important role that the Land Commission played in virtually every rural community in post-independence Ireland in the vesting of unpurchased holdings after 1923, the settling (or creating!) of disputes over such things as rights-of-way and turbary, its involvement in programmes of land improvement schemes and so on. Until then, if this study stimulates others to break more ground, so to speak, then it will have served its purpose.

The Irish Land Commission had been established under the terms of the 1881 Land Act as 'a body corporate and a court of record with the powers, rights and privileges of the High Court relating to matters within its juris-diction'.[37] Essentially it began life as a rent-fixing body and in this respect helped considerably to stabilise agrarian society during the turbulent years of the Land War. R. V. Comerford succinctly describes its importance at that time:

> With agrarian issues being so central to Irish public life the various functions of the Land Commission had a large political significance. It can be seen as a stabilizer in volatile circumstances, mediating a change with an imperturbability unachievable

by politicians increasingly susceptible to public pressures. Thus, in determining the thousands of cases referred to it in 1881 and 1882, the commission tacitly took 'fair rent' to mean 'politically acceptable rent' and was the main agent in the deflation of the Land War.[38]

To put this into perspective, 275,525 tenants with an aggregated rental of £5,883,904 entered the land courts to have their rents fixed during the first statutory term after 1881. They succeeded in having their aggregated rental reduced to £4,649,918, or by 21 per cent. First terms rents should not have been reviewed for 15 years, but continued depression forced the Land Commission to begin the process much earlier and thus 92,881 tenants had their rents reduced by almost 18 per cent in the late 1880s. In the 1890s, during the third statutory term, 3,143 tenants had their rents reduced by just over nine per cent.[39] For many who were successful in having their rents reduced in all three terms, this represented a highly significant saving on rental outlay. Of course, by reducing rents below what the annual repayment on the capital value of the land would be, it also acted as a major disincentive to tenants to purchase their holdings under the land acts up to 1903. It was only when the Wyndham Land Act of that year guaranteed that future annuities would be less than former rents that a revolutionary, though by no means complete, transfer of land-ownership took place. The fixing of judicial rents diminished as land purchase increased but the Land Commission retained this responsibility up to 1923 when the land act of that year prohibited the further fixing of rents under section 64.[40]

Soon after its establishment, the Land Commission was also developed by law into a land purchase agency charged with facilitating the transfer of agri-cultural holdings from landlords to tenants. Under the Land Acts of 1881 to 1896 the Land Commission advanced in the region of £23.4 million to almost 73,000 tenants to purchase 2.45 million acres.[41] However, the most significant transfer of ownership took place under the terms of the Land Acts of 1903 and 1909 when the Commission advanced £77.3 million to almost 124,000 tenants to purchase 7.3 million acres, as well as £7.5 million to the Congested Districts Board to purchase 729 estates encompassing 46,700 holdings.[42] The work of the Land Commission (both before and after 1923) provided other incidental advantages to tenant purchasers. For example, before the Commission finally vested holdings in tenant purchasers a vast amount of work had to be done in fixing boundaries, settling rights-of-way and turbary rights, allocating liabilities for drainage, and determining who retained mineral and sporting rights. When a tenant farmer became an owner-occupier, many areas of potential friction, dispute and litigation had, therefore, been removed and he was left in possession with a well-defined title to his land and appurtenances.

Following independence, the Land Commission was reconstituted and assumed the land purchase and other land law functions of its predecessor as well as those of the Congested Districts Board. All the manpower, property, assets and finances were transferred to the new commission under the terms of the Land Law (Commission) Act of 1923.[43] For almost seventy years thereafter the Commission remained a state body with responsibility for operating government policy in relation to land structure reform, subject in its early years to the control of the Minister for Agriculture and afterwards of the Minister for Lands.

After 1923, the Commission's two main functions were to complete land purchase and ostensibly to deal with the problem of congestion (on a national rather than a western scale) through the acquisition of untenanted estates (and later larger holdings resumed from those who had purchased under previous land acts) and their redistribution into appropriate parcels among selected allottees, in the main for the enlargement of uneconomic holdings but also for the provision of new holdings for persons specified as being entitled to them under the post-1922 land acts. It is with the latter process that the main body of this text is concerned.

While the minister had administrative control over the Commission, there were certain matters excepted from his brief, clearly defined in the 1933 Land Act, most importantly the determination of the persons from whom land was to be acquired or resumed; the determination of the actual lands that were to be acquired; the determination of the price to be paid for them or the price at which they were to be sold; and finally the determination of the persons to be selected as allottees.[44] All those decisions were to be the sole prerogative of the Land Commission, at least in theory. However, as chapter 7 illustrates, procedure was very much open to political manipulation and there is irrefutable evidence to suggest a great deal of political interference in land reform decisions.

Under the terms of the 1923–31 Land Acts,[45] there were four senior land commissioners, all of whom were appointed by the government.[46] Under the terms of the 1933 Land Act two extra commissioners were appointed ostensibly because the new Fianna Fáil government wanted to expedite acquisition and division but just as likely because the government wanted to ensure the placement of two of its own sympathisers.[47] (It seems that new appointments were made throughout the Land Commission that year. P. J. Sammon recalls a new second clerical officer being appointed to the Acquisition and Resales branch, P. J. [Paddy] Brennan, who was actually one of the founding members of Fianna Fáil.[48]) Continuity and experience were regarded as being essential to the success of the commissioners, so that up to 1950 they had life tenure. Under the land act of that year, retirement age was introduced at 65.[49] However, just four years later, Joseph Blowick[50] (Clann na Talmhan), Minister for Lands, asked that this age should be raised to 67 as 'a matter of urgency'.[51] The reason was quite simple: the existing commissioners were all approaching retirement age and Blowick did not want to lose them at around the same time.

The commissioners had responsibility for the discharge of the various statutory functions and duties assigned by the various land acts. It was they, for example, who set the procedure of the acquisition of lands in motion. They did so on their own inquiries, at the behest of their field workers, or as the result of representations made to them by politicians, local committees or individuals.[52] In his evidence to the Commission on Banking in 1935, Commissioner Michael Deegan pointed out:

> We are very careful and very particular before moving in any direction. We have investigations constantly in progress in regard to land in every county; we have information from various departments as well as from our own inspectors and, in addition, we have . . . representations made to us constantly, questions raised in the Dáil, letters to the Land Commission etc. When we have in mind any particular part of the country or any particular land that should be made the subject of investigation, we, first of all, get a preliminary report from one of our inspectors. That report has to be authorised by a commissioner and the inspector is not permitted to enter on the land for the purpose of that preliminary report.[53]

The members of the Banking Commission were rather surprised to find from Deegan's evidence that there was no formal policy, no written document setting out the role of the land commissioners other than directions issued in the various land acts. The chairman, Joseph Brennan, asked: 'They give no directions to you? They do not tell you to exercise them? They do not tell you to go out and get 10,000 acres of land?'[54] Deegan bluntly informed him that the commissioners made their 'own rules and regulations'.[55] There was also a certain amount of incredulity that decisions regarding the actual land to be acquired, the price to be paid for it, and the people to whom the land was to be given were entirely at the discretion of the land commissioners.

But Deegan's evidence was very much based on the theoretical interpretation of the duties of the commissioners as laid down in the acts. In reality, the land commissioners were not as independent as Deegan led the Banking Commission to believe. Invariably, Ministers for Lands frequently made applications on behalf of applicants.[56] It would be rather ridiculous and naïve to contemplate that civil servants did not consider the minister's recommendations. Furthermore, ministers continually issued directives to the land commissioners as to how government policy on land acquisition and division should be implemented. Government input was much more vigorous than Deegan claimed.[57]

Under the terms of the 1923 Land Act, one of the land commissioners fulfilled the role of judicial commissioner who heard appeals regarding objections to compulsory acquisitions or proposed prices to be paid by the Commission for estates. Under the terms of the 1933 Land Act, an appeals tribunal, composed of three of the land commissioners, was established to replace the judicial commissioner. For the years from 1934 to 1938, the tribunal heard an average of 470 appeals a year in sittings held throughout the country. By the late 1940s, this number had fallen dramatically to less than 50 per year, largely as a result of the tightening of land legislation but also because of the overall decrease in the number of acquisitions.[58] This decrease left the lay commissioners with very little work to do and so under the 1950 Land Act, they were detached from the appeals tribunal to continue the ordinary work of lay commissioners, leaving the judicial commissioner the sole arbiter of appeals.

One of the commissioners also acted as chief inspector. In 1948, a Department of Lands memorandum pointed out:

> The position of chief inspector in the Land Commission is one which calls for specialised knowledge and experience and for personal qualities of a high order if the holder, who should be a sound organiser, is to be successful in guiding and controlling the inspectorate and survey staffs to the satisfaction of the department and in earning and retaining the respect and loyalty of those staffs. It is a key post on which may depend to a large extent the success of work such as land acquisition and division.[59]

The inspectorate staff were probably the most important members of the Commission, certainly in regard to acquisition and division. When a land purchase scheme was decided upon by the commissioners, an inspector was sent down to the area to value the lands for acquisition, building his aggregate price field by field, which, in the case of untenanted lands, meant coming to a price that would be fair both to the owner as vendor and the Land Commission as purchaser. It was not always easy to reconcile the two interests. Nor was it easy to carry out the other practical tasks, such as providing access to all lands and ensuring water supplies for each farm. As Kevin O'Shiel, himself a land commissioner, put it, an inspector's task called for 'the tact of Machiavelli and the patience of Job'.[60]

For purposes of division, the inspector had to gather all the facts he could about each prospective allottee who lived within a mile radius of the estate or farm proposed for division. Each applicant had to be interviewed in order to determine the number in his family, the amount and type of stock that he held, and evidence of capital available to him to invest in his holding. Potential allottees were, it seems, often more revealing about their neighbours who were in competition with them than they were about themselves: one land commissioner claimed that 'when the inspector is going his rounds at this work he inevitably hears the whole truth, for the competition for land is so keen that each applicant will see to it that his neighbour will not get away with his particular story.'[61] The inspector carefully recorded his allotment scheme on a map and sent it to headquarters, along with a schedule giving the name, address and reference number of each proposed allottee. It was not easy for an inspector to come into an area and draw up a scheme independently of any local influence. As Timothy Linehan TD (Cork, Fine Gael) remarked in the Dáil in 1938:

> They [inspectors] are in the midst of a seething mob of people, every one of whom expects to get land and every one of whom has at the back of his own mind the idea that he is able to work a little greater pull than another.[62]

Indeed, it was not unknown for inspectors to receive death threats from disgruntled applicants for land.[63]

One of the most difficult tasks inspectors had was settling migrants[64] in an area. The *Land Commission Report 1932–33* concluded that in planning such a scheme an inspector was obliged 'to draw liberally from his reserves of tact and patience especially when he seeks to prevail upon holders to move to a different part of the country where everything is strange to them'.[65] In the 1930s, S. J. Waddell (who had joined the Land Commission in 1909 and had risen to the position of land law commissioner by the mid-1920s) wrote: 'To deal justly with those who have to give up their land so necessary for the relief of the congests, to allot this land equitably to the numberless applicants and to install the migrants in the teeth of what is often determined and strenuous opposition, is not an easy task'.[66] In Waddell's play, *Bridge Head*, written under the pseudonym Rutherford Mayne, a local informs the recently arrived inspector: 'You'd be wise to be putting no migrant up into that country. Begor the Rising that was in [nineteen] sixteen will be nothing to what's coming on yous if you plant strangers up in that bedlam'.[67] The locals, according to another character, Mrs Morrisey, 'have it all planned out. Who is to get and who isn't'.[68] The plight of the inspector and his staff is best captured in his assistant's tirade:

> It's a rotten life. All right for some maybe, but out there at Tubber – all hours of the day – and often at night . . . knock-knock-knock, someone at the door. 'If yous don't repair the kish that was put down for the right of way at Ballindine bog, we'll have a question asked in the floor of the Dáil – the drain between Pat O'Flaherty and Mick Hennigan is choked and Red Jack Dempsey has the water stopped on them below – the big wind of Friday last has stripped the slates off Mick Dolan's

new house – Tim Casey has put on a jennet for grass where he had only the right
of a donkey.' I wonder do they ever think up in Dublin of all that we ever go
through down here.[69]

Until the mid-1930s, no woman had applied for the position of inspector.
At the time, the Fianna Fáil Minister for Lands, Joseph Connolly, was unper-
turbed. In fact, he felt that there were both moral and physical objections to
the employment of women in this capacity: they were unsuited to physical
exertion, to working outdoors in all kinds of weather, walking over bogs and
drains sometimes carrying spades and they could not 'be expected to convey
that sense of strength and responsibility which the duties of the post demand'.
Furthermore, because inspectors had to work together in the evenings he felt
that it would 'be readily understood that serious objection could be raised to
male and female officers working together in those conditions after normal
hours, particularly in remote parts of the country'.[70] The idea of them sharing
the same hotel would send shock waves through Catholic Ireland!

In 1934, the Executive Council gave consideration to the potential repercussions of excluding women from a forthcoming competition for inspectors.
The secretary of the Department of Finance did not think that women could
be excluded on either physical or moral grounds, but he was reasonably confident that women would not apply for the post anyway, and even if one did
and was successful:

> If she proved unsuitable she could be discharged on probation and if her unsuit-
> ability showed the anticipation of the Minister for Lands to be well grounded,
> then there would be one instance at least to support the suggestion that women
> should be totally excluded from the employment.[71]

The inspectorate was therefore to remain a male preserve.

It was very important that inspectors were pillars of propriety. In November
1930, an inspector was discharged by the Executive Council when it was
discovered that he was 'financially indebted to a subordinate officer'. Martin
Roddy,[72] parliamentary secretary to the Minister for Lands at the time, told
the Dáil:

> Indebtedness of this nature on the part of a high official constitutes a grave
> impropriety and especially so in the case of a land commissioner about whose
> financial stability and independence there must be no possible doubt.[73]

Another scandal was to erupt in 1930 when it was proved that a Land
Commission official had accepted bribes in Sligo from certain applicants

when dividing lands there.[74] The Minister for Lands elaborated in a letter for 'private information':

> The resident inspector was dismissed by Order of the Executive Council following upon an investigation of grave irregularities over a series of years connected with the allotment and distribution of land. For example, parcels of land had been allotted and parties placed in possession without the authority and knowledge of the Land Commission, and, as a consequence, no payment in respect of such lands had been received by the Land Commission for a number of years and when the matter came to light early this year the arrears amounted to almost £2,000.[75]

The system of division was undoubtedly open to such temptations and inevitably there were numerous allegations of corruption and, it seems, a number of subsequent inquiries; unfortunately the records of these enquiries have proved elusive.[76]

The Land Commission staff members were full-time civil servants, recruited through the Civil Service Commission, and divided into several branches or sections. While these branches were altered from time to time to cater for changing circumstances, the main ones were: the secretariat which controlled the management and regulation of the personnel of the Commission, prepared the statistics which had to be presented to the Dáil and dealt with all correspondence of the Commission; the accounts branch which dealt with the financial dealings of the Commission; the collection branch which collected purchase annuities; the solicitors' branch which looked after all legal proceedings including, for example, the recovery of arrears of annuities; the purchase branch which catered for the purchase of tenanted lands; the sub-division branch which decided upon requests made by farmers to sub-divide their holdings; the records branch which filed all documents relating to land purchase, title deeds, maps, reports and so on; the surveying and mapping branch which was responsible for the survey of tenancies and untenanted lands to be sold or acquired; the examiners' branch which dealt with any queries regarding the distribution of purchase monies; and finally, the acquisition and resale division, the section most central to this study as it dealt with the acquisition and division of lands. In 1933, the Fianna Fáil Minister for Lands, Frank Aiken,[77] singled out the 170 employees of the latter section: 'On the whole the Land Commission officials – particularly those engaged in the acquisition and distribution of land – have the most arduous work assigned to them of any body of civil servants I know, the difficulties of which are not appreciated by those who do not know it intimately.'[78]

In the mid-1930s, at its peak of operations (in terms of acres divided), the Land Commission employed in the region of 1,350 people, around 1,200 in the branches listed above and a further 150 in the inspectorate. This number was an indication of the scale of work involved; land acquisition and division was a hugely complex procedure, a fact that was also reflected in the need for 14 further land acts after 1923 to refine legislation to prevent its being open to interpretations that would hamper the Commission in its work. It was not always easy to appreciate the difficult, and, indeed, highly technical work that was involved in the acquisition of estates and their redistribution. But patience was at a premium in rural Ireland; as Martin Roddy (Leitrim–Sligo, Cumann na nGaedheal) pointed out in the Dáil in 1925: 'They [people] want to have the lands divided immediately, and no other argument will convince them of the effectiveness of the work of the Land Commission'.[79] The Commission could not create the miracles that some expected of it. None more so than Simon P. O'Rorke, an estate agent on 154th Street, New York, who wrote to Kevin O'Higgins in 1923, who, in turn, told his Dáil colleagues:

> He [O'Rorke] was quite candid as to his requirements. He said that he understood there would be a certain pressure of business for some time upon us, but that he would ask me to write to him to say when it would be convenient for us to entertain his claim to Leitrim, Cavan and certain areas around there, as he was quite sure that he was a lineal descendant of O'Rorke of Breffni.[80]

III HISTORIOGRAPHY OF THE LAND QUESTION IN INDEPENDENT IRELAND

The Irish land question from the mid-Victorian period to around 1912 looms large in Irish historiography. This is understandable given that as well as being hugely important in its own right, it could not of course be disentangled from the wider political developments of the time that saw the land and national questions merge.[81] Received wisdom has largely accepted that the 1903 Land Act and acts amending it passed by the British government effectively solved the land question; in other words, the rather dramatic transfer of land-ownership post-1903 diffused the potential for agrarianism because by 1914 over two thirds of Irish tenants had become proprietors of their holdings. Implicit in this orthodoxy is the assumption that the land question was primarily about peasant proprietorship. But of course it was about much more than that: owning a farm was one thing, securing a livelihood from it was another. The establishment of the United Irish League in the late nineteenth century and its subsequent campaign in the early years of the twentieth century, particularly for large ranches to be broken up, was more to do with the economic viability of farms than peasant proprietorship.

Could the land question have simply disappeared by 1914 after bestriding Irish socio-political life for so many generations? The answer is quite simply no. In the early 1980s, Charles Townshend, writing on the Irish revolution, contended that perhaps 'the real dynamism which underlay the national movement remained the pressure of population on the land' and that land hunger 'remained the only force which generated large scale popular action'.[82] A few years later, Paul Bew's sapient conclusions in an article entitled 'Sinn Féin, Agrarian Radicalism and the War of Independence' (1988) might have pointed the way for a much more thorough examination of the agrarian dimension of the revolution.[83] But other than acknowledging some contribution of agrarian issues to the revolution, historians have failed to take up the challenge of exploring them in greater detail or, indeed, to be fully convinced of their existence.[84]

Instead, most historians stuck to the traditional hypothesis, which seems largely to have stemmed from an influential article written in 1966 by Patrick Lynch. He questioned why the Rising of 1916 had not produced a social revolution of corresponding significance and consequence and concluded that 'most agricultural holdings had been purchased by their occupiers, subject to land annuities, which were not then a matter of contention. The tenant had become a proprietor, the owner of his land; and little land remained, to which the system of voluntary purchase could be applied.'[85] Thus over thirty years later, John M. Regan in his *The Irish Counter-revolution, 1921–36* (1999) argued that 'any chance of real social revolution had been substantially undermined by land reform and the creation of an increasingly conservative peasant proprietorship in Ireland sponsored by various British Governments in the four decades before independence'.[86] More recently, Peter Hart has argued that: 'Not only did the Irish revolution not bring social transformation, there was no socially revolutionary situation in Ireland even in prospect', and like his precursors concluded that this was because 'most farmers owned their farms by 1922'.[87]

It is arguable that the importance of the land question in the Irish revolution should be more fully appraised. The legacy of the various land acts from 1881 to 1909 was the creation of a mass of peasant proprietors, a significant proportion of whom, while they may have got what they wanted in terms of owner-occupancy, did not get what they really required – *enough* land to make their holdings economically viable. The new phase of agrarian agitation that broke out in 1917, and which will be dealt with in more detail in chapter 2, could be seen as an extension of the agrarian revolution that began forty years before. Previous outbreaks had the organisational support structure of a Land League, a National League or a United Irish League or, even, the support of a constitutional political party that knew the importance of the land question to maintaining the momentum of the national question. With the demise of the parliamentary party during the Great War, Sinn Féin moved to fill the vacuum by attempting to manipulate the land question for similar purposes as the Home Rule Party had done for earlier generations. Traditional agrarian ideals were pushed a step further with claims that an independent republic rather than a Home Rule parliament was what would settle the land question once and for all. The geography of agrarianism remained essentially as it had been in the past – confined largely to the west and midlands. Those most aggrieved remained the smallholders and the landless. Their targets were still predominantly the landlords and the graziers, but farmers of all sizes were by no means secure, particularly those who had been in any way associated with the taking over of farms from which families had been evicted since the late 1870s. With the legal apparatus largely paralysed because of political developments and military activity, the agrarian outbreak of 1917–23 was at different times and in different places, particularly in the spring and summer of 1920, at least as violent as previous outbreaks.

It is not a function of chapter 2 to test the 'social revolution' hypothesis systematically. That would require a much more detailed and independent study. Rather it sets out to offer an explanation of why the first post-independence government should place the enactment of land legislation so high on its priority list. It concludes that the widespread nature of agrarian agitation and its aggressive nature made it incumbent on that government to enact the 1923 Land Act that contributed to the return to more peaceful ways in the Irish countryside.

The 1923 Land Act was one of the most important pieces of legislation passed by an independent Irish government, and probably the most important piece of social legislation.[88] Yet political, social and economic historians have tended to associate the 1923 Land Act merely with the completion of land purchase.[89] It was, indeed, ostensibly introduced as a land purchase act but its terms acknowledged that it had to tackle an issue much more controversial, pressing and ultimately intractable than the completion of land purchase – the relief of congestion through the compulsory acquisition and redistribution of lands. Because the 1923 act has been seen as a land purchase act, this has fuelled another misconception that it disposed of the grievances underlying land agitation and that logically the issue of land reform subsequently faded from national politics.[90] Nowhere is this hypothesis more clearly pronounced than in J. J. Lee's *Ireland 1912–1985: Politics and Society* (1989) in which the author contends that at independence:

> There was no longer a viable landlord system. Most Irish farmers became the effective owners of their holdings before 1921. The 1923 Land Act permitted the remaining tenants to purchase their holdings quickly but the major changes in

land ownership occurred before independence, contrary to frequent eastern European experience. The government was not therefore exposed to the temptation to manipulate land reform extensively for political purposes, which might have spawned massive corruption and provoked widespread grievance. Such limited land redistribution as occurred continued to be channelled through the safer conduits of the Land Commission. Communities were not generally rent asunder by rival claims to land.[91]

This virtual disallowance both of the importance of the 1923 Land Act in terms of the acquisition and redistribution of lands, and of the subsequent centrality of the land question to Irish life and politics for decades thereafter needs to be reappraised.[92] This book will show that there were momentous changes in landownership after 1923 as a result of the working of the Irish Land Commission. First of all, there were 114,000 tenant farmers who had not had their holdings vested in them. In respect of this completion of the transfer of proprietorship, the sheer scale of the financial burden that the 1923 act placed upon the state, and its willingness to carry that burden, is simply more evidence of the perceived importance of the land question to contemporaries. In May 1923, the Minister for Agriculture, Patrick Hogan, estimated that it would cost the state up to £30 million to complete land purchase at a time when the country was 'only just emerging from an atmosphere of unreason and irresponsibility'.[93] This money could only be raised through a loan from the British government.[94] In a Dáil speech in 1925, Hogan put the scale of the operation into perspective for his fellow TDs:

> It is an enormous loan, when compared with ordinary development, say, with the development of the Shannon, a gigantic scheme, but at the outset which is only going to cost about five million pounds. Thirty million pounds for land purchase is a very expensive matter, very much more expensive than any other . . .[95]

It is also worth noting that the Department of Lands budget during the 1930s equated to approximately 5.4 per cent of the total annual budget, which is a very significant proportion.[96]

If no other issue dominated Irish rural society as much as access to land, no other body was as important to the people living in the Irish countryside for most of the twentieth century as the Land Commission. It is hardly an exaggeration to claim that its impact on Irish society was matched only by that of the Catholic Church. In 1943, a civil servant, commenting upon the amount of 'irrelevant' correspondence that arrived in the Land Commission offices every day, stated: 'Unfortunately the Land Commission is regarded in the rural mind as a sort of universal benefactor, competent to deal with every requirement from the cleaning of a drain to the repair of an embankment, from the trespass of a neighbour to the making of a road'.[97] The sheer volume of correspondence arriving at the office of the Commission's secretariat – around 400,000 letters per annum – illustrates the truth of the civil servant's observation.[98] To put this into perspective: in 1946, the total rural population of the 26 county area was around 1.12 million people, of which just under 250,000 were returned as farmers.[99]

It was in the area of acquisition and division that the Land Commission had greatest impact on the majority of rural families. By the time the Commission published its final report in 1987, over 1.5 million acres had been acquired and redistributed under the various land acts from 1923, while another 840,000 acres acquired under previous land acts (for which the Land Commission became responsible after 1923) were also divided. That is a total of 2.34 million acres. Given that there was at most 11.6 million acres of agricultural land in the 26 counties (that is the area under crops, pasture and grazing) throughout this period, this represents a very significant 20 per cent of land affected by acquisition and division.[100]

Furthermore, for the years for which statistics are available (1937–78), the Land Commission migrated (or moved) over 14,500 farmers mainly from congested areas of the west onto lands totalling over 382,000 acres in uncongested areas primarily in the east and midlands.[101] In total, 45 per cent of the area acquired by the Land Commission in County Kildare and 54 per cent in County Meath were allotted to such migrants.[102] Add to these figures the thousands of families who lost land through compulsory acquisition (not just landlords but many large farmers who had purchased their holdings under the pre-independence Land Acts[103]), and it becomes very clear that after 1923 the working of the Land Commission impacted positively or negatively on a significant proportion of families living in rural independent Ireland.

It is argued in chapter 7 that, for most of the period under study, no other social issue was as important to political survival – not only that of individuals but also that of political parties – as land division. The very nature of the procedures involved in land division left it open to widespread manipulation by many local and national political dignitaries who could at least pretend some degree of influence in the division of an estate, thereby cementing their political futures.

Yet despite the immense importance of the Land Commission in economic, social and political terms, one will search largely in vain to find even the most cursory reference to it in any of the standard text books. Remarkably, even the much-heralded *Encyclopaedia of Ireland* (2003) has no entry for the Land Commission. This book is therefore intended to address a lacuna in the current state of knowledge and awareness of both the working of the Commission from its reconstitution in 1923 and the wider land question in independent Ireland.

IV STRUCTURE, TERMINOLOGY AND SOURCES

Basically a chronological structure is followed in this book, but within each chapter certain themes are dealt with such as land division policy and implementation with a statistical analysis of how land was divided amongst the various categories of allottees over certain periods of time. While this book examines acquisition and division on a national scale, specific local case studies are often referred to in order to illuminate on how land division policy or implementation affected localities. It is hoped that the book will provide a broad framework for more specialised local studies that are so necessary to understanding the importance of the working of the Land Commission at local level.

Ministerial responsibility for the Land Commission initially lay with the Minister for Agriculture who in 1923 was Patrick Hogan.[104] It soon became apparent, however, that a portfolio that included agriculture as well as the Commission, land acquisition and division was far too much for one minister and so in 1927 responsibility was transferred from Agriculture to a newly created Department of Lands and Fisheries. Ironically, however, successive Ministers for Lands[105] were usually burdened with other portfolios as diverse as Fisheries, Industry and Commerce or the Gaeltacht. Rather than referring to these ministers by their full titles (for example Minister for Lands, Industry and Commerce), it has been decided for convenience simply to use Minister for Lands throughout this work.

In the present day, terms such as 'colonist', 'migrant' and 'congest' may not only seem quaint and archaic, as Patrick Commins has pointed out, but they may also seem very unflattering to the people they describe.[110] This was, however, the terminology of the time and for that reason it will be adhered to throughout the book.

The findings in this book are based upon a wide range of primary sources. Statistical information, for the most part, is derived from the annual published reports of the Irish Land Commission. There are, however, a number of difficulties regarding the availability of statistics. First of all, and rather unfortunately, the Land Commission did not begin to publish annual statistics until the 1930s. This causes some difficulties for the period of administration of the Cumann na nGaedheal government from 1923 to 1932 in respect of determining how much land was allotted to specific categories of allottees. Secondly, governments were, of course, not so considerate to this author as to have changed according to the accounting year (1 April to 31 March) used by the compilers of Land Commission statistics. There are therefore some discrepancies regarding the acquisition and division statistics during the administrative periods of the various governments, but these are negligible. Thirdly, there are no statistics currently available on the number of applications made to the Land Commission from people in individual counties seeking transfers to holdings in other counties or for that matter even the number of applications for parcels of land within the county. In fact, it may be the case that such statistics were never even compiled. In answer to a question regarding the number of applications for land in County Leitrim in 1947, the Fianna Fáil Minister for Lands, Sean Moylan, replied:

> The position generally is that the Land Commission receives numerous applications for allotments throughout the country. These applications mostly relate to definite lands in course of acquisition and they are considered in relation to the lands they specify. The keeping of detailed statistical records of the applications would be laborious and would serve no useful purpose.[107]

Land Commission annual reports are also immensely valuable from the point of view of understanding how the Commission implemented government policy. But even more enlightening is the large corpus of official government records available in the files of the Department of the Taoiseach, Department of Finance, Department of Justice and the Department of Agriculture. Extensive use has been made of published records, in particular the *Dáil Debates* and to a lesser extent the *Seanad Debates*. Findings have also benefited from the richness of published reports carried out by various committees inquiring into a wide variety of aspects of Irish life such as emigration, the preservation of the Irish language, agriculture and banking,[108] all of which contain surprisingly large amounts of data and information on land reform policy, emphasising once again how the working of the Land Commission impacted upon all spheres of Irish rural life – economic, social, political and cultural.

I have benefited immensely from formal interviews and informal chats with people who either profited from division or suffered from compulsory acquisition. Unfortunately, the only published memoirs of a Land Commission official are those of P. J. Sammon who began his civil service career as a clerical officer in the Land Commission in 1933. Sammon rose to the position of principal officer and retired in 1978.[109] His memoirs contain nuggets that only someone who worked within the system could possibly provide. Finally, newspapers, national and provincial, were richly illuminating and the latter are an ideal starting point for any local historian interested in land division issues.

It may seem surprising to some readers that the Land Commission records have not been given priority in this survey of sources. After all, the records branch of the Land Commission contains an estimated eleven million records including title documents, maps and related papers, records of Land

Commission proceedings, correspondence, inspectors' reports on individual holdings and families, and a myriad of other types of documents some – such as title deeds – dating at least to the fifteenth century.[110] The Land Commission inherited the records generated by the Ecclesiastical Commissioners who conducted the disposal of church lands after disestablishment in 1869, as well as the records of the Congested Districts Board set up under the 1891 Land Act and disbanded in 1923, which are hugely important in elucidating the social, economic and cultural circumstances of people living along the western seaboard. The reason for not giving these records priority in this survey of sources is very simple – they are not freely accessible. Indeed, their anomalous position down through the years may very well help to explain why so little research has been carried out on the working of the Land Commission since 1923.

As far back as the 1950s, the importance of these records was widely accepted within political (and academic) circles. In July 1958, James Dillon, the then leader of Fine Gael, expressed his concern in the Dáil regarding their safekeeping and he suggested that the records should be microfilmed.[111] He was given the assurance of the then Minister for Lands, Erskine Childers, that he would approach the national librarian and 'some of our historians' for their views but that in the meantime:

> The importance of these documents is fully appreciated in the Land Commission
> and every possible care is taken of them. The documents are preserved in a special
> records branch of the Land Commission where they are fully indexed and filed in
> steel boxes which are kept in strong-rooms. I can assure the deputies these docu-
> ments are in good hands. Occasionally, they are consulted by research students
> from the university, people claiming to be descendants of former estate owners and
> people interested in genealogy. That disposes of the humorous suggestion made
> that if the Land Commission were compelled to move their offices, nobody would
> ever be able to find the files again.[112]

It might be unfair to claim that Childers was being disingenuous, but certainly not everybody shared his appreciation. According to P. J. Sammon the suggestion of microfilming the documents was mooted from time to time 'with a view to conserving storage space' but this never happened; instead, Sammon tells us 'the pruning of estate files was authorised in the late 1960s', a task undertaken by the revesting branch (the final branch to handle estate papers). What was pruned? How much was pruned? Has there been further pruning? Will there be pruning in the future? These are all questions to which answers have proved somewhat elusive.

Since Dillon's time, other politicians have made enquiries regarding the accessibility of these records. In 1992, Senator Thomas Hussey proposed that the Minister for Agriculture should 'ensure that those records will be available, that somebody will be responsible for them and that they will be passed to the people when they need them'.[113] When John O'Connor (Fine Gael) once again highlighted the importance of these records during the debate on the Dissolution of the Land Commission Bill 1989, he was assured by Minister Liam Hyland that

> every care is being taken to preserve all the very important and, in many cases, historic documents and to ensure that they are transferred and filed in a way which will make them as accessible as possible to the public and to the legal profession. I hope all these important documents will be properly stored in the new home we have found for them and that the public will have full access.[114]

On 17 August 1992, the Records Branch of the Land Commission was closed to allow for the relocation of its records to the National Archives building in Bishop Street.[115] The public have not yet been given 'full access'.

Section 8 (2) of the 1986 National Archives Act excludes from the terms of the act records over thirty years old that continue to be working records or which contain information that might cause 'distress or danger to living persons on the grounds that they contain information about individuals, or would or might be likely to lead to damages for defamation'. Thus, at the beginning of 2003, when former leader of the Fine Gael Party and Taoiseach, John Bruton, enquired of the Minister for Agriculture, Joe Walsh, the reasons why the records 'are not open to scholars and others', he received the following reply:

> These records have not been formally handed over to the National Archives as they contain title documentation of all land acquired by the former Commission for distribution under the Land Purchase Acts. These records are referred to on a daily basis by my staff who deal with ongoing queries relating to current and past transactions involving the former Land Commission.[116]

It is section 8 (2) that is most often cited to would-be researchers who, as a body, it is safe to conclude, are becoming increasingly frustrated by not being able to gain access to vital information that is necessary to progress scholarly research. It seems remarkable that, even though the Land Commission has been officially disbanded, *all* of its records are still considered 'working records'.

Surely section 8 (2) cannot and should not be interpreted to apply to the millions of documents on hand. After all, the fundamental purpose of the 1986 legislation was to enhance scholarly research. It is something of an anomaly that the act should now be used as a pretext to limit access to such an important source. And while there may be a case for a longer closure period on the more sensitive records, such as the inspectors' reports, there is surely a case for making open to the public the vast majority of other records. There is most certainly a very strong case for the appointment of an archivist, or better still, a number of them for the records branch.

However, to finish this introduction on a much more positive note, while the Land Commission records are a veritable goldmine in their own right, and while they will, when eventually opened, undoubtedly enhance primary research in every aspect of Irish social, political and economic life from 1881 to the end of the twentieth century (at least) and become the basis for numerous books, it should be emphasised that access to them was not deemed essential for the completion of this book. Because the focus here is fundamentally on land division and government policy and its implementation, the rich vein of other sources already in the public domain are more than ample to compensate and to have justified its writing. In fact, there is a distinct possibility that had the Land Commission archive been fully accessible, this book might not have been written at all.

TWO

CONTINUING THE LAND QUESTION
AGRARIAN DISORDER 1917–23

The struggle with the English invaders had been as much a fight for land as for political supremacy, and, therefore, every uprising of the people after the conquest partook largely of an agrarian character. The hope of driving back to England, or to perdition, the foreigner who played the rural tyrant and made their lives miserable, had as much to do with stimulating the Irish farmer and agricultural labourer to participation in revolutionary conspiracies, as any idea of the benefits to be derived from national self-government.

JOHN DEVOY

The Land of Eire (1882), p. 20.

—

I THE ROOT CAUSES OF AGITATION

During the 1880s, politicians and humanitarians had drawn attention to the grave social problems posed by the uneconomic holdings in the counties of Donegal, Mayo, Galway, Clare and Kerry, over 50 per cent of which were rated at less than £4 in valuation, and where around one million people struggled to survive. Official attempts to relieve congestion in the west were given impetus with the establishment of the Congested Districts Board under the Purchase of Land (Ireland) Act of 1891. Eighty-five regions along the western seaboard were identified as being in urgent need of rural development, particularly with regard to a reform of land structure.[1] Between then and 1909 (when under the Birrell Land Act of that year the congested districts were redefined to include all of the counties of Donegal, Sligo, Leitrim, Roscommon, Mayo, Galway, Kerry and six rural districts in Clare and four in Cork, see map 2.1), the board was practically given unlimited discretion over the yearly income placed at its disposal of between £50,000 and £95,000 a year.

Under the 1909 Land Act, the board's annual budget was increased rather dramatically to £250,000.[2] But even this was far from satisfactory. To compound the problem of congestion, land in these counties was very often still held on the rundale system. For generations, local communities, usually on their own initiatives, had divided fields into strips in an attempt to provide local farmers with an equal share of good (and bad) lands. There were no

Map 2.1 The congested districts of Ireland, 1909

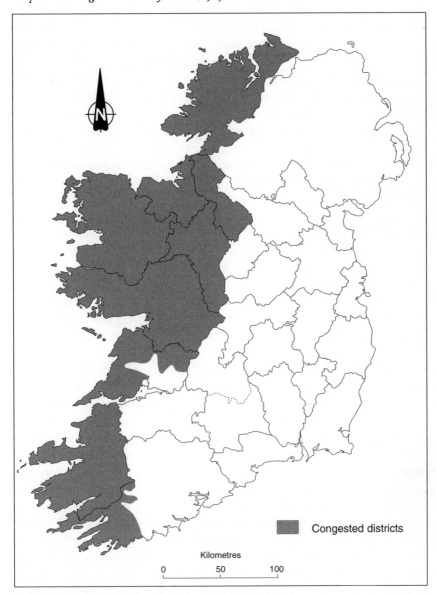

Congested districts

Kilometres

0   50   100

Source: T. W. Moody, F. X. Martin, F. J. Byrne, *A New History of Ireland* IX *Maps, Genealogies, Lists: A Companion to Irish History* (Oxford, 1984).

fences, just a series of intermixed plots constructed with very little foresight for long-term planning. A field of one acre, for example, could be divided into 12 strips, each belonging to a different farmer. As late as the 1930s on one Mayo estate, there was a 284-acre townland that was held by 27 tenants in 450 separate plots. One tenant held 14 acres in 11 different plots spread over four miles; another held 19 plots covering just over six acres and the remainder were in much the same situation.[3] (This could only provide a nightmarish scenario to anybody in the future with responsibility for consolidating such scattered strips, especially if one farmer remained intransigent and refused to give up his holdings to facilitate the process.)

The prevalence of uneconomic holdings and the rundale practice were serious obstacles to agricultural development. Most of the western small-holdings consisted of nothing more than rough grazing land, with potatoes and oats being the only crops usually grown. In 1908, the Royal Commission on Congestion in Ireland concluded in its final report that tenants 'pay rent for a holding not so much for its agricultural value as because it furnishes a home for their family'.[4] Thus, while the Land League began in the west and the Land War spread from there, the truth of the matter was that the league's ideological aspirations for reductions in rents, fixity of tenure or ultimately the transfer of land ownership could do very little to alleviate the plight of these impoverished farmers unless they either had alternative sources of income or they received more land to make their holdings viable.

Aggravating the frustration of smallholders was the fact that they existed side by side with huge grazing ranches, particularly in Roscommon, East Galway, parts of Mayo and the midland counties of Westmeath, Meath and Offaly (then King's County). By 1917, an estimated 33,400 holdings over 100 acres in size remained in Ireland (representing 7.5 per cent of the country's total number of holdings), of which 8,231 were between 200 and 500 acres and 1,967 were over 500 acres.[5] (See Appendix 1, table 2.1, p. 233). At the very least this represented a total acreage in excess of 7.3 million acres, which was approximately one third of the country's total acreage and more significantly about 63 per cent of its arable acreage. According to popular nationalist rhetoric of the time, even where it was expounded by politicians who were themselves large graziers, the break-up of these ranches was desirable for two reasons: firstly, they were of little economic value to the local community because they created very little demand for labour and secondly, and more importantly, if they were to be broken up smallholders would benefit from their redistribution.

Furthermore, the designation of particular districts as congested was an arbitrary one. There were electoral divisions in a relatively poor county such as Cavan where conditions were much worse than in some of the officially desig-nated congested districts. In fact, in 1921 an average of around 65 per cent of all agricultural holdings in each of the 19 counties outside the designated congested areas came under the definition of 'uneconomic' as set out by the Land Commission, that is below £10 valuation or roughly 20 acres of 'reasonable' land.[6] Added to the smallholders of the west, this represents a very high proportion of farmers throughout the country whose holdings were unviable. It was not, however, until the early 1930s, that it became more widely accepted that congested areas were not confined to the scheduled areas of the west and the term was more readily applied to 'any district in Ireland where a considerable number of holdings [were] of such a size or quality as not to afford a reasonable means of livelihood to the families of their occupiers'.[7]

There were also around 114,000 tenants who had not yet been able to purchase their holdings, comprising 3 million acres, under the land purchase acts.[8] Many of these were uneconomic holders who, it seems, had no hope of purchasing their holdings because the Land Commission was refusing to advance the purchase money in the belief that the holdings were unlikely to sustain the repayment of annuities. From 1 April 1919 to 31 March 1920, for example, the Commission refused 3,568 applications for full advances amounting to £841,000, and in 13,196 other applications the Commission refused to advance the full purchase price. In both cases, the reason cited was insufficient security on the tenant's behalf.[9] (Inspectors' reports in the Land Commission records, if and when they become available to the public, will undoubtedly show a great variety of reasons for the Land Commission refusing advances to the occupying tenant.)

The crucial point in all of this is that the achievement of peasant proprietorship for over two thirds of Irish tenants on the eve of the First World War should not be accepted as the solution to agrarian ills. The point has earlier been made that legacy of the British land purchase acts was the creation of a mass of peasant proprietors, many of whom did not have the qualifications to cope with proprietorship or, more importantly, either the capital or the requisite amount of land to make their holdings viable.

Nor should the continued existence of so many large graziers and tracts of untenanted lands be underestimated as a source of continuing grievance.[10] Traditional landlords alone retained an aggregated total of approximately two million untenanted acres by 1922, much of which was let on the eleven months' system to graziers.[11] In the earlier part of the twentieth century, the failure of the Wyndham Land Act of 1903 to address the grazier issue had resulted in the outbreak of the so-called 'ranch war' organised through the United Irish League founded in 1898 to agitate for the break-up of western ranches.

UIL activity in areas of the west and midlands (and its subsequent decline) has attracted a good deal of scholarly attention in recent years[12] but it is important to recognise that UIL activity at a local level did not just focus attention upon the typically large graziers of the midland and eastern counties.

In County Monaghan, for example, the failure of the 1903 Land Act to fulfil
the ambitions of the uneconomic holders and the landless attracted over 6,600
members to the UIL by 1907.[13] There any farmer with more land than was
necessary to rear a family in relative comfort was deemed a grazier. Thus, in
January 1917 the UIL-dominated county council enthusiastically welcomed
the compulsory tillage order of that year because it would provide the opportunity to break up the 300 or so holdings in the county which were in excess of
fifty acres in size. The majority of councillors agreed that: 'The large grazing
farms are spread all over the county, and are in most cases surrounded by small
tillage farms, which makes such a scheme as proposed an ideal one for this
county.'[14] When a Unionist representative, Michael Knight, acutely aware
that the Protestant community owned a disproportionate share of the larger
farms, proposed that the council 'ought to make their position perfectly clear
and not leave themselves open to any charge that they were utilising this cry
for increased tillage for the purpose of injuring any particular class of people',
he could not find a seconder for his resolution.[15]

When economic conditions prior to 1914 continued to deny the new class
of small farmer proprietors a reasonable standard of living, they found that
their new masters, the Land Commission, as a bureaucratic state body, did
not grant any of the assistance formerly available from benevolent landlords,
however scarce or plentiful the latter might have been. The Commission did
not, for example, take a particularly bad harvest into consideration when considering farmers' needs for annuity abatements. Mainly, it proceeded with
uncompromising severity against all the little devices and pretexts formerly
used by tenant farmers when dealing with landlords.[16] In Tipperary, for
example, Dan Breen could recall the 1903 Land Act bringing 'great joy to the
farmers' which was soon dissipated by the realisation that annuities were no
easier to pay than the former rents.[17] This became a much more serious problem
during the 1920s as a result of the post-war economic depression that severely
affected Irish agriculture. In 1926, Conor Hogan, Farmers' Union representative for County Clare, summed up what had effectively happened:

> It appears to me that these people who were put into occupation of the land are
> defaulting now, not so much because the land was bought at an excessive price, but
> because in most cases they were poor men without any capital. Without capital,
> with the holdings too small and trying to put too many men on the land, trouble
> arose, because they were given uneconomic holdings at a stiff price, which they
> were unable to bear.[18]

By 1932–3, the new proprietors were £2.9 million in arrears on a collectable
annuity of £4.6 million (total annuities plus accumulated arrears), a very dramatic 59 per cent. However, the post-independence and reconstituted Land

Commission was forced to tread more carefully – a Free State government could not afford to be associated with evictions by its state body on the same level as those that had accompanied earlier periods of agricultural depression. Thus, instead of resorting to large-scale resumptions (or evictions under a different name), the government extinguished most arrears and halved annuities under the 1933 Land Act.

Land hunger in Ireland had remained just as great after 1903 as it had been before. The uneconomic holders were not the only disgruntled rural class in this respect. There were tens of thousands of landless men, the younger sons of farmers denied access to landownership by the fact of birth. Many of these and thousands more besides were agricultural labourers whose envy of farmers increased as time passed (and especially from 1914 to 1918 when wartime profits accruing to farmers grew dramatically). There were thousands more, described in contemporaneous terms as 'the dispossessed', those tenants or their representatives who had been evicted since the beginning of the Land War in 1879 and who considered it to be their right to have their holdings returned.

The Great War had a number of significant consequences, all of which fed into an intricate web of agrarian unrest. First and foremost, the virtual closure of emigration outlets during the Great War meant that a higher proportion of rural malcontents were housed in Ireland than had been the case for generations. Secondly, the war effectively stopped land purchase when the British Treasury curtailed advances, its priority now being with financing the war effort. As it was, there had been huge delays in expediting purchases under the 1903 and 1909 Land Acts because of inevitable logistical difficulties – there was such a number of holdings to be transferred that it was impossible for civil servants to deal with them any more quickly than they were doing. By 1921, there were 1,248 estates encompassing 46,600 holdings on 1.5 million acres that sales to the value of £10.7 million had been agreed upon but for which advances had not yet been made.[19] In 1923, Joseph McGrath, then Minister for Industry and Commerce, enlightened the Dáil on one such case in Cork where an agreement to sell under the terms of the 1903 Land Act had been signed by the landlord and his tenants on 1 November 1906. As under the terms of the act, estates pending for sale were proceeded with 'in order of priority, so far as may be practicable', preliminary requisitions were not actually issued until 1915; the property was not inspected until 1917; requisitions of the estates commissioners arising out of these inspections were not disposed of until 1922 and the purchase money was not advanced until May of that year.[20] It was delays such as this that caused much annoyance. Thirdly, during the war, the Congested Districts Board was forced to withdraw its unaccepted, but still pending, offers for ninety estates comprising 112,000 acres of tenanted land and 32,500 acres of untenanted land. The board had also made preparations to issue offers for a further 69 estates comprising 123,000 acres but again was forced to withdraw.[21] From the board's point of view, the suspension of land purchase therefore involved a postponement of the acquisition of 159 estates comprising 267,500 acres.

At the same time, the war reinvigorated a flagging agricultural economy as prices rose to unprecedented levels for agricultural products.[22] Irish agriculture had rarely, if ever, had it so good, certainly not since the beginning of agricultural depression in the late 1870s, but the boom only increased the hunger for land. The landless wanted access to land to benefit from the increased demand for tillage, while the smallholders wanted more land to increase their incomes. It is difficult to gauge to what extent influences from Europe fashioned attitudes in rural Ireland but it may be worth considering that from 1917 radical contemporary commentators such as Aodh DeBlacam and Selina Sigerson maintained that 'a large majority of the Irish proletariat is now becoming Socialistic in hope and policy. . . . Today the erection of Socialist republics throughout Europe has kindled an enthusiasm in the Irish proletariat that has burnt away all doctrinaire hesitations.' Sigerson wrote that 'every day outside events press more strongly on Ireland, and urge us to a decision. We cannot, even if we would, make Ireland an island of calm amid the world-changes'.[23] But to claim that outside influences were hugely important would be to deny the existence of potential for agrarian revolution in Ireland that had continued to be present from the Land War days of the 1880s. One thing is more certain: while Arthur Griffith, the original founder of Sinn Féin, had expounded that 'a mere agricultural state is infinitely less powerful than an agricultural-manufacturing state',[24] his economic principles were quickly reshaped by those who saw the potential of using the land question as a catalyst towards the promotion of the national question of independence in the form of a republic.

There were historical precedents for such an ideology. R. V. Comerford in his *Fenians in Context* (1985) argued that 'a secondary but nonetheless important aspect of the appeal of Fenianism in the 1860s was the prospect of material reward, essentially in the form of land. There was a virtually universal assumption at the time that a successful political revolution would result in the re-division of Irish land.'[25] Even more remarkable is the evidence that he presents of contemporary fears regarding the return of exiles clamouring for their recently lost holdings, seeking the same rewards as the home-based soldiers if they partook in revolutionary activity. As the quotation from John Devoy (Fenian recruiter of the British soldiers in Ireland in the 1860s and later leader of the Clann na Gael in America[26]) that opens this chapter suggests, Fenians and some of the later separatists understood that promises of the expropriation of Irish landlords would fuel revolutionary intent amongst the masses.[27]

II SINN FÉIN AND AGRARIAN AGITATION, 1917–19

As the Irish Home Rule Party went into irreversible decline during the years of the Great War, a vacuum was created to allow rising Sinn Féin to exploit the link between party and the land movement that had worked successfully for constitutionalists since the 1870s. Arguably, in the last quarter of the nineteenth century, the sections of Irish rural society that had benefited most, in turn, from the alliance were the middle to large-sized farmers both in terms of improving their economic situation and achieving a commensurate share in political authority at local and national levels. There remained, however, a sense of resentment amongst the lower strata of rural society that the Home Rule Party had done very little for them.[28] By 1918, with a post-war general election looming and the Representation of the People Act having given the vote to all men at 21 and women at 30, it was clear to Sinn Féin that much of its appeal, particularly to the smallholders and labourers, might lie in the land question.

Since 1917, Sinn Féin had, in fact, made significant moves in this direction. By that year, the genuine fear of a food shortage led to a popular demand for increased tillage in Britain and Ireland. The government had little choice but to introduce a compulsory tillage order at the beginning of that year. The new tillage regulations required all occupiers of ten or more acres of arable land to cultivate ten per cent more of it than they had done in 1916, although no occupier was required to cultivate more than 50 per cent of his total holding.[29]

The idea of compulsory tillage appealed to smallholders and landless labourers. It meant, in theory at least, that large graziers would have to set aside lands for tillage, which, in turn, would mean that they would have to employ extra labour in a country starved of industrial outlets outside the north-east, or alternatively they would have to rent part of their estates on conacre that would allow smallholders and labourers access to (extra) land and therefore an opportunity to share in the prosperity of the wartime boom. More importantly, it could set the precedent for the break-up of the grazier ranches, something that had been advocated for many years.

A variety of responses to the order are worth considering because they compounded rural exasperations. Firstly, some graziers did begin to let plots of their grazing lands to the landless but at exorbitant rents. Land hunger and the prospects of increased earnings/income had greatly inflated the letting (and sale) price of Irish land over the previous three years or so. In County Monaghan, for example, lands were being let on the eleven months' system for £20 an acre in 1916–17, at a time when the county council suggested that £3 an acre would be more than enough.[30] Elsewhere, conacre auctions failed because people abstained from bidding in the expectation that the lands would be compulsorily acquired from their owners and let in tillage plots at a nominal rent.[31]

Secondly, the Congested Districts Board and the estates commissioners[32] who had large tracts of land under their control (which they had acquired for sale under the land acts but had not disposed of due to the postponement of land purchase for the duration of the war) also let plots on conacre, although reportedly at more moderate rates than the graziers.[33] However, the fact that the board was using the conacre market (as admittedly it had done in the past) only focused more resentment upon it and led to accusations of profiteering. Smallholders felt that if the board could rent lands, it could just as easily divide them.

Thirdly, the majority of graziers in western counties such as Galway as well as midland counties such as Roscommon, Westmeath and Offaly were opposed to the compulsory order, arguing that it was being used 'as a lever for renewed agitation' to compel the Congested District Board and estates commissioners to purchase their holdings and to redistribute them amongst small farmers.[34] (In practical terms, many were not prepared to make the necessary outlay on ploughs, harrows and so on to begin tillage farming or to employ labour.)

During 1917, it was hardly surprising that agrarian agitation for the break-up of grazier lands and their redistribution should originate in the west where this latest phase of popular agrarian revolt was orchestrated by alleged Sinn Féiners, most likely drawn from the small farmer and landless class who had most to benefit from the break-up and redistribution of grazier land.[35] Sinn Féin was simply manipulating the land question for the same purposes as the Home Rule Party a few short years before. Indeed, one could justifiably argue that there were many elements of direct continuity, both in terms of policy and that offered by defections from one side to the other.[36] For example, new converts to the Sinn Féin cause such as Laurence Ginnell, a veteran of the Land War, toured much of the country encouraging evicted tenants to take whatever action 'was appropriate to local conditions' to regain their holdings; advising unpurchased tenants not to pay any more rents but to lodge their money with trustees in order to pursue a policy akin to the Plan of Campaign of the 1880s; and urging that young people were to be ready 'to clear cattle off every ranch and keep them cleared until distributed'. 'The simultaneity of the operations' he argued, would 'paralyse opposition of every kind and command success, with little personal risk'.[37] There was nothing new in his message; he had preached it all before but in the past as a Home Ruler.

Ultimately Sinn Féin's political priority was the establishment of an independent Irish republic and by 1917 it was preaching that the 'true remedy for the land problem' was the 'exclusive control of our own resources which

sovereign independence alone can win'.[38] According to its adherents, constitutional means were no longer the way forward. In the past, as we have already
seen, separatists had preached the importance of recognising the pivotal
position of the land question, more particularly its resolution, in the struggle
for independence, especially in its role of enticing young men to become active
revolutionaries. When Sinn Féiners encouraged agrarian agitation, they also
emphasised the need 'to ignore British authority'.[39]

Historians have acknowledged that agrarian issues played at least some
role in motivating young men to join the Volunteers (later the IRA).[40] This is
not, of course, to deny the simultaneous existence of other more patriotic
reasons, for after all the land question and the struggle for independence had
been so closely connected in previous generations that patriots and land agitators were regarded as one and the same. But the possibility that young men,
particularly small farmers or farmers' sons destined for the labouring class or
the emigrant ship, were attracted to the IRA by the prospects of securing land
in the event of the establishment of an independent Irish republic is not
beyond reason. John Devoy's quotation which opens this chapter suggests
that there was a Land War generation that would gladly have driven back to
England 'or to perdition the foreigner who would have played the rural tyrant
and made their lives miserable'. That generation's children and/or grand-
children soon became aware of how easily that could be achieved through the
burning of big houses or the terrorising of their inhabitants that drove hundreds of landlords from rural Ireland from 1920 to 1923, effectively leaving
their untenanted and demesne lands to be divided amongst locals, initially
with or without the official sanction of the Irish Land Commission.[41]

Arguably, some at least of the more prominent rural IRA leaders were very
much tuned in to the agrarian needs of the people they purported to represent
or understood the land-related psychology that was necessary to entice young
men into the movement. A Clare IRA leader, Michael Brennan, later claimed
that he 'hadn't the slightest interest in the land agitation, but I had every
interest in using it as a means to an end . . . to get these fellows into the
Volunteers'.[42] In Cork, Liam Deasy was educated at national school to rid him
'of the attitude of servility and subservience towards the landed gentry'.[43] He
was quick to acknowledge 'the small farmers and cottiers of West Cork and
elsewhere who, throughout the entire campaign, sheltered and fed our fighting
men, often at the price of great hardship and loss to themselves'.[44] Without
them victory, he felt, would not have been achieved; the underlying notion
being that they deserved some form of reward as a result. Even the likes of
Ernie O'Malley, who was not born into a farming background, was not entirely
oblivious to the correlation between the land and national questions. In *On
Another Man's Wound* (1936), O'Malley conceded that: 'There is a hunger for

the soil, an elemental feeling that even the stranger or the foreigner can sense'. In his own inimitable style he wrote:

> There was a strange passionate love of the land amongst the people. Material possessions were low or gone, the arts were a broken tradition, the ideal of beauty had gone into the soil and the physical body. Their eyes had long dwelt on the form, colour and structure of the landscape. It had become personal; its praise had been sung by joyous or despairing poets, and had been felt by the people. An old soil well loved had given much to them, and they had put much into it. They clung to this last treasure and solace with imagination and with physical senses.[45]

On a more earthly level, O'Malley met Volunteers in Clare who told him 'bloodthirsty tales' of the bitter land war in that county and who could identify every 'land-grabber' in a locality, a person perceived to be even more vile and odious than the dreaded informer.[46] Even contemporary police reports acknowledged the allure which the prospects of a revolution had for potential recruits to the Volunteers: in February 1918, for example, the county inspector for Galway East Riding reported: 'Sinn Féin is now being worked in this riding as an agrarian movement for the forcible possession of lands. . . . This new phase of Sinn Féin will bring many young men into the movement which had no attraction for them heretofore'.[47] They recorded with some trepidation that the likes of Eamon de Valera were promoting the establishment of Volunteer companies not only to prevent conscription but also 'to help to divide the land evenly' and that notices were posted by local Sinn Féin clubs throughout the west and midlands assuming responsibility for the letting of estates on conacre 'in the name of the Irish Republic'.[48]

Obviously not all active or potential agrarian agitators joined the Volunteers but this did not prevent many from falsely using the authority of the republican movement to bolster their claims. In March 1918, a notice was posted on Patrick Deviney's land at Gort that it had been taken over by 'the Irish Republic'; it was actually taken over by Deviney's brother (who had recently been evicted from this farm) with the help of some of his friends.[49] Anonymous letters, often signed 'IRA', sometimes 'Sinn Féin', demanded the recipients to surrender all or part of their lands. Again, in March 1918, the county inspector of Galway's west riding claimed regarding the rise of Sinn Féin:

> At the back of the whole procedure is greed for land and it has been necessary to take strong precautions to prevent the forcible entry and ploughing up of lands. Threatening letters, threatening notices and intimidation are rife at present and they are caused in most cases by this greed for land and in the county they are sinister and ominous.[50]

It must be understood that this was a time in Ireland when no other material reward was as alluring as land. Ironically, before the end of the Great War and before the Anglo-Irish military struggle began, the British government had recognised the potential of land grants as reward for recruitment to the army. Thus, in June 1918, after all thoughts of conscription had been abandoned, Lord Lieutenant French issued a proclamation aimed at replenishing the Irish divisions at the front by 50,000 men before 1 October. One particular inducement made a potent appeal – the promise of landownership. According to the proclamation: 'Steps are, therefore, being taken to ensure, as far as possible, that land shall be available for men who have fought for their country'.[51] Significantly, the appeal was aimed 'almost entirely' at young men in urban areas – shop assistants, publicans' assistants and so on – who were 'mostly transplanted countrymen, the sons of small farmers'.[52] According to the editor of *The Irish Times*: 'The instinct of the land is strong in them and they are told now that its gratification will be the reward of honourable service in their country's cause'.[53] However, the editor felt that the government had acted 'tardily' in this matter; it should have noticed the potential of the promise of land as an inducement to recruitment long before. In December 1919, as a follow-up to the proclamation, the British government introduced an act to facilitate the provision of land in Ireland for Irish men who had served in the British army, navy or air forces during the course of the First World War.[54] Up to March 1921, the commissioners had purchased 5,046 acres of untenanted land under the act for £125,000 and were in negotiations to purchase a further 10,600 acres to accommodate former soldiers and sailors. By then, 134 ex-servicemen had been given possession of holdings comprising 2,700 acres (or a respectable average of just over 20 acres each).[55]

In the meantime, the general election of December 1918 saw Sinn Féin win 73 out of 105 seats. In January 1919, Sinn Féin established a parliament in Dublin, styled Dáil Éireann, and a government that declared independence. At the beginning of April, the Dáil turned to the agrarian commitments that Sinn Féin had made to the electorate and the following resolution was introduced:

> That this assembly pledges itself to a fair and full redistribution of the vacant lands and ranches of Ireland among the uneconomic holders and landless men. That no purchase by private individuals of non-residential land in the Congested Districts, or other land essential for the carrying out of any such schemes of land settlement as the Dáil may decide upon, which has taken place since Easter Monday, 1916, be sanctioned now or subsequently by the Irish Republican Government. That this resolution be taken as conveying a warning to those who have recently availed themselves of the crisis in national affairs to annex large tracts of land against the will and interests of the people.[56]

After discussion (the records of which are not available) this motion was withdrawn, ostensibly because the question of land policy had yet to be discussed
by the Department of Agriculture, although it is more likely that Dáil members were acutely aware of the potential hazards in attempting to promise
what they did not yet have the machinery to deliver. But the motion itself is
arguably significant. First of all, a democratically elected government representing an Irish republic deemed land redistribution to be one of the most
important duties to be performed by it. Vacant lands undoubtedly referred to
untenanted and demesne lands, still in the ownership of traditional landlords.
It was to be expected that these would be targeted, given that they were owned
by a class that was perceived to be representative of what the republic aimed
to overthrow.

To target the ranches had, of course, long been a political catch-cry. But in
a Dáil resolution it could very well have been construed to indicate that the
Dáil was dangling a carrot in front of younger sons of farmers as well as
labourers inviting them to partake in the rewards of a political revolution. Yet
at the same time, there was a warning to those who were grabbing land. This
was becoming a worrying aspect to the politicians: by producing rural anarchy
that would pit smallholders against strong farmers and labourers and the
landless against both, agitation could undermine the primary aim of Sinn Féin
to secure political independence.

In March 1919, a number of isolated incidents over a wide geographical
spread had suggested to the inspector-general of the RIC that there was
a danger of an increase in violent agrarian crimes. John O'Hara's house in
Kilmainhamwood County Meath was fired into because he ploughed boy-
cotted land; in Westmeath, shots were fired into the home of Peter Deegan to
compel him to give up a purchased farm; in Mayo, a resident magistrate was
murdered because he had convicted several Sinn Féiners allegedly involved in
local agitation; in Galway a herd was beaten to death for not giving up his
employment, a Franciscan brother attached to the agricultural college in
Kilkerrin was severely assaulted as he tried to gather his herd of cattle that had
earlier been driven, and a large grazier at Carnalough who did likewise was
stripped naked and beaten through the street on the day of the fair of Creggs.
The police were severely handicapped in what they could do to prevent crimes
of this nature. The inspector-general wrote:

> The police from their complete local knowledge supplemented by confidential
> information are almost invariably able to spot the offenders but except in rare cases
> where some tangible clues are found, the latter cannot be made amenable when
> witnesses are either afraid or unwilling to give evidence.[57]

But as the statistics below suggest, it seems that for the rest of 1919 the police were, in fact, able to keep agrarian crime in check. It was only when the IRA began to target the RIC systematically in the spring of 1920, forcing them to close rural barracks and retreat to larger garrisons, that a rather dramatic increase in agrarian crime occurred.

III AGITATORS AND VICTIMS, 1920–3

Agrarianism seems to have reached its zenith in the spring of 1920; Kevin O'Shiel later reflected that agrarian fever 'spread with the fury of a prairie fire over Connacht and portions of the other provinces sparing neither great ranch nor medium farm and inflicting on its headlong course sad havoc on man, beast and property'.[58] The limited statistics that are available neither substantiate Shiel's claim nor reflect the true extent of agitation – given the chaos of the time and the levels of intimidation the police were simply not able to compile statistics as they had been in the past – but, nevertheless, they are informative.

The total number of agrarian crimes reported for the period from 1 January to 19 May 1919 was 156. For the same period in 1920, the number rose to 712. No agrarian related murder was recorded for 1919 (note, however, the example of the Mayo resident magistrate above which indicates the unreliability of these statistics), but there were four recorded for the first five months or so of 1920 (and three more later that year). The number of cases of 'firing at the person' rose from seven in the 1919 period to 28 for the 1920 period; the number of threatening letters from 72 to 254; the number of injuries to property from 25 to 205 and the number of cases of firing into dwellings from nine to 91. (See Appendix I, table 2.2, p. 234).

A précis of agrarian outrages reported on a daily basis thereafter (for the period from May 1920 to December 1921) is really no more revealing regarding the true extent of crime but again it is informative in that it indicates the primary motive for agrarian crime throughout the country was undoubtedly the division and redistribution of lands. Of a total of 491 crimes reported for the period, 287 (58.5 per cent) were put down to the fact that an estate, a demesne or a farm was wanted for division; 106 (21.5 per cent) were categorised as disputes concerning evicted tenants who wanted to repossess their former holdings; 74 (15 per cent) were put down to local disputes or family disputes, many of which might very well have had something to do with division also, while the remaining 24 (5 per cent) were put down to a variety of other reasons.

It would be foolish to flag the widespread nature of agrarianism in terms of geographical spread or, indeed, intensity during the War of Independence

based on such unreliable statistics. What seems certain, however, is that the
extent of crime was much greater than these statistics suggest. Notably during
this phase, which was to continue until the end of the Civil War in 1923,
agrarian agitation was neither concerted nor organised through any national
central authority. Landless associations and evicted tenants' associations
sprang up throughout the country but no attempt seems to have been made to
co-ordinate their activities. Their members drove cattle, knocked fences,
burned outoffices and houses, sent threatening letters, dug graves outside the
front doors of private residences, beat and, in more extreme cases, murdered
people and seized land. But they set out no more organised aims than
declaring that the land was for the people. They proposed programmes for the
amelioration of grievances at local level but did not see beyond those to
national level. This was dangerous from the point of view of the burgeoning
separatist independence movement because local considerations overruled
national considerations. In other words, there was a higher degree of
separation between the land movement and the national movements –
particularly, as we shall see below, after the establishment of Dáil Éireann in
January 1919 – than there had been during any previous outbreak when the
Land League, the National League and the United Irish League were more
closely associated with the Home Rule Party.[58]

In comparative terms, the 1917–23 outbreak was most prevalent in the west
but everywhere carried out along similar battle lines: landlords versus tenants;
small farmers versus graziers; small farmers versus large farmers; labourers
versus farmers. It affected Catholic as well as Protestant landowners, those
who had bought farms under the land purchase acts, as well as those who had
taken over farms from which families had been evicted during and after the
Land War. Even employees and local shopkeepers were affected. A few
examples will suffice.

In June 1920, J. D. Blake was shot and seriously wounded as he walked to
mass at Kilconly in Galway because he would not sell his grazing lands to
some of his tenants. In May 1920, a man named Cooney employed on the
Kennedy estate in Waterford received a letter threatening him to give up his
job because the estate was wanted for division. In Sligo, an employee on the
Duke estate was treated even more harshly when he was put on his knees by a
gang of armed and masked men and threatened that he had to resign from his
job there. In July 1920, the herd on the Hanly estate in Tipperary was murdered as the land was wanted for division. Having been shot at in June 1920,
H. V. MacNamara's steward was the last of the estate employees to leave
owing to intimidation aimed at having the estate divided. The same month,
Bridget Shea, a shopkeeper in Tipperary, received threatening letters warning
her not to supply any more groceries to two men who held evicted farms in the

locality. In August 1920, the home of William Lonergan of Tinlara in Waterford was forcibly entered by a group of masked men and his son was murdered. Lonergan held an evicted farm that he had been warned to give up. Farm animals suffered just as much: cattle were often driven for miles, cows had their teats cut off, bullocks had their legs broken, their tendons cut or their tails lopped off.[59]

And as with earlier phases of agitation, unpurchased tenants refused to pay rents to their landlords. Thus, in December 1922 Patrick Hogan told his parliamentary colleagues that:

> For the last couple of years, there has been practically a general strike by tenants against the payment of rent to landlords. Generally speaking the cause alleged was the inability to pay due to the depression in agriculture. Possibly the desire to force land purchase has given its chief strength to this no rent movement.[60]

Landlords and their properties continued to be targets for agrarian agitators. A significant proportion of the 300 burnings of big houses during the 1920–3 period can be put down to local agitators who simply wanted to be rid of the resident landlord so that his untenanted and demesne lands could be distributed.[61] A Galway landowner who had lived through much of the extended land war of the late nineteenth century felt that conditions were much worse in the early 1920s:

> Even demesnes and land immediately round the owner's house, and already farmed by him may be considered suitable for division. In many cases the landlord has been compelled to give up farming altogether, owing to threats from those who consider that he is in possession of too much land, while others have not sufficient.[62]

When in March 1920, his fellow Galway landowner, Frank Shaw Taylor, reputedly told a deputation of locals who wanted him to sell his estate: 'You'll never see a perch of my land', he was found murdered a short time later.[63] Following the eruption of agrarianism in the west from the spring of 1920, 'large numbers of terrified landowners came up to the city for the purpose of seeking interviews with responsible Republican officials' and beseeching the Dáil for protection.[64] They rarely got either.[65]

Their position did not improve during the Civil War; in fact it deteriorated even further when in 1922 the British army pulled out of Ireland, the RIC was disbanded, and no official police force was ready to take its place.[66] It is perhaps in this respect, more than any other, that this phase of agrarian agitation from 1917 to 1923 differed from the outbreaks which had preceded it in every decade since the 1870s: during no previous outbreak were landlords forcibly ousted from their homes or their lands. Similarly, during no previous outbreak was land grabbing so endemic: in the past, land grabbers were those who took possession of evicted holdings with the consent of the landlord; they rarely, if ever, took forcible possession of occupied holdings. Civil war created the anarchical conditions for agrarian radicals to operate freely.

The anti-Treaty section of Sinn Féin refused to accept the legitimacy of the new state. In the west (where socio-economic conditions were so bad that the Irish White Cross set aside £25,000 for the relief of distress in the spring of 1922[67]), the IRA went predominantly anti-Treaty and drew the bulk of its support from small farmers and agrarian radicals.[68] The treaty had not promised any economic gains to the landless or the uneconomic holders and Tom Garvin points to evidence that some IRA leaders and their followers therefore joined the anti-Treatyites for fear of losing what they had been promised earlier by Sinn Féin.[69]

The corollary may also be true, that the political principles of the anti-Treatyites drove them to seek support for their cause through an agrarian movement. In May 1922, Col. Maurice Moore wrote a revealing letter to the Minister for Defence:

> The anti-Treaty politicians and IRA finding themselves in a hopeless minority, have adopted a policy very dangerous to the country and to the present ministry, though it has not been openly avowed. They are now making a bid for support through an agrarian movement.[70]

To members of the government this was of particular concern. Later that year, Patrick Hogan contended that: 'it would have the advantage of being much more popular, in fact quite in the best traditions. The "land for the people" is almost as respectable an objective as the "republic" and would make a much wider appeal.'[71] Hogan had his finger very much on the rural pulse. While land and political issues had traditionally been inextricably entwined in Ireland, it was arguably land issues that had provided the momentum to political movements rather than vice versa. For the majority of people living in rural Ireland, access to land continued to be possibly a more desirable commodity than independence and the Anglo-Irish Treaty of 1921 had made no provision for the completion of land purchase or the redistribution of large untenanted estates.

The perpetrators of agrarian crimes did not necessarily have to have had any political affiliations. In March 1922, agitation was completely out of control in the Clogheen area of Tipperary, but William Rochfort, a local landowner, writing to the Minister for Home Affairs, advised him that 'the men in question have no connection with the anti-Treaty party'.[72] In January 1922, Lt Col. Raleigh Chichester Constable wrote to Arthur Griffith that agitators on his estate were 'all young men . . . sons of my agriculural tenants'.[73] A report regarding the 'eviction' of Protestant farmers at Luggacurren in County Laois concluded that those responsible were

> a set of young 'hooligans' drawn from a district of some 3 miles radius, and comprising herds, farm labourers and miners from the adjacent Wolfhill collieries, none of who have anything to lose, and who are absolutely beyond the control of their clergy or of any lawful authority.[74]

This latest phase in the turbulent history of the Lansdowne estate at Luggacurren was itself instructive: it suggested that sometimes politico-religious considerations were at least as potent as purely political ones. The extended land war from the 1880s had reinforced confessional divisions even if there were Protestant supporters of the Land League or unsupportive Catholics.[75] During the Home Rule crises, particularly the third one from 1912, politico-religious divides were widened as Protestant Unionists faced up to the challenges presented by a Catholic dominated Home Rule movement. In the 26-county area (and particularly outside the three Ulster counties of Monaghan, Cavan and Donegal), there was a small minority of Protestant farmers (as distinct from landlords) who invariably owned larger farms than their Catholic neighbours. In the past, periods of social or political crisis had traditionally tended to heighten sectarian tensions in mixed communities. The revolutionary period was no different.[76] While southern Protestants were targeted for a variety of reasons – because they were loyalist, because they were suspected of co-operating with the British forces, because they were revenge targets for anti-Catholic atrocities in Belfast – it seems that land and ancestral grievances were very much to the fore as the root cause of many attacks.[77] Nowhere was this more obvious than around Luggacurren.

In the mid-1880s, during the Plan of Campaign, Lord Lansdowne had evicted a number of Catholic families from his Luggacurren estate in County Laois and replaced them with Protestant tenants taken mainly from Ulster. From then on, predictably, there was 'bad feeling between these Protestant colonists and their immediate Roman Catholic neighbours'.[78]

Early in 1922, two Protestant farmers on the estate, William Stanley and George Stone, were served with anonymously written notices to give up their farms within a week. They refused to do so. Early in April, both these men and their families were forced by armed gangs to leave their homes. Their furniture and belongings were 'turned into the road, their cattle were drived [*sic*] off the land, one or two men were left in occupation, and notices were posted on the doors that anyone entering the house or land did so at their peril'. Between 19 and 26 April, 16 more Protestant families in the area were similarly evicted. In all cases, these evictions were reportedly carried out by between 100 and 150 persons ('chiefly boys and young men'), many of whom carried guns and revolvers. On 28 April, Henry Sythes and his family were evicted, his cattle and horses were driven off the land. In this case, Denis Brennan, the son of a tenant evicted during the Plan of Campaign in the late 1880s was left in possession of house and holding.[79] One woman who feared she would be next to be evicted wrote to the Minister for Home Affairs: 'These poor creatures will not be allowed to shelter anywhere. No one dare take them in.'[80]

A short distance away at Stradbally, on the Cosby estate, four other Protestant farmers who had taken 'evicted farms' during the 1880s were now themselves 'evicted'.[81] On 25 April 1922, Richard Pearson, who rented 400 acres on the Scott estate near Rathdowney for grazing, was visited by an estimated crowd of between 300 and 400 men. They drove off his 80 cattle and 18 horses and then evicted him and his family of nine children warning them that if they returned they would burn his house down and murder him and his family, one of the raiders adding: 'it's shooting you and the rest of your sort deserve'.[82] Although this type of activity was denounced by the local Catholic clergy, it had no effect: land hunger it seems was much greater than the fear of eternal damnation. Those involved in the evictions and cattle drives had few moral scruples about driving Protestant farmers from their homes In a climate where land-hunger prevailed, taking land from so-called 'Protestant colonists' merely acted as a form of moral justification for taking land without having to pay for it. What is more, they received little support from the new enforcers of law and order. In April 1922, Joseph Johnston, a Fellow of TCD, wrote to the Minister for Home Affairs: 'I understand that the Republican police of Luggacurren do not take a strictly impartial view of their functions where questions concerning the Protestant colonists are concerned.'[83]

Similar developments in Cork are also instructive. There the IRA took forcible possession of at least 11 farms purported to belong to loyalist spies found 'guilty' and subsequently executed by the IRA during the War of Independence. At least nine of these were extensive Protestant farmers. These lands were subsequently let out to locals by the anti-Treatyite IRA, ensuring support for the Republican wing during the Civil War. To take one example: John Good of Barryroe, Timoleague, a farmer with 150 acres had been executed by the IRA and his land confiscated. In 1923, it was reported that 'there would not be an Irregular in the parish of Barryroe where [*sic*] it not for the grazing rights given to the local people on Good's confiscated farm'.[84]

While there is perhaps an argument to be made that Protestant land-owners suffered disproportionately and that land agitation was often fuelled

by sectarian bitterness, it was also true that Protestants owned a disproportionate share of large holdings that, politics and sectarianism aside, were
deemed suitable, in the eyes of smallholders and the landless, for division: the
1926 census report showed that Protestants who made up only 8.4 per cent of
the population of the Free State owned 28 per cent of the farms over 200 acres
in size. In 1917, before the revolution broke out in earnest, and before Protestant
farmers migrated in large numbers, this proportion was undoubtedly much
higher. In May 1922, Col. Maurice Moore told the Minister for Defence that
the rise in agrarian crimes in Mayo directed against local Protestants was not
dictated by a nationalist desire to exact revenge for the Belfast pogrom
directed against Catholics:

> reprisals for Belfast are only the cover for these acts, the real reason is to give the
> lands to the people and thus gain their support. The real reason is not that they are
> Protestants but because they are landholders.[85]

He was adamant that 'the people of the west have no ante [*sic*]-Protestant
feeling, but they have a strong desire to take the land, and that is being utilised
to raise an agrarian agitation, to popularise the ante treaty [*sic*] party'.[86]

Other groups of vulnerable people were also targeted. For example, police
reports for the western counties after 1917 make numerous references to attacks
on migrants who had been transplanted to new holdings by the Congested
Districts Board. They were not welcomed by locals who felt they had a prior
claim on any divided local estate. In May 1918, three migrant families were
forced to give up their farms at Brockloon in County Galway because of intimidation.[87] By 1922, the board was unable to operate any type of migration
scheme in that county because of intimidation of its workers. Local landless
men were simply moving into and confiscating the holdings making it impossible to deal with migration.[88]

Widows were also vulnerable. For example, there were numerous cattle
drives on the farm of Kate McGuinness at Garristown County Dublin from
1919 to 1922. During one drive on 10 March 1922 her cattle were driven six
miles from her lands, then divided into two lots and driven a further six to
seven miles in opposite directions.[89] In May 1923, Henry Colclough, a large
farmer in Tipperary, was the victim of an agrarian murder. Immediately afterwards, his farm implements were stolen, his gates removed and his stock
attacked: 'Under these intolerable conditions, and in view of the local hostility
shown to her, the widow sold all her belongings (including farm stock) and
left the place'. The lands were subsequently grazed by 'promiscuous trespassers
without let or hindrance'. Nobody was tried for the murder of Henry Colclough
or taken to court for trespassing.[90]

IV ATTEMPTS TO DEFUSE AGITATION

Local agitation flourished as a result of the IRA's successful campaign against the RIC in early 1920. But revolutionary contemporaries feared it was also detracting from the IRA's military campaign. In 1921, Erskine Childers, former director of publicity for the IRA and then the Dáil's Minister for Propaganda, wrote:

> While the IRA were establishing their authority as a national police, a grave danger threatened the foundations of the Republic. This was the recrudescence in an acute form of an agrarian agitation for the breaking up of the grazing ranches into tillage holdings for landless men and uneconomic smallholders.... There was a moment when it seemed that nothing could prevent wholesale expropriation.[91]

His fear was that 'the mind of the people was being diverted from the struggle for freedom by a class war', and there was a probability that this class war might be carried into the ranks of the IRA itself.[92] Arthur Griffith felt that if agitation were not dealt with, it would 'wreck the entire national movement'.[93]

It is, of course, notoriously difficult to quantify whether such fears were more real than imagined. But the fact that they existed in the minds of leading politicians is perhaps just as significant. The perceived need to deal with agrarianism suggested the uneasy alliance that existed between local agrarian radicals and their Dáil representatives since the 1918 general election. In July 1919, Robert Barton, Director of Agriculture, made a public appeal to the patriotism of Irish farmers and labourers who were becoming embroiled in wage disputes. Barton propounded that the closure of emigration outlets during the Great War had broken the nexus of emigration and that it was now up to farmers to do all in their powers to keep labourers at home for 'the goal of an Irish Volunteer is to live in Ireland as well as to die for Ireland'.[94] Barton was arrested a short time later but the following month his successor, Art O'Connor, made a similar appeal to farmers to co-operate with labourers for the common patriotic good.[95]

When such individual efforts failed to have a salutary effect, the Dáil was awakened 'from its lethargy like an angry mother to punish an unruly child'.[96] And so in June 1920, it decreed:

> That the present time when the Irish people are locked in a life and death struggle with their traditional enemy, is ill-chosen for the stirring up of strife amongst our fellow-countrymen; and that all our energies must be directed towards the clearing out – not the occupier of this or that piece of land – but the foreign invader of our country.[97]

Sinn Féin TDs went to their constituencies and warned recalcitrants of the consequences of their ignoring the Dáil's decree. Brian O'Higgin told the people of West Clare:

> After the victory has been won the Dáil will do everything to do justice to all, so that no Irishman will have to go to seek a livelihood far from his native land. . . . But this must be clearly understood, any individual who, after today, continues an endeavour to enforce his claims, to give rise to disputes, to write threatening letters in the name of the Republic to a fellow-countryman, must be aware that in so acting he is defying the wishes of the representatives elected by the people and is injuring the national cause.[98]

In May 1920, the Dáil took a more calculated dual approach of establishing a system of arbitration courts to deal with land disputes (amongst other crimes) and ordering that 'the forces of the Republic be used to protect the citizens against the adoption of high-handed methods by any such person or persons' engaged in agrarianism.[99] These courts were not a new idea in Ireland; courts along similar lines had operated during the Land League days and had continued in many areas under the auspices of the UIL until at least 1918. 'Semi-official Republican courts' had actually been in operation in Clare and Galway during 1919. The idea behind the land courts, whose structure was designed by Art O'Connor from a scheme proposed by Robert Barton in October 1919, was to fix non-occupying people – uneconomic holders, landless and small tradesmen living in rural areas with knowledge of farming but whose trade or business did not provide him with a decent livelihood – on untenanted land.[100] O'Connor's scheme now seems somewhat naive in its inception, but it did acknowledge that congestion would have to be dealt with, provision would have to be made for the landless and that both could be achieved only through the redistribution of untenanted lands.[101]

On 17 May 1920, the first land court was held in Ballinrobe, County Galway to deal with a claim to divide the 100-acre Hyland and Murphy farm at Kilmaine among a number of local landless men and uneconomic holders who had recently 'grabbed' it. Art O'Connor and Kevin O'Shiel presided and to the surprise and the chagrin of most of those present they decided against the claimants, decreeing that the holding was barely sufficient for the maintenance of the two joint owners and their large families. The court also considered the fact that beside the Kilmaine farm was a 700-acre estate in the hands of the Congested Districts Board towards which the claimants 'should have turned their gaze'. The claimants were indignant at the court's decision and continued to occupy the farm. However, about two weeks later, the local

IRA was given orders to arrest four of the ringleaders who were subsequently taken to 'an unknown destination'. This action by the IRA effectively ended the dispute.[102]

The following month O'Shiel was appointed a special commissioner for the land courts and throughout the summer of 1920 he held sittings throughout the west and midlands in towns such as Ballinrobe, Claremorris, Ballyhaunis, Roscommon, Castlerea, Mullingar, Castlepollard, Birr, Portlaoise, Tullamore, Granard, Longford, Manorhamilton and in Dublin. O'Shiel later described one held in Roscommon:

> The hotels were packed with counsel, solicitors, land valuers and litigants, whilst the streets of the town swarmed with hundreds of witnesses. Every single solicitor in the county, despite politics, and many from neighbouring counties, appeared professionally at some time or other during the sitting. The court was crowded with the general public, who took the greatest interest in the proceedings, and from the very start the peoples' courts were everywhere enthusiastically welcomed by all classes of the community, and their awards were, with a few exceptions, largely accepted and carried out.[103]

A similar report of a court in Galway appeared in the *News Bulletin*[104] of June 1920. A reporter wrote (in a sympathetic tone) that the court operated 'in a common sense way, relying not upon a complete and formal code of legal precedent, but upon considerations of equity and of the normal law as generally understood'. Before litigants entered the court (a room in a local hotel which was draped with 'Sinn Féin colours' and decorated with photographs of the leaders of the 1916 Rising), he observed that they signed a pledge to abide by its findings. At a table in the centre of the room sat the registrar of the court and three arbitrators (the local priest and three local businessmen/professionals). The court proceedings were conducted in both Irish and English. After the first case was heard, the litigants and their friends were asked to leave the room. They stood smoking in the street while the arbitrators deliberated. The reporter found that there was

> no pomp or ceremony of any kind – no theatrical gesture such as might be expected from men who deem themselves citizens of a young republic and creators of a new social order. It was simply an affair of busy men giving up their evenings to help out their neighbours to the best of their ability, reconstituting a native law where British law had collapsed. I believe that the decisions are perfectly fair and that political bias does not colour any verdict.[105]

Land courts were remarkably successful in bringing stability to threatening circumstances in many parts of the country, possibly because they appealed to Irish patriotism. At least this was the view of Sylvain Briollay, a French traveller to Ireland at this time:

> Above all, over these bitter quarrels of self-interest, there hovered an atmosphere of Irish brotherliness, a feeling that it would have been too degrading to appeal from the justice of one's own countrymen to that of the foreigner. . . . Republican justice derives its strength from the fact that it is not submitted to unwillingly, but accepted and loved as a proud token of freedom – and that here as elsewhere every heart beats in unison.[106]

Because the land courts decided upon cases in which tenants were given the right to purchase holdings, the Dáil, being responsible for the courts, had to set up a National Land Bank to finance these purchases. Again, the purpose of the bank, according to Patrick Hogan was 'to prevent . . . the land agitation from cutting across the national struggle and reaching unmanageable dimensions'.[107] The bank was eventually responsible for the purchase and resale of just under 16,000 acres to 850 people (who were organised in co-operative societies) for £340,000, at seven per cent interest. By 1923, this interest rate made repayments to the bank extremely difficult to meet. These lands were excluded from the terms of the 1923 Land Act, but the government made special provisions to repurchase this land from the societies and then it resold it to them under much more favourable terms.[108]

It is perhaps ironic that the revolutionaries of the First Dáil did more to quell agitation during the War of Independence than constitutional parliamentary leaders had done during the earlier phases of agrarianism. This was a fact not lost on western agrarian radicals. As Paul Bew has penetratingly concluded: 'when it became clear in the summer of 1920 that the revolutionary nationalist leadership was not prepared to sanction land seizures, the west responded by a relatively low participation in the War of Independence'.[109]

The revival in crime during the Civil War seriously perturbed the government. From the establishment of the Dáil to the truce in July 1921, the Sinn Féin government felt it had at least some control over the localities. Through a simultaneous appeal to the patriotism of agrarian radicals, the introduction of a system of land courts and the co-operation of local IRA units, it rather successfully dampened agrarian radicalism after the spring–summer of 1920. But the potential for agrarian anarchy remained. The treaty split revived it. The land courts became less effective, the IRA in the localities could no longer be relied upon and appeals to patriotism simply depended upon what side of the divide individuals wanted to take. Thus the Provisional Government watched with nervous apprehension as the latest conflagration of agrarian disorder, feeding off anti-Treatyite support, swept through the west and other parts of Ireland in 1922–3, fearing that if it was allowed to grow unchecked, it would do irreparable damage to the position and authority of the new government. It would certainly lose the Provisional Government the electoral support of the larger farmers who were becoming increasingly indignant at the state's inability to protect them.[110] There was also an acknowledgement that while the anti-Treatyites may have been fuelling agrarianism, they were merely exacerbating an existing situation in which a mass of uneconomic holders and landless people were harbouring agrarian grievances that needed remedial attention. After all, the Anglo-Irish Treaty of 1921 had made no provision for the completion of land purchase or the redistribution of large untenanted estates.

Patrick Hogan for one believed that government failure to stamp out immediately the renewed agitation would make it impossible to deal with the land question in the years ahead. He was concerned that the growing number of Irish refugees in Britain, at this stage reputedly running into tens of thousands, would impact negatively upon the British public's perception of the Provisional Government.[111] As it was, southern landlords were continually informing the British government, for example, of the chaotic social conditions in the country during the Civil War. Lord Midleton wrote to Winston Churchill:

> The farmers who have purchased their tenancies had begun in the last two months to pay their instalments again . . . but the general spirit of Bolshevism, which is being cultivated by the revolutionaries all over the West, will undoubtedly land the Provisional Government in further difficulties, while the land-lords in the districts affected are living on their capital and have not the money to pay their labourers.[112]

More importantly, Hogan realised that part of the solution to the land question lay in the completion of land purchase and that this could not be contemplated by an effectively bankrupt state without financial credit 'on easy terms' from Britain.[113]

From December 1922, the government adopted a number of approaches to combat disorder. By then, Hogan was convinced that dealing with land seizures was no longer a concern of the Department of Home Affairs or the civil courts; the situation was so ungovernable that it was now a matter for the army to take 'immediate and drastic action against people who [had] seized other people's land'. Hogan proposed that in early January 1923 the army should clear simultaneously three of four 'grabbed farms' in each county, transport the cattle they would seize on them to Dublin and have them sold. He thought it would be wiser not to arrest the grabbers at that stage. Obviously, a plan such as this would cause great resentment towards the soldiers involved, particularly if they were from the area, so to overcome this Hogan suggested that the raids should be carried out by 'flying columns' made up of men selected from outside the county. In February 1923, the Minister for Defence, acting on Hogan's suggestion, established a Special Infantry Corps specifically to tackle agrarian disorder.[114]

The Special Infantry Corps operated in large areas of the country but particularly in the west and in the areas of Cork where the so-called 'spy farms' had been taken over by the local IRA. By April 1923, Hogan was praising the work of these columns, particularly in Galway ('probably the best [county] at the present moment as a result of the operations of the Columns'). In June, he reported that all the 'spy farms' were cleared of trespassers. In most cases, these trespassers had been allowed to retain their stock on their paying substantial fines and signing an undertaking not to interfere with the lands in future.[115]

Naturally, such action was resented in some quarters. In March during a number of simultaneous raids on lands in Roscommon, the Special Infantry Corps ran into trouble at Runnamoat where men, women and children rushed at them while others attempted to drive the stock away so that the unit would not be able to impound them. The troops fired shots into the air, which had the desired effect; the crowd dispersed and the stock was rounded up and moved to Dublin where it was sold off.[116] During the debate on the 1923 Land Bill, Daniel Vaughan criticised the government for sending in the Special Infantry Corps to support bailiffs seizing cattle from three farms in Clonbannin, County Cork:

> These farmers . . . were the men on whose land the Clonbannin ambush took place, and where Colonel-Commandant Cummings lost his life. These people gave us assistance when we were out on the hills fighting against an alien government. I think it is a very bad action for the government to seize cattle on these farms for arrears of rent due to English landlords.[117]

There was strong opinion within government circles that force alone was not going to quell agrarian disorder (there was always the likelihood that sustained activity by the Special Infantry Corps would aggravate unrest[118]) or general lawlessness. In March 1923, the government took its first major legislative step towards the restoration of law and order with the enactment of the Enforcement of Law (Occasional Powers) Act and the District Justices (Temporary Provisions) Act.[119]

The Enforcement of Law Act was passed to undo the paralysis that had adversely affected the executive machinery of the courts. It was intended to tackle those 'people taking advantage of the political and national situation, withholding payment to their neighbour for value received, withholding money due in various forms, whether through debts, rents, Land Commission annuities, or in any other form'.[120] With bailiffs granted increased powers, landlords began to resort to the courts to have their rents paid. This put the new government in an invidious position; it could hardly be seen to favour the old landed class over the new order. If landlords were granted the opportunity to press for arrears or alternatively evict their tenants, the new government was likely to be accused of being no different from British governments in the past.

Ultimately, it was accepted that only land legislation could provide the final solution. Back in July 1922 a government spokesperson had written that 'the completion of the land acts is the most earnest concern of the Government of Ireland. As soon as internal affairs are sufficiently stable to warrant a step forward, measures will be taken to settle finally the land question.'[121] However, by the following spring it was recognised that it was more urgent that land legislation should be introduced to stabilise internal affairs.[122] Already, the first tentative steps had been taken towards the formulation of a new land bill as a matter of 'importance and urgency'.[123] By promising to complete land purchase and initiate compulsory land acquisition and redistribution, it was hoped that this might negate the popular support of the anti-Treatyites and initiate a return to more peaceful ways in the countryside. In this respect it could be argued that the new government followed the example of the British governments of the past who addressed various phases of agrarian agitation through the introduction of land legislation: the 1881 Land Act to quell the Land War; the 1885 and 1891 Land Acts to deal with continued agitation and the Plan of Campaign; the 1903 Land Act to counter the growth of the United Irish League and the 1909 Land Act to stabilise the volatile circumstances that centred on the slow progress of the transfer of tenant proprietorship under the 1903 Land Act and the growth of the so-called 'ranch war'.

There was one other major consideration as far as the new government was concerned. If civil war did not soon end and stability were not reintroduced to the countryside, the new government would have great difficulty in attracting long-term future investment.[124]

If the new land bill was to solve the land question in Ireland once and for all, it should have been very carefully formulated. Possibly it was not and this observation is not intended as a reflection upon the abilities or intentions of those who formulated it but rather upon the extreme complexities of the issues with which the bill had to deal and which would have required much longer than a few months' deliberation and planning (although, of course, few bill are

actually afforded such a luxury). While Hogan was aware that it was unlikely
to be the last land bill introduced to the Dáil,[125] he hardly envisaged it would
be followed by a dozen or so more over a 40-year period. It seems that the
anarchical climate of the time dictated that it would have to be pushed
through before the impending general election on 27 August 1923. In the
aftermath of the Land Purchase and Arrears Conference of 10–11 April that
had been established in an attempt to negotiate common ground between
landlords and tenants, Hogan had announced the mood of a significant proportion of the electorate to the government:

> They [the tenant representatives] informed the landlords in all moods and tenses
> that a great change had come; that they were now in a small minority, and an
> unpopular minority; that they could take the land from them for nothing if they
> wished; that the people meant to have the land cheaply, *and that if the present
> government did not meet the wishes of the people in this respect, they would put in a
> government the next time who would* [my italics].[126]

The conference failed to establish any middle ground between landlords
and tenants. For example, tenants demanded a 50 per cent reduction on first,
second and third term judicial rents, 60 per cent reductions on non-judicial
rents and on holdings in congested areas, while the landlords responded that
they considered the purchase terms as set out in the report of the Irish
Convention in 1917–18 and in the Irish Land Bill of 1920 were much more
reasonable and should not be reduced. Patrick Hogan admitted to President
W. T. Cosgrave that the tenant representatives wanted a bill 'on terms which
would amount to confiscation'.[127] While confident that the 'reasonable
landlords' were prepared to take what they could get 'providing it is anything
approaching fair play, rather than take their chance of what they can get from
the next parliament', he urged the immediate introduction of the land bill.[128]

The formal introduction of the land bill to the Dáil in May 1923 coincided
with the ending of the Civil War. Arguably, its anticipation significantly contributed to the decline in support for the anti-Treatyites' agrarian campaign.
The point had already been well flagged by the government that those who
continued to involve themselves in land grabbing and similar lawless pursuits
would be excluded from the benefits of the bill, a fact reinforced by the
Minister for Home Affairs, Kevin O'Higgins, in a powerful speech upon its
introduction in which he warned against recalcitrancy:

> Within the last year, under cover of activities against the Government, men have
> gone out in an entirely selfish, wilful and criminal spirit to seize land by the strong
> hand, or by the hand which they thought was strong. . . . [I will urge] on the

Minister for Agriculture from my department, that the people who go out in that spirit, who go out in the defiance of the law and in defiance of the Parliament to press their claims by their own violence and their own illegalities be placed definitely outside the benefits of this Bill.[129]

Dáil rhetoric during the debate astutely emphasised that the introduction of the bill marked the end of the agrarian revolution, the beginning of which was dated, with some justification, to 1870. In many respects, deputies from all parties were attempting to create something of a legacy for themselves: they, the first constituent members of a national parliament since the passing of the Act of Union would, as one deputy forcefully put it, 'dispose of the last remnant of Irish landlordism'.[130]

On 8 August 1923, President W. T. Cosgrave introduced a special resolution to both houses of the Oireachtas. This resolution was considered necessary in order to prevent the suspension of the bill for 90 days which could technically have happened on the written demand of two fifths of the members of Dáil Éireann or of a majority of members of Seanad Éireann unless, according to article 47 of the 1922 constitution, the bill was declared by both Houses to be 'necessary for the immediate preservation of the public peace, health or safety'.[131] Introducing the resolution, Cosgrave told the Dáil:

during the last two or three years a good deal of dislocation of the ordinary administration has been attributable to the land agitation . . . This is a Bill on which the maximum amount of agreement has been brought to bear by all the parties to it. . . . But I think the general consensus of opinion in the Oireachtas and in the country is that the measure is one that will go far towards making for much more peaceful conditions and much more ordered conditions and for greater security and greater stability than perhaps any other measure we have had under consideration here. We consider that the public peace is ensured by the passing of this Bill.[132]

Cosgrave's speech was strongly suggestive of the fact that the bill would have a more salutary effect than even the Public Safety (Emergency Powers) Acts passed the same month.[133] But was the bill really that necessary as a means of ensuring public peace or was it more of a political expedient at a crucial time in the genesis of the new state, or more particularly in the con-solidation of the Cumann na nGaedheal Party as the party of government? If the referendum clause was not bypassed, the bill could technically have been suspended for 90 days, which would have given landlords the time to follow through on the thousands of writs that allegedly had been processed during the previous months. This could possibly have had disastrous electoral consequences for the government in the general election fixed for 27 August. Back in April, Hogan had urged upon Cosgrave the necessity of an immediate introduction of the land bill before landlords began to issue writs for arrears of rent that would cause 'a very big row'.[134] If the bill was enacted all arrears of rent up to the final gale day in 1920 would be immediately cancelled, all those accruing from that gale day to the one preceding the passing of the act would be compounded at 75 per cent of the total, and no proceedings against tenants for the recovery of arrears could be begun or continued after the passing of the act. It therefore made good political sense to have it enacted before the general election.

The special resolution was passed by both Houses and the 1923 Land Bill passed into law on the following day, 9 August.[135] In the long term this act and those which followed would redesign the social structure of Irish rural society; in the short term it contributed to the return to more peaceful ways in the Irish countryside at least as much as any other legislative measure introduced by the government in the first eight months of 1923.

Obviously a considerable number of factors need to be taken into consideration when analysing the reasons why electors *might* have voted one way or another in the 1923 or any election, but it seems rather significant that Cumann na nGaedheal, the party which had evolved from the pro-Treaty faction of Sinn Féin, polled a higher percentage of first preference votes than the Republicans, or anti-Treatyite faction, in eight of the 11 constituencies that were coterminous with the designated congested areas, the very areas most associated with republicanism during the Civil War. The exceptions included Cork North. Here the Republican share of the first preference votes was double that of Cumann na nGaedheal but more significantly the Farmers' Union Party polled almost seven per cent more first preferences than the Republicans. Cork North was 'cow country', an area dominated by large predominantly dairy farmers who presumably did not want to see the break up of their farms. In Clare, the Republican share of first preferences was 47.4 per cent (about five per cent more than Cumann na nGaedheal and the Farmers' Party combined). Here de Valera polled over 17,000 first preferences, almost twice as many as his nearest rival, Eoin MacNeill (Cumann na nGaedheal). Perhaps more revealing is the fact that the other four Republican candidates polled less than 1,000 first preferences between them. One of these, Brian O'Higgins, subsequently elected because of the transfer system, polled only 114 first preferences; this was the TD who in 1920 had gone to Clare and warned his constituents against any further participation in agrarianism.

In total, Cumann na nGaedheal polled a higher percentage of first preferences than the Republicans in 18 out of 25 rural constituencies. It had significant first preference majorities in counties such as Cavan where congestion was recognised as being as bad as in the west; similarly in neigh-bouring Monaghan; and in the grazing, dairying and large tillage farm counties of Carlow–Kilkenny, Limerick, Louth, Meath and Tipperary where small-holders would have anticipated that the 1923 Land Act would work to their advantage. In all of these counties, a significant proportion of first preferences also went to the Farmers' Party (from almost 12 per cent in Limerick to over 23 per cent in Cavan), probably a fair indication that the large farmers hoped that political representation would lessen the blow to their property rights.[136] Equally as interesting is the fact that in the 1932 election, as we shall see below, most of these constituencies swung to Fianna Fáil after it promised a more revolutionary transfer of land under the terms of its proposed land legislation.

THREE

THE 1923 LAND ACT, ITS ORIGINS, PURPOSE AND SIGNIFICANCE

It may be too much to say that it is the first Land Bill [1923] ever introduced in an Irish parliament, but at least it is the first for more than a hundred years. It may be also too much to expect that it will be the last; but such as it is, its main purpose is to complete the work that was begun in 1870, and which was continued during the latter half of the last century, and which is still unfinished.

PATRICK HOGAN
Minister for Agriculture,
Dáil Debates, vol. 3, 28 May 1923, 1146.

———

I INTRODUCTION

There was, as President W. T. Cosgrave's 8 August speech emphasised, general consensus amongst the parties regarding the main aims of the 1923 Land Bill, which were designed to complete land purchase and to relieve congestion. Then, of course, those who initially were likely to lose most, the landlords who retained substantial tracts of demesne and untenanted lands, were unrepresented in the Dáil chambers. Even if their representatives had created much of a fuss in the Seanad, which they did not, it would have been largely futile and in the socio-political climate undoubtedly unwise. Because the Republicans refused to take their seats on the Oath of Allegiance issue, it is arguable that agrarian radicals were also largely unrepresented. There is also one other point that is worth considering: the issues that the bill attempted to deal with were so complex, as well as numerous and varied, that probably only a very few TDs fully understood the implications of the legislation they were dealing with.

It should also be emphasised that in formulating new land legislation, the government had to tread carefully regardless of the mood of the un-purchased tenants or agrarian radicals. The point has already been made in chapter 2 that this was determined by the need for British financial support to complete land purchase.[1] The sheer scale of the financial burden that the completion of land purchase alone would place on the state was enormous; the government's willingness to carry that burden is merely more evidence of the perceived importance of the land question to contemporaries. As noted already, in May 1923, Patrick Hogan estimated that the completion of land purchase was going to cost the state up to £30 million, a truly colossal figure for the implementation of any social policy, and undoubtedly one that constrained the political ambitions of Cumann na nGaedheal and, indeed, their expenditure in other areas of social policy. As one contemporary later wrote: 'it was realized that individual and national prosperity and stability, anticipated as the fine fruit of proprietorship, would be deferred'.[2]

It was unlikely that the British government would guarantee the stock required to finance the bill if it did not concur with its contents.[3] Secret negotiations were held in February 1923 between Hogan, President Cosgrave and members of the British cabinet, as a result of which the British government undertook to provide the cash and stock and, in return, the Irish government undertook to collect the full amount of annuities due each year and to hand them over to the British Treasury.[4] In April–May 1923, further negotiations were held to secure British acceptance of the terms of the bill; Hogan met with the Duke of Devonshire, while Judge W. E. Wylie (a future land commissioner) had, according to the minutes of the Executive Council, 'already secured from the British government unofficial acceptance of the main points'.[5] Memoranda circulated to members of the government suggested that it was determined to keep these negotiations secret, otherwise 'it would simply be interpreted by interested parties to mean that the terms of the Land Bill were to be virtually settled in England'.[6]

II FRAMING THE 1923 LAND ACT

In light of these developments, it was not surprising that the framing of the 1923 Land Bill drew much of its inspiration from proposals put forward by the land purchase sub-committee of the Irish Convention of 1917–18 (which ostensibly had been organised by Lloyd George to offer Ireland an opportunity to 'try her hand at hammering out an instrument of government for her own people') and later embodied in the 1920 Land Bill which, of course, due to the circumstances of the time, had not been enacted.[7]

The convention failed in its main objective of reaching agreement on the desired form of government, but it did produce a unanimous report on the completion of land purchase that made some notable recommendations. For example, it recommended that all untenanted land in the congested districts should be immediately transferred to the Congested Districts Board for redistribution. (A wholesale transfer of untenanted lands outside these areas was not considered practicable.) The report recommended that ownership of tenanted lands should be automatically transferred to occupying tenants or to the state.[8] Landlords should be paid in five per cent stock with a bonus added that would yield an income which would be adequate as compared with the landlord's net rental.[9] On the appointed day (a day fixed by the Land Commission for the taking of possession of land), the landlord would cease to be entitled to rent but he would have the right to sue for arrears.[10]

Most of the convention's recommendations were embodied in the 1920 Land Bill. However, the bill went a stage further by recommending the compulsory acquisition of lands necessary for the relief of congestion with the exception of land purchased under previous land acts (1870–1909), residential holdings, demesnes, home farms, parks, gardens and pleasure grounds, potential building ground and land held in trust by any government department.[11] Of course, compulsory acquisition was not altogether a novel idea. The 1907 Evicted Tenants Act, though a short and rather minor one in the land code, was the first measure to give parliamentary approval to the idea of compulsory acquisition of lands for the reinstatement of tenants (or their representatives) who had been evicted during the Land War. The 1909 Land Act increased and extended the compulsory powers of acquisition, though its application was limited and confined to the counties within the jurisdiction of the Congested Districts Board.

As already noted, the 1923 Land Act[12] has been primarily associated with the completion of land purchase that had been begun by the British land purchase acts.[13] Its title suggested that it was focused upon the 'occupation and ownership of land'. It was introduced by Patrick Hogan as an act: 'to complete the work that was begun in the year 1870, and which was continued all during the latter half of the last century [nineteenth], and which is still unfinished'.[14] It was, however, much more significant than a mere facilitator of the completion of land purchase. In its very ambitious attempt to solve the land question once and for all, it gave the newly constituted Land Commission powers to compulsorily acquire and redistribute lands with the anticipated results of the new agricultural order being economic prosperity and social and political stability. The act recognised that the completion of land purchase was only one stage in the solving of the land question; the other stage, which was much more complex and would remain intractable, was the relief of congestion.[15]

The relief of congestion had long been a utopian ideal. It had political appeal and it had patriotic appeal. Its adherents delineated the nation as being those descendants of Catholic Gaelic landowners dispossessed during the plantations of the sixteenth and seventeenth centuries who considered the untenanted and demesne lands of landlords to be prime targets for acquisition as a form of retribution. Thus when William Sears (Mayo, Cumann na nGaedheal) learned that under the terms of the 1923 Land Bill the Minister for Agriculture proposed compulsory acquisition, he felt free to tell his parliamentary colleagues:

> It is but fair to ourselves and to the nation that they [landlords] should get the treatment proposed by the Minister. Perhaps it is fitting that they should have held out until a National Parliament would dispose of the last remnant of Irish landlordism. This Oireachtas will put an end to a system that was the curse of this country, and I hope we will hear no more of it in that shape.[16]

Patrick Hogan was much more of a pragmatist, yet he, too, harboured a serious desire to translate this utopian ideal into a reality. This was reflected in the terms of the 1923 act: all untenanted lands in congested districts and such untenanted land elsewhere required for the relief of congestion, that is the enlargement of existing uneconomic holdings of less than £10 valuation or the creation of new viable holdings, could be compulsorily acquired by the Land Commission with a view to division and redistribution.[17] But Hogan was somewhat naive in his belief that: 'The difficulty in the way of effecting that purpose is not so much the shortage of land, but the shortage of land in the right places'.[18] The assumption here was that there were not enough untenanted lands in the designated congested areas, but he (and obviously other interested parties) had totally underestimated the extent and geographical spread of congestion elsewhere, which meant there was not enough land anywhere: by the early 1920s, uneconomic holdings comprised an average of 65 per cent of all holdings in each of the other 19 counties outside the congested areas.[19]

The exceptions, almost identical to those proposed under the 1920 Land Bill, partially benefited the remnants of the old landed class, in theory at least, allowing them to retain the trappings of demesne and untenanted lands.[20] The 1923 act made two further significant exceptions: untenanted lands that were run as stud farms or 'intermingled with woodland'.[21] Few of the great houses in Ireland had untenanted lands that were not intermingled with woodland. Regarding stud farms, this exception was understandable as the whole horseracing industry in Ireland was growing in importance and the government was well aware of the need to continue to promote it. It was not difficult for many landlords to establish stud farms or at least to claim that a stud farm was in operation. By the late 1920s, Lord Dunraven's Fort Union Stud at Adare was highly successful, as was Charles Moore's stud at Mooresfort in Tipperary. The Marchioness Conyngham established a stud at Slane. Sir Gilbert Greenall continued breeding horses and pedigree cattle at Kilmallock in Limerick, while Lord Mayo established an extensive stud farm at Palmerstown.[22]

Holdings owned by large tenant-purchasers who had availed themselves of the terms of the earlier British Land Acts were also considered legitimate for acquisition and division (the 1917–18 Convention had recommended likewise). It might seem political madness that Cumann na nGaedheal should also target the large farmers who provided the party with so much support. But in reality, such tenant-purchasers were safeguarded. If the Land Commission was to take up purchased lands, the proprietor had to be provided with a new holding which 'in the opinion of the Land Commission . . . shall be equally suitable for the said proprietor or tenant and of not less value than the declared land'.[23] Nor could the Land Commission compulsorily acquire land from an owner 'so long as there [was] other un-acquired land in the same locality suitable for relieving congestion which [did] not come within the exceptions.'[24]

It has been pointed out earlier that there were in the region of 114,000 unpurchased tenants. Many of these were substantial holders, usually graziers, whose farms, either as a single holding or a combination of holdings, exceeded £3,000 purchasable value and were therefore mainly in excess of 200 acres. Many of these had not purchased under previous land acts because, for example, under the 1903 Land Act the Land Commission could not advance more than £3,000 for the purchase of any individual holding. The 1923 act legislated that these holdings could be 'retained' by the Land Commission (which now replaced the landlords and became the owner of all unpurchased tenanted land) and divided for the relief of congestion in the same way as untenanted lands. The large unpurchased tenant was significantly worse off than the large purchased tenant; he was not entitled to an alternative holding but instead was compensated in 4.5 per cent land bonds. His security of tenure was therefore questionable, because it was much easier to compensate with land bonds than provide an alternative holding.[25]

Exceptions were invariably going to make it difficult for the Commission to acquire a great deal of land. So was the legal right of owners to object to the acquisition of lands through appeal to the judicial commissioner. Up to March 1928, there were 148 appeals to the judicial commissioners against the price fixed by the Land Commission in respect of untenanted land, 384 applications by motion for judicial declarations as to whether the 1923 Land Act applied to certain holdings and a further 3,667 objections to the accuracy of particulars of rent lodged by owners.[26] All of these caused a huge bureaucratic headache and obviously slowed down the process of acquisition and division. If, for example, the government had been serious about appropriating vested lands, where was it going to find equally suitable holdings as compensation? In 1933, during the debate on the land bill of that year, Frank Aiken, acting Minister for Lands, told the Dáil:

The words 'equally suitable' in the 1923 Act rendered the section inoperative. Even though the Land Commission wanted it very badly for the relief of congestion, they could not take vested land simply because no one would be satisfied that the land they were getting was 'equally suitable'. It was only in very few cases that the owner would be satisfied that the alternative holdings were 'equally suitable'. Usually, unless the owner got a holding that was two or three times the value of his original holding, he was not satisfied. In cases where the Land Commission was compelled to give the alternative holding, that holding was worth several times as much as the holding he was giving up.[27]

The terms of the 1923 Land Act were therefore somewhat ambiguous. With regard to compulsory land acquisition they were not nearly as draconian as resident landlords and large farmers might first have feared. While, on the one hand, the act appeased the masses of uneconomic holders and landless persons with promises of compulsory acquisition, on the other hand the terms were couched so as to offer protection to certain sectors of the rural population. The act embodied much of what was in the 1920 Land Bill and thus many of the recommendations of a sub-committee six years previously that had been largely dominated by the landed interests. It protected the class of large farmers that the government drew the bulk of its support from (a government that recognised the importance of the graziers and large farmers to the economy, particularly the cattle export trade, a huge contributor to fiscal revenue).[28]

Finally, given the secretive nature of negotiations between the Irish and British governments over the funding of land purchase, it seems quite probable that both agreed on the need to offer safeguards and assurances to the more politically conservative large farmer and landed classes. Back in December 1922, when Hogan had called upon the Provisional Government to deal with the growth in land agitation, he told his colleagues that the future stability of the state depended upon the support of such conservative elements:

> If we miss this chance of getting English credit on easy terms because the tenant and the landless men refuse to see anything like reason, it will be an incalculable loss. . . . It will alienate from us all conservative support in Ireland and this will probably have serious reactions on the financial settlement which we must make this year with England.[29]

III THE HIERARCHY OF ALLOTTEES

'The land for the people' had become a catch-cry for Sinn Féin in its early days of advocating agitation, but, of course, this catch-cry had been around long before Sinn Féin was even founded. The difficulty with it, whether it was used in the 1880s or the 1920s, was that its proponents did not fully calculate its potential repercussions. It promised land to 'the people' as if the amount of available land was a proverbial bottomless pit when, in reality, it was nothing of the sort. At any rate, who constituted 'the people' who were to be deserving of land? Back in 1908, the influential Dudley Report, recognising the difficulties that could be associated with such a promise from nationalists stressed that

> it cannot be said that the sons of tenants and other landless young men in any particular district have any better claim to the land in their neighbourhood than men in other parts of the country, unless they are direct representatives of men who were unjustifiably cleared off the land.[30]

The Dudley Report effectively consigned the landless to the bottom of any redistribution pile, by making a case for evicted tenants and suggesting that uneconomic holders from different parts of the country (migrants) were entitled to be given consideration in a divisional scheme before the local landless men.

This brings to the fore once again the whole question of congestion. Patrick Hogan continually emphasised that as far as he and the government were concerned the basic premise of land division was 'primarily for the relief of congests'. His consistency on this issue led Frank Aiken to tell the Dáil shortly after Hogan's untimely and tragic death in a car accident in 1936 that: 'His name will always be honoured for his work in connection with the Land Act of 1923 and for his efforts for the completion of land purchase and the provision of land for congests'.[31]

The relief of congestion, particularly in the west, was a very emotive issue in post-independence Ireland. Western congests were eulogised in the Dáil by politicians such as William Sears as the direct descendants of the victims of Cromwell, 'greedy landlords' and 'usurping colonists': 'There are a million people in the Congested Districts of Ireland, and if any man went through them he would think that the system of land tenure was specifically devised to see how much human nature could be degraded and still live'. Sears contended that the only solution to the existing problem was 'the reversal of Cromwell's policy, which drove these people over into the lands of Connaught'.[32] Similarly, another TD told the Dáil during the debate on the 1923 bill:

I believe that implicit in this event alone [the passing of the bill into law] is the undoing of the conquest of Ireland. For the conquest of Ireland was the conquest of the land of Ireland, held by Irish tenure, from the people of Ireland by foreigners who held by foreign tenure from a foreign king.[33]

Whether this is an acceptable analysis of the history of the land question in Ireland or not is irrelevant; it was more an indication of how emotional politicians were with regard to the relief of congestion and, indeed, the expropriation of landlords.

It is true that the population of these designated congested areas was dependent on land to a much greater extent than was the case in the rest of the country. According to the 1936 census, only 16 per cent of the population in congested areas was resident in towns and villages with a population of over 1,500 persons. To put this into context, the corresponding figure for the rest of the country was 46.4 per cent.[34] Farmers and their relatives constituted 66.4 per cent of the population gainfully employed in South Kerry, 66.2 per cent in West Galway, 71.1 per cent in East Galway, 74 per cent in West Donegal and 78.2 per cent in West Mayo. In comparison, similar figures for the counties of Leinster averaged 34.8 per cent and in the Munster counties of Waterford, Cork, Limerick and Tipperary, 35.5 per cent.[35] Congests had to survive on desperately poor holdings; only 53 per cent of the land in the congested districts as a whole could be classified as arable and so the Inter-departmental Committee on Seasonal Migration to Britain 1937–8 concluded:

> Few [holdings], if any, are capable, of providing a livelihood for a family, and only emigrants' remittances, pensions, unemployment assistance, relief, tourist expenditure, fishing, the rural industries which have been established here and there, and the wages of seasonal labour in other parts of the country and in Great Britain, keep the standard in these districts above the level required to support life.[36]

Migration was considered the only possible solution to the relief of congestion in the west. For this, untenanted land would have to be secured not only within the western counties themselves but also elsewhere, particularly in the counties of the midlands and the east where large grazier farms comprised significant proportions of the total number of holdings (see Appendix I, table 3.1, p. 235). But this did not take into account that the receiving counties also contained large numbers of uneconomic holders who felt, with a great deal of justification, that they were just as entitled to enlargements as migrants.

It was not until the committee stage of the 1923 Land Bill that Hogan produced specific details on the hierarchy of allottees (having made some tentative suggestions in the Dáil during the earlier readings).[37] In order of priority, local congests were first on his list. These were followed by labourers (more usually referred to as ex-employees), who would become redundant when the estates upon which they worked were acquired for division. Next came evicted tenants (or their representatives) and, finally, 'any other suitable persons'. Obviously 'any other suitable persons' included the landless but suitability was a stated prerequisite to ensure that potential landless allottees could satisfy the Land Commission of their competence to work the land, their intention to do so, and their guarantee that they would not sell, let or assign it in the future.

Hogan seems to have had great difficulty in deciding the actual fate of the landless in land division schemes. In June 1923, he responded to a Dáil question that 'outside the congested districts . . . though untenanted land will be bought, in the first instance for congests, nevertheless the major portion will be available for landless men'.[38] If at the time he genuinely believed this, he was again being somewhat naive; if he did not then his disingenuousness was a case of simply attempting to placate the landless, or more immediately the TD who raised the question, with false hope. Less than a month later, his actual intentions became clearer; he categorically stated that he was not in favour of compulsorily acquiring lands on behalf of the landless:

> We would find that the Land Commission would be faced with an organised demand to take land here, there and everywhere for landless men who are more numerous and who have more influence, and perhaps, organising ability than the ordinary congested tenant.

He emphasised that the government was prepared: 'to withstand any pressure that may come to deal with the more numerous and less deserving class in the first instance'.[39]

This is a quite revealing and in some ways quite extraordinary statement. For the first time, this was an admission by the Minister for Agriculture that all landless men would not be catered for, shattering the myth of pre-independence Sinn Féin propaganda. It was a throwback to the conclusion of the Dudley Report of 1908 that giving land to the landless was nothing more than satisfying their geographical contiguity to an estate that was up for division 'to the exclusion of other generations and other classes'.[40]

Hogan's recommendation that land be made available for evicted tenants or their representatives was earlier accompanied by another exaggerated claim that: 'We have made provisions to acquire sufficient land to deal with all genuine cases of evicted tenants within the period which is prescribed in the Bill'.[41] There was a precedent of providing land for evictees that had been established by the 1903 Land Act (and later endorsed by the Dudley Report of

1908).[42] Initially Hogan suggested 1881 as the cut-off point for the claims of evicted tenants (in acknowledgement of the granting of fixity of tenure under the land act of that year), arguing that 'if you go back behind 1881 you will have, not only a claim for each evicted holding, but you will have four or five'.[43]

Thus, the final hierarchy in order of priority as specified in the 1923 Land Act comprised local congests, migrants, ex-employees, evicted tenants and their representatives, and the landless.

IV ACQUISITION AND DIVISION: THE MECHANICS INVOLVED

After 1923, the mechanics involved in acquisition and division essentially remained the same throughout the whole of the period under study. However, neither the 1923 Land Act nor Cumann na nGaedheal's second land act in 1931[44] specifically set out the relationship between the government and the minister responsible for the Land Commission with regard to land acquisition and division. It was Fianna Fáil's first land act in 1933[45] that did so; it gave statutory recognition to practices that were already established.

Section 6 of the 1933 Land Act set out that the Land Commission was answerable to the Minister for Lands *except* in respect of the determination of the persons from whom land was to be acquired or resumed; the determination of the actual lands to be acquired; the determination of the price to be paid for lands acquired; the determination of the persons to be selected as allottees; the determination of the price at which the land was to be sold to the allottees; the determination of a new holding to be provided for a proprietor (or tenant) whose existing holding was acquired and, finally, the determination 'whether or not a holding has been used by the tenant thereof as an ordinary farm in accordance with proper methods of husbandry' (if it had not been it could be compulsorily acquired). Apart from these excepted matters, the Land Commission carried out all of its other duties in accordance with the directions of the Minister for Lands.

While the commissioners had excepted powers in relation to land acquired and its division, they took direction from the minister and his department as set out formally in statute or conveyed in ministerial orders and directives regarding the hierarchy of allottees. At various stages, different ministers found it necessary (or helpful) to establish internal committees to enquire into best land policy practice and to advise the minister on it. For example in 1936, the minister, Senator Joseph Connolly, established such a committee to advise on 'whether it is desirable to concentrate on the improvement of the position of the uneconomic holders and congests to a greater extent than we are doing at present or to give primary consideration to those rather than to landless men'.[46] Such committees as well as interdepartmental committees established by the government, of which more will be said in this book, advised on what direction policy should take.[47] Once formulated, new policy changes were passed on to the commissioners who were asked to implement them. Thus in 1933, the acting Minister for Lands, Frank Aiken, wrote to the secretary of the Land Commission praising the fact that in the past: 'The commissioners have quite properly followed the policy laid down for them by the government and the land code.'[48] It should be added that he was careful to act somewhat deferentially towards the commissioners: 'I shall be glad if in considering schemes of land division from now onwards, the commissioners will take cognizance of these proposals.'[49]

Having received policy changes regarding, for example, changes in the hierarchy of allottees, the commissioners through the chief inspector (who was also a commissioner) passed these changes on to the inspectorate by way of directives that were 'strictly private and confidential and under no circumstances to be shown or divulged to others than Land Commission agents authorised and on service'.[50] It was these directives that determined which category of allottee was to be given priority in the division of an acquired estate.

Estates and large farms required for the relief of congestion could either be compulsorily acquired under section 24 of the 1923 Land Act or acquired through voluntary purchase under section 36.[51] In the period from 1923 to 1978, 5,686 estates comprising almost 847,000 acres were compulsorily acquired for £45.3 million and a further 4,346 comprising over 510,000 acres were voluntarily sold for £26.5 million.[52] Of course, to what extent most of the latter sales were 'voluntary' in the strictest sense of the word remains to be seen: many owners, aware that the Land Commission was contemplating the compulsory purchase of their land, may very well have pre-empted the compulsory acquisition.

In the early years, the non-residential estates of the landlord class were the primary targets of the Land Commission but, as land reform policy changed during the 1930s and 1940s, any large farm deemed to be unproductive or failing to provide adequate local employment was just as likely to be targeted.[53] Because the 1923 act stipulated that an estate/farm could be acquired for the relief of local congestion, it followed that uneconomic holders in an area would be keen to petition the Land Commission for the division of large local estates/farms. Thus many acquisition cases were initiated by an individual smallholder, a group of local smallholders, or representatives of various evicted tenants' associations, or of landless associations writing to the Land Commission or simply calling to the nearest Commission office.[54] It was claimed that it was simply a matter of a number of people in a locality coming together, deciding that they wanted a farm divided for their benefit, telling the Land Commission that it was not being worked properly and the Land Commission would issue a notice of inspection.[55] Frequently locals drew the Commission's attention to estates/farms whose owners were deceased with no obvious relatives, or whose owners had abandoned them and emigrated.[56] In 1948, for example, the lands of David Frame at Lamberton Park in Laois were inspected with a view to acquisition and division shortly after his death.[57] In 1949, Bridget Rice (Monaghan, Fianna Fáil) asked the Minister for Lands if the Land Commission was going to inspect the lands of the recently deceased Mary McCann in Inniskeen, County Monaghan.[58]

Alternatively, interested individuals or groups often approached their local TD to make representations on their behalf either to the Land Commission directly or to the Minister for Lands. Thus, during the 1920s and the 1930s, parliamentary question times in the Dáil were largely dominated by requests from TDs as to when estates in their constituencies were to be acquired and divided.[59] Finally, Land Commission inspectors, during the course of their fieldwork, frequently came across land that they reported as being suitable for acquisition and division purposes.[60]

Once lands came to the attention of the Commission, the next step in the procedure was the drawing up of an acquisition report, a detailed document running to about 20 pages, that was completed by an acquisition inspector who effectively surveyed the land to be acquired field by field determining such things as the quality of the soil, the crops grown (if any), water supplies, and rights-of-way. (In the case of a voluntary sale, a proposal to purchase was issued to the owner.) He also valued the land and computed the price to be offered to the owner, which only the land commissioners had the power to vary. Until the introduction of the 1950 Land Act,[61] the price paid for untenanted land was a figure considered by the Land Commission to be fair to it and the vendor, hardly an arrangement that inspired optimism in the latter. Only after 1950 was the price determined by the market value of land.

When residential lands of traditional landlords were targeted for acquisition, the Land Commission, it seems, was generally willing to allow owners to retain 'a suitable area' around the house which was then excluded from acquisition or it could actually, upon the request of the owner, be purchased by the Land Commission and then resold to the vendor 'as if he were a person to whom advances might be made for the purchase of a parcel of land under this Act'.[62] A similar clause had existed in the 1903 Land Act that had allowed landlords to sell their demesne lands to the Land Commission for up to a maximum of £20,000 and repurchase them under the same terms as purchasing tenants. The obvious advantage was that landlords retained ownership while at the same time securing what was effectively a large low-interest loan. Under the 1923 act, the advantage was not so materially rewarding (vendors were paid in 4.5 per cent land bonds instead of cash), but it legally ensured that as purchasers under the act, their demesne lands could not be targeted again in the future. Thus there remains to this day in Ireland an ever-dwindling number of predominantly Georgian country houses with sizeable demesnes attached.

Where acquisition was compulsory, the Land Commission then published a provisional list of the land and a certificate that it was required for the statutory purposes of the Commission in the *Iris Oifigiúil.* The owner had one month to lodge an objection, which was heard in the Land Commission Court by two of the commissioners whose decision was subject only to an appeal to the judicial commissioner (after 1933, the appeals tribunal). In the event that a price could not be agreed upon, a notice fixing the price was published in the *Iris Oifigiúil* and served on the owner. When the price was determined, arrangements for possession followed. The Land Commission accountant placed the purchase money to the credit of the estate. Inspectors then arranged to let the lands until such time as a scheme for the disposal/division of the estate could be arranged. This was simply for revenue purposes. Occasionally there were cases, surprisingly rare it seems, where owners refused to allow the Land Commission take possession of their lands. In such cases it was up to the sheriff, sometimes with the help of the gardai, to take forcible possession.[63]

Where the time limit for the lodgement of an objection elapsed, or when the objection had been disposed of, instructions for the preparation of a resale (or division) scheme were issued by the acquisition branch to the inspector-in-charge. It was not always a case of immediate redistribution; very often, acquired estates were in extremely congested areas, where the acquisition of one estate was not enough to relieve the problem. In such cases, inspectors often waited until more land was acquired and in the meantime let what they had on hand until a total scheme could be arrived at.

It was the job of the inspector-in-charge to draw up an allotment scheme in consultation with his district inspector. This was, without doubt, the most complex and controversial of Land Commission tasks. The extent to which such schemes may have been determined by political favouritism is discussed in chapter 7; here follows an outline as to how schemes should have been implemented according to official policy.

All eligible applicants living within a mile of an estate to be divided were supposed to be interviewed by an inspector. For nearly every parcel of land there could be at least ten and perhaps up to 100 applicants. If there were large numbers of uneconomic holders in the vicinity, then the radius was cut down to half a mile in order 'to eliminate the very detailed enquiries into the circumstances of those beyond that limit given that there was no scope for providing land for those more remote smallholders'.[64] By the early 1940s, it had become obvious that it would be impossible to satisfy all claims and so where acreage available for distribution was insufficient to bring all the qualified 'and

genuinely deserving smallholders within the prescribed distance [one mile]'
up to the optimum level, the land was distributed 'in a fair and reasonable
manner amongst as many of such qualified smallholders as is practicable'.[65]

The inspector-in-charge then drew up an official list of applicants. From
the beginning, it seems, these lists were accompanied by the names of the
persons recommending each applicant (politicians, members of the local
clergy and other local dignitaries.)[66] An allotment schedule was then set out
detailing every applicant under headings such as marital status; particulars of
family (age, sex and so on); full particulars of parent holding (townland,
acreage, valuation, distance from estate to be divided and so on); details of
how the parent holding had been farmed in the past; details of the present
condition of the farm house and buildings; an evaluation of the character of
the person seeking (more) land – whether he would be industrious, have the
capital to expand and the willingness to work.

The final column stipulated whether each applicant was successful or
rejected. The main reasons for rejection included: there were more deserving
applicants (it will be interesting when the Land Commission records finally
become open to the public to ascertain upon what grounds were some applicants less deserving); the applicant did not have the means to work additional
lands, which usually meant he neither had the capital nor the support of
family labour; the parent farm, meaning the one to be enlarged, was not being
worked in a satisfactory manner, which by extension meant that the Land
Commission was not going to waste valuable resources on a farmer they deemed
unworthy of an enlargement; the applicant failed to disclose important information (which, it seems, was often withholding the fact that he had land
elsewhere, which not only highlights once again the hunger for land that would
motivate some to effectively lie but also begs the question as to how many
actually got away with it); and, finally, the applicant would be able to apply for
an addition on another neighbouring estate in the future.[67]

According to the terms of the 1923 Land Act, the land commissioners had
to assign lands in accordance with the hierarchy of allottees that had been
decided by the Minister for Agriculture in 1923 and embodied in the act. Later
ministers would change the emphasis in the order of priority from time to
time (sometimes upon the advice of the land commissioners[68]) usually, as
chapter 7 suggests, as a political expedient rather than a consideration of the
need to address social policy. Although the emphasis changed, the categories
remained intact and various cases were being made for all of them right up to
the end of the period under study.[69]

The commissioners were expected to take into account the farming competence of applicants, their marital status and family circumstances. During
much of the 1920s and the 1930s extra preference was given to men who had

IRA service during the revolutionary period.[70] Preference, as a general rule, was given to married men with families over married men without families, and both of these over single men, although how this rule applied to the IRA veterans remains to be examined. Bachelors who promised to get married in the near future had preference over those who did not. At one stage in the Dáil in 1953, Sean MacEoin suggested resuming the holdings of those who had broken their promises to marry: 'There is no point in allocating land to people who are not going to make use of it in that direction. It is a waste of time and energy'.[71] Any allottee that the Land Commission officials suspected might let, sell or otherwise dispose of an allotment was automatically disqualified (although how this could possibly be determined also remains to be elucidated.)[72]

From 1923 right up to the end of the period under study, the allocation of lands to migrant farmers was a recognised imperative in land reform policy. The removal of migrants from congested areas, particularly in the west, freed up farms that were redistributed to form more economic holdings in localities they left. They were not always welcomed in the receiving areas, particularly if there were local uneconomic holders who felt that they should have first priority on the lands to be divided.[73] Thus the relief of congestion through migration and the abiding need to bring all uneconomic holdings up to standard meant that uneconomic holders, migrants and the relief of congestion remained very much the foci of land reformers. So much so that while the remainder of this chapter examines the other categories of allottees in the hierarchy, a separate chapter (5) has been set aside to deal with migration.

V EX-EMPLOYEES

Once again, the earlier British land acts passed for Ireland had established certain precedents in relation to ex-employees. Under the terms of the 1909 Land Act, the Congested Districts Board was empowered to sell parcels of land to 'any herdsman employed on or in connection with the land'. Similar privileges were granted under the terms of the Labourers (Ireland) Act 1906 to labourers who had been employed on an estate for not less than five years prior to its sale. In order to benefit under the terms of the 1923 Land Act, employees had to be working on the estate at the time of its acquisition. (This stipulation did not prevent former employees trying their case. In 1926, William Crowe, for example, a former employee on the Scully estate in Tipperary was refused an allotment when it was discovered that he had been working as a county council employee since shortly before its acquisition.[74])

In the 1920s and early 1930s the bulk of the acquired untenanted estates belonged to the old landlord class. To give just a few examples: in Donegal, Sir John Leslie (of Glaslough in Monaghan) had 12,250 acres acquired; in Galway W. A. Persse had 5,700 acres acquired; In Limerick, W. C. Trench had 4,500 acres acquired; in Mayo, Shaen Carter had 19,600 acres acquired. Most of these had continued to be let on conacre with parts of them run as large farms, often giving a good deal of employment to stewards, bailiffs, herds, gardeners and agricultural labourers. By the mid-1920s, Mount Juliet estate in Kilkenny, for example, was a very efficiently run farm of over 1,000 acres giving employment to members of at least 50 families in the surrounding area.[75] Much debate centred on whether it would be more beneficial to divide such farms or allow them to continue offering employment. In 1929, M. R. Heffernan (Tipperary, Farmers' Party), who most likely had the large farmers at heart rather than the landlord class, argued in the Dáil that the provision of lands for former employees had not been a success and that:

> Serious consideration should be given to the fact whether more useful work could not be done by leaving the land in the hands of a man who is giving considerable employment on those lands than by placing a number of agricultural workers without capital on the same land. It is undoubtedly a fact that the particular type of experience that an agricultural labourer gets as a workman on a large estate is not the type of experience which fits him to be a success as a small farmer later on.[76]

Because no relevant Land Commission statistics are available for the 1923–32 period, it is impossible to determine exactly how many allottees during the Cumann na nGaedheal administration were ex-employees. There is, however, ample evidence to suggest that ex-employees were certainly considered in land division schemes during this time. When the Ballinlough estate was divided in Meath in the mid-1920s, for example, ten of the 16 allottees were former employees.[77] But there is just as much evidence to suggest that ex-employees were not always successful. In 1927, David Hall (Meath, Labour) pointed out to the Dáil that the acquisition of lands had resulted in large-scale unemployment and that 'with few exceptions, those who have lost employment . . . have not received holdings'. He was right to point out that many labourers were probably reluctant to take up allotments because they had not the necessary capital to sustain them.[78] It was, in fact, incumbent upon inspectors to ensure that potential allottees were capable of working a holding in a competent manner and that they had a certain amount of capital available to them to stock their holding and get it up and running. Thus, in 1929, when a Dáil question was raised as to why an ex-labourer on the Glenbeigh estate in Kerry did not receive an allotment, Martin Roddy, parliamentary secretary to the Minister for Lands, replied: 'The Land Commission consider that he was a most undesirable applicant, considering the fact that he has not paid rent for five years, and does not own any stock, not even a hen'.[79]

By the mid-1920s, questions were continuously being asked in the Dáil as to whether access to capital was, in fact, a *sine qua non* before a grant of land was given. The official Land Commission line was that while capital was not essential it was 'obviously a very important element that must be taken into account when considering the suitability of a proposed allottee'.[80] In fairness to the Land Commission, this was a serious consideration: it made sense that inspectors should enquire about the availability of capital to a prospective allottee lest they might be quickly forced to sell or assign their new holding. The corollary to this, of course, was that there were very few labourers in the 1920s in rural Ireland, particularly if they were married with a family, who had any significant savings (although Patrick Hogan contended that three or four sons willing to work with their father was capital enough).[81]

There is also the major consideration that labourers lacked any significant political clout. They were very much second-class citizens who, more often than not, were overlooked in local land division schemes in favour of local dignitaries such as shopkeepers, teachers and even members of the Catholic clergy.[82] They did not complain. Often reliant upon local shopkeepers and publicans for credit facilities, they felt they were not in any position to complain.[83] As one ex-employee from County Louth told me:

> I knew more about farming than any man in the parish. I kept farms going for years for them who were too lazy to work them themselves. But I got paid pittance. So I had no money saved and no stock. They wouldn't give me a divide but they gave it to them big shots who already had plenty of land.

When asked who were the 'big shots', he replied: 'The local shopkeeper and publican was one. He already had a farm. And a couple of big farmers who could change a pound note in the pub at night when the rest of us had to work nearly a month to see one.'[84]

There were many others who felt just as aggrieved. In 1927, Thomas Derrig (Carlow–Kilkenny, Fianna Fáil) drew attention to the division of the Burton Hall estate in Carlow where

> people who never tilled an acre of soil in their lives, and who had forty acres of land – private gentlemen with private incomes – got parcels of the land while 10 or 12 labourers who were living and working on the estate, through the operations of the

Land Commission have not alone lost their weekly wage of 30/- or whatever it was, but it is now proposed to throw them out without giving them a garden.[85]

One other point needs to be considered: because so many of the estate employees, particularly stewards, bailiffs and gamekeepers, were English or of recent English origin, giving lands to them was often bitterly resented by locals. In 1927, for example, some of the Leitrim–Sligo TDs (including Martin Roddy, parliamentary secretary to the Minister for Lands) and the Land Commission secretariat received copies of a letter signed by 19 Leitrim persons who protested against 'the giving of land to English and Scotch planters, game keepers and such people, and also English army officers'.[86] Most opposition was reserved for the so-called 'emergency-men' who had come to the aid of landlords during the Plan of Campaign days of the mid- to late 1880s when no other labour could be secured. Many of these were Ulster Protestants (and often Orangemen) who stayed on in the south working on landed estates. In 1927, D. J. Gorey (Carlow–Kilkenny, Farmers' Union) told the Dáil: 'I do make the plea that the emergency-men should get no consideration from the state. . . . He was the bulwark of the landlord – the most objectionable man in the district – and his continuance there must be always regarded as a slur and an insult.'[87]

VI EVICTED TENANTS

As was the case with ex-employees, earlier land legislation had established certain historical precedents regarding the claims of evictees. Under the terms of the Wyndham Land Act of 1903, tenants (or their representatives) who had been evicted in the previous 25 years were eligible to purchase loans provided that they were considered by the estates commissioners to be 'fit and proper persons to become purchasers'. If they could not purchase their original holdings, they could buy alternative holdings. The terms of the 1903 act were not enough to cope with the subsequent demands from evicted tenants and their representatives, and so in 1907 the government introduced the Evicted Tenants (Ireland) Act which gave power to the estates commissioners to compulsorily acquire land for evicted tenants:

who, or whose predecessors, were evicted from their holdings before the passing of the said act [1903 Land Act] in consequence of proceedings taken by or on behalf of their landlords and who made application to the estates commissioners before the first day of May 1907 to be put in occupation of holdings and whom the commissioners consider to be fit and proper persons to become purchasers under the Land Purchase Acts not exceeding 2,000 in all.[88]

Compulsory acquisition was limited: no tenanted lands were to be acquired nor lands subject to land purchase annuities, or untenanted land which formed part of a demesne, home farm, town park garden or pleasure ground. If evicted tenants were not happy with the parcels of land offered to them they could apply to be compensated for their interest. The act gave the estates commissioners the power to negotiate with new occupiers of evicted holdings to entice them to surrender their farms for an alternative holding in order to accommodate the former tenants.[89] By March 1919, 1,914 tenants or their representatives had been reinstated as purchasing tenants in their former holdings or other holdings supplied by their former landlords and 1,662 were reinstated or provided with alternative holdings by the commissioners on estates purchased by them, making a total of 3,581. This represented only about one quarter of all those who had applied to be reinstated.[90]

If the plight of the evicted tenants had been a burning issue beforehand, it became a highly charged, emotive one during the revolutionary period. They were ideal subject matter for propaganda purposes. They were exalted as victims of 'capricious eviction' and 'of rackrent so unendurable that eviction only precipitated a catastrophe which was bound to come'.[91] Thus, in his pamphlet *The Land Question* (n.d., [1917]), Sinn Féin propagandist, Laurence Ginnell, referred to the thousands of evicted families 'still unprovided for scattered from end to end of Ireland, living on charity, on sufferance, in uncongenial occupations, and in wholly different circumstances from what would be theirs if they had not been evicted', and argued that their reinstatement was 'a special right due "to the wounded soldiers of the Land War", by whose heroic self-sacrifice substantial benefits have been won for the rest of the agricultural community'.[92] Of course, whether they were all victims of rack rents or capricious evictions is debatable. But many of them had made a genuine sacrifice and considered themselves (perhaps with some justification) the martyrs of the Land War who sacrificed a great deal while some of their fellow tenants were secretly paying rents behind the Land League or the National League's back. Ginnell, appealing to the emotions of certain sections of the rural classes with his references to the inherent ills of landlordism, the greed of the graziers, the misfortunes of the labourers and the plight of thousands of evicted families could, therefore, conclude:

> The claim of the evicted and their descendants has been, and must until satisfied continue to be, beyond all question the strongest and most urgent of all the victims of the English garrison. The failure to satisfy those claims is the greatest blot on land legislation, and the greatest disgrace to the representatives who acquiesced in that most ungrateful neglect.[93]

This type of rhetoric was at least indirectly responsible for fuelling agitation throughout the country from 1917 to the early 1920s. Evicted tenants' associations sprang up in many parts of the country during the revolutionary period (it is impossible to enumerate how many were established but it is quite certain that they operated at local level in most counties), their aim being to restore evicted families to their 'rightful homes'. Of a total of 491 crimes reported in a précis of agrarian outrages for the period from May 1920 to December 1921, 106 (21.5 per cent) were disputes concerning evicted tenants who wanted to repossess their former holdings.[94]

In many cases the name of the IRA was used by local agitators to give authority to their anonymous claims. In April 1922, for example, Philip Houlihan of Urlingford in County Kilkenny received the following: 'Just a line too [sic] give you a final warning if you have not the land giving [sic] up in six dayes [sic] your house and your self has too [sic] take the consequences. Signed the IRA.'[95] Elsewhere, local tensions were heightened by sectarianism where Protestant families had taken over evicted farms during the Land War. At Luggacurren on 28 April 1922, the Protestant Sythe family was evicted by a gang of armed men who drove their cattle and horses off the land and installed Denis Brennan, the son of a tenant evicted during the Plan of Campaign, in their place.[96] During the spring and early summer of 1922 at Ballinagh in Cavan, two Protestant farmers, George Cartwright and another man named Carleton, were violently threatened on numerous occasions. They pleaded with the Minister for Home Affairs for assistance who, in turn, ordered the Free State army to protect them. However, the captain of the local unit made it quite clear in no uncertain terms that the two farmers were held in odium in the area for good reason. Back in 1886, Cartwright had taken over the evicted farm of the Masterson family (in which there had been 12 children ranging in ages from one to 18 years). He allegedly 'entered the place, carrying arms, in a defiant manner, driving cattle to the lands'. The hostility of the locals towards these 'grabbers' is best illustrated in the Free State captain's letter: 'Cartwright is a staunch Orangeman, and I may mention a typical "Cromwellian" who never tires of ridiculing Catholics. He has a family of six, two of whom are [B] Specials.' Regarding Carleton, his demeanour

> until recently was most aggressive. He always carried arms and indulged in firing shots along the country roads with a view to terrorising the inhabitants. He is an Orangeman of the blackest type and never at any time displayed a friendly feeling towards his R[oman] C[atholic] neighbours.[97]

The import of the message was quite clear: the army was in sympathy with the local Catholic nationalist community and had little intention of helping these men.

In April 1923, Patrick Hogan condemned the role of evicted tenants' associations in the most recent phase of agrarian crime, contending and probably rightly so that many of those who participated in these associations were neither genuine evicted tenants nor their representatives. It infuriated him that their role in social disorder might have serious repercussions for his impending land legislation.[98] This was possibly one reason that led him to believe that evicted tenants (and landless men) were 'in the main persons who have neither a first nor a second claim to land'.[99] Another reason was that he believed there to be at least 100,000 evictees (or their representatives) who had lost their holdings during and after the Land War who would have to be catered for.[100] The number of eventual applications from evictees or their representatives for reinstatement under the Free State/Irish Republic land acts never came near this figure, but in Hogan's mind it simply convinced him that evictees could not be catered for.

Within the parliamentary party, the question of the evicted tenants had the potential to be a very divisive one. There were Cumann na nGaedheal TDs who were reluctant to forget the promises that had been made by Sinn Féin from 1917. In May 1923, M. J. Hennessy (Cork, Cumann na nGaedheal) drew on one of the more emotive Land War eviction cases to enforce his point that evicted tenants had to be given special consideration:

> Recently I met some evicted tenants from the Ponsonby estate. We were all young at that time, but at the same time we have read of the Ponsonby tenants. I think that estate was a landmark in that war. . . . I found that these people had a very just case.[101]

Public and parliamentary pressure thus forced Hogan to reconsider and so he introduced evicted tenants into his hierarchy of allottees under the 1923 Land Act behind congests and ex-employees. The problem of the most appropriate cut-off date to choose of course remained. In a Dáil debate in October 1924, Thomas Nagle made the impractical suggestion that they should go back to the Famine, only to be reminded by Hogan that such a policy would entail the eviction of a very large percentage of tenants and tenant purchasers, the necessity to reclaim a considerable area of the Irish Sea so as to make more land available and an amendment to the 1923 Land Act so as to exclude all labourers, landless men, and a very large number of existing congests.[102] Many were aggrieved at setting the eviction post 1881, as Hogan had originally recommended. For example, P.J. Ward (Donegal, Cumann na nGaedheal) brought up the case of the infamous Derryveagh evictions of 1861 and expressed concern that those tenants or their representatives would not come under the terms of the act.[103] That had been one of the most notorious clearances of the post-Famine period when John George Adair, one of the new class of post-Famine entrepreneurial landlords, evicted 47 families, totalling 247 persons, from 11,600 acres of virtually barren land because he believed they were in some way implicated in the murder of his Scottish steward, James Murray.[104] For many, Derryveagh symbolised everything that was detestable about the system of landlordism.

The cut-off point was eventually set at 1878 but exceptions were made. In 1927, the government agreed that allotments should be provided to represen-tatives of the Derryveagh evictions still living in the area.[105] By 1935, allotments had been provided for eight people. One woman, Mary Sweeney from Creeslough, had not been provided for, so James Dillon (Donegal, Centre Party) asked in the Dáil:

> Will the parliamentary secretary bear in mind that while it would be impossible for a tenant evicted in the Derryveigh [sic] evictions to be still alive, this particular woman was, in fact, then a child living in one of the houses from which the tenants were evicted and is, in that sense, the only surviving person actually evicted in the Derryveigh evictions and would, therefore, seem to have a pre-eminent claim to reinstatement on that land when an opportunity of reinstating evicted tenants presents itself?[106]

By the 1920s, there were hundreds of evicted holdings which had remained vacant in the country since the Land War, the Plan of Campaign days or the ranch war of the early twentieth century,[107] which landlords had not rented out either by choice or because they could not get new tenants to take them over. The 1923 Land Act provided no concrete guarantees that all such holdings would be sold to the original tenant or his representative.[108] The commissioners were instructed to choose men competent to work such holdings, not men with little or no farming experience who just happened to be the descendant of the evicted tenant.[109] When an amendment to the 1926 Land Bill was proposed by James Cosgrave (Galway, Independent) 'that the Land Act of 1923 shall be amended to make provision for the reinstatement to their holdings of *bona fide* evicted tenants whose holdings are now in posses-sion of the respective original landlords, their successors or other persons', Hogan objected strongly on the grounds that it would mean evicted tenants would be given priority over all other potential allottees. Nor was he in favour of giving land to a representative who was successfully engaged in business or who was wealthy enough to be able to do without land. This was understandable. Land division, after all, came as close to a form of rural social policy as Cumann na nGaedheal managed in its term of office. Land division was regarded as a means of alleviating unemployment and controlling emigration. Thus there was no sense in giving land to somebody gainfully employed. In May 1924, Hogan gave the example of a tenant named Cahill who had been evicted from his 130-acre farm (probably in the 1880s) and who subsequently emigrated to Argentina where he made his fortune and died a wealthy man. Under the 1923 act, his brother applied to be reinstated in this farm as Cahill's representative. He was a middle-aged, unmarried, reputedly wealthy man living in Dublin. Hogan argued that it made more sense to divide the 130 acres amongst five or six congests that to provide this man with a holding.[110]

James Cosgrave's amendment was eventually defeated on the grounds that to cater for all evicted tenants would represent a serious threat to the existing security of tenure of those who had purchased evicted holdings without any intimation whatever that there would be an objection in the future. Not pleased with the outcome, Cosgrave dramatically (and unfairly) proclaimed 'a glorious victory for the Clanricarde and Smith-Barry planters'.[111]

In February 1924, Patrick Hogan had actually used the Clanricarde estate in County Galway to illustrate the difficulties involved in appeasing evicted tenants at local level. Patrick Gallagher had been evicted from his holding at Traeneerla on the Clanricarde estate during the Land War. Sometime before 1914, his nephew applied to the estates commissioners to be reinstated as his representative under the terms of the 1909 Land Act. Because of the First World War and the revolutionary period, nothing had been formalised. Michael Gallagher died sometime before 1923. Upon his death, and with news that the new land act made provision for evicted tenants, several persons applied to take Michael Gallagher's place as the representative of Patrick Gallagher. These included Michael's brother who resided in New York; a cousin (whose mother was a purchaser on the Clanricarde estate); another cousin who was a shop assistant in Aughrim; a man (no relationship specified) who had lived with Michael Gallagher until his death and who forwarded a copy of the latter's will to the Land Commission as proof that he had been given the rights to the evicted holding. His cousin, a shop assistant in Aughrim, also furnished proof that Gallagher had made a will in his favour and that he had defrayed the funeral expenses in consequence. Eventually, the Land Commission took the easy option: they took no action with regard to any of these applications and instead sold the holding to another evicted tenant.[112]

In fairness to the Land Commission inspectors, they had to be discerning about whom they chose as potential allottees. In April 1925, the case of Michael Whelan of Kilkea in Kildare who had been evicted from the Verschoyle estate in 1903 was turned down because he was eighty years old, physically unable to work the land and with no next of kin.[113] In 1926, a representative of Thomas Clarke, a tenant supposedly evicted in 1881 from the Bury estate at Edenderry, County Offaly, applied to be reinstated. The investigation carried out by the Land Commission into the eviction found that Clarke had in fact surrendered his lease, so it took no action.[114] There was undoubtedly a reluctance to reinstate those who were considered 'poor', that is with no capital to invest in a new holding, just as there was a reluctance to reinstate those who had alternative access to wealth.[115] And, as in every other aspect of Land Commission work, it was impossible to please everybody. In 1931, an evicted tenant offered reinstatement on the Woodford estate in Galway refused to take up his holding because his annuity would be substantially higher than his old rent.[116]

By the end of 1926, only 21 evicted tenants or their representatives out of a total of 1,284 applicants had been reinstated in their former holdings and 27 others provided with alternative holdings. Between them they received a mere total of 2,166 acres.[117] The Land Commission's perceived reluctance to deal adequately with evicted tenants continued to give rise to isolated outbreaks of agitation throughout the 1920s as evicted tenants' associations continued to adopt an aggressive stance in many areas. In August 1923, for example, four men were charged at Greenstreet Courthouse in Dublin of having conspired with others, styling themselves the Evicted Tenants and Land Settlement Association, to take possession of farms in various parts of the country, particularly Louth and Dublin, by 'means of menaces and threats of violence'.[118] The men were found guilty but only bound to the peace for three years, perhaps an indication that even the judicial system believed there was some ancestral justification for their actions.[119]

Similarly, in 1924 the Louth Evicted Tenants' Association met with Land Commission officers in the Imperial Hotel in Dundalk to discuss the division of the Robson estate. They were assured that their claims would be considered; subsequent disappointment led to a great deal of local tension and unrest.[120] In the spring of 1927, an agitation broke out in mid-Tipperary for the reinstatement of a group of local evicted tenants.[121] Another agitation broke out in County Wexford around May 1928 when 156 evicted tenants or their representatives made application to be reinstated in their former holdings or to be provided with alternative ones. The scale of this protest led the Land Commission to hold an inquiry; upon its recommendation only 12 of the tenants or their representatives were reinstated.[122] In 1927, the Department of Agriculture found it necessary to send out letters to evicted tenants associations throughout the country in an attempt to quell the growing tensions, promising that: 'It is the intentions of the Irish government to deal completely with the question of the evicted tenants . . . Those who are concerned on their behalf may rest assured that no genuine evicted tenant will in the end be unprovided for.'[123]

Despite the fact that this letter was issued from Hogan's department, the minister remained reluctant to consider evicted tenants or their representatives to be as deserving of lands as congests. Time after time, he was criticised in the Dáil by the opposition for having 'forgotten the sacrifices made by the people who took part in the Land War' and for having 'congests on the brain'.[124] In March 1927, M. J. Corry (Cork, Fianna Fáil) reminded the government of promises made during the revolutionary period:

> I remember in 1920 that guarantees were given by the Republican government of the day to the evicted tenants that their claims would be first considered. I have seen estates divided in my district and nobody knew where the gentlemen came from to whom these estates were given, whilst there are evicted tenants in that district, men who went out in the Land War – and in consequence of fighting landlordism lost their farms – in order that some benefit might be derived from the land by the unfortunate people who slaved and worked on it. I notice that these evicted tenants' claims are absolutely ignored at the present day.[125]

There was possibly more than an element of truth in the allegation made by R. S. Anthony (Cork, Labour) in 1929 that the reason evicted tenants had not been catered for was simply because they had 'small voting power when a general election comes on'.[126]

VII THE LANDLESS

From the 1920s, the most aggrieved sector of rural society from the point of view of land division was the landless. But who exactly fell into this category? In August 1923, speaking on the land bill, Patrick Hogan told the Seanad that: 'Under every Land Act since 1903 landless men had to be dealt with and were dealt with. You have to deal with the herd, with the ploughman, and with evicted tenants, a certain number of them. This demand from landless men has been growing every year'.[127] The problem with Hogan's speech was that he categorised the herds, the ploughmen and the evicted tenants as landless men. These were, of course, separated in his own hierarchy from the landless: the herds and the ploughmen came under the category of ex-employees (those who were working on acquired estates), while provision was specifically made for the evicted tenants. In the strictest sense of the word, landless persons were those with no access to land, the younger sons of farmers who generation after generation, especially with the ending of subdivision after the Famine, were faced with the dilemma of whether to drop into the class of labourers, possibly secure employment in urban areas or emigrate. Similarly, generation after generation, they had been involved in agrarian agitation attempting to secure for themselves access to land whether at the expense of landlords or large farmers.

The 1903 Land Act acknowledged that there was a need to go some way towards appeasing the landless in order to curb the growth of agitation that had coincided with the establishment of the United Irish League. The act empowered the estates commissioners and Congested Districts Board to purchase untenanted land to divide among uneconomic tenants and where there were surplus lands to sell small parcels, not to exceed £5 in valuation, to farmers' sons. This was highly significant: by making provision for farmers' sons, the 1903 act gave hope for the future to claimants who were landless. But the Congested Districts Board had rarely any surplus land available for distribution. Up to 31 March 1919, only 219 parcels of land had been sold to the landless sons of farmers by the estates commissioners (152 in Connaught of which 102 were in Galway; 33 in Leinster, the same number in Munster and one in Ulster), the average price of the plots being £480.[128]

In 1917–18, the Irish Convention also recommended that land should be set aside for the landless. In June 1919, the Dáil passed a resolution that: 'The provision of land for the agricultural population now deprived therefrom is decreed, and a loan fund under the authority of the Dáil may be established to aid the purpose'.[129] In December 1919, the aforementioned National Land Bank was launched with its first social objective, according to Robert Barton, 'to facilitate the transfer of untenanted land to landless men and uneconomic holders and thus to prevent emigration and rural congestion'.[130] Forty societies, comprising a total of 850 members, were subsequently formed (seven in Galway; six in Offaly; four in Mayo; three each in Limerick and Kildare; two in Kilkenny; and one each in Leitrim, Meath, Westmeath, Roscommon, Carlow, Sligo, Kerry, Dublin, Tipperary and Louth) and loans advanced to them to purchase 15,750 acres. By August 1921, Barton assured the Dáil that:

> The bank and its land operations has worked harmoniously with the Land Commission [meaning Sinn Féin] courts and those who were concerned over the land agitation which sprang up in the spring of 1920 will agree that the concerted efforts of the two authorities probably averted an outbreak of violence which might have had very serious national consequences.[131]

The success of the National Land Bank in quelling agitation through its acquisition of just under 16,000 acres is, of course, highly debatable. But again it is significant that a Sinn Féin-dominated Dáil should be continuing the rhetoric of the land for the landless. During the term of the Provisional Government, former Sinn Féin deputies, now holding their seats on the Republican ticket, continued to argue in favour of land for the landless. In a debate in March 1922, David Kent introduced the motion that land formerly occupied by the military should be divided amongst the landless with, as we shall see below, preferance to be given to IRA veterans.[132] By then, numerous local landless associations had mushroomed throughout the country, simultaneously with evicted tenants associations. They were symptomatic of the growing disappointment amongst the landless that independence had not delivered all that Sinn Féin had promised.

Local landless associations canvassed and threatened on behalf of individuals, families and whole communities to have lands divided, sometimes working in tandem with the local evicted tenants association.[133] In 1925, in Clare, for example, a Land Commission inspector named Thompson was subjected to 'a considerable amount of intimidation' from local landless people when he attempted to divide an estate solely amongst congests.[134] Agitation in this county continued throughout the 1930s in the Lisdoonvarna area because the Commission had not divided ranch lands at Gowlaun, Ballyconnoe, Ballygastle and Ballydonoghue amongst the local landless, uneconomic holders and evicted tenants.[135]

Patrick Hogan was not a supporter of the compulsory acquisition of land for the landless, often pointing to the dangers posed by the organisational power of landless men.[136] His views were strengthened in 1924 with the publication of the report of the Commission on Agriculture that had been appointed by him (with J. P. Drew as chairman) two years previously, ostensibly to enquire into the causes of the agricultural depression of the early 1920s and to offer recommendations for its alleviation. Its terms of reference were laid down before the passing of the 1923 Land Act, but its final report attempted to set out some of the main factors that affected the proposed land division schemes.

The report urged upon the government not to admit men to land division schemes who had no experience of agriculture and not to allot small farms to men whose only experience was working on grasslands, namely herds who were entitled to land divisions according to policy as it existed: 'The settlers must be drawn from men and from families in whom the habits of industry and hard work attaching to tillage farming have been strongly implanted'.[137] The report strongly recommended that men be not given land simply because of the fact that they were 'contiguous to the land to be divided or because of their influence or importunity'.[138]

Landless men became increasingly frustrated and angry at the slow progress of the Commission in addressing their grievances. Again, because of the lack of satisfactory statistics, it is simply impossible to determine how much land the landless received during the Cumann na nGaedheal administration from 1923 to 1932. It is almost certain to have been negligible. In reality, it would of course have been impossible to provide farms for all the landless men who sought them. Those in political office and the Land Commission were aware of this. Members of the opposition were not simply being naïve when they continued to promote the policy of land for the landless as if the amount of land available for division knew no end; they were instead being politically astute for such policy made for an excellent electioneering ploy. Were the landless naïve enough to believe that land existed for them all? Possibly. The physical world of the landless very often did not extend beyond their native parish where most landless men could see large tracts of demesne and/or untenanted lands. That was enough for them. They did not have to think of the other categories of prospective allottees or even the collective national volume of their own numbers.

VIII THE IRA

Before proceeding with an examination of land division policy and the IRA, it must be pointed out that this section and later sections relating to this issue concentrate upon government policy devoted to rewarding with land those who had taken part in the independence struggle from Easter 1916 to the calling of the Anglo-Irish truce in July 1921. The role of the New IRA in the land struggle during the 1920s and 1930s is not considered, although there is plenty of evidence to suggest that they too, like all separatist organisations before them, saw the intrinsic value of involvement in local land issues as a means of garnering support. It is an area that possibly requires more detailed examination in its own right.[139] It was official policy to allot lands only to the Old IRA and so it is only they who are considered in this work.[140]

Before the Civil War broke out in earnest, the first significant debate on providing land for the IRA took place in the Dáil on 1 March 1922. David Kent (Cork, Sinn Féin, later Coalition Republic) introduced a motion:

> That it be decreed [by Dáil Éireann] that all lands which were in the occupation of enemy forces in Ireland and which have now been evacuated, except those that may be retained as necessary training grounds for the IRA, be divided up into economic holdings and distributed among landless men; and that preference be given to those men, or dependents of those men, who have been active members of the IRA prior to the Truce, July 1921.[141]

Kent argued that it was the first duty of the Dáil to the people of Ireland (and he specified the landless and the unemployed) to fulfil any promise made to them in the past in terms of putting people back on the land. The division of military lands, he claimed, was a step in the right direction; the break up of large estates would follow. He went on:

> I want to make myself perfectly clear that in giving the land to landless men, preference should be given to active members of the IRA who, during the trying times of the last two or three years, have given their services to the country. . . . These men and their dependents are entitled to anything we can do for them. These men came out not for any pecuniary gain, but for love of country. And the first duty of a nation should be to the soldiers who fought for them.[142]

Kent's speech perhaps suggested that the landless class played a more significant role in the IRA than has been assumed, although he may very well also have been considering the small uneconomic holders who certainly were attracted to the IRA. In reality he was not proposing that all landless men should be rewarded, but rather the younger sons of farmers. Thus, he accepted an amendment from Constance de Markievicz (Dublin, Sinn Féin, later Republican) that as well as being members of the IRA, landless allottees should also have a working knowledge of farming.[143]

Richard Mulcahy, the Minister for Defence, supported Kent's qualification clause that prospective IRA allottees should be confined to those who saw active service prior to the truce of 11 July 1921. So-called 'trucileers', those who had joined the IRA in great numbers immediately after the Anglo-Irish truce, were not to be included. At this stage there was no argument.[144] Then again, by March 1922, there were still hopes of avoiding a civil war. When the Civil War had ended, the whole question of which IRA members were deserving of land was raised to a different platform.

Kent's proposal of March 1922 was never implemented, largely because of the outbreak of the Civil War the following month. When Patrick Hogan formulated the terms of the 1923 Land Act and set out the hierarchy of allottees to whom land was to be given, there was no mention of the IRA. It is arguable that the Civil War did much to change the notion that IRA veterans should be entitled to land. A pragmatist such as Hogan undoubtedly realised the potential dangers of legislating that land should be given to those who had fought in the IRA, particularly if due regard was not to be paid to their previous farming experience. Hogan's policy, as we have seen, was that the maximum number of uneconomic holders, particularly in the designated congested areas of the west, had to be catered for at the expense of the minimum number of landless men. In 1926, he had to travel to his own county,

Galway, because of agitation on the Pollock estate by landless locals who objected to the bringing in of migrants. These migrants had given up their holdings elsewhere in the county in order to help relieve congestion. As such they were entitled to alternative holdings elsewhere but the landless men in the vicinity of the Pollock estate felt that they should have first preference. Hogan described the difficulties he and – of course – the Land Commission faced, claiming that it would be easier to divide an estate according to the wishes of 'a few super-landless men' in the district rather than in an objective way.[145] The 'few super-landless men' were probably those who had risen to prominence in the local IRA, whose sympathies had been with the anti-Treatyites, and who were now fuelling agitation on the estate. Hogan despised such tactics. He was, in fact, extremely suspicious of the Republican IRA's intent with regard to the land question. Peadar O'Donnell had 'a contact' in Hogan's office who supplied him with scraps of information. From these O'Donnell deduced that 'Hogan seemed to consider the [Republican] IRA was lurking in the shadows'.[146]

The first mention of land for IRA veterans in the Dáil after the passing of the 1923 act was not until December 1925 when John Nolan (Limerick, Cumann na nGaedheal) made the point that:

> there is one class who seems to be nobody's children and they are the ex-army men of the old Volunteers. I think if any class of people are entitled to consideration as regards land, they have first claim, because the Act of 1923 would not have been in existence at all, and we would not be here, were it not for them. They seem to have been forgotten in every department, and I hope when the minister sends his inspectors out that he will give them directions to have these men given special consideration.[147]

Rather significantly, only D. J. Gorey (Carlow–Kilkenny, Farmers' Union) and David Hall (Meath, Labour) responded to Nolan's remark. Gorey rather flippantly referred to: 'the new class [of allottee] who has been brought into the discussion – the national heroes'.[148] Hall took exception and responded: 'Had it not been for some of those heroes whom Deputy Gorey was hitting at he would not be here today'.[149]

Gorey's flippant remark epitomised the Cumann na nGaedheal government's negative attitude towards the IRA that had been causing so much disgruntlement amongst those who had fought in the independence struggle. Back in January 1923, the government's reluctance to reward IRA veterans for their efforts prompted General Liam Tobin and some others to establish the organisation that became the Old IRA.[150] It was not a political move; it was more an attempt to bring to the government's attention the widespread grievances of a body of men who felt that they had not been compensated for the sacrifices they had made during the War of Independence. While Tobin and his allies were embittered by the fact that they had been gradually excluded from key positions within the army, there were hundreds, if not thousands, of rank and file veterans, particularly former Republicans, who felt just as aggrieved about the lack of employment opportunities available to them (especially in the public sector) as they did about the slow progress of land division.

Outside the Dáil, grievances gave rise to a dramatic growth in Old IRA associations at local level, mainly composed, it seems, of Old Republicans.[151] In 1928 an Old IRA association was formed in Westmeath because there were 'a good many of the men who did their bit in the Anglo-Irish war unemployed in this area. . . . [and] there are several other grievances that need redressing'.[152] By then, there were too many like Paddy Hennessy, formerly of the third Kerry Brigade, who died destitute in Liverpool of tuberculosis and who was, according to the Sinn Féin newspaper, *An Phoblacht*: 'as much a victim of the slave state as any soldier who died in action'.[153] In the mid-1920s, this newspaper continually criticised the land division policy of the Cumann na nGaedheal government 'that preferred bullocks to people'.[154] A preliminary survey suggests that Old IRA organisations were strongest in counties such as Tipperary, Laois, Limerick, Offaly and Galway where there was a high proportion of large estates yet to be divided and where pre-Truce IRA men were hoping to receive parcels of land. By the early 1930s, the West Limerick Brigade of the Old IRA had drawn up a list of 34 landless members who were 'selected' as being suitable for holdings.[155]

At the Fianna Fáil *ard-fheis* in 1934, a speaker from County Offaly made the bold claim that under the Cumann na nGaedheal administration 'most of the people who fought against the Republic in the Civil War were placed in mansions and on broad acres, while other men were left out in the cold'. Unfortunately there are no reliable statistics available to confirm how much land IRA veterans received from the Land Commission between 1923 and 1932, but there is certainly evidence to suggest that those who became Free State army officers were well looked after. In 1925 a Land Commission official in charge of dividing an estate in Sligo is supposed to have given the lands to:

> ex-officers of the Free State army, some of who were living miles away, and in receipt of pensions from the government. Two ex-captains of the Free State army, each in receipt of a pension of £70 per year, received allotments on the Knockbrack farm. Several other members of the Free State army were brought in from other estates were given portions of this farm, with the result that the unfortunate congests on the mountain-side were deprived of the land . . .[156]

A document drawn up by the Old IRA Association of County Meath in the 1930s listed 'Free State army pensioners and gratuitants (who took up arms against the Republican troops) and who are resident in County Meath and environs', at least ten of whom had reputedly received land in Meath, although the size of allotments is not specified in most cases. Amongst these was Seán Boylan, possibly the most prominent IRA leader in Meath during the War of Independence and later a Free State army officer, who received fifty acres from 'a "grateful" Land Commission'. (According to an earlier Dáil debate Boylan had allegedly received 140 acres of the Cloncurry estate in Kildare much to the chagrin of local TD, Donal Ó Buachalla, who wanted to know why this land had not been divided amongst the smallholders in the area.[157]) A former captain in the Free State army, named Haughey, who was referred to as 'a Mayo migrant', received another farm and Sylvester Duffy from Monaghan, an ex-captain in the same army, received 60 acres.[158] Sean Collins, brother of Michael, took up residence at Roselawn mansion situated on around 300 acres in Celbridge, County Kildare.[159] To this day, there is an area of the former Cloncurry estate in Kildare between Athgoe and Newcastle that is known as the 'Free State' because those who received land divisions there in the mid-1920s were formerly Free State army officers. Given that demobilised Free State soldiers were given preferential treatment on roads and drainage schemes set up by the Cumann na nGaedheal government in the 1920s as well as in the newly established Gárda Síochana, there is no reason to believe that similar preferential treatment was not given to them in land division schemes.[160]

IX THE LOSERS

To put it simply: from the late 1870s a series of land movements – the Land League, National League and United Irish League – had all demanded the transfer of ownership of farm holdings from landlords to tenants and the break up of the large grazier farms for redistribution amongst the uneconomic holders and the landless. By independence, the land purchase acts had facilitated the transfer of the majority of holdings but there remained around 3 million untenanted acres to be dealt with.[161] As long as congestion remained a problem, both landlords and graziers would attract negative attention as they had done in the past and the revolutionary period had served to highlight this fact.

On 4 April 1919, the First Dáil proposed 'a fair and full redistribution of the vacant lands and ranches of Ireland among the uneconomic holders and landless men'. Given the nature of the inextricable ties between the Irish land

and national questions since the nineteenth century, and particularly from the 1880s, when militant separatists such as John Devoy argued that the final solution to the Irish land question could only be achieved in an independent Ireland,[162] it was inevitable that there would be a certain moral as well as social and political pressure upon the Dáil to deliver. It was no surprise then that in 1922 Arthur Griffith should have received the following reply to his query regarding the benefits of ending landlordism:

> It is of the utmost importance that landlordism be abolished; that no person should be permitted to own agricultural lands, except he used such for cultivation and lived on the soil. No person should be allowed to use arable land for speculative purposes or rent the same to another for a consideration. It should be distinctly understood that the land of Ireland, is for the use and support of the people of Ireland, not for the purpose of enriching or supporting landlords – whether foreign or native.[163]

Contemporary sentiment, as has already been noted, very much espoused the notion that the erosion of landlordism was in itself an integral stage in the move towards independence. Thus in the Third Dáil, when the 1923 Land Bill was under discussion, Williams Sears (Mayo, Cumann na nGaedheal) announced that he thought 'it is fitting that they ["die-hard landlords"] should have held out until a national parliament would dispose of the last remnant of Irish landlordism'.[164] This, in turn, gave rise to a popular consensus that tenants and smallholders had to be considered first and landlords second under the terms of the 1923 Land Bill.[165] There were those who would gladly have expropriated landlords' lands and who venomously denounced them as 'bloodsuckers' and the 'descendants of Cromwellian planters'. Some TDs harped upon Cromwell's edict of 'To Hell or to Connaught' and reminded their parliamentary colleagues of the 'emigrant ship' and 'the blood spilled by our forefathers' during the Land War. Patrick McGoldrick (Donegal, Cumann na nGaedheal) summed up the feelings of members of his generation:

> We are the children of the people who had to fight the power of landlordism in the past, who have had to stand up against it, who had to put up with the hardships that it meant, and who had to consider and feel a great deal of the sufferings and penalties that it had imposed.[166]

Previous land legislation passed by the British government, most notably the 1903 Land Act, had attempted to recompense landlords for the sale of their lands by artificially raising the price through the provision of a 12 per cent cash bonus upon the sale of estates. In 1908, the Dudley report had concluded that a landlord 'should not be put in a worse financial position than he was in before' by the compulsory acquisition of part of his estate. It proposed that the price paid to him should consist of two parts: a sum sufficient to pay off all his charges and a sum that when invested at a certain rate would yield the equivalent of his former net profit rent.[167] By 1923, attitudes in the Dáil towards compensating landlords in this way were, as could be expected, much harder. But if pro-landlord sympathies were not current, there was an acceptance, albeit a grudging one, that lands could not be expropriated without some form of compensation. As vendors, they had legal rights, which could not be ignored without running the risk of diminishing the credit of the new state, frightening off potential investors in Ireland or more significantly – as I have already suggested – losing British financial support necessary for the completion of land purchase.[168] Perhaps fortunately for landlords, Patrick Hogan felt strongly that the government was morally obliged to compensate landlords for their lands. Nevertheless the ambiguous nature of the government's 'generosity' was best summed up by President W. T. Cosgrave in July 1923:

> The question is this, are the tenants getting off too cheaply and are the landlords getting too much? . . . in one case they are giving all they can afford and . . . in the other case they are getting as little as it is possible to give them with any degree of justice.[169]

Those surviving landed families who have managed to retain their ancestral homes up to the present are all acutely aware of the problems which arose for the future of their houses as a result of the diminution of their estates below a level that was viable for maintaining houses of the size of Glin Castle, Ballinlough, Temple House and Clonalis. They are highly critical of the policy of the Land Commission that denuded them of the lands necessary to maintain their houses. They also condemn the fact that where the Commission acquired lands and accompanying houses, all too often it simply demolished the house with no consideration for its architectural or heritage value. They dismiss payment in 4.5 per cent land bonds during an extended period of worldwide economic depression as having been little better than expropriation.[170]

What of the graziers? Many had weathered earlier agrarian storms only to be thrown into the eye of another one from 1917. During the ranch war, they had effectively been protected by the vacillation of the Home Rule Party in which, significantly, many of them played prominent roles at both national and local levels. Sinn Féin was not likely to be as sympathetic from 1917 – Sinn Féiners, as is evident in Art O'Connor's speech below, regarded ranches as being anathema to the national conscience - and it became evident in the early days of the Second Dáil that a distinction would be made between large farmers who offered employment (largely through tillage or mixed farming) and those who operated extensive grazier farms that were not as labour intensive. Thus in August 1921, Art O'Connor, then Director of Agriculture, asserted in the Dáil:

> the national conscience would feel easier if the ranch lands were invaded, and it seems to me that a sharp line of division will need to be struck between the farmer who has done, is doing, and intends to do his duty by the state in working his land, and the man who, by keeping large tracts of land out of cultivation is a menace to the whole community. Voluntary operations with the former and the equivalent of compulsion with the other would seem to be the most suitable line.[171]

Again, O'Connor's speech at this time draws heavily upon the dramatic rhetoric of revolution: the ranch lands should be 'invaded' and the lazy grazier evicted for the sake of the 'national conscience'. Verbal hostility to the grazing system and the concentration of large tracts of lands in the hands of so few continued to stir passions and give rise to a great deal of rhetorical verbosity, usually from Cumann na nGaedheal backbenchers and members of the Opposition after 1923. But talk was cheap. Could a conservative-minded Cumann na nGaedheal government actually carry through the threat of expropriating the grazing lands of the country, and if so what consequences would this have for the Irish economy, so heavily dependent upon beef production? In the late nineteenth century the Home Rule Party was in theory committed to the break up of large grazing farms and their redistribution. During 1898–1903 and 1906–10, the party leadership had offered its support to the United Irish League during the ranch wars, but as Bew *et al.* have argued: 'In reality, despite much verbal hostility to the allegedly evil grazing system, the Irish nationalist leadership was forced to recognise at all the key points that the cattle trade was crucial to the livelihood of the great majority of Irish farmers.'[172] In this respect it is worth emphasising again that the 1923 Land Act was used to protect as well as to attack.

In 1924 it was acknowledged by the Commission on Agriculture that the place of ranching and the eleven months' system in Irish agriculture was still regarded as 'one of the most controversial of rural problems'.[173] But the commission also recognised the contribution of large cattle farmers to the economy. (Within the Dáil the Farmers' Party, while not opposed to land division, was keen to protect the interests of large farmers. The party's central line was that it was better for the economy of the country to leave the lands in the hands of men who were giving substantial employment rather than placing a number of agricultural workers without capital on the land.[174]) The conclusions of the

Commission on Agriculture possibly had a much more important bearing on Cumann na nGaedheal land division policy than has previously been acknowledged. The evidence the commission received, admittedly from interested parties, pointed to the fact that the first class pasture lands played an important and vital role in the rural economy as they provided the market for the younger stock reared by small farmers who on their own could not bring that stock to maturity.[175] The report concluded:

> We are inclined to support the view that either greater profit to the occupier or greater advantage to the community at large will not follow from their use in any other way, and we therefore recommend the government to proceed with due caution in the matter of their re-division.[176]

The report was much more pragmatic in its approach to land division than were many TDs. It recognised that 'no schemes of redistribution, however drastic, would ever effect more than a partial solution, as there was insufficient land to give every existing occupier an economic holding'.[177] And it did not promote the creation of a mass of small subsistence tillage farms. These could only be characterised by drudgery. The report pointed out that the average tillage farmer in the 1920s worked 'harder and harder for longer hours, and denies himself even necessary nourishment until he reaches a standard of subsistence far below that of the most poorly-paid wage earner, possibly far below that of those in receipt of public assistance.' The most suitable type of farm economy in Ireland would therefore be one composed of both small and large holdings that would facilitate the practice of mixed farming. But land division was too potent a political necessity for such recommendations to be universally accepted.

Did Cumann na nGaedheal subsequently protect the large farmers? There is no doubt but that Hogan was a proponent of large commercial farms – he came himself from large farming stock – a fact that often made him unpopular with many of his own backbenchers and members of the Opposition. So did many of his agricultural policies, which disproportionately favoured the large commercial farmer.[178] For example, while the passing of the Live Stock Breeding Act of 1925, the increased funding made available to the Irish Agricultural Organisation Society and the establishment of the Agricultural Credit Corporation in 1927 were intended to benefit the agricultural community as a whole, they were disproportionately beneficial to the strong farmers. The establishment of the Agricultural Credit Corporation [ACC] to advance working capital to farmers favoured those whose extensive properties offered better collateral as security for credit. In fact, Hogan told the Dáil in 1928 that the ACC was not intended to help the 'down and outs', but those with security.[179] The Livestock Breeding Act was of little benefit to small farmers who bred cattle simply to pay the rates and annuities. Egg production was a means towards self-sufficiency as well as a continuation of the barter-type economy of rural Ireland in which a basket of eggs was exchanged for credit with the local shopkeeper. Poultry farming in rural Ireland was not an industry; it was merely a means to making ends meet.

While it may not have been very popular to talk about the bullock in the Dáil, the reality was that cattle rearing brought £20 million a year to the economy. Hogan saw no wisdom in deflecting Irish farming into other areas of production. In fairness, such a deflection could only be brought about at somebody's cost: cost to the farmer if he was forced to grow crops at his own expense; cost to the taxpayer if diversification was subsidised by the government; cost to the urban consumer if it was funded by import duties upon food.

More and more there was a sense amongst the electorate as well as parliamentarian backbenchers that the 1923 Land Act had been something of a political smokescreen, promising revolutionary land division in return for social order. The government was continually barraged by its own backbenchers for not expediting acquisition and division. In November 1925, Martin Roddy (a very outspoken critic who seems to have been silenced by his appointment as parliamentary secretary to the Minister for Lands in 1927) moved that 'the Dáil is of opinion that the purchase and division of land under the Land Act 1923, and previous land acts, should be expedited so that tenants and congests shall be dealt with as soon as possible'.[180] By putting down this motion, Roddy was drawing attention 'to the very grave discontent that exists throughout the *Saorstát* [Free State] and particularly in the western counties because of the dilatory methods of the Land Commission in dealing with the distribution of land'.[181] The rather ineffectual Opposition inquired incessantly as to why estates were not being acquired. In May 1926, Hugh Colohan (Kildare, Labour) demanded that Hogan do something about an estate at Lullymore in Kildare that belonged to 'one of the old type of landlords' who it was 'nearly time to deal with'.[182] In 1928, Daniel Corkery (Cork, Independent) claimed there was no respect for the Land Commission anywhere in the country because 'their ideas seem to be to turn the country again into ranches'.[183] From its entry to the Dáil in 1927, Fianna Fáil attacked the perceived efforts 'to keep the midlands safe for the grazier'.[184]

Reasons had to be given when estates were not acquired. In 1926, the Land Commission made an inspection of the 2,000-acre demesne and untenanted lands in the possession of Lady Howard Bury of Charleville in Tullamore but on finding that 38 local families were employed thereon decided not to acquire it.[185] The following year, Hogan told the Dáil that the Commission was not going to acquire the substantial Franks estate in Cork because of the

progressive manner in which the land was farmed and because it gave employment to a substantial number of labourers.[186] More often the argument put
forward was that an estate could not be acquired because there was no congestion in the immediate area, which often led to accusations of favouritism.[187]

Indeed, different pretexts were used at different times: in 1927, the Dáil
was told that the Commission was not going to acquire the 600-acre estate of
George Mansfield at Caragh in Kildare because 'this man tills considerably
and gives a lot of employment'.[188] Two years later, the reason given for its non-
acquisition was that there was 'practically no congestion in that district'.[189]
Many were very cynical about the rather sudden establishment of stud farms
on untenanted lands such as those at Ballinlough, Killeen and Slane.[190] When
Martin Roddy told the Dáil in 1927 that the Gill estate in Offaly was not to be
divided, William Davin (Leix–Offaly, Labour) enquired sarcastically: 'Is this
another of the many stud farms supposed to be allowed in this particular area?'[191]
The protection afforded demesne lands meant that the earl of Dunraven held
on to 1,160 acres in Limerick; Lord Rossmore retained 1,430 acres in Monaghan;
the absentee Lord Harewood retained 1,400 acres around Portumna in
Galway; and Lord Rathdonnell retained 1,290 acres in Carlow, to name but
a very few.[192]

X WHY SUCH SLOW PROGRESS?

From 1923 to the year ending 31 March 1932 (a month after Fianna Fáil came
to power), the Land Commission acquired and divided a total of 491,501
untenanted acres (an average of 54,611 per annum) which was allotted to an
estimated 12,421 allottees (an average of 39.5 acres each). These statistics are
misleading, however, as they include lands (160,676 acres) inherited from the
estates commissioners and the Congested Districts Board. Thus the newly
constituted Land Commission itself acquired and divided 330,825 acres (an
average of 36,758 per annum) amongst 16,587 allottees (an average of just under
twenty acres, regarded at the time as the standard holding).[193] According to
the annual report of the Land Commission for 1933, roughly half of the
acquired land was utilised for the enlargement of uneconomic holdings while
the remainder was allotted to evicted tenants, migrants, discharged labourers,
herds and other 'suitable persons' (unfortunately no breakdown is given).[194]
Thus, an average of 1,843 people per annum had benefited from acquisition
and division. These statistics might seem rather impressive now, but they did
not impress land-hungry contemporaries who were growing increasingly impa-
tient with what they considered to be the dilatory progress of the Commission.

Furthermore, there were geographically determined grievances: land acquisition and division were heavily concentrated in the western counties (with particular activity in Galway) and in the midland counties of Westmeath, Kildare and Meath. Much less land was being acquired in the dairying and tillage counties. David Seth Jones argues that:

> the geographical pattern of acquisition and resumption thus was largely as expected. In areas noted for commercial grazing or ranching, tenure was much less secure than in those regions associated with dairying and tillage. It appears that both tillage and dairying, in contrast to commercial cattle and sheep grazing, provided some protection from acquisition or resumption because they were considered types of farming based on 'proper methods of husbandry.'[195]

The most practical problem was that there was never going to be enough land to satisfy all the uneconomic holders in the country, let alone the other categories of allottees as well. Patrick Hogan had, in fact, come to realise this by June of 1925: 'When we have completed land purchase we will only be able to deal . . . with about 60,000 congests out of a total number of 120,000'.[196] By November he had refined his figures even further. There were now according to his calculation 140,000 congests in the country, but the Land Commission would be able to acquire only around 1.2 million acres, which would provide the 140,000 with an average of only 8.5 acres each. Hogan therefore admitted that there were 'the elements of a very serious problem'.[197]

Cumann na nGaedheal or the Land Commission should not be unduly criticised for the tardy pace of acquisition and division from 1923 to 1932. In 1929, Martin Roddy, now conspicuously wearing his parliamentary secretary's hat, told the Land Commission's detractors:

> The alleged dilatoriness of the Land Commission has recently become quite a popular catch-cry, but those who are so ready to criticise have really no conception of the enormous amount of survey, inspection, administration, clerical and legal work involved in the purchase, improvement and resettlement of half a million acres of untenanted land.[198]

It was a reasonable argument, given the circumstances. First of all, the Commission was hampered by a depletion of staff following the establishment of the Free State; secondly, there was a huge amount of legal and technical work to be done in regard to tenanted estates (which had formerly been carried out by landlords' solicitors and agents[199]); thirdly, the machinery was further clogged by the requirement to open accounts for payments in lieu of rents, formerly payable to landlords, in the case of 114,000 holdings which had been vested in the Land Commission under the 1923 Act (together with the task of collecting arrears).[200] Fourthly, there were so many sections to the Land Commission that a high degree of bureaucracy was inevitable and bureaucracy is often the enemy of efficiency and speed.

In fairness to the Land Commission, it had to administer an enormous amount of work in the early years. Forms of rentals had to be prepared to enable landlords to make returns of their tenants and of the rents payable by them and of the arrears due. Forms had to be prepared giving all the particulars necessary for the vesting of tenanted holdings which had to record the area of holding, the nature of tenancy, whether the rent was judicial or non-judicial, whether sub-tenancies existed and so on. When these forms were lodged with the Land Commission, they had to be carefully checked. If for example, a rent was returned as judicial, the Commission clerical staff had to check their own records to see when the fair rent had been fixed because if it was fixed before 12 August 1911, the standard purchase annuity would be 65 per cent of the rent whereas if it was fixed after that date it would be 70 per cent. If the rent was non-judicial, an inspector had to adjudicate on the price. The appointed day could not be declared until all particulars had been checked, the purchase money determined and boundaries settled.

And there were a myriad decisions or procedures that could produce delays. For example, disputes often arose as to whether or not somebody returned as a tenant by a landlord had, in fact, become the owner of his holding by reason of non-payment of rents over an extended period.[201] Holdings had to be surveyed, maps examined and boundaries checked. In some areas, particularly in the west where rundale still existed, certain tenants had unofficially exchanged holdings with their neighbours without their landlords' consent. (These holdings were not actually legislated for until 1939 when the land act of that year enabled the Land Commission to treat these exchanges as if they had originally been legally carried out.[202]) Rights of way had to be decided upon, an extremely important issue in rural Ireland. As H. J. Monahan, a barrister and former legal adviser to the Land Commission, pointed out in 1944: 'The machinery was there all right, but it could not cope with such a multitude of cases at the same moment'.[203]

During the first few years of the administration of a land act that contained so many novel features, it was inevitable that time would be taken up in elaborating the machinery and in preparatory work for bringing the act into operation. It was also inevitable that legislation dealing with a subject as complex as land division and redistribution would require much fine-tuning. Amending acts in 1927 and 1929 were necessary to remove some of the legal difficulties that delayed the vesting of lands. It was found, for instance, that there were numerous farms near cities and towns with a certain frontage to the road (perhaps nothing more than a couple of acres) that could be deemed suitable for building. For that reason the whole farm, which could run to 100 or 200 acres, was excluded from the terms of the 1923 act. The Land Act of 1927 revised the clause stipulating that they could no longer be excluded if they had not been used for building within three years of the passing of the 1923 act.[204] It also prohibited sub-letting and sub-division without the consent of the Land Commission and prevented any farmer who had purchased under earlier acts sub-dividing or sub-letting until such time as he had repaid the money advanced to him to purchase his holding.[205] The 1929 Land Act obviated a considerable amount of inspection and other work in respect of non-judicial tenancies by fixing the rate of standard purchase annuities at 65 per cent of non-judicial rents (in the absence of objections). Up to the end of March 1928, schedules of particulars had been obtained in respect of 86,983 holdings situated on 5,583 estates comprising an area of 2.76 million acres with a previous rental of £1.24 million. But of the above, only 2,994 holdings on 134,140 acres with a rental of £90,700 had been vested in the Land Commission.[206] The process had to be speeded up. The much more substantial 1931 Land Act was the last important enactment relating to land purchase as distinct from land division or resettlement. Power was given to vest all unpurchased tenanted holdings in the Land Commission on the strength of the completed forms presented to it by the landlord, without further investigation.[207]

Interpreting the 1923 Land Act and the amending acts caused great difficulties. There was even a general consensus amongst politicians of all parties that the land acts and land law were 'most confusing' and that 'every new section makes confusion more pronounced'. Of course, for those wanting to exploit loopholes this was fortunate. There were many landlords and large farmers who had very good legal connections, able minds who could quite easily provide legal pretexts to circumvent the law. In 1927, William Davin (Leix–Offaly, Labour) proclaimed in the Dáil that 'whenever the commissioners announce their decision to acquire land in Leix and Offaly, more particularly in Offaly, an organised band of landlords with their expert advisers, get to work and, so far as I can see, they seem to be successful in every case'. He noted that this was particularly evident in the Edenderry area of Offaly where landowners, solicitors, their advisers and friends allegedly gathered together in a hall in the town and 'put their heads together with a view to beating the commissioners'.[208]

In 1933, Frank Aiken (Louth, Fianna Fáil) summed up the frustration caused by the procedures: declaration had to be made that the land was required for the relief of congestion; this was followed by publication in the *Iris Oifigiúil*; a hearing of the owner's objections by the Land Commission; a decision followed often by an appeal by the owner; a hearing of the appeal by the judicial commissioner; a decision on the price and so on. As Aiken pointed out: 'All this takes a very long time even under the most favourable circum-stances. It is necessary to make sure that legal requirements are complied with in every detail and legal business is always slow'.[209] By the 1930s, calls were being made for one comprehensive statute that would be 'comprehensible to the ordinary person' and above all solve an interminable problem.[210]

Finally, one should consider the fact that the hands of the Minister for Lands were often tied by the financial purse strings of the Department of Finance. Successive Ministers for Lands and Finance often found themselves at loggerheads with each other over expenditure on land division, an issue to be dealt with in more detail in succeeding chapters. It was possibly unfor-tunate for Cumann na nGaedheal that at the end of 1931, the Department of Finance dictated that there was to be 'no new expenditure, e.g. on pensions, housing, land purchase or division'.[211] It was an announcement that was badly timed with a general election just around the corner.

FOUR

FIANNA FÁIL AND LAND REFORM POLICY, 1932–48

I was brought up to believe that the Land Commission was the friend of the people, that the small farmer had the Land Commission behind him as against the landlord who tried to deprive him of his rights. I do not want a situation to develop in which the Land Commission, instead of being the friend of the small farmer, becomes a substitute for the landlord who used to oppress him.

JAMES DILLON

Dáil Debates, vol. 63, 22 July 1936, 1643.

—

I FIANNA FÁIL AND LAND DIVISION, 1932–9

In April 1926, a month prior to the first official meeting of the Fianna Fáil Party[1] in the La Scala theatre in Dublin, a statement of the fundamental aims of the party was issued. These were: to secure the unity and independence of Ireland as a republic; to restore the Irish language as the spoken language of the people and to develop a distinctive national life in accordance with the Irish tradition and ideals; to make the resources and wealth of Ireland subservient to the needs and welfare of all the people of Ireland; to make Ireland, as far as possible, economically self-contained and self-sufficient; to establish as many families as practicable on the land and to promote the ruralisation of essential industries as opposed to their concentration in cities.[2] The party machine intimated that Fianna Fáil would tackle the land question much more forcibly and radically than Cumann na nGaedheal. On 24 November 1926, at the first formal *ard-fheis*, de Valera pledged *inter alia* to 'complete land purchase, break up the large grazing ranches, and distribute them as economic farms amongst young farmers and agricultural labourers, such as those compelled at present to emigrate'.[3] The fifth plank of its policy – 'to establish as many families as practicable on the land' – was the promise that appealed most to the small farmers and agricultural labourers who were on the whole more concerned with improving their standards of living than, for example, achieving a 32-county Ireland. In ideological terms Fianna Fáil, by promoting this policy, regarded itself as following in the tradition of Sinn Féin and the first Dáil Éireann.[4] In more practical terms, Fianna Fáil was creating

99

a power basis in rural constituencies that was fundamentally based on numerical strength. In the constitution of 1937, de Valera ensured that the fifth plank of the party's policy was enshrined in article 45.2. It was highly symbolic of his personal commitment and that of the party to acquisition and the creation of as many economic holdings as was practicable.

By the early 1930s the political landscape had changed considerably from 1923. The founding of Fianna Fáil had arguably been the most decisive development, as it effectively eclipsed Sinn Féin (which after 1923 had merely been 'an uneasy combination of extremists and (relative) moderates, of ideologues and politicians, of fundamentalists and realists'[5]). By August 1927 the Fianna Fáil TDs elected in the June election were prepared to take their seats in the Dáil and it looked as if the party would provide the parliamentary representation denied to those who had clung on to their anti-Treatyite politics, which, in turn, was good news for small farmers, the landless and agrarian radicals who, along with a number of other interest groups, had become increasingly antagonised by Cumann na nGaedheal's style of government. (Of course, Fianna Fáil would also make sizeable gains in the Dublin constituencies, which reflected its growing appeal to certain of the electorally mobilised urban classes.)[6] Another general election in September 1927 helped consolidate Fianna Fáil's standing as a parliamentary party but Cumann na nGaedheal hung on tenuously thanks to its formal alliance with the Farmers' Party. But even though its position was precarious – in 1927, its average loss in terms of the popular vote in each constituency was almost 12 per cent[7] – Cumann na nGaedheal's tenure in office was not seriously challenged until 1932.

The 1932 general election was fought during a period of considerable political tension. The rise of paramilitary activity had forced the government to introduce draconian legislation that provided for military tribunals with the power to impose the death penalty on those threatening the security of the state. Cumann na nGaedheal did itself no political favours by introducing a budget that raised taxes and proposed cuts in public service pay. Its ideological vagueness and its lack of social policy (possibly curtailed by its huge expenditure on the completion of land purchase) was a source of disillusionment to all who had looked forward to radical change in an independent Ireland.

The unpopularity of the government played into Fianna Fáil's hands. Since 1927, Fianna Fáil had refined its own economic and social policies The party's continued promise to expedite land acquisition and division arguably made a major contribution to its victory in the 1932 general election.[8] So did its commitment to withhold the annuities payable to the British government for loans advanced under the pre-1922 land acts. The annuities question allowed de Valera to link once again the land question with Irish nationalism. In 21 out of the 25 rural constituencies Fianna Fáil secured a higher percentage of first preference votes than Cumann na nGaedheal. It could not though carry its promise until it could pass a new land act, but initially its narrow majority, dependent upon the Labour Party, was too tenuous to introduce the radical type of land legislation that was necessary. The new government, therefore, continued to garner support by proclaiming its commitment to a radical land division policy. During a political rally in County Mayo, de Valera launched a stinging attack on the previous land division policy of Cumann na nGaedheal, ironically (or perhaps deliberately) in the county where the Land League had first taken root in the 1880s:

> What about the rich lands? Have they been divided? In Meath, the richest land in Ireland, 5 per cent of farmers own 41 per cent of the land. These are the farmers who own 200 acres each; 631 persons own 234,575 acres: 631 own practically a quarter of a million acres of the best land in Ireland . . . In Tipperary 485 persons own 200,000 acres and in Kildare 6 per cent of farmers own over 172,000.[9]

This type of Fianna Fáil rhetoric was very much anti-grazier. And in line with this rhetoric, the party committed itself to a policy of directing agriculture towards domestic subsistence rather than international trade.[10] (One of the first occasions that de Valera publicised this policy was in January 1927; when speaking in Drogheda, he said that the party's 'guiding principle' was to make Ireland 'as self-contained and as self-sufficient as possible'.[11]) This would necessitate the expansion of tillage at the expense of grazing and the obvious consequence would be the break-up of ranch lands to facilitate the creation of smallholdings.[12] No less than seven resolutions (out of a total of 45) passed at the Fianna Fáil *ard-fheis* in November 1932 related to land acquisition and division and the working of the Land Commission.[13]

This reorientation of policy was deemed necessary in light of the growing economic recession that was worsened by, amongst other things, the growing reluctance of many farmers to pay their annuities which they now considered to be unaffordable, and the virtual closure of emigration outlets as a result of continued worldwide depression. The new government felt that an urgent employment outlet within the agricultural sector had to be found for an estimated 15,000–20,000 young men.[14] Land division was seen to be the most obvious solution. In May 1932, the first Fianna Fáil Minister for Lands, P. J. Ruttledge[15] (Mayo), informed the Dáil that it was now the aim of the government

> to provide an opening and a living for every man of character and conduct who is willing and able to work. It will be the aim of the Land Commission not only to divide land but to divide it in such a way that it will enable the people put on the

land to derive an economic livelihood from it. Every effort will be made to speed up the acquisition and distribution of land.[16]

(In February 1933, P. J. Ruttledge was replaced by Joseph Connolly – an usual choice in that, as a city-born man, he admitted himself that he 'knew little about land problems'[17] – who continued Ruttledge's policy and who quickly called numerous conferences of the land commissioners and the inspectorate staff to demand that they expedite land acquisition and division in each county.[18]) Fianna Fáil social policy aimed at rural regeneration, the curbing of unemployment, the reduction of emigration and alleviation of poverty was therefore to be very much tied to land reform policy.

Having laid the foundations, it was no coincidence that in January 1933 de Valera called a snap general election after the party had clearly publicised the fact that the expediting of land acquisition and division was dependent upon a new land act. An election manifesto distributed to the electorate in Tipperary on behalf of Fianna Fáil candidates Dan Breen, Sean Hayes, Andrew Fogarty, Timothy Sheehy and Martin Ryan announced: 'Arrangements are being made to end the unchristian system whereby a man and a dog looks after numerous bullocks and hundreds of acres of the best land in the world while thousands of our people are struggling on uneconomic holdings or existing in poverty in our towns and villages'.[19]

Significantly, Fianna Fáil captured an additional five seats giving it a safe overall majority. In 22 out of the 25 rural constituencies, Cumann na nGaedheal's share of first preference votes declined rather dramatically, in 14 of them by at least ten per cent. The constituencies most affected were in the west (Donegal, Clare, Galway, Leitrim–Sligo, Roscommon and Mayo North and South) where Cumann na nGaedheal had not been successful in relieving congestion; in the east-midland counties of Longford–Westmeath, Louth, Meath and Carlow–Kilkenny and the south-midlands county of Tipperary, all characterised by the existence of large grazier and dairy farms; and the border counties of Monaghan and Cavan where there was a very high concentration of smallholders clamouring for more economically viable holdings. In 24 out of the 25 constituencies (Cork West being the exception), Fianna Fáil candidates secured a higher percentage of votes than their Cumann na nGaedheal opponents (an average of 48.2 per cent to Cumann na nGaedheal's 28.3 per cent). In 15 out of the 25 constituencies, Fianna Fáil's share of first preferences over Cumann na nGaedheal was in excess of 20 per cent. Again, these were the constituencies where land acquisition and division were most likely to have played a key role in determining election results (Cavan, Clare, Cork East and North, Donegal, Galway, Kerry, Leix–Offaly, Limerick, Longford–Westmeath, Louth, Mayo, Meath, Monaghan, Roscommon and Tipperary).

In August 1933, Fianna Fáil passed its own land act,[20] with the intention of making 'a very definite progressive stride towards the completion of the process of land settlement in Ireland' and to clear what Frank Aiken (acting Minister for Lands in the absence of Connolly who was in America) termed the 'congested slums'.[21] In a letter to the secretary of the Land Commission in 1933 Aiken revealingly claimed that the act was framed specifically to tackle unemployment.[22] It provided the Land Commission with more draconian powers regarding the compulsory acquisition of lands and allowed for the expropriation of purchased farms as well as untenanted estates, with limited restrictions.

According to Aiken, section 29 was designed to confer powers upon the Land Commission to 'sweep away a number of the legal and administrative technicalities that clog progress'. Restrictions on the acquisition of particular classes of lands were repealed. The privilege of demanding an alternative holding was restricted to residential owners who worked their lands themselves as ordinary farmers. These residential owners would be entitled to a holding of similar market value, subject to a maximum of £2,000, anything above that to be paid in land bonds. It worked as follows, to quote an example given by Aiken himself:

> If, for instance, a man has £2,400 worth of land and the Land Commission propose to take £400 worth of it from him, they can take it . . . and give him the value of the £400 in land bonds. If, however, they want £500 worth of it from him, thereby reducing the market value of his holding to £1,900, the owner can compel them to give him £400 in bonds and £2,000 worth of land elsewhere.[23]

The definition of 'residential' was modified to remove from this category lands upon which there were only derelict residences. The veto against the acquisition of land if there was other suitable untenanted land in the district was also repealed. Purchased owners could no longer escape the net unless they were practical farmers, farming their lands in a proper manner (that is giving adequate employment and producing an adequate amount of food for the community) and residing on or adjacent to them. Thus, the 1933 act greatly reduced the protection previously afforded under the 1923 act and, it could be argued, reduced proprietorial security, although Aiken was quick to point out that 'the interests of the *genuine* [my italics] working farmer are specially safeguarded'.[24]

The perceived reduction of proprietorial security provided the focal point for the Opposition's criticism. Quite evidently, the act was aimed specifically at the break up of large estates and ranches and the appropriation of lands that were not serving the common good in favour of the creation (or extension) of a mass of smallholdings that would go some way to appeasing the uneconomic holders, the landless and the labourers. Patrick Hogan, the former Minister for Agriculture, saw the act as being 'a purely political' one, pandering to the small farmer and labouring classes in an attempt to secure votes.[25] G. C. Bennett (Limerick, Cumann na nGaedheal) saw it as a desertion of the principles that had been fought for during the Land War and after:

> We should not undo all that our forefathers fought for and won. Think of all the misery that was endured in the [18]70s and [18]80s and the [18]90s to win security of tenure for the Irish farmer. Surely an Irish government is not going to undo the great work that was accomplished in that respect when the people of this country were under an alien government, and the great results that were achieved by the Irish parliamentary leaders of a past generation, the great fight that they made in an outside country to make the position of the Irish farmers secure in his homestead.[26]

This threat to proprietorial security was critical. If one were cynical enough, one might claim that this was a deliberate attempt by Fianna Fáil to break the political elitism of the large farming class and that there was something of a Machiavellian strain in the party's attitude towards the Economic War – in other words that the bankrupting of large farmers would lead to cheaper and more land for division and subsequently more mass appeal for the party.

What is more certain, however, is that the new threat gave impetus to organisations such as the Blueshirts, as we shall see in chapter 7, and stimulated the representation of the Land Commission as the 'bogey-man' of rural Ireland by those sections of the rural community most likely to lose out. In 1935 James Dillon[27] (Donegal, Centre Party) told the Dáil:

> Hitherto, the Land Commission has been looked-up to by the people as their friend and champion as against the landlords. It is now becoming an infinitely worse landlord than Clanricarde ever was. You shake the confidence of the people in the personnel of the Land Commission if you make the Land Commission appear in the minds of the people as a menace and a threat to their fixity of tenure; you are going irretrievably to injure the Land Commission as a power for good in this country and that would be a great disaster.[28]

Dillon was one of the most astute observers of the Irish attachment to land. He lamented the fact that people would now have to learn to live with the fear that the Land Commission might take over a holding if it decided a farmer had too much land and that some of it could be used for the relief of local congestion; if a land-hungry neighbour reported that a farm was not being worked in an efficient manner; or if a farmer fell on hard times owing, perhaps, to a lack of capital input or even illness or infirmity. As Professor George O'Brien told the Commission on Banking in the late 1930s:

The question of whether a person will continue in possession of his holding at the present time in the last resort depends on the opinion of some official guided by some policy regarding the utility or otherwise of the type of agriculture he is pursuing?[29]

There were inherent difficulties here, which were quite clear from Commissioner Michael Deegan's evidence to the same commission. Deegan was one of the newly appointed commissioners who came in under the Fianna Fáil administration. It is obvious that he was favourably disposed to Fianna Fáil policy, believing that 'raising cattle and grazing will not give the same employment and the land will not support the same number of people as it would if we took it and divided it'.[30] Firstly, he pointed out that the Land Commission did not take into consideration whether a large farmer was producing for export or the home market; he believed it was more economically desirable to have a farmer who employed a great deal of labour than one who exported a great deal of cattle. Secondly, no consideration was given to the fact that a man employing only a few labourers in a given year might have plans to expand his labour force in the coming years: 'I am afraid', Deegan told the Banking Commission, 'we do not concern ourselves at the moment with that. We take the situation as we find it at the moment the man comes under our notice'.[31] Thirdly, there was no definition laid out as to the fair valuation of lands to be acquired; it was determined by the valuation reports of individual inspectors:

> From the Land Commission point of view we inquire as to what price we can resell the land – what is the maximum annuity we can recover on the land and that, by and large, is the price that is fair to us. We have also a statement from the man [owner] himself. . . . We have a statement from him as to his profits; what he has made out of the land for five or ten year periods. And we then try to arrive at a price fair to us and him.[32]

This was again a crucial admission. In a prolonged period of economic crisis where agricultural profits were falling – through no fault of hardworking farmers – the basis upon which the Commission therefore determined fair market value was of more benefit to the state as purchaser than to the farmer as vendor. Of justifiable concern was the fact that no economist was attached to the Land Commission or even an expert to keep it informed of land policy developments in other countries.[33] In fact, little thought appears to have been given to long-term planning. When Professor O'Brien asked Deegan about the possibility of an increased population leading to the necessity of creating even smaller holdings in the future, Deegan replied:

The future will have to look after itself and we hope that when we reach that stage – that you must give out land in smaller quantities than would constitute an economic holding – the people of the land will have other means of subsistence – industries, towns, or something to equalise matters.[34]

Little wonder then that John Costello (Dublin, Fine Gael) was reminded of the old tag: 'Large fleas have little fleas upon their backs to bite them, and little fleas have lesser fleas and so on *ad infinitum*', implying that it would only be a matter of time before Fianna Fáil supporters would clamour for the break up of even 30-acre farms.[35]

II A CHANGING HIERARCHY OF ALLOTTEES

With the passing of the 1933 act, the hierarchy of allottees was amended. Preference was now to be given to discharged employees, followed by evicted tenants 'who are competent to work land', uneconomic holders in immediate proximity of the estate to be divided, landless men 'of a deserving class' in the immediate vicinity and, finally, migrants.[36] In all cases, preference was to be given to married men with families to support, especially those whose wives and children would be capable of co-operating in working the farm. When a large untenanted estate was acquired for division, there would not be that many discharged employees to take a significant proportion of the land. Legitimate evicted tenants and their representatives, as we shall see below, were becoming scarce. Thus the uneconomic holders (local congests) were still largely catered for as before. The point of the new hierarchy was, it seems, to ensure that local uneconomic holders and the landless were appeased before migrants could be taken in. The new hierarchy placed emphasis upon the need to cater for the landless (with those who had national service in the pre-Truce IRA to be given priority), which represented a major departure from Cumann na nGaedheal's policy.[37] Thus, in 1933, Frank Aiken wrote to the secretary of the Land Commission:

> I wish . . . the commissioners to take into consideration to a greater extent than has, perhaps, been possible hitherto the claims of cottiers and agricultural labourers and of farmers' sons who are capable of working land. In selecting allottees for these classes the Land Commission should be guided solely by the experience, fitness and character of the applicant, by the nature and value of any farming effort he has already been able to make (e.g. taking conacre or grazing, keeping pigs, fowl etc.) by the capital he has accumulated or can readily find, by the extent to which his being given a holding will assist his family. . . . I fully realise that the selection of suitable landless men will be a more difficult task than

the selection of congests but unless he is suitable there is no gain to the state in giving land to any man and consequently I attach the greatest importance to this particular point.[38]

Patrick Hogan quickly pointed out the dangers of the new hierarchy:

You are accepting landless men quite apart from herds and other suitable persons. That is good politics, I admit, but it is rotten economics and rotten national administration. . . . No matter how ignorant you are there is not a single man on the opposite benches who does not know perfectly well that you cannot even make a beginning of dealing with this problem of the landless men by land purchase.[39]

Hogan's observations were pragmatic: landless men may have been experienced agricultural labourers and extremely hard workers, but they did not always have the experience of managing a farm. They had little capital for investment and probably even less experience in organising financial affairs. More importantly, if they were to fail where would they then turn if the labour market from which they came had been taken away by the removal of large farmers in favour of the creation of small subsistence, family-run farms? Hogan might have been right in his observation that it made for 'good politics.' In 1935, when the terms of the act began to make an impact, the government also introduced the Local Government Act,[40] which for the first time gave the vote to all adults over 21 in local government elections. Property restrictions no longer applied so that the landless and agricultural labourers, who had just been moved up the hierarchy of allottees, now formed an important component in the local electorate and carried much more numerical power than the propertied classes.

It is not difficult to understand why the terms of the 1933 Land Act would have such appeal for the masses in rural Ireland. In a country where rural status was defined by landownership and virtually everybody's desire was to own their own patch of land, the 1933 act promised a great deal. When its terms kicked into place, the rate of acquisition and division increased dramatically. For the year ended 31 March 1935, an unprecedented 102,000 acres of untenanted lands were divided amongst 6,244 allottees.[41] The following year, the achievement was even greater, 104,000 acres amongst 7,712 allottees. For the first five-year period of Fianna Fáil's administration (ending 31 March 1937) almost 353,000 acres were divided amongst 25,802 allottees, over 100,000 acres more than in the preceding five-year period (see Appendix I, table 4.1, p. 236).

Until the Land Commission records become more accessible, there are no means of assessing the criteria used by the inspectors in choosing landless allottees. Unfortunately, neither are there any statistics available regarding the class of allottees who received allotments for the period 1933–7. But there are for 1937–8 and 1938–9. During those two years a total of 102,652 acres was divided amongst 8,333 allottees. Of this total 41,967 acres was allotted to 3,755 uneconomic holders as enlargements, each receiving an average of just over eleven acres; 13,626 acres were divided amongst 640 migrants, each receiving an average holding of just over 21 acres; 9,486 acres were divided amongst 372 ex-employees, an average of 25.5 acres; 370 acres was divided amongst eight evicted tenants or their representatives, an average of just over 46 acres each; and 18,098 acres were divided amongst 642 landless men, each receiving an average of over 28 acres. The remainder of the lands were allotted in sports fields (mainly, if not exclusively, for the Gaelic Athletic Association), turbary plots, forestry plots and accommodation plots.

The significance of these figures is that almost 27 per cent of the lands divided went to ex-employees and the landless and it is probable that they had benefited even more in the period 1933–7. That so few evicted tenants received holdings during these years was a reflection of the fact that the supply of genuine applicants was now coming to an end. In December 1950, the Minister for Lands in the First Inter-Party government, Joseph Blowick, was asked if there were 'any verified claims of victims of the Land War' still outstanding. He answered that the 'vast majority of claims' had been disposed of and that those which remained would 'receive such favourable consideration as the Land Commission may find possible'.[42] In fact, after 1939 only 13 more applications were accepted between that year and 1961 (and only two after 1950.) Between them they received a total of 379 acres or an average of just over 29 acres each.

III THE IRA

The existing published Land Commission statistics offer no indication as to how many allottees during the Fianna Fáil administration were members of the Old IRA, but the number would seem to have been significant. Richard Dunphy has suggested the pivotal role that the IRA played in the rise of Fianna Fáil from the mid-1920s: the most important source of recruitment of supporters to the party was 'the large pool of disillusioned republicans who had not been politically active at all since the end of the Civil War; many of them may not even have voted in 1923'.[43] From the mid-1920s, Fianna Fáil organisers toured the country, contacting local IRA commanders who more often than not were highly regarded in their local communities 'as heroic or charismatic figureheads' because of 'their (real or legendary) exploits during the War of Independence and Civil War'.[44]

An analysis made by this author of the republican backgrounds of the Fianna Fáil TDs who were successful in the 1932 general election shows that at least 45, or 62.5 per cent of them, had been involved in the independence movement (including the Civil War) from 1916 to 1923.[45] Amongst these were many of the most prominent members of the pre-independence Sinn Féin movement and/or the IRA including Dan Breen (who was amongst the Volunteer leaders at what is generally regarded as the first encounter of the War of Independence at Soloheadbeg in Tipperary); Oscar Traynor who played a pivotal role in both the War of Independence and Civil War; Sean Moylan, later Minister for Lands, who was commander of the North Cork flying column and Republican Director of Operations during the Civil War; and Frank Aiken who became OC of the 4th Northern Division of the IRA in 1921 and who also played a key role in the Civil War. Many others were prominent local leaders: Patrick Smith who had led the IRA in Cavan and who was to be re-elected in every election until his retirement in 1977; Dr Con Ward, a senior member of the IRA in Monaghan during the War of Independence and IRA representative on the Border Liaison Commission in 1922; Frank Fahy of Galway who had been sentenced to death after the 1916 Rising and who played a prominent role in the IRA from 1919 to 1923; Thomas McEllistrim from Kerry who led the ambush at Headfort Junction in March 1921 in which over 20 British soldiers were killed; Gerald (Gerry) Boland who represented Roscommon was involved in the independence struggle from 1916 to 1923 (he was also a brother of Harry Boland); and P. J. Ruttledge who led the anti-Treaty forces which captured Ballina from the Free State forces in September 1922. The others included de Valera, of course; Sean Lemass, future Taoiseach, a veteran of the 1916 Rising and later independence movement; Sean T. O'Ceallaigh, later president of Ireland, founding member of Sinn Féin and the Irish Volunteers; and Conor Maguire who had drafted the constitution of the Sinn Féin courts and served as a judge on them in 1920–2.

Many of these, in turn, were to hold key cabinet positions in Fianna Fáil governments during the 1930s and 1940s, including Aiken, Moylan, Boland and Ruttledge who were all to become Ministers for Lands. It was hardly surprising that they would seek certain preferential treatment for IRA veterans in the hierarchy of land division allottees.

As explained in chapter 3 there was a growing proliferation of Old IRA associations in many areas from the mid-1920s. The membership was drawn from the same social classes as the rank and file of Fianna Fáil – small farmers, labourers and clerks. After Fianna Fáil entered the Dáil for the first time in 1927, giving the party political legitimacy, established Old IRA associations simply evolved into local Fianna Fáil *cumainn* offering support to the party.[46] From November 1926 to the summer of 1927, the number of *cumainn* rose from 460 to over 1,000.[47] Very soon a *cumann* existed in nearly every parish in the country. As we shall see in chapter 7, the role of the local *cumann* was often crucial in securing farms and allotments for individuals.

Support for Fianna Fáil was largely conditional upon the reversal of the perceived discrimination against Republicans during the Cumann na nGaedheal administration. In 1932, the Meath Old IRA Association argued that in the allocation of farms under the Cosgrave administration, Old IRA men (meaning Old Republicans) had been victimised while the lands were given to Free Staters. Now they demanded 'the preferential treatment, all else being equal, of Old IRA members in the division and allotment of lands' as material recognition of their Old IRA service and a compensation for losses for such services.[48] On 2 October 1932, a conference of the South Tipperary Old IRA, held in Thurles, passed a series of resolutions proposing *inter alia* that the 1923 Land Act should be abolished; that the ranches of Tipperary should be distributed immediately amongst local uneconomic holders and landless men with 'first preference [to] be given to Republican soldiers'; that the farm at Castleffogarty offered for sale by the Land Commission should be handed over to a local Republican; and, finally, that the two migrant families brought on to the Bailey and Carew estates should be removed and replaced by local landless men and uneconomic holders.[49] In April 1933, the Tipperary Old IRA demanded that their members should get first preference in any appointments in the county for 'the Cosgrave gang were being catered for long enough in the way of land, pensions and positions'.[50]

It became fashionable for Fianna Fáil politicians to make promises that members of the Old IRA would be rewarded for past sacrifices. In 1935, Dr Con Ward (Monaghan, first Fianna Fáil parliamentary secretary to the Minister for Local Government) told a rally in Monaghan: 'He would see that those who fought for their country had first claim in the division of land in the county, and they would also have first preference in the division of large ranches in Meath and Roscommon.'[51] This is largely what many veterans of the revolutionary period had come to expect as is exemplified in the following resolution passed by the Tipperary Old IRA in 1933 which clearly shows that if men fought for patriotic reasons they also fought in the hope of bettering their economic futures:

> Governments in the past have proved themselves notoriously ungrateful and convinently [*sic*] forgetful of the men who made them and as our only hope of compensation is through the medium of land, we mean to see it, as far as in our power lies that a reoccurence [*sic*] of this treatment is not meted out to those who gave the best years of their lives to make this country a land without footing or shelter for slaves.[52]

If IRA veterans were to be catered for, the right men, so to speak, had to be placed in strategic or influential positions. In his Land Commission memoirs, P. J. Sammon claimed that the aforementioned Paddy [P. J.] Brennan joined the Acquisition and Resales branch in the spring of 1933 having passed the clerical officer grade examination that was 'open to applicants with certain pre-truce IRA service'.[53] Brennan was prominent in the founding of Fianna Fáil and a former Republican, and it is quite clear that Fianna Fáil in attempting to redress the anti-Republican discrimination that had taken place under Cumann na nGaedheal was anxious to place its own sympathisers within the civil service. In the same year the number of land commissioners was raised from four to six. One of the new appointees was Eamonn Mansfield who, it seems, worked feverishly on behalf of the IRA veterans.[54]

In May 1935, Commissioner S. J. Waddell issued 'strictly private and confidential' instructions to the Land Commission inspectorate, that seem to have been passed down from the Minister for Lands, which widened the scope for providing lands for veterans. National service in the pre-Truce IRA was now to be taken into consideration in each class of allottee. This meant, for example, that congests with pre-Truce IRA service were to be given preference over those who had none. While Waddell's instructions made it clear that it was to be difficult for anybody with a pension (or other source of income) to receive land, he pointed out that: 'Pre-Truce IRA men who have been awarded small pensions for national service under *Saorstat* Pensions Acts are not affected if eligible for land and capable of working it'.[55]

Once it became known from the mid-1930s that IRA veterans were to get preference in all land division schemes, it was always going to be the case that there would be considerably more men (and in some cases women) claiming to have seen active service in the pre-Truce period than had been the case. It was difficult to determine what constituted active service. Did one have to have taken part in an ambush in which members of the crown forces had been killed or was it enough to have carried dispatches? Was the cutting of roads or the purchasing of arms as important as the shooting of a member of the RIC?[56] The government faced the same type of difficulty with regard to the issuing of military service pensions to IRA veterans, so that when the Minister for Lands recognised that one could work in conjunction with the other, he decided in August 1936 that preferential treatment for IRA members should be 'definitely confined to men with pensions and to men in respect of whom the army pensions authorities are prepared to issue certificates of first-class meritorious service'.[57]

The first four years of Fianna Fáil's administration seem to represent the heyday of land allotment to IRA veterans. A Fianna Fáil statement issued through the Office of the President in 1937 claimed that 'in addition to provision for pensions, the gov[ernmen]t has, as no doubt the Old IRA organisations are aware, given special consideration to Old IRA men in the important matter of land division'.[58] It is probably safe to conclude that Fianna Fáil was much more favourably disposed to Old Republicans than their predecessors in government. For example, in 1935, the editor of the *Meath Chronicle* wrote:

> We are able to give the names of some of the allottees on the Deerpark and at Dunmoe and for those of us who lived in and had a fair share of our being in the resurgent years from 1916 to 1922 and 1923, it is pleasant to see amongst them brave men and brave families that took their full share of the perils of that glorious if dangerous epoch . . . families that sheltered the soldiers of the Republic when the hounds of England were at their heels. . . . Too long were many of these men forgotten and the Land Minister can rest assured that there are few indeed who begrudge the restoration of the land to the men, and to the breed of men, who fought and wrought and bled for Ireland.[59]

Two years later at a meeting of Dunboyne Fianna Fáil *cumann*, David Hall, an Old IRA member and president of the *cumann*, announced that during the previous two years 'not a single Old IRA man who had made application for land was turned down'.[60] To appease local opposition to a migration scheme at Emly in Tipperary in 1942, the Land Commission set aside the O'Connor estate for locals including five Old IRA men.[61]

By the late 1930s, a number of high-ranking officials and civil servants were pragmatic enough to realise that allotting land based on military service did not make sound economic sense. In 1936, the aforementioned Land Division Committee recommended that IRA men should be placed at the bottom of the hierarchy.[62] In May 1937, Gerry Boland,[63] the Minister for Lands, was asked if he was aware of a resolution passed by members of the Tipperary Old IRA:

> alleging that a hostile element within the Land Commission was deliberately endeavouring to obstruct the government's declared policy of settling suitable Old IRA men on the land; whether he has instituted an inquiry into the allegation, and with what result; and, if not, if he will state what action he intends to take in the matter.[64]

Boland replied that he was aware of the resolution but unimpressed by the fact that it was an attack upon the impartiality and loyalty of the staff of the Land Commission and that he had no intention of taking any further action.[65]

By the end of the 1930s, coinciding with the beginning of the Emergency, it was becoming even more apparent that many of those Old IRA men who had received farms were not cut out to be farmers. When Sean Moylan[66] became Minister for Lands in August 1943, his policy regarding land division was more pragmatic and directed in the main towards agricultural development. Although Moylan and other representatives of the Fianna Fáil government met during the 1940s with various organisations representing the Old IRA from different localities, as well as with representatives from the United Conference of Old IRA Organisations[67] who were seeking lands, nothing concrete came from these discussions. Fianna Fáil's tough anti-IRA stance undoubtedly contributed to a change in policy. Fighting the IRA at one level did not stand easily with rewarding IRA veterans on another level. Old IRA members began to look for patronage in the form of jobs rather than land.[68] From the late 1950s, the Old IRA stopped lobbying for land and concentrated more upon their pension entitlements.[69] It had become obvious that they had received all the favouritism in respect of land division that they could hope for. Writing in 1957, an embittered Seosamh Ó Cearnaigh, a member of the Leinster Council of the Old IRA, complained to de Valera:

> Over a year ago we decided that we would not in future seek any concessions from any of the political parties which constituted an Dáil at that time, and we wish to let you know that we still adhere to that decision. We are convinced more and more of the hostility of successive governments to the pre-Truce IRA. This was very evident in the allocating of land and positions in which we did not even get equal treatment with the rest of our countrymen.[70]

IV 'GRIT IN THE LEGAL MACHINERY'

Despite the record acquisition and division successes of the mid-1930s, there were warning signs that progress was going to be hampered in the future by continued legal restraints. A new bill was therefore introduced in 1936. This was more an amending and interpreting measure than one that contained fresh land legislation and was probably prompted by a Dáil motion of 1934 which stated that:

> The land acts and land law generally are most confusing and every new section makes confusion more pronounced. Should it not be possible to have one comprehensive statute framed in such a way that it would be comprehensible to an ordinary person, and not a puzzle as at present.[71]

The bill aimed to eradicate loopholes that landowners had been exploiting in order to retain their lands. For example, following the 1933 Act, some large farmers had signed over parts of their farms to their wives, thereby creating two separate holdings and so avoiding the £2,000 threshold. Clause 27 of the 1936 act legislated that the lands of a husband and wife now had to be bulked. Clause 36 was necessitated by a test case brought before the Supreme Court in the mid-1930s by an owner who had purchased his estate under the 1923 Land Act. When the Land Commission attempted to compulsorily acquire it, the Supreme Court decreed that lands, once vested in purchasers under the 1923 Land Act, could not be subsequently acquired by the Land Commission under their compulsory powers. Clause 36 of the 1936 act enabled lands purchased under all land acts to be acquired, including lands purchased since 1923 (providing seven years had elapsed since purchase).[72] Similarly, any lands that had not been used as demesne lands, home farms and pleasure grounds for a period of five years or more lost exemption from acquisition.

Tighter restrictions were also imposed on those claiming to be breeding thoroughbred stock in order to evade compulsory acquisition. The Minister for Agriculture was given the responsibility of deciding whether or not the stock was of a nature and character suitable to the requirements of the country. One of the land commissioners, Kevin O'Shiel, noted that this was 'an obviously wise precaution, because . . . there could be a thoroughbred herd of elephants, camels or ostriches, which could hardly be deemed suitable for Ireland', a much less harmless remark than it seemed on the surface, directed as it was against those who had exploited technical loopholes to safeguard their untenanted estates.[73]

However, even after four significant land acts (1923, 1931, 1933, 1936) there remained interpretive difficulties. Legal objections continued to slow down the work of the Commission. Two of the most notable of these were the Potterton case and the Maher cases. Thomas E. Potterton was an unvested tenant on the estate of Lord Darnley in County Meath who objected to the resumption of his holding by the Land Commission. In the subsequent hearing a question of law was raised as to what body had the power to make an order for resumption, and it was legitimately argued that two sections of the 1933 Land Act appeared to be contradictory. Section 11 of the act purported to transfer to the Appeal Tribunal the powers of the court for resumption whereas section 31 purported to make it obligatory on the Appeal Tribunal to order resumption upon the certificate of the lay commissioners of the Land Commission.[74]

The other case arose out of Mrs K. M. Maher's objection to the Land Commission's proposed acquisition of her untenanted land. During the Appeal Tribunal hearing, a question of law was again raised as to whether the certificate of the lay commissioners declaring the lands to be acquired had to be signed by two of the lay commissioners (as had been the case in the past) or by all six of them. The judicial commissioner held that because the Land Act of 1936 in prescribing the procedure for the compulsory acquisition of land mentioned 'a certificate by the lay commissioners' without specifying how many had to sign it, signature by all was legally necessary.[75]

One of the most outspoken critics of the defects in the land legislation of the 1920s and 1930s was Commissioner Eamonn Mansfield. In 1943, in a memorandum prepared for the government, he argued that 'faulty draughts-manship appears to be an outstanding feature of many of the land bills'.[76] He and his fellow land commissioners were invariably frustrated by their unsuc-cessful attempts to have what they considered to be 'glaring flaws' removed from the various bills; he wrote: 'If the lawyers and draftsmen time after time are permitted to insert in bills sections with obvious flaws, the man-in-the-street can only come to one conclusion'.[77] By the early 1940s, Mansfield was vehement that it was 'nearly time to cut away the rolls of red tape in which the Irish Land Commission have permitted themselves to be strangled'.[78]

Besides legislative restrictions, the most obvious reason for the deceler-ation of land acquisition and division was that the amount of land available for acquisition, particularly in the form of large estates, was dwindling. From 1923 to 1937, the Land Commission had targeted scores of untenanted estates scattered throughout the country, such as the massive 20,000-acre Shaen Carter estate in Mayo, the 12,300 acre untenanted estate of Sir John Leslie in Donegal, the the 6,000-acre Persse estate in Galway, the 4,000-acre estate of Lord Ashtown in the same county and the 3,600-acre McCann estate in Meath. By the late 1930s, most of these large estates had been acquired and divided and, as the table 4.2 illustrates (see Appendix I, p. 236), the size of estates left to acquire were substantially smaller. After 1937, the rate of division slowed just as dramatically as it had risen three years before, falling to less than 42,000 acres amongst 3,374 allottees in 1939 (which was still, of course, a very respectable figure). In 1939, the Land Commission pointed out that 'acqui-sition was . . . for all practical purposes, confined to those lands which we were able to purchase by negotiation with the owners'.[79]

More important, however, was the fact that huge sums of money were being expended by the Land Commission on the erection of dwelling houses, fences, the construction of roads, the supply of farm implements, fuel, seeds and the general improvement of holdings, particularly those of the thousands of migrants who benefited from free grants. Each new holding in the Meath migration schemes cost just over £900 in the late 1930s (see Appendix I, table 4.1, p. 236). Financial pressure on the state was also heightened by Fianna Fáil's 1933 Land Act which, in response to the growing economic depression and the party's pre-election promises to the electorate to reduce annuities, resulted in the extinction of arrears in excess of three years, the establishment of a funding annuity of 50 years' duration to fund the payment of arrears of up to three years, and, most significantly, the halving of all future annuities. From then, the increase in cost of improvements meant that the allocated budget to the Department of Lands was rarely enough to meet expenditure, with the result that the Minister for Lands had to ask for additional funds each year. As might be expected this gave fodder to whoever was in opposition to attack the government, but it also, as we shall see below, led to much division within government circles.

V THE LANDLESS AND DISCHARGED EMPLOYEES

By the mid-1930s, the smallholders of the west had become as disillusioned by Fianna Fáil's attempts to expedite land acquisition and division in Connaught as they had been with Cumann na nGaedheal in the past. The enormous difficulties associated with the continued existence of the rundale system could only be solved through migration and the redistribution of lands. But in August 1936, Frank Aiken, the Minister for Lands, informed the government that:

> The order of priority . . . requires the Land Commission to consider the claims of 'landless men of a deserving class in immediate proximity' to the lands being divided before those of migrants. Considerable difficulty is resulting from adherence to this rule and an amount of criticism, which, in the Minister's opinion is justifiable, has been experienced, particularly in the west.[80]

These difficulties prompted Aiken to establish a Land Division Committee in 1936, composed of representatives of the Land Commission and other government departments, to tease out what changes in land division policy were necessary. The committee was not favourably disposed to the continued allocation of lands to the landless and so it put increasing pressure on Gerry Boland, who replaced Aiken as Minister for Lands in November, to restore priority to uneconomic holders and congests over the landless. This pressure was increased following the publication of the 1938 Inter-departmental Report on Seasonal Migration that made a similar recommendation.[81] In 1939, Boland was forced to admit that giving land to the landless had been a failure:

> Where the failures have been is where a lot of people, landless men, who were supposed to be good allottees – they may have deceived some inspector – got land and did not avail themselves of the opportunity given to them. Some have not

gone to live in their houses – I will not say a great number – but the Land Commission is determined that if they do not live in these houses and work these holdings, the holdings will be taken from them again. Whatever opposition there may be to that, we will insist that they either work the holdings, and work them properly, or make way for somebody else who will. They have been given the opportunity, and if they are not going to avail of it, we will get plenty of people who will.[82]

Landless allottees failed for a variety of reasons: lack of initial capital investment; lack of experience – it was one thing to work a farm for somebody else, it was quite another to manage it; the prolonged agricultural crisis of the 1920s and 1930s that stifled growth and inhibited expansion; and not least the fact that by the 1930s it was evident that standard twenty-two acre holdings were not large enough to assure a farmer of his being able to keep his family 'in reasonable comfort without recourse to outside assistance'.

By 1936, Commissioner S. J. Waddell defined an economic holding as one which would bring in from the sale of livestock, crops and other agricultural products enough to pay the cost of production and would leave such a margin as would allow the farmer to pay annuities, rates and taxes, to educate his family and to keep them 'in fair comfort'. That would require 25 to 35 acres. On an average 30-acre holding where mixed farming was practised, 14.5 acres would be devoted to grazing, six acres to corn, six acres to hay, two acres to root crops, one acre to potatoes, and the remainder to catch crops and orchards. It would support six cows, five calves, five yearling cattle, two two-year-old cattle, seven sheep, nine lambs, a pony/donkey, a sow, three pigs, eighty poultry and twenty turkeys. It would yield an estimated £100 per annum from which £20 would go towards annuities and rates, leaving £80 per annum for the keep of the family.[83] As it was, most smallholders survived only by taking conacre (which seems to have been in plentiful supply despite Land Commission restrictions), borrowing their neighbours' horses and farm implements, and depending on the labour of their children who worked for nothing more than their subsistence. In 1936, Commissioner S.J. Waddell pointed out to the Minister for Lands that:

the present regulations are in my opinion creating holdings that are not up to economic standard. . . . If the division of land does not create holdings capable of maintaining the members of the families put into the same, and they are compelled in whole or in part to eke out additional and external means of subsistence by the unemployment dole etc., the huge cost of land settlement on the state is only increasing and perpetuating all the evils of agricultural slums for the following generations.[84]

The following year, an amendment in policy was suggested by the Department of Lands and the minimum size of holdings was increased to 25 acres of good arable land.[85]

There were by now clearly divisions within the government regarding land reform policy. That de Valera himself continued to retain romantic notions of a countryside resplendent with 'cosy homesteads' offering no more than 'frugal comfort' is evident from his oft quoted St Patrick's Day speech of 1943.[86] Similarly, within the Land Commission, there was still an influential body of opinion, including Kevin O'Shiel and Eamonn Mansfield who argued that landless men, particularly agricultural labourers, could not be overlooked.[87] In 1943, Mansfield argued:

> The Land Commission treats the agricultural labourer practically as an outcast. He may be a descendant of those cleared off the ranch. He may have a cow or two. He may have been taking for years grazing or meadow on conacre thereon. His family may be numerous and industrious. All these do not count. An old bachelor or an old maid comes first if possessed already of an acre or two. The agricultural labourer must remain in the class to which he belongs, and then after refusing him any, he is cynically advised by our public men to stay on the land.[88]

However, when Sean Moylan became Minister for Lands in 1943, he was determined to develop land division policy so as to improve Irish agriculture. This, he believed, would necessitate relegating the landless to the bottom of the allotment hierarchy. He wrote to de Valera:

> It has also been the policy of the Land Commission to allot land to landless men. A sound reason can be given for so doing but I am afraid that very often the reason for allotting portions of land to this particular class is because of local agitation and a complete misconception as to what the use of land should mean. It seems to me to be quite useless to give land to a landless man who has neither experience of agricultural work, capital or stock or who lacks any of these qualifications.[89]

Moylan believed that 'a better type of man' had to be chosen in future and that such applicants could only be found 'amongst the sons of working farmers who may have sufficient capital to start their sons on the land'.[90] The following year he once again reiterated that results were 'unsatisfactory and disappointing, often shamefully so' and pointed to the fact that 'hundreds of new houses' built for landless allottees had been left unoccupied for years or else sublet.[91] This type of land division policy, he felt, was only creating 'subsistence holdings, which add little or no expendable surplus and allow no appreciable cash margin'.[92]

From the late 1930s, we begin to see a significant decline in the number of landless allottees. In 1939–40 the number fell to 177 from 226 in 1938–9 and 416 in 1937–8. The 177 received 4,912 acres (an average of almost 28 acres each) whereas an average of over 9,000 acres had been allotted to the landless over the previous two years. The number of landless allottees was to plummet even further to 30 in 1943–4, the year Moylan took over as Minister for Lands, and thereafter continued to decline until 1976 when the last of the landless allottees received a parcel of only seventeen acres. From 1940–1 to 1975–6, a total of only 346 landless allottees (an average of less than ten per year) received 11,395 acres (an average of almost 33 acres each), representing an average annual allotment of only 316.5 acres, way behind every other category. From the 1940s, the landless were essentially no longer considered in land division schemes as the focus returned firmly to the relief of congestion and migration schemes.

Moylan's attitude to ex-employees was much the same. It angered him that many of them had taken up an allotment but resold it on the open market for a profit within a short time.[93] The same trend is obvious in relation to ex-employees as it was for the landless from the 1930s. For the years, 1937–8, 1938–9 and 1939–40, a total of 482 ex-employees received 12,272 acres (an average holding of 25.5 acres each). That represented an average of 161 ex-employees a year. By 1940–1, the number had fallen to 59 (who received a total of 1,403 acres). From then until 1972–3, a total of 675 ex-employees (an average of only 21 per annum) received 18,881 acres (an average of almost 28 acres each). Granted, part of the reason for this decline was the fact that by the late 1930s most of the large estates had been divided and there were subsequently fewer ex-employees to be dealt with.

At the end of the Emergency in May 1946, Moylan made his position quite clear:

> in my experience, men employed on estates acquired by the Land Commission and proposed to be divided, should be compensated by some other methods than by giving them land. Numbers of them have made good, but it is my personal experience that most of them do not make successful farmers.[94]

This idea seems to have been suggested to him by a Department of Finance proposal in March 1945 that 'ex-employees except those who, in the opinion of the Land Commission, are likely to be good farmers and to retain possession of their holdings, should be given monetary compensation instead of being provided with holdings'.[95] The proposal was to be later adopted by the Inter-Party government when it introduced its own land act in 1950. Under section 29, gratuities determined by the Land Commission were awarded to displaced employees instead of land, although some received gratuities and small plots of lands. In 1951, 12 ex-employees received a total of £1,482. One of them also received a cottage and garden while another was provided with an accommodation plot.[96] From the passing of the act to June 1954, a total of 89 ex-employees were awarded gratuities averaging around £125 per person. A further 77 were awarded holdings of land.[97]

It is only a matter of conjecture but it is probable that many landless applicants were given lands for the wrong reasons, for their political or IRA connections, for example, rather than their ability to farm. Given the importance of landownership in Irish rural society there is no need to speculate why they might have accepted land without the availability of capital grants. There were those who were genuinely determined to make a living from their new holdings but who failed simply because Irish agriculture, particularly subsistence agriculture, was in such a depressed state that it was difficult to eke out a living to support a family, let alone have the necessary surplus to pay annuities and rates. (This applied equally to those who inherited farms; one must acknowledge that there were also varied levels of managerial ability amongst inheriting sons, not all of whom were cut out to be successful farmers.) While prevailing economic conditions, attitudes towards drudgery and lack of education in agricultural methods are certainly factors the lack of government support should not be overlooked. In theory, landless applicants were expected to have around £200 in capital or stock before they could be considered suitable allottees (or an average of around £10 per acre). Commissioner Michael Deegan told the Banking Commission in 1935: 'We do not give land to a man who has nothing'.[98] It must be remembered that £200 was then a huge sum of money for a strong farmer let alone a landless person to gather (particularly one married with a wife and a family).

In retrospect, the policy of giving land to landless men without initial grants seems to have been self-defeating. In 1933, William Davin (Leix–Offaly, Labour) had suggested that the government provide an interest free loan of £300 to £500 to the landless for a period of five years or so to get them established.[99] His idea was scorned as being impractical; yet the government gave free grants to migrants for farm improvements, the building of outoffices, the stocking and cropping of farms. How was a landless or discharged recipient of a farm expected to pay £40 for a cow or £10 for a suckling calf when lending institutions would not deal with him? They seemed to be defeated at every turn, for when some allottees let a portion of their farms in an attempt to improve their financial positions, they found themselves liable to have their holdings resumed by the Land Commission. In the mid-1930s, to cite just one example, two herds ('two of the greatest workers on a farm') who had received lands at Rathcarne in County Meath were threatened with eviction by the Land Commission because they did not have 'the wherewithal to run their farms since they lost their wages'.[100]

VI THE EMERGENCY AND AFTER, 1939–48

By the late 1930s, the Fianna Fáil government was gradually being forced to concede the importance of the cattle trade to the economy so that the party's anti-grazier rhetoric and promotion of tillage was now being challenged from the inside. (By 1939, the area under tillage was, in fact, only two per cent above its 1930 level.[101]) David Seth Jones has concluded that for those who were increasingly sceptical of the benefits of division:

> the overriding priority was to raise the output and efficiency of Irish agriculture, which required large-scale commercial farming based upon modern farm practices and technology. Land distribution, by breaking up extensive commercial grazing farms and replacing them by traditional family farms of limited productive value, was inimical to those aims.[102]

Whatever momentum was gathering was arrested by the Emergency, 1939–45, which in many respects threw the Land Commission into disarray. Firstly, under the Emergency Powers Act of 1939,[103] the acquisition and division work of the Commission was curtailed. The government, or more particularly the Department of Finance, decided to limit the cost of resumption and acquisition of lands to £250,000 a year whereas prior to this there had been no limitation.[104] The revesting of lands was discontinued. Save for urgent cases of forestry and turbary, the acquisition of lands to complete rearrangement schemes and the completion of the acquisition of lands offered by owners, no further approvals were given for preliminary reports or resumption reports.[105]

It was one thing for Finance to curtail the expenditure of the Department of Lands; it was quite another for it to interfere in its working.[106] Thus, when Finance suggested that because the Land Commission was a categorised 'non-emergency department', it should be the main one drawn upon for the staffing of emergency services, a series of standoffs developed between Thomas Derrig,[107] Minister for Lands, who had assumed the portfolio in September 1939 (himself no stranger to controversy following his time as Minister for Education in the 1930s and described by Charles Townshend as 'an uncharismatic minister with a tendency to hector rather than inspire Irish teachers'[108]) and Sean T. O'Kelly,[109] Minister for Finance (and Tánaiste).[110] For example, in April 1941, the Department of Finance issued a memorandum for the government that read:

> To enable the maximum release of staff to be secured at an early stage it would be necessary for the Land Commission to suspend action on all schemes of division which have not reached a stage at which suspension would hold up or seriously

interfere with the production of food. Land so retained by the Land Commission could be let in conacre or resumed by the former holders under specific agreements or, in the rare cases in which neither of these courses is feasible, could be administered by the Land Commission in accordance with the government's policy regarding food production and turbary.[111]

Derrig was furious but despite his vociferous objections the staff of the Land Commission inspectorate was reduced from 247 to 129 by 1943 and the staff of the Acquisition and Re-sales branch from 211 to 101, with obvious consequences for land acquisition and division schemes.[112] When, by 1944, the Land Commission was informed that its staff would not be returning in the near future, a Commission official responded: 'Any short term planning by the Land Commission is thus impossible and long-term planning is, in the peculiar circumstances of the Land Commission, so hypothetical as to have little practical value.'[113] (Of course, even if staff had been available it is likely that acquisition and division would have been restricted by the deterioration in transport facilities available to staff. The monthly petrol quota for inspectors, for example, fell from 7,500 gallons in 1939 to 344 gallons in 1943.[114])

Table 4.3 (see Appendix I, p. 236) clearly illustrates the retarding effect that the Emergency had on acquisition and division. From a high in 1935–6 of almost 104,000 acres divided, the acreage plummeted to 13,359 in 1944–5, and while 7,712 allottees benefited in 1935–6, only 861 benefited in 1944–5. It was not until December 1945 that the acquisition of new lands in the congested areas was resumed, and not until the spring of 1948 that the Land Commission resumed operations outside the scheduled congested districts.[115] (Operations in 1947, it should be added, were also seriously impeded by the arctic conditions of that winter and spring which made travel or inspections impossible.[116])

In 1943, Sean MacEntee, who had replaced O'Kelly as Minister for Finance, opposed any further land division schemes. In a letter to *The Irish Times* on 8 December, MacEntee said he was not in favour of further multiplying the number of small farms in the country. For him, de Valera's ideal was no longer practicable; in fact he was later to claim in an interview that de Valera's ideal was 'one man's dream, never party policy'.[117] MacEntee had the support of the newly appointed Minister for Lands, Sean Moylan, who the same year pointed out to de Valera that 'the Land Commission had been altogether too generous with public funds' and that free grants given to migrants could no longer be justified.[118]

Both MacEntee and Moylan were acutely aware that the state of the post-war economy would clearly impact on all future land division policy. The war had seen a dramatic increase in the market value of agricultural land. In the pre-war period, land was sold for around £9–12 a statute acre; by 1945 the price had risen to £25–40 an acre. Furthermore, building supplies had doubled in price during the war years and their scarcity had repercussions for the preparation and improvement of holdings.[119] In 1945, the Cabinet Committee on Economic Planning (established in the autumn of the previous year to discuss, amongst other things, post-war agricultural policy) pointed out that this rise meant that 'the position of the Land Commission during the years immediately following the Emergency will be one of considerable difficulty as regards the price to be paid for lands compulsorily acquired'.[120] The Appeals Tribunal was sure to fix the price of lands at their market value but the Land Commission was restricted by statute to charging the lands with an appropriate purchase annuity, in other words one that would be affordable to the occupier. In March 1945, the Department of Finance pointed out that this would mean that 'as this annuity is fixed on a long term basis the charge falling upon the Exchequer in respect of the service of the land bonds covering each acre divided will have multiplied'.[121]

Prior to the war, the new occupier serviced less than half of the purchase price (usually about £5 per acre), leaving the state to bear the charges upon the other £5–£7. When the Emergency ended, the tenant would continue to service only £5 an acre but the state would be faced with a charge several times greater. According to a Department of Finance memorandum in 1945: 'It may be taken that division of moderate sized farms into holdings of 25–30 statute acres is an uneconomic proposition as the operations give rise to an inordinate overhead expenditure, including small contracts for the erection of buildings'. It was estimated that the cost of dividing 250,000 acres (roughly what was thought to be the area of untenanted lands remaining to be divided) at the rate of 50,000 per year over a five-year period would cost the state £6.34 million or £25 per acre.[122] Significantly, the Department of Finance argued that 'even if land division is regarded in some measure as a social service the cost would be altogether excessive in such circumstances'.[123] As far as the Cabinet Committee on Economic Planning was concerned, the need for the division of land on the pre-Emergency scale had ceased.[124] And as far as Sean Moylan was concerned in 1945: 'Deputies must never again expect that land acquisition and land division will assume the volume it did before the war'.[125] Nor did it. From 1944–5 to 1947–8 inclusive (when Fianna Fáil's long term in office ended), a total of only 53,494 acres was allotted (an average of 13,374 per annum) to 3,651 allottees (an average of only 913 per annum), each receiving a reduced average of just under 15 acres each, reflecting the fact that Emergency land division policy concentrated largely on the enlargement of existing holdings rather than the provision of new ones.

Fianna Fáil, as we have seen, had been forced to face up to the fact that many of the allottees who had received lands during the record-breaking days of the mid-1930s had turned out to be unsatisfactory farmers (and there were probably a substantial number of what Alexis Fitzgerald – lawyer, senator and son-in-law of John A. Costello – called in 1956 the 'agrarian skinflints, usually a bachelor, who runs his broad acres with a below par quota of employment and that generally vilely remunerated'.[126]) At the beginning of the war, the government had demanded that the Land Commission carry out inspections of farms to ensure the success of the Compulsory Tillage Order introduced as a result of the exigencies of war that made extra food production a necessity. A series of random inspections made between 1940 and 1943 showed that in 20 per cent of the cases examined, allottees had not been working their lands properly and that a large number of houses built for allottees by the Land Commission remained uninhabited. This caused enough concern to lead to the establishment of a special section within the Land Commission to deal systematically with investigations for 'usership' and residence.

During 1944 and 1945, 6,900 holdings were visited by Land Commission officials. They were satisfied with 5,660 of these (82 per cent) but found that 1,120 (16 per cent) were 'not being worked satisfactorily generally because they were being sublet by the allottees'.[127] (There is no reference to the other two per cent.) There were, in fact, many cases throughout the country of original owners leasing from allottees, which allowed the original owners to continue as large farmers, while providing the lessors with an income without the work.[128] High Court decisions in the early 1940s laid down that lettings for conacre or temporary grazing were not in fact breaches of conditions in the purchase agreement with the result that allottees could not be dispossessed for these practices. That only 16 per cent were deemed to be unsatisfactorily worked farms does not seem that bad. But one gets the impression that this might very well be a case of the books being cooked. Any more would reflect very badly on recent land division policy and, indeed, cause monumental headaches regarding resumptions and reallocations. At any rate, it was not just the numbers found guilty of neglecting their holdings that were important, rather it was the fact that a fairly systematic survey of farms had been carried out. There is no breakdown available as to where the inspectors visited but even averaging visits based on the number of counties it comes to over 265 for each of the 26 counties. One can only imagine the fear that such a sweeping survey could have had on farmers, particularly those who, perhaps through no fault of their own, were having difficulties in maintaining farming standards or even eking a living. In fact, subsequent to these inspections, 500 further individual cases of bad husbandry were reported to the Commission during 1946, the bulk, no doubt, by neighbours, whose land-greed had been stimulated by the inspections.[129] After this initial flush of inspections, a further 25,000 were carried out between 1945 and 1985, a third of which eventually led to partial or full dispossession.[130] It should be added that the vast majority of these inspections were geared towards the resumption of lands from large farmers/graziers, an issue which will be dealt with in more detail below.

Moylan was determined to get rid of those who were not performing adequately as farmers:

> I am altogether in favour of getting rid of those failures ruthlessly. Men who get land and houses from the Land Commission and who refuse to live in these houses, who let the land to former owners, who merely regard as a legacy and windfall accruing to them the amount they can get out of the land by setting it and by letting the house, are a menace. I think that we should have no pity for them.[131]

Other influential figures within the party such as Sean Lemass felt likewise. A memorandum prepared for the government in January 1945 stated that Lemass believed: 'Only a limited number of families can be settled on the land, on economic holdings, and policy must be directed to ensuring that ownership will be confined to persons willing and capable of working them adequately.'[132] At least this was now a pragmatic acknowledgement that land division was not a utopian scheme.

In April 1945, the Department of Lands produced a report on 'Economic and social aspects of land policy' that began with the argument that a changing social outlook coupled with experiences learned during the war years had led to the conclusion that 'an unlimited and irresponsible ownership of land can no longer be admitted'.[133] There was a dangerous implication here for land-owners in that land was regarded as being too vital to the national economy 'to permit of its utilisation being regarded as the sole concern of its owners and its ownership must be limited by a responsibility directed towards appreciation of national need and subject to specific commitment'.[134] The security of tenure that had been a fundamental demand of land movements in Ireland for gener-ations was being questioned once again, even more specifically than under the 1933 Land Act. The report referred to the deep-rooted feeling amongst farmers that land ownership was sacrosanct and to the prevailing attitude that any restrictions made on landowners could be morally resisted. It concluded that while security of tenure was essential to the proper working of land:

> There are, implicit in this recognition of ownership and guarantee of security, certain commitments on the part of the owner to the community, certain limits beyond which that recognition does not apply nor that guarantee operate.[135]

This effectively amounted to a threat that the state would no longer allow land to be held out of or below production for it was 'definitely detrimental to the state to have land utilised below its potential capacity'.[136] The government had seen the potential for control of agriculture through the working of the Compulsory Tillage Order during the course of the war and it now wanted to continue to exert this control even if in a modified form.

> Land administration must in future take a more specific cognisance of the contribution to national income which economic policy demands of agriculture and must on the one hand forcibly combat the misuse or inadequate use of land and on the other hand must endeavour to make such provision and create such conditions as will enable farmers to make an adequate contribution. Powers for the acquisition and resumption of land not being utilised according to proper methods of husbandry are already in existence. These powers should be re-examined. . . . This is particularly necessary if those who have acquired land in various parts of the country either speculatively or with a view to running them as natural grass farms in post war years are to be dealt with.[137]

In 1945, Moylan introduced a land bill to deal with neglected holdings. Passed into law in 1946, it gave the Land Commission specific and definite powers in relation to allottees who did not reside in the houses provided by the Land Commission, who sublet their lands, or who did not work them in 'a satisfactory manner'. After the inspection of what was termed an 'under-worked holding', the inspector followed one of two procedures: he either issued letters of warning where there was a chance that the owner might improve his farm management policies or he issued a termination of agreement where the case seemed hopeless which gave the Land Commission the right to repossess. Where repossession was obtained, the lands were let on temporary contract until a resale scheme was organised. Where possession was not given up voluntarily, the Land Commission solicitor initiated legal proceedings. If after that the owner refused to give up his holding, the sheriff was called in and possession taken forcibly.

It was inevitable that Land Commission action in repossessing (or resuming) holdings would result in strong opposition. (Although the Irish legislation was by no means as draconian as the Agricultural Act of 1947 in Britain, which introduced a policy of expropriation without compensation that was much more radical than that in Ireland where the inefficient farmer had at least to receive full market value for the land resumed from him.) To accuse a farmer of not working his holding in a satisfactory manner was a very delicate matter. There could be a number of holdings in any given parish that fell below a reasonable productive capacity and how was that ever to be judged fairly and consistently? Some of these holdings might have become derelict because of a complete lack of capital (not necessarily the result of a lack of effort on the owner's behalf) or because an owner was aged, senile or even mentally incapacitated. But what of cases, as the Minister for Agriculture asked, where a farmer was currently falling upon hard times but who had a young family, one member of which in time might 'pull the place together and become in due course a first-class farmer'.[138]

When the Land Commission sent the sheriff and bailiffs in, they were often met by the same type of communal opposition that had been fashionable during the Land War. A farmer explained to me how the 'grippers' [bailiffs] had come to his father's farm in 1949 because his father had allowed the land to fall into dereliction largely because of his 'drink problem'. He was young at the time, just gone 12, but he remembered a neighbouring farmer and two of his labourers arriving in their yard, who drove the 'grippers' away with pitchforks. 'I'll never forget what that neighbour shouted after them. He shouted, "there's a young fellow here that'll make a fine farmer some day, now get the f— out of here and don't come back!"' They didn't and the young boy did subsequently become a very successful farmer. When, twenty years later, his neighbour's farm was put up for sale (ironically because his son 'drank it out'), he felt morally obliged not to buy it out of a sense of loyalty 'to the man who ran the grippers'. [139]

The opposition played the well-worn tune that the bill amounted to an attempt to expropriate lands from Irish farmers and thereby negated all the work and sacrifices made by the Land League and the tenants of Ireland from the late 1870s. Joseph Blowick (Mayo, Clann na Talmhan) told the Dáil: 'I tell the minister and the house that too many sacrifices have been made in the past for the land of this country to allow anybody to come in to a farmer and tell him that he is working his farm well or badly.'[140] Moylan attacked as nonsense the Opposition's claims, arguing that the three Fs won in 1881 still applied.

> As to fair rent, they are asked to pay what is, after all, only a very attenuated annuity, which is a purchase annuity, and will end in the year on which the annuity expires and the land becomes their absolute property. They are given fixity of tenure. The land is theirs forever. No one can disturb them, if they will face up to the written contract which they have signed with the Land Commission. . . . They are completely different from the tenants of the Land War. These are men who are beneficiaries, chosen arbitrarily by an independent tribunal, secure in its office, protected legally in its acts, independent of any government or any political party. They are provided with a valuable gift of the most fundamental property in this State – the land of the country.[141]

Although, as noted above, hundreds of inspections were carried out each year after 1946, it seems that the Land Commission trod very carefully regarding the resumption of neglected holdings. In 1947, it recovered only 390 acres from unsatisfactory allottees who had been persistently non-resident, who had sub-let, practised bad husbandry, not paid their annuities or had breached their purchase agreements in some other way.[142] As table 4.4 shows (see Appendix 1, p. 237), an average of 383 further holdings were under review in the first four years of the operation of the act. Thereafter the numbers kept under review following inspection gradually dwindled. A comparison of cases under review with the number of holdings recovered clearly shows that the threat of resumption of neglected holdings was much greater than the action; this was similar to landlord policy in the nineteenth century. In fact, by 1968, after which year the resumption of holdings ceased, only 7,300 acres on 540 holdings were resumed and re-allotted under the 1966 act, an average of only 348 acres per year.

It can be argued that it was not the actual number of holdings resumed that was important, but rather the fear of resumption hanging like the sword of Damocles over the heads of Irish farmers. One can only imagine the level of suspicion and fear, often retarding neighbourly relations in small rural communities, as the ever-present fear stalked the countryside that badly worked land would sooner or later result in inspection and attempted acquisition.[143] As one farmer informed me: 'There were certain neighbours you dared not let into your yard lest they saw a cow with red water or a broken plough that there was no money to mend in case he might report you to the commission for negligence.'[144] Patrick Kavanagh's semi-autobiographical *Tarry Flynn* (1948), set in the mid-1930s, offers a revealing insight into such land-hunger. When the Carlins ran into financial difficulties, and Tarry's mother became interested in purchasing the smallholding to consolidate their own, Tarry remembered that: 'He often heard it said that the Land Commission would let a man have a farm by merely paying the arrears of Annuities. Wouldn't it be marvellous if she got it for forty or fifty pounds?'[145]

VII CONCLUSION

In 1950, James Dillon, the then Inter-Party Minister for Agriculture, sardonically referred to 'the halcyon days of 1934, 1935 and 1936'.[146] The acerbic Dillon was being critical of the Fianna Fáil policy that had allotted lands hastily and without due consideration for the future economic and agricultural prospects of the country. Dillon's speech is worth quoting at length, even if only for its entertainment value:

With the academic approach, which is by no means alien to his nature, he [de Valera] tells us that he summoned the Land Commission [in 1932] and desired to know if they had 500,000 acres, what digit they proposed to divide into that and the resultant sum. Being given a very tentative calculation, he deplored their lack of precision, and said he did not want to talk in 'ifs' and 'buts' . . . As a result of this mathematical operation, the division of land rose from the 50,000 acres per annum, which had been the rule in the previous decade, in 1934 to 101,000 odd, and in 1935–36 to 103,000 odd, and the votaries of the god proclaimed a miracle again. Behold, what was declared to be impossible was now possible; that which no one else could do, a Daniel come to judgment had done. . . . The story did not finish in the halcyon days of 1934, 1935 and 1936. The story was not finished until his own Minister for Lands, Deputy Moylan, came to this House in 1946 and said that he must ask the House to enact an Eviction Bill of a character that no minister had ever dared to lay before this House before. For what purpose? . . . It was to evict the allottees of 1934, 1935, 1936 and 1937.[147]

From the late 1930s there were signs of a growing rift within the government over land reform policy. David Seth Jones's pioneering article on 'Divisions within the Irish government over land-distribution policy, 1940–70' examines this rift in some detail. He divides the two factions into those who remained faithful to the established land policy, including de Valera, who were fully convinced of its merits and the contribution it could continue to make to 'maintaining a traditional rural culture based upon the small family farm; and sustaining economic self-sufficiency through tillage production suited to small scale farming' and those such as Moylan, Lemass, MacEntee and O'Ceallaigh (the latter two significantly Ministers for Finance) who became unconvinced of the merits of land division to the agricultural economy. The latter faction saw the merits of large-scale commercial farming inimical to the aims of Fianna Fáil.[148] Towards the end of the war, Moylan and Lemass were shaping up towards an alliance. In 1944, Moylan wrote to Lemass: 'Some people hold the view that the greater number of acres of land divided the greater the success. I don't hold that view. The creation of records has resulted in ill-advised schemes the evils of which are now apparent'.[149] But, as we shall see in chapter 6, while Moylan remained true to his beliefs, Lemass's attitude was much more ambivalent and he shifted position very quickly as the political need arose.

There was also amongst social commentators and agricultural experts a growing realisation that small-farm life could no longer be painted in idyllic terms; harsh reality had intervened in the form of reports by agricultural experts and experienced members of the Land Commission.[150] In 1942, a committee was appointed under the chairmanship of Professor T. A. Smiddy to consider agricultural policy in the aftermath of the Emergency 'with special reference to measures for increasing the fertility of the land, promoting efficiency in the industry and making the various branches of the industry self-supporting'.[151] The committee reported in 1945 and emphasised that 'the prosperity of the agricultural industry in this country will depend in the future, as it has done in the past, on intensive production of livestock and livestock products and on the disposal of a large proportion of such products in the export market' and recommended the expansion rather than the contraction of the livestock market.[152] In 1947, the Cabinet Committee on Economic Planning argued that the small standard farms of £20 poor law valuation (or 25 acres of good land) were 'only subsistence holdings which add little to the agricultural wealth of the country, provide little or no exportable surplus and allow no appreciable cash margin'. These holdings were now deemed uneconomic.[153] There was a clear change in thinking here for the committee argued that to divide 200-acre farms into holdings of less than 30 acres had no lasting effect: 'Quite apart from any other result, at the first opportunity these small holdings will tend to coalesce once more under the force of economic attraction.'[154]

The highly influential Department of Finance similarly argued in 1948 that before any further reduction in the small number of large farms now left in the country was brought about, 'the possible repercussion on the agricultural economy as a whole should receive exhaustive examination'.[155] Finance further suggested that the Land Commission should not acquire any more land for division except in the congested districts or where the land was needed for the relief of congestion by migration from these districts to contiguous areas.[156] It was now acknowledged that in a country where so many smallholdings had been created, it was necessary to preserve the remaining large farms in the richer agricultural areas to provide a market for the cattle produced in the poorer agricultural lands of the west and south.[157] Furthermore, it was argued that the breaking up of large farms would have unwelcome social as well as economic consequences. It would tend to deprive farmers of all hope of leadership, and leave them at the mercy of other sections of the community. It would

> reduce and perhaps finally eliminate that small relatively well off and well educated minority from which alone the example of scientific and progressive farming can be expected and it would lead to a lowering of the general standard of culture in rural areas.[158]

More will be said of the political factions in chapter 6, but suffice it to say at this stage that anti-divisional rumblings tended to take place at cabinet level or in committee rooms. There was an unspoken agreement that such dissenting views should not be made public; that would certainly not be good politics. Fianna Fáil TDs who ventured outside the terms of this agreement were quickly admonished by their leader. Thus, when Sean MacEntee in 1943 suggested in a public speech that land policy might in the future be re-orientated towards large farms, fewer farms and fewer farm workers, the Taoiseach, Eamon de Valera announced in the Dáil:

> I am aware that in a speech delivered on the 26th November last the Minister for Local Government and Public Health, speaking on national planning, referred to two conceivable land policies for this country – one that of a highly mechanised agriculture with large farms, fewer farms and fewer farm workers. The other, that of smaller farms, more farmers, and more farm workers. The choice between these two policies, he said, had been made. I think it was quite clear from his speech that the policy which the Minister referred to as having been chosen is that indicated in Article 45 of the Constitution directed towards establishing on the land in economic security as many families as in the circumstances shall be practicable. This policy which puts the social above the narrow economic aim, has been the basis of the activities of the Land Commission for a large number of years and it is the policy of the government to maintain that basis.[159]

FIVE

REVERSING CROMWELL'S POLICY

MIGRATION SCHEMES, 1923–48

Only a few years ago it was practically impossible to induce tenantry in congested localities in the Gaeltacht to migrate even a few miles from their old homes, but many hundreds of small holders now are expressing their willingness to exchange into new holdings even where the latter are situated at a large distance from their present domiciles.
ILC report, 1931, p. 11.

—

I INTRODUCTION

Some brief references have already been made in this book to migration schemes, which were not unique to the period after independence. From the late nineteenth century, it was widely accepted that migration was one of the few viable solutions to the relief of the chronic congestion that existed in large areas of the west of Ireland. Tenants would have to be removed from congested areas and provided with new holdings elsewhere, so that their original holdings could be redistributed amongst their former neighbours in order to bring them up to economic levels. The migration of large individual landholders and, later, whole families after 1923 became something of a social phenomenon that ultimately represented a remarkable piece of social engineering by successive governments, particularly Fianna Fáil in the late 1930s, to solve the Irish land question. And yet, like all aspects of the Irish land question post-independence, these internal migration schemes have attracted very little attention from historians.[1]

II PRE-INDEPENDENCE MIGRATION SCHEMES

Migration schemes had been tried in the past through both state and private initiatives. There is plenty of evidence of landlords such as Lord Lansdowne in Kerry, the Shirleys in Monaghan and Lord Clonbrock in Galway, removing tenants from their estates through assisted migration schemes during and after the Great Famine. The 1881 Land Act acknowledged that the plight of western congests could be alleviated by empowering the Land Commission to advance loans to assist the emigration of families from 'the poorer and more thickly populated districts of Ireland'.[2] In 1882, the establishment of what became known as 'Mr Tuke's fund', inaugurated at the Duke of Bedford's home in London and subscribed to by many of the leading Irish landlords of the time, promoted 'assisted emigration' from these areas. By 1882, £8,000 had been subscribed and by June over 1,200 families had left from County Galway for North America (including 350 from Connemara on board the *Nepyon* in May 1882 and another 430 on board the *Winnipeg* two weeks later).[3]

Of course, any type of landlord or British government involvement in emigration schemes for Ireland attracted the wrath of the more intense nationalists who became alarmed at the loss of numbers to the nation.[4] The promotion of emigration schemes was viewed suspiciously as an attempt to sap the energy of the Irish nation. Thus for generations there was 'a contradiction between attachment to an economy that required the emigration of many of the sons and daughters of the land, and a nationalist ideology that viewed emigration as almost tantamount to treason'.[5] During the Great War, the channels of emigration were effectively closed to prospective emigrants. During the revolutionary period, particularly up to the truce in July 1921, Sinn Féin and the IRA tried to ensure that emigration levels were kept to a minimum so that young, energetic potential recruits could be kept in the country.

In the meantime, the continued plight of western congests remained an emotive issue. The influential Dudley report of 1908 concluded that western congests were 'to a large extent, the wrecks of past racial, religious, agrarian and social storms in Ireland, and of famine catastrophes'.[6] The establishment of the Congested Districts Board in 1891 to promote agriculture and industry in designated areas along the western seaboard where poverty was most acute gave a certain amount of impetus to migration. One of the more influential members of the Board, Sir Henry Doran, the senior land inspector, argued that the migration of large landowners should be the first objective.[7] He was soon made aware, however, of the potential difficulties facing any migration scheme. In 1894 the Board's baseline reports from inspectors, asked to inquire into the availability of suitable land 'to which families could be migrated with a reasonable prospect of success', made frequent reference to the fact that there was very little land in the scheduled areas, that large graziers were reluctant to give up their holdings and that without the movement of large occupiers, migration schemes would be useless.[8] The reluctance of the large occupiers to migrate became an intractable problem.[9]

But reluctance to migrate was not just the preserve of the large landholders. The reasons for not wanting to depart their homesteads were, probably, common to all classes. Writing in 1904, Horace Plunkett, one of the most able agricultural commentators of his time, thought that 'there is, no doubt, a poetic justice in the Utopian agrarianism which dangles before the eyes of the Connaught peasantry the alternative of Heaven or Leinster'.[10] (Plunkett was obviously playing on the phrase attributed by folklore to Cromwell that encapsulated Cromwellian land redistribution policy: 'To Hell or to Connaught'.) One would have thought that given the conditions of life on small uneconomic holdings, farmers would have relished the opportunity of escaping the poverty trap but they seem to have been no more willing to leave their homes than large holders. Why? Was it simply an attachment to a plot of land where their ancestors were born? Contemporary commentators attempted to understand a mentality that put pride of place before a favourable change of circumstances, and largely failed to do so. In 1887, one social commentator argued that the work of the Congested Districts Board was made difficult by 'a population intensely agricultural in its instincts, and clinging to the soil with that tenacity so marked in the history of the Irish tenant'.[11] Similarly, Horace Plunkett wrote:

> What the Irishman is really attached to in Ireland is not a home but a social order. The pleasant amenities, the courtesies, the leisureliness, the associations of religion, and the familiar faces of the neighbours, whose ways and minds are like his and very unlike those of any other people.[12]

One can rightly be sceptical about some of Plunkett's reasons; nevertheless his attachment theory was hardly misplaced. And if prospective migrants were to be enticed to leave they had to be provided with some sense of security that would allay their fears for as Enda Delaney has concluded regarding external migrants:

> To assume that migrants had detailed information about their prospective destination is, at best, a naïve starting point, yet it was only either a foolhardy migrant or one seeking refuge from distress of some form (famine, religious persecution, etc.) who would have left their home country without at least some information on the conditions in the prospective receiving society.[13]

Delaney goes on to point out the crucial role of kin and personal networks in the migration process; the existence of a family member in the receiving society lessened the trauma of a move to a strange environment. Studies have shown that Ireland traditionally exhibited a low rate of internal migration by international standards and continued to do so right up to the 1970s, when even then only about one in five of those leaving provincial Ireland was likely to move to Dublin. The remaining four were more likely to emigrate.[14] People from rural Ireland, it seems, emigrated with much less apprehension, simply because they more often than not went to communities already composed of members of their families, former neighbours and friends. Again, Plunkett related a revealing anecdote in this respect:

> Recently [c.1904] a daughter of a small farmer in County Galway with a family too 'long' for the means of subsistence available, was offered a comfortable home on a farm owned by some better-off relatives, only thirty miles away, though probably twenty miles beyond the limits of her peregrinations. She elected in preference to go to New York, and being asked her reason by a friend of mine, replied in so many words, 'because it is nearer'. She felt she would be less of a stranger in a New York tenement house, among her relatives and friends who had already emigrated, than in another part of County Galway.[15]

In this respect County Meath was probably more alien to prospective western migrants in the 1920s than was Boston, Chicago or New York. In 1924, Dr Bartley Ó Beirne (Tuberculosis Officer for Galway) in his evidence to the Gaeltacht Commission emphasised that inhabitants of Connemara would be much happier to move to East Galway than to Meath as they 'would be nearer the old home' and 'Meath would be out of their world as far as their lives are concerned'.[16] As late as the 1950s, the Commission on Emigration (1948–54) recognised this same phenomenon:

> Tradition and example have also been very powerful influences. Emigration of some members of the family has almost become part of the established custom of the people in certain areas – a part of the generally accepted pattern of life. For very many emigrants there was a traditional path 'from the known to the known', that is to say, from areas where they lived to places where their friends and relations awaited them.[17]

As a further barrier to the encouragement of the migration of farmers within Ireland, Horace Plunkett astutely and rightly placed emphasis upon 'the possible opposition of those who live in the vicinity of the unoccupied land about to be distributed, and who feel that they have the first claim upon the state in any scheme for its redistribution with the help of public credit'.[18] In the early twentieth century, when the Congested Districts Board began to purchase untenanted lands outside the designated congested areas, its commissioners quickly realised that 'those who lived in the vicinity of the grazing lands expressed with increasing strength their disapproval of the utilisation of those lands for relieving congestion in other parts of the country'.[19] (Negative attitudes towards migrants were by no means a phenomenon of rural Ireland. Mary E. Daly has found, for example, that migrant labourers in Dublin in the early twentieth century were made just as unwelcome.[20])

And such negative attitudes were not to change easily. We have already seen how the revolutionary period heightened tensions between migrants and locals.[21] This continued throughout the 1920s and into the early 1930s: in 1934, S. J. Waddell, a senior member of the Land Commission (writing under the pseudonym, Rutherford Mayne) declared in the introduction to his play *Bridge Head*: 'But the clan feeling of territory still exists, often in a narrow parochial form, and the advent of the congested migrant into a new holding in a strange district is rarely welcome to the local people.'[22]

On a more practical level, the Congested District Board was faced with other inherent difficulties regarding the implementation of migration schemes, chief amongst which were the attendant expenses of equipping holdings, fencing them and erecting buildings.[23] Much needed state aid in the form of capital to stock farms and instructors to educate farmers in the ways of commercial farming was not forthcoming. With no money or agricultural implements (and annuities to be paid) too many of these migrants seem to have been forced into mortgaging their stock to local shopkeepers and publicans.[24] Thus, from 1891 to 1903, the board effected only 207 migrations.[25]

After the passing of the 1903 Land Act, the board became more successful in the acquisition of untenanted estates outside the scheduled areas for the relief of western congestion. Up to the date of its dissolution on 24 July 1923, it had purchased 2.25 million acres of which 1.6 million acres were still in its possession for resale and/or redistribution purposes to be dealt with by the reconstituted Land Commission after 1923.[26] The 1903 act allowed the board to utilise whatever land was left over after migration schemes had been effected for the enlargement of uneconomic holdings (below £5 valuation) in the vicinity of the purchased estate. But continued logistical problems, related largely to the fact that there were too many congests and not enough land, and then the curtailment of the board's activities by the outbreak of the First World War meant that migration schemes progressed ineffectually prior to independence.

After independence, public representatives from western constituencies continually urged the need to relieve the congestion problem through migration. In 1923, Joseph MacBride (Mayo, Cumann na nGaedheal) was the first TD to propose publicly that families should be migrated in groups or colonies: 'They will not then be absolutely alone in their new holdings, but will have the help and advice of those who go along with them'.[27]

III 'THE GAELTACHT INVADING THE PALE'

By the early 1930s, 43 per cent of the land in Kildare was held in estates of over 200 acres in size; in Meath, 40 per cent; in Westmeath, 30 per cent and in Tipperary, 22 per cent. In other words, over 75,000 acres in these four counties were divided into holdings of over 200 acres.[28] Those who proposed the implementation of migration schemes from west to east saw the possibilities of utilising lands in these counties where the population was generally less densely situated than that of many western regions (although, arguably, they were not fully alert to the extent of local congestion in each of these counties). There were the idealists, such as William Sears (Cumann na nGaedheal), who considered west to east migration an effective means 'to lift the curse of Cromwell'. Sears described western congests as being 'of the old stock of the Irish race [who] have kept the language alive' and for this deserving of consideration.[29] His rhetoric was very much born of the D. P. Moran school which had insisted in the early twentieth century that 'the foundation of Ireland is the Gael, and the Gael must be the element that absorbs'.[30] In this context it is interesting to look at how the first Free State government contemplated the idea of using migration as a means of reviving the Irish language outside the Gaeltacht areas before moving to a discussion of more pragmatic (if less patriotic) reasons for such schemes.

Since the last quarter of the nineteenth century, the Irish language had been promoted as an essential ingredient of Irish nationality. The influence of the Gaelic League, formed in 1893, and its successful campaign in 1910 to have Irish made a compulsory matriculation subject within the recently formed National University of Ireland system ensured, as one historian has put it, that 'deference to Irish as the national language was required of nationalist politicians and of anyone else who needed to cultivate the undivided support of nationalists'.[31] Similarly, the role of the Gaelic League in nurturing revolutionaries has been widely accepted by contemporary Volunteers and later historians alike.[32] In January 1919, despite the seeming impracticalities involved, the first meeting of Dáil Éireann was conducted in Irish. Under the 1922 constitution, Irish was designated as the official language of the Free State. That same year the reform of the Irish educational system began which saw Irish become a compulsory subject at primary and secondary levels by 1924.

Government policy towards the Irish language also manifested itself in another more audacious proposal – the migration of farmers from the Irish speaking areas of the country, more generally referred to as the Gaeltacht areas, which were essentially confined to the west coast, to the east as a possible means of consolidating the strength of the spoken language. In July 1924,

Patrick Hogan (Clare, Labour) suggested to his namesake, the Minister for Agriculture, that he should

> give some consideration to the possibility of transferring colonies of Irish speakers from Irish-speaking districts into districts that are not Irish-speaking, and putting the colony together so that it would be self-supporting, and that instead of the Pale invading the Gaeltacht, we will have the Gaeltacht invading the Pale, and spreading the light there.[33]

Subsequently, in 1925, a commission was appointed by the Executive Council to inquire into the preservation of the Irish language and to enquire simultaneously into the economic problems facing Gaeltacht areas. These areas were largely coterminous with the originally designated congested districts. The report concluded that 'the land is the sole permanent basis of livelihood of the Gaeltacht population'; the estimated 10,650 men employed in the fishing industry could be described only as farmer-fishermen.[34] It described districts where the land was so poor and the holdings so small that no amount of migration or resettlement would make the holdings economic. These included areas around Erris in County Mayo and Connemara in County Galway. Connemara was almost entirely insulated from the rest of the country by Lough Corrib and Lough Mask, the entire centre of the area 'a barren desert of mountain and moor', with no market town except Clifden, very little cultivable land and no natural diffusion of population into surrounding areas. From it there was a constant stream of emigration to America. The remittances sent home made potential émigrés 'look to America as an El Dorado',[35] in stark contrast to 'the gloom and lack of amusement in the Gaeltacht'.[36] The Donegal Gaeltacht areas were no different. Here children from the age of ten were regarded as 'economic assets', sent at this early age to work in the Lagan area during the summer and autumn months while their fathers went to Scotland as migratory labourers.[37] Consistent with the thinking of the time, the Gaeltacht Commission's report concluded that the congests in such areas were 'the evicted tenants of the race' and that the terms of the 1923 Land Act would have to be amended to provide some form of restitution to undo 'a great economic injustice' of the past. If not, the life of the Irish speaker would be

> one of continued poverty and degradation in his native surroundings, involving dependence on American money, old age pensions, migratory labour in Britain, or elsewhere and government relief; or emigration with the consequent loss to the living language position.[38]

The commission concluded that there could be 'no effective settlement of the economic conditions in the Gaeltacht without a satisfactory arrangement of the land into economic holdings' and urged the break-up of all the grasslands in the west. It recommended that only Irish-speaking families should be resettled in Gaeltacht areas, that resident English-speaking families with claims to lands should have their claims satisfied outside the Gaeltacht and that 'the large holders and the English-speaking holders should, as far as possible, be migrants, as it is important that the population remaining locally may be as homogeneously Irish-speaking as possible'.[39] These recommendations were obviously underpinned by the belief that there was no room within the cultural boundary of the Gaeltacht for English-speaking graziers.

The recommendations of the commission were not unanimous. Those who dissented did so largely on cultural and linguistic grounds rather than on grounds related to land division. A professor at University College Galway, for example, stated that 'I am not an economist or a businessman. . . . However, I am against transplanting people out of the Gaeltacht into the Galltacht. I believe their language would have no chance.'[40] Seán Ó Muirthile disagreed entirely with the notion of colony migration. He argued that:

> The largest colonies that land distribution facilities could permit could not in my opinion – no matter how loyal they were to the language movement – withstand the continuous crushing influence of the English language around them on all sides.[41]

On a more practical level, he contended that farmers from the Gaeltacht would have great difficulty in adapting to different farming methods in counties such as Meath and that the cost involved in equipping their farms and training them in new agricultural methods would be more expensive than developing local industry.[42]

Indeed, it was the estimated financial costs of the colony migration schemes that had the greatest impact upon the Cumann na nGaedheal government. Patrick Hogan calculated that it would be necessary to migrate 20,000 families from the Gaeltacht regions to Dublin or Meath, at a cost of £700 per family, or a total of around £14 million. (The largest outlay would have been on the construction of houses and outoffices on the new holdings, averaging in 1930 between £350 and £700 for smallholdings and between £700 and £1,800 on large holdings.[43]) Significantly, the influential Department of Finance, even though headed in the late 1920s by an Irish language enthusiast, Ernest Blythe, was opposed to the proposal of a Gaeltacht migration scheme.[44] Thus, in 1927, President Cosgrave wrote:

The extensive migration schemes proposed by the [Gaeltacht] Commission do not commend themselves to us. There is only a limited amount of land available for distribution in the country. There are congests both inside and outside the congested districts. Migration, even when there is no opposition or hostility, either on the part of the migrants themselves or on the part of the owners of the land to which they are being migrated, is costly. Any scheme of wholesale migration to lands which could only be rendered available by a second migration of the present occupiers is, to our minds, unthinkable.[45]

The Gaeltacht Commission's recommended scheme was subsequently shelved by the government.[46]

From 1923 to 1932, the government's policy (promoted as 'the only wise and sane policy for the Land Commission to follow'[47]) was to migrate individual extensive farmers from the west to the east where they were compensated with 'lands equally suitable and of no less value'. The belief was that it was cheaper to migrate one large farmer and to divide his lands amongst local congests than to migrate a number of smallholders.[48] Unfortunately there are no reliable statistics available regarding the numbers migrated from west to east during the Cumann na nGaedheal administration or, indeed, regarding local migrations (the occasional movement of smallholders from one parish to another), but the number almost certainly ran into hundreds.[49] By March 1930, 17 farms, with an average size of 160 statute acres, had been allotted to migrants in County Meath whose lands in other counties had been acquired by the Commission for the relief of congestion.[50] In February 1926, the Land Commission had acquired over 500 acres in Meath which Patrick Hogan claimed was wanted urgently for the settlement of a large farmer being brought from Mayo giving relief to 70 families in the area of his old holding.[51] The same year the Land Commission purchased the 660-acre Butler estate at Dunshaughlin in County Meath to accommodate two migrants from the west.[52] In November 1927, 270 acres of the Rathregan estate in Meath were acquired for a migrant from Mayo.[53] Around the beginning of 1927, a large farmer from the west was given the Elmgrove farm in Ballivor, the acreage of which was not specified.[54] In 1928, P. K. Joyce received 270 acres on the Wallis estate in Meath in compensation for the lands he surrendered in Mayo.[55]

Outside the Dáil, the government had to contend with a great deal of opposition from various lobby groups in the receiving counties. From the beginning, there was widespread criticism of what was perceived to be the establishment of 'a new plantation' in the eastern and midland counties. The minister was reminded time and again that these receiving counties had their own congests. In July 1924, for example, John Conlan (Kildare, Farmers' Union) pointed out to Patrick Hogan that:

Anybody who travels through counties such as Meath, Westmeath, Kildare etc., must know that here and there you run into a tract of inferior land, bogland, and so on, and find that that tract is studded with the little houses of people who are living there under very miserable conditions, indeed. I know of one estate in County Kildare, surrounded by a rich district, in which there are 180 tenants with valuations of £5 and under. Before bringing migrants from distant places, I think that these people should be placed in possession of economic holdings. If that is not done, I am sure it will create a great deal of dissatisfaction, and the state of the country, to use a moderate term, will not improve.[56]

In February 1927, David Hall (Meath, Labour) objected to the proposed 'planting' of migrants on the Dobbett estate in Meath given that the demands of local congests had not yet been satisfied.[57] In June 1927, Hugh Colohan (Kildare, Labour) told T. J. O'Connell (Galway, Labour) to 'keep his migrants in his own county . . . I hope that he [the Minister for Lands] will put a stop to the planting of these men in Kildare until Kildare men are first satisfied'.[58] In 1931, Matthew O'Reilly (Meath, Fianna Fáil), referring to growing dissatisfaction in Meath, pointed out that: 'We have no objections to migrants getting portions of an estate, provided that a sufficient number of uneconomic holders of the county get lands surrounding them . . . it leads to peace and contentment in the county'.[59]

Appeasing local uneconomic holders became by necessity an accepted part of Land Commission policy. When, for example, the McVeagh estate in Meath was divided in 1927, 334 acres were first divided between locals before 380 acres were divided amongst migrants.[60] When the Cloncurry estates in Meath and Kildare were divided around the same time, 600 acres were divided amongst 24 local uneconomic holders and 1,438 acres were divided amongst eight migrants who had surrendered a total of 2,027 acres in the west.[61] During the four years from 1927 to 1931, an area of 7,200 acres was acquired by the Land Commission for division in Kildare, 1,950 acres of which was divided amongst migrants and the remainder amongst local uneconomic holders.[62]

Cumann na nGaedheal's failure to promote migration schemes on a much more ambitious scale, and, therefore, to relieve congestion, led to disillusionment in the west. On 22 March 1930, a resolution was passed by Mayo County Council expressing 'grave concern' at the delay which had occurred in the provision of lands in other counties for the migration of large landholders from that county and calling upon the government to put its compulsory powers of acquisition to better use.[63] By now Dáil question times were dominated with queries from TDs regarding the reasons for the delays in acquiring estates or breaking up large farms (and not, it should be emphasised, just in the west). While Cumann na nGaedheal had toyed with the idea of group or colony migration, it had not actively promoted it. From 1923 to 1932, it was, it seems, almost exclusively large farmers who were moved out of western areas to the midlands and the east where they were given lands of at least equal value (and in a lot of cases probably of substantially greater value). It was not until Fianna Fáil came to power in 1932 that colony migration was again contemplated.

IV FIANNA FÁIL AND COLONY MIGRATION

From the late 1920s, Fianna Fáil saw in migration schemes the possibility to achieve three aims simultaneously – the preservation and spread of the Irish language, the relief of congestion and the stemming of emigration – all of which formed parts of the party's wider social policy.[64]

By the early 1930s, as the opening quotation to this chapter, taken from the Land Commission Report of 1931, suggests, attitudes towards migration seem to have been changing. Families had come to realise the possible advantages of receiving a fertile farm in the east of 20-odd acres in exchange for a few miserable acres in the west. (Evidence of this is suggested by the fact that in 1937 68 applications were made from tenants in North Mayo for 12 holdings in Gibbstown in County Meath.[65]) But Fianna Fáil's hands were largely tied until it passed its own land act in 1933 and it was not until 1935 that the new land division policy had an impact on acquisition and division.

In the meantime, the ever-impatient smallholders of the west were becoming increasingly frustrated.[66] Their frustration was symbolised in December 1934 by the protest of 40 congests who made the arduous journey by bicycle from Connemara to Dublin in order to draw the government's attention to their needs and to the necessity for immediate and extensive migration schemes. When they met de Valera, he allegedly told them that the people of Meath would probably react negatively to the establishment of a colony in their midst, to which one of the deputation, Máirtin Ó Cofaigh, reputedly replied: 'Abair leo gur chuir Cromwell siar muid agus anois go bhfuil muid ag teacht aniar' [Tell them Cromwell sent us there and now we are coming home].[67] This was a small but very important and highly symbolic demonstration.

At about the same time as the Connemara protest, the Minister for Lands, Senator Joseph Connolly, promised at the party's *ard-fheis* that there would be spectacular increases in the acquisition of lands and that when the demands of local uneconomic holders were met, he would ensure that surplus lands would be used 'as a reserve for the migrants from the Gaeltacht'.[68] Significantly, Connolly tied land division policy to the restoration of the Irish language – the second fundamental aim of Fianna Fáil. For Fianna Fáil idealists, this was important. Charles Townshend argues that de Valera, for example, 'assumed that language was not just the primary badge of nationality but that it offered the only vehicle through which the nation's essential spirit could shape its everyday life'.[69] While Fianna Fáil, in its drive to restore the Irish language, did, of course, direct most of its attention to the educational system, there were those within the party who believed that there could be some benefit (perhaps political as much as social) to be achieved from establishing Gaeltacht colonies.

In 1935, J. C. Gamble was placed in charge of preparing the Gaeltacht colonies migration scheme.[70] But news of the proposed scheme sent what could only be described as shock waves through the receiving counties. When the first rumours of a proposed migration scheme to County Meath broke in January 1935, a writer styling him/herself 'Tara' wrote to the editor of the *Meath Chronicle*:

> I wonder are the Meath folk asleep or are they content to be driven as sheep? Their birthright is being filched from them to help in the spoon-feeding of that section of our people who seem to be only capable of sponging on the remainder of the community . . . Wake up, remember there is a cuckoo in the nest, and that we have uneconomic holders of our own at Meath Hill, Kilmainhamwood etc.[71]

Land division policy at this time, it must be remembered, gave priority to discharged employees, evicted tenants, local uneconomic holders and the landless in that order over migrants (with special provision to be made for the Old IRA.) Thus, when the first group of prospective migrants visited the county in 1935 to view their holdings, they were met by a deputation led by Seamus Finn, president of the Meath Old IRA Association who did little to assuage their anxieties by telling them that: 'It is generally urged that the Old IRA men have first claim with landless men and uneconomic holders. These having been fairly satisfied, the congests from the western seaboard will be cordially welcomed.'[72]

Other protestations were more forthright. Slogans appeared on walls: 'Warning, no more migrants allowed here'; 'This land is not for Connemara people. It is for Meath men'.[73] Local politicians saw the potential for stirring local passions for political gain. Few were as adept at this as Captain Patrick Giles in Meath. Giles, a former commandant in the IRA during the War of Independence, a captain in the Free State army during the Civil War, the county director and member of the national executive of the Blueshirts during the mid-1930s stood (successfully) as Fine Gael candidate in the 1937 general election.[74] Opening his election campaign in May 1937, he delivered a defiant speech:

The migrants of the west were getting the lands of Meath. The people of Meath deserved first choice . . . They were brought up to make a Fianna Fáil victory certain . . . Keep the stranger out until you are satisfied. The people in the Gaeltacht are supposed to be the purest men in the world. The people of Meath were as good as ever they were – they were the people who stood in the bogs and hillsides and defied Cromwell to put them out. These colonies would be English-speaking colonies in five years.[75]

The government's proposed land settlement policy in Meath provoked widespread opposition amongst its own supporters. In January 1937, Moylough Fianna Fáil *cumann* passed a resolution 'protesting in the strongest possible manner against the action of the government in bringing migrants into Meath until all the deserving applicants for land in Meath are satisfied'.[76] In June of the same year, F. J. MacCabe, a Fianna Fáil county councillor, proclaimed at Nobber: 'I maintain that Meath people have first claim to Meath land and I now believe that every family who can satisfy the statutory requirements will have land allotted to them before we hear of any more migration.'[77] Following the general election of 1937, the Dunderry Fianna Fáil *cumann* allegedly foiled an attempt to put migrants on lands in the area through a cocktail of intimidation and political pressure and informed the Land Commission that 'any intrusion on these lands to the prejudice of the local applicants would be strongly resented by the people' in the future.[78] At the Fianna Fáil *ard-fheis* later that year, a Meath delegate made the relevant point that there were other counties in Ireland that could facilitate migrants as well as Meath:

> I believe in concentrating all the industries possible in the Gaeltacht, but leave the land of Meath for the people of Meath where ancestors fought and in some instances died for it. They should try the valleys of Limerick or the plains of Kildare; but for goodness sake, they should leave poor old Meath alone and give the people there breathing space.[79]

While opposition was initially concentrated in Meath, simply because it provided the first experimental location, it gradually spread to other receiving counties and remained vibrant and often violent until migration schemes were scrapped in the 1970s. In 1938, for example, 17 people were arrested after a 'pitched battle' between the gardai and locals near Ballyhaunis when the Land Commission attempted to introduce migrants to the area.[80] In March 1940, locals in the Ballymeelish area of County Laois objected strongly to the introduction of migrants with the result that some of these migrants subsequently refused to take up their holdings in the interest of their own safety.[81] In March 1941, William Norton (Kildare, Labour) asked the Minister for Lands:

Whether he is aware of the dissatisfaction which exists in the Kilcock area at the transfer to the area of migrants who have been allotted holdings on estates for which many qualified local persons were applicants . . .[82]

The following month, the Kilcock Parish Council forwarded a resolution to James Hughes (Carlow–Kildare, Fine Gael) objecting to the division of the Gannon and Thorpe estates amongst 'people from other counties, while we have so many deserving applicants in our own district'. In 1950, the Land Commission's proposals to settle migrants in the Edenderry parish in Offaly met with 'strong objections from the clergy and general public' and Joseph Blowick, the Minister for Lands (Clann na Talmhan) was reminded in the Dáil that 'previous experiments of bringing migrants into this area ended in failure' when it became evident that the local smallholders were to be left out in the cold.[83] In February 1952, William Norton (Kildare, Labour) enquired of the Minister for Lands if plans had been put in place for the division of the Hemmingway estate at Clane, County Kildare, and if it was proposed to bring in migrants considering 'the undesireability [*sic*] of creating local ill-feeling by migrating into this area persons from other areas, when there is a clamant demand from local uneconomic holders for this estate'.[84] It took a long time for migrants to become accepted in receiving communities and even where this happened more readily, there remained a stigma of sorts attached to the fact that one was a migrant, a 'blow-in'.

Local opposition placed Land Commission officials in an invidious position. Local claims had first of all to be satisfied; if they were not, tensions between locals and migrants would probably have become even more unbearable. Thus, the first priority that J. C. Gamble and his colleagues faced was the appeasement of local claimants in the receiving areas.[85] In 1935, in the environs of Rathcarne, the first Gaeltacht colony established in County Meath, 4,000 acres were divided amongst local uneconomic holders and landless people before migrants were introduced.[86] In 1942, S. J. Waddell, one of the senior land commissioners, claimed that:

> There would have to be a considerable area of land allotted to local deserving applicants in the localities to which migration took place. In previous years when allotment of land rose to an unprecedented degree, it took almost 80 or 90 per cent of the area distributed in any non-congested county to satisfy local clamour before any migration could be effected.[87]

By the late 1950s, it had become standard policy to deal with local uneconomic holders before congests were brought into an area and thus in April 1957, the Minister for Lands, Erskine Childers, calculated that: 'On average, when an estate is divided, about 70 per cent goes to uneconomic landholders in the area and about 30 per cent to migrants who come from western counties'.[88]

V A CASE STUDY: THE MEATH GAELTACHT COLONIES

Rathcarne lies about four kilometres from Athboy (its nearest town), ten from Trim, 15 from Navan and about 60 from Dublin. Here, in April 1935, the Land Commission acquired its first large estate for the purposes of a colony migration scheme. It was 776 acres in extent. Of this, 187 acres were allotted to discharged employees (an unspecified number of herds).[89] The remaining 589 acres were divided amongst 27 migrant families (totalling 177 persons) from Connemara, giving each family an average of around 22 acres.[90] Most of these were large families, the average size being 6.5 persons. The Land Commission regarded sons and daughters as sources of capital investment because they provided the necessary labour. John MacDonagh and his wife, for example, had twelve children; Patrick Folan, Thomas MacDonagh, Michael Conroy and their wives all had eleven children each. Only two of the families had one son each; each of the others had an average of four sons.[91]

According to contemporary reports it was a wet spring morning as the migrants prepared to leave Connemara on three specially arranged Coras Iompair Éireann buses, while six lorries of the Great Northern Railway were used to transport their belongings. Their neighbours gathered around them in Connemara to bid them farewell, the scene reminiscent of the traditional 'American wake' that preceded the departure of family members for America in the past. The local parish priest, Fr Concannon was glad that something had at last been done for his parishioners: 'The young people are naturally discontented with the lives they have been forced to lead in this lonely district. They do not live; they only exist. In my opinion, the best thing the government could do is to take all the people from this district and leave it to the gulls.'[92] But despite the fact that they were leaving desperately poor agricultural land to live on farmland that was eminently more productive, there was still the traditional sense of loss associated with leaving the 'family acres' behind. As Micheal Ó Conghaile put it:

> Agus nuair atá talamh ag duine, fiú más talamh bocht féin é, is féidir a rá go bhfuil seilbh phearsanta ag duine, seilbh nach le éinne eile agus nach feidir a ghoid ná a bhaint amach le láimh láidir. Is luachmhaire go mór aríst talamh a bheith ag duine más falamh atá ann a tháinig ón tseanmhuintir anuas o ghlúin go glúin den sloinne céanna agus gach glúin acu ag fágáil a ainm agus a lorg féin air le claí anseo, leacht ansiúd, nó clais in áit eígin eile, agus chuile ghluín acu ag cur a bhfeabhas féin ar an ngabháltas.[93]

[When a person owns land, no matter how poor it is, it is safe to say that they have a strong personal attachment to it, an attachment that nobody else has and that is impossible to steal or break by force. The attachment to land is much stronger if it has been handed down from generation to generation of the same name, particularly when each generation has left its own mark upon it with the planting of a hedge here, the laying of a flagstone there or the digging of a ditch somewhere else.]

Thus, in April 1937 two of the migrants supposed to move from Mayo as part of the Gibbstown colony opted out at the last moment. It was reported that Bridget Naughton of Carratigue and Michael Beodrick of Emlybeg 'found it beyond them to part with their friends. . . [and] leaving behind them a district where for hundreds of years their forebears had toiled for a miserable existence'.[94]

The state provided the funding necessary to prepare the farms and equip them at Rathcarne (something it was not prepared to do for local uneconomic holders) at an average cost of £431 per farm and £1,010 for equipment (see Appendix I, table 5.1, p. 238). For the 27 holdings this involved total expenditure of £11,637 on the land and £27,270 on equipment. On each holding, a substantial four-roomed dwelling house was built together with a stable, piggery, poultry house and dairy. A new approach road was made, the lands were fenced, water installed and an adequate supply of turf banks supplied within a reasonable distance of the settlement. A playing field was set aside and a school was constructed by the Office of Public Works. The maximum amount of stock provided to each colonist was three cows, two heifers, 12 sheep, one sow, two bonhams, 21 fowl, a horse and cart, a donkey and cart, a harness, a plough, two harrows, a scuffler, a roller, a ploughing tackle, a wheelbarrow, a turf barrow, dairy utensils and shares in a mowing machine and potato sprayer.[95]

In 1937, 13 more families were migrated from Galway to nearby Kilbride and fifty families were migrated from Donegal, Kerry, west Cork and Mayo to Gibbstown. In 1939 and 1940, another 50 families were migrated from Kerry, Donegal and Galway to Allenstown and Clonghill. In total the Meath Gaeltacht colonies comprised 122 families and 767 persons (see Appendix, table 5.2, p. 238). The lands divided amongst these families had originally comprised seven grazier estates totalling 5,233 acres.[96] The total cost of preparing the lands and equipping the holdings was in excess of £78,000 (taking the average cost for equipment per holding at Clongill to be £936).

The migrants faced a variety of problems in the initial settling-in period. Many were homesick and missed aspects of Connemara that they had taken for granted all their lives. Fifty years after moving, Colm Seoige told a television interviewer: 'Tá mo chroí thiar is tá m'intinn thiar agus bím ag plé le báid agus is dóigh go bhfuil an fharraige thiar; airím uaim i gconaí í.'[97] [My heart is there [in Connemara] and my mind is there and I continually think of the boats and I imagine what the sea is like; I long to be back there.] Not least of their difficulties was the hostility shown towards them by locals. The Gaeltacht colony was surrounded by a community that was not always culturally sympathetic to the migrants or their language needs, and, indeed, that in many cases simply resented them receiving lands that locals felt could have been theirs. Occasionally tensions came to a head in Athboy, the nearest market town, particularly during fair days. In November 1939, the aforementioned Captain Patrick Giles asked the Minister for Justice, Gerry Boland, if he was aware that a number of the Rathcarne Gaeltacht migrants had

> repeatedly created ugly scenes in the town of Athboy by fighting and using bad language and threatening the lives of local residents, and whether, in view of their repeatedly very bad behaviour, he will see that extra guards are stationed in the vicinity of the colonies for the purpose of protecting the lives and properties of the local residents and the better enforcement of the law.[98]

The Minister for Justice was satisfied that the gardai were in charge of the situation,[99] but it was Giles's question that was revealing about local attitudes towards the migrants: it suggested that it was they who were creating the ugly scenes and using threatening behaviour, not, by extension, the law-abiding locals. Giles's anti-migration rhetoric became more vitriolic as the years passed. In 1946, he told the Dáil:

> I will not help to flood my county with men from Connemara who never saw anything but a fishing hook. Some of these men were given land on the best farms in Meath which should never have been divided. They are now being brought into police courts, morning, noon and night, and they are a disgrace to me, to the Minister and to Connemara. I am not saying that they are all of that type, but many of them are. It is not alone Moore Street and Gloucester Street that are dangerous at night time, where you might be knifed in the back. I defy the Minister to go on a dark night through the streets of Athboy after a fair day. He would be lucky if he came out of it with his life. Then we are told that land division is a success. I have been telling the minister for the past ten years that it is a failure and a fiasco, creating bitterness and enmity.[100]

It was, it seems, migrants who were much more often the victims. Migrant children had stones thrown at them as they walked to and from school; they were ridiculed by local children – one told how he learned to fight hard very young because he could not always run fast enough to escape.[101] Threatening notices were painted on walls of migrant houses and on roads approaching their allotted lands warning them to stay away. Similar warnings were posted on chapel gates.[102] The anti-migration campaign in Meath, supported by politicians of all parties, probably contributed to the decision taken in October 1937 by the Minister for Lands, Gerry Boland, to abandon all further migration schemes to Meath until local congestion had been solved.[103] That year an internal migration scheme was put in place in County Meath whereby congests from elsewhere in the county were settled on the Dunne–Cullinane estate at Scurlockstown.[104]

Although the debate on whether Rathcarne contributed to the preservation of the Irish language in that area of County Meath belongs to a different forum, the fact that the families who migrated were Irish speaking brought its own problems that had wider repercussions. Bilingualism, for example, became a practical necessity. As a Meath County Council report was later to point out, the community was so small, it could not support a full range of services performed exclusively in Irish. For the same reason, it was difficult to establish a range of recreational facilities.[105] Such a colony could not exist as a self-contained unit, isolated from local market towns in which the first language of shopkeepers, publicans and other merchants was English. By 1937, the colonists were complaining that 'the policy of isolating them in an all-Irish speaking colony has worked ill from the stand-point of developing their knowledge of farming technique'. One of them argued that 'if, side by side with each Gaelic farmer there was a Meath farmer accustomed to the soil and its treatment then we would have learned quicker how to properly cultivate this land'.[106]

Farming methods were totally different from those with which the migrants had been reared. As one of them, Mícheál Mac Craith, later pointed out:

> The Meath farmer harrowed before he sowed. We in Connemara dug and sowed. Here we ploughed and sowed, then harrowed. The seed went too deep. The yield was not so good. We would not have made that mistake if side by side we had Meath farmers, locals.[107]

Most were coming from a farming society where labour was entirely manual. They had no knowledge of machinery (some had never, for example, seen a plough). Farm implements did not arrive on time during the first year: ploughs did not arrive until November; it was six months before horses arrived and no donkeys arrived at all. In April 1936, Coleman Kane and Bartley Curran refused to accept the carts supplied by the Land Commission on the grounds that they were 'of inferior workmanship'. When the Land Commission refused to supply them with alternative carts, Curran's son and Kane seized two new ones from a consignment that arrived at Athboy railway station. The Land Commission had to institute legal proceedings to have them returned.[108] In the spring of 1937, Micheál Mac Craith told a journalist: 'We could not get the work done in time this year. Last year, I got 20 barrels of wheat at £1 per barrel from the land, and only one acre of potatoes. No man can make a good living for an increasing family on our 20 acres. Another 10 acres would do.'[109]

In 1936, Martin Roddy (Leitrim–Sligo, Fine Gael), now in Opposition, told the Minister for Lands that if he took the trouble

> to look up the records in the Land Commission he will find that there is ample evidence, going back to the days of the Congested Districts Board, to prove that it is quite impossible to colonise successfully with that type of people districts which contain land of a different quality from that on which they have been brought up and where the marketing conditions are so different from those which obtain in the west of Ireland.[110]

Within two years it was being argued that the colonists had found themselves 'translated into a life which, on the surface, offered greater prospect for them and their young children, but which turned out unexpectedly costly and complex'.[111] In Connemara, they caught fish, in Meath they had to buy it; in Connemara they had seaweed manure and plenty of turf, in Meath they had to buy manure and their turf banks were flooded; in Connemara they had free medical services, in Meath they paid a doctor £1 a visit. Annuities and rates, which were obviously much higher than they had been in Connemara, were no more affordable despite the more productive quality of the land. Shortly after their arrival in Meath some of the Gaeltacht colonists found themselves in court at Athboy for the recovery of arrears of annuities and rates. One of the defendants, Micheál Mac Craith, said that the migrants 'all thought the rates would have been much lower. They had been promised that the rates would be £5, and now they were £8.'[112]

By now, there were also criticisms that farms were too small to support the large families that had been chosen and that the farming methods they were advised to follow limited their ability to increase their incomes. Inspectors kept a close watch that migrants were adhering to the Land Commission stipulations that they should follow an intensive tillage policy. This meant they could not raise cattle to sell in the off-season and without cattle they had no manure to fertilise the soil, as they could not afford to buy artificial manure. It was also argued that intensive tillage made their holdings in Rathcarne just as uneconomic as their old ones in the west because of the expense involved in transporting grain to the Dublin market. A colony representative pointed out that 'it was a bad start for the [Land] Commission which apparently doesn't realise that to disappoint in a bargain is to create distrust and enmity'.[113]

In 1939, the annual Land Commission report concluded:

We are satisfied that the experiment, though somewhat costly, has been justified by the results obtained. The migrants generally have now definitely made good in their new holdings and are able to maintain themselves and their families at a higher standard of living than heretofore.[114]

The Commission was being rather disingenuous. Besides the disillusionment of the colonists themselves, the whole question of colony migrations was causing controversy in government circles and the future of the schemes was at that stage very much in doubt. Perhaps more significantly, by April 1937 Rathcarne was being labelled 'Half way house to England', which raises a question mark over its success. Thirty-six persons under 30 years of age (or 12 per cent of the Rathcarne group) had either emigrated to England or were preparing to do so.[115] Mícheál Mac Craith, a father of four emigrants, claimed: 'There's nothing in Rathcarne for them; they'll only return if England fails them . . . it was like a funeral when the last fifteen went off together'.[116] An official government memorandum had stated the previous year: 'At the present time practically every family is sending members across the water to England to assist the occupiers in living on these holdings and help to pay the annuities and rates and to exist on them.'[117] The population of the colony was to decline from 340 in 1937 to 264 in 1961. Obviously there were social factors involved other than migration but it was a significant demographic decline of over 22 per cent.

The years of the Emergency brought some prosperity as a result of the rise in agricultural prices and the demand for more tillage. Most of the migrant families began to take land on conacre to supplement their own holdings. However, when the war ended, land on conacre became scarce once again, wartime prices fell, unemployment rose and it became obvious that their 22-acre farms were slowly but surely becoming less viable.[118] By the early 1950s, the migrant farmers began to move away from tillage into dairying, a move facilitated by the establishment of dairies firstly in Lucan County Dublin and then in nearby Athboy. This transition was further facilitated by the rural electrification scheme of the 1950s that was to make dairying much easier.[119] By 1952, the stock on hand of the colonists consisted of 1,792 head of livestock of which 415 were milch cows and 631 stores.

There is little doubt that, despite their occasional protestations, the overall long-term material welfare of the majority of the colony was substantially improved by their move east. While temporary conditions of hostility had to be overcome and families had to adapt to new methods of farming, the opportunities available to them were increased. The migrant surrendering a poor farm with poor outoffices usually gained a holding up to perhaps four times the value of the one he vacated, equipped with a good dwelling house and outoffices. Based as they were in the midlands, many were also able to secure part-time employment in turf production schemes and on local tillage farms. And they eventually learned to cope with homesickness. (To this day migrant families have tended to hold on to a measure of sentimental attachment to their home counties. A trip through areas of Kildare and Meath in the lead up to a major football or hurling match in which either Mayo or Galway is involved is clearly suggestive of this: migrant houses are easily distinguishable by the Galway or Mayo flags flying outside them, as indeed are those of the more recent settlers who have come in search of easy access to the city of Dublin rather than land.)

By 1960, the Gaeltacht migrants had another fight on their hands for official recognition of Rathcarne and Gibbstown as Gaeltacht areas entitled to the various Gaeltacht grants available to Irish-speaking communities else-where in the country. Time and again such requests were rebuffed by the claim that as the Gaeltacht colonies were not included in the Gaeltacht Areas Order of 1956, they did not qualify for the benefits available to other Gaeltacht regions.[120] Amazingly, it was not until 1967 that Rathcarne was officially designated a Gaeltacht region by the government.[121] The grants available to the migrant families (to extend their homes, install bathrooms and so on) and the establishment of local industry there (two factories were set up by 1980 providing eighty jobs) further consolidated their position.[122]

By the 1960s, most of the migrant families were said to 'have become relatively prosperous'.[123] Of course, there were others who were finding it difficult to make a living from mixed farming on the standard 22 acres and who could not afford to buy more land because of escalating prices. In 1969, 70-year-old James Mellett, one of the original migrants, complained that small-holders were continually outbid by large farmers around Athboy whenever a suitable farm came up for auction. He said:

> It is virtually impossible for the Gaeltacht people to get any more land. Not so long ago a 122-acre farm was put up for auction and was taken over, lock, stock and barrel by one of the big guns for tillage. The Land Commission should have stepped in and divided up among the colonists. We have got no extra land since we came here.[124]

The real problem here was that the standard holding of thirty years before was now no longer viable. But this was not, as we shall see, a problem confined to the Gaeltacht colonies.

VI CONCLUSION

This chapter has looked at migration schemes in Ireland up to the Emergency (and beyond in the case study of the Meath Gaeltacht colonies). It is an area worthy of a complete study in its own right, as the scope of this book allows for nothing more than an overview. Of particular note was the great struggle that Gaeltacht migrants faced in their early years not only in regard to the hostility of locals towards them (again an interesting study in its own right), but their very struggle against nature. Their long experience of having to eke out a living in the harsh lands of Connemara and other western regions left them experienced only in drudgery; it was remarkably difficult to adapt to new methods of farming, coming to terms, for example, with different soil types, rearing different breeds of cattle, dairying on a larger scale and managing productive lands. Land Commission agricultural advisors were, of course, made available to them in the early days but some of these were not fluently conversant in Irish, which caused its own particular problems.

In general, however, migrants seem to have coped remarkably well. This applies equally to the non-Gaeltacht migrants who also settled in counties such as Kildare, Meath and Dublin. Above all they proved industrious.[125] In the early 1950s, Commissioner O'Shiel declared of western migrants: 'If every proprietor in the country worked his lands anything like as well as these people it would be exceedingly difficult, not to say impossible, to acquire any land compulsorily.'[126] Many of the succeeding generations reaped the reward of their industry and thrift. While the bulk of the population of the Rathcarne colony, for example, remained employed in agriculture as late as 1971 (58 per cent of the 105 employed), there were signs that second and third generation members of the original families were moving more into other occupational spheres such as the construction industry (12 per cent), industry, commerce, public administration and the professions (between them 24 per cent).[127] Invariably, success depended on the ability to keep pace with the commercialisation of farming – increasing their asset base by investment in land and machinery, improved farm practices and so on. The second generation abandoned intensive farming, largely for dairy farming that allowed them the flexibility of working during the day between milking times. More became part-time farmers, exploiting their proximity to the capital and other urban centres to avail themselves of full-time employment opportunities. Their work ethic, their determination to succeed, and perhaps, above all, their efforts to educate the succeeding generations in an attempt to stem the tide of migration became characteristics of migrant communities, facts which were revealed in an interesting study by Hannan and Commins in 1990.[128]

No other Gaeltacht colony like that in Meath was established elsewhere. By the late 1930s, the expenses involved in colony migration schemes were leading to a great deal of friction between the Department of Lands and the Department of Finance. Matters came to a head in 1938 when an inter-departmental committee was appointed to examine the problem of seasonal migration of labourers from certain areas of the west to Great Britain. Its report recommended that a much more ambitious programme of land resettlement through colony migration had to be undertaken as 'the occupants of uneconomic holdings in the Congested Districts remain in such poor circumstances as to require state assistance on a liberal scale'.[129] The committee proposed the migration of 8,000 families.[130] Subsequently, on 13 December, the Minister for Lands submitted the following proposal for the consideration of the government:

> That the Land Commission be instructed to provide with all reasonable speed some 6,000 holdings outside the scheduled congested district for allotment to migrants from the scheduled congested districts and to endeavour to provide some 2,000 holdings within that area for a similar purpose.[131]

Personnel in the Department of Finance were shocked as this scheme would cost an estimated £8 million of which £7 million would have to be provided in the form of free grants. The Minister for Finance felt that this cost was pro-hibitive; it was, he contended, too much to invest in a scheme, the feasibility of which was uncertain. He suggested a much less ambitious scheme that would be restricted to an experimental five-year plan. He proposed that instead of free grants 'a greater proportion of expenditure should be charge-able on the holdings as recoverable advances'.[132] He further recommended that 'no public announcement which might prove embarrassing at a later stage should be made as to the possibility of ultimate adoption of the full scheme proposed by the Land Commission': this might either lead to immediate agitation in the receiving areas or future agitation amongst those who might be disappointed if the scheme were to fail.[133] As the Department of Finance had control over the purse strings, the Department of Lands had really little option but to accept these proposals.[134]

However, the Emergency, as we have already seen, threw the Land Commission into chaos. Operations were severely curtailed, and instead of a new scheme of migration there were dramatic cutbacks. From 1940–1 to 1950–1 a total of 1,359 families were migrated, an average of only 124 per annum in comparison to an average of 332 per annum in the three years immediately preceding the outbreak of the Second World War. In the post-Emergency period, from 1 April 1946 to 31 October 1951, the Land Commission acquired

5,446 acres on 66 estates or resumed holdings in County Meath and allotted 4,038 acres to 287 allottees. Only 34 of these (less than 12 per cent) were migrants from other counties, the remainder were locals.[135]

For those opposed to colony migration, it is arguable that the Emergency offered the pretext to curtail it. One of these opponents was the influential land commissioner, Eamon Mansfield, a consistent and outspoken critic of migration, who believed that the suitable claims of local smallholders and labourers, especially married men living in close proximity to an estate, had to be settled before migrants could be taken in. There was, in the past, he contended: 'too much spoon-feeding'.[136] In other words, he believed that the state was doing too much for migrants and that they should be made responsible themselves for improvements carried out on their holdings such as the construction of fences, the gravelling of paths and the clearing of drains.

From the beginning of the Emergency to the end of Fianna Fáil's 16-year tenure in office in 1948, the government came under pressure from their own backbenchers, as well as members of the Opposition, to expedite both the relief of congestion and the number of migration schemes. Sean Moylan consistently argued that neither lands nor funds were available. In truth, there was undoubtedly more land that could have been made available (if one accepts that it made good economic and agricultural sense to break up all the large grazing and dairying farms) for division in the midland counties, as well as the large dairying counties such as Tipperary, but Moylan, amongst others, was becoming less convinced of the value of the break up of all large farms in favour of the creation of a mass of smallholdings.

SIX

AMBIVALENT ATTITUDES AND CHANGING POLICIES 1948-73

We have a land congestion problem here which it is national policy to solve.
MICHAEL MORAN
Minister for Lands quoted in *Dáil Debates*, vol. 188, 4 May 1961.

Unless we maintain machinery for land distribution what will inevitably happen is that certain speculative persons will gradually become landlords again. They will buy up holdings so that gradually one man will have 60 or 70 holdings, all of which had been at one time the subject of Land Commission transactions, so that perhaps in a period of fifty years we will be back in exactly the same position as before, with a series of large landholders having tenants on their land...
JAMES DILLON
(Donegal, Centre Party), *Dáil Debates*, vol. 43, 24 July 1936.

'the Land Commission as presently constituted [c.1983] is a luxury the country can no longer afford'
DES MAGUIRE
The Land Commission, p. 16.

———

I THE FIRST INTER-PARTY GOVERNMENT, 1948-51

At the end of the Emergency, it looked as if Fianna Fáil might continue in government for a long time to come. De Valera's successful policy of neutrality, it has been argued, 'greatly enhanced his appeal to voters outside the original decisive western support basis'.[1] A widening geographical and social class support base was important, for now Fianna Fáil could move more to the right. But a characteristic post-war desire for change initiated a shift away from Fianna Fáil for a variety of reasons already set out by historians, including *inter alia* a serious balance of payments deficit in 1947, disillusionment that the post-war economy was not improving, a disastrous winter in 1947, a serious energy crisis as coal supplies from Britain were curtailed, and perhaps popular reaction to Fianna Fáil's growing arrogance that manifested itself in the need to demonstrate that power was revocable and that Ireland would not be turned into a one-party state.[2]

These reasons were undoubtedly important but the continued role of the land question should not be underplayed, most notably Fianna Fáil's failure to convert its promises of the early 1930s of sweeping land division into reality. Most obviously, this had given rise to the establishment in 1939 of a new political party, Clann na Talmhan, in the west where disillusionment and disappointment were strongest. In the 1943 General Election, Clann na Talmhan won ten seats: one in Cavan; one in Cork North; one in Cork West; one in Donegal East; one in Galway East; one in Kerry North; two in Roscommon; one in Tipperary; and one in Wicklow.[3] Its most notable achievement was in Roscommon where it won two out of the three available seats, here certainly reflecting the anger in the county that large tracts of grazing land had not been broken up and divided amongst local congests.

By 1948, there were signs that Clann na Talmhan was in decline, but this was probably more as a result of its own inadequacies as an effective party than a change in western attitudes towards the land question. It secured only seven seats in the general election of that year: one in Cork North; one in Cork South; one in Galway North; one in Kerry North; two in Mayo South; one in Roscommon.[4] But with the simultaneous growth in Clann na Poblachta, founded in July 1946, again as the result of widening disillusionment with Fianna Fáil, the hegemony of the latter party was being threatened. After the 1948 election, Fianna Fáil held 68 seats; it could be unseated by a coalition of all other parties in the Dáil. While this might have looked improbable, it did not prove to be impossible. And so after 16 years in power, Fianna Fáil made way for the First Fine Gael-led Inter-Party government that also encompassed Clann na Talmhan, Clann na Poblachta, Labour and Independents.

Joseph Blowick, leader of Clann na Talmhan and representative for South Mayo, who had been an ardent campaigner for continued land division as the only viable means of relieving congestion, was appointed Minister for Lands. Shortly after taking up his portfolio in 1948, he referred to congested areas as 'an evil in our midst that has to be eradicated' and informed the Dáil that it was to be 'the policy of the present government to place in first priority the ending of congestion and the raising of uneconomic holdings to economic level'.[5] Blowick too had 'the greatest contempt' for those who had been allotted lands and who had failed to work them productively; he was determined to give them 'short shrift'.[6]

The new Minister for Finance, Patrick McGilligan[7] (Dublin North–Central, Fine Gael), was, however, no more receptive to raising the budget for Lands than Sean T. O'Kelly had been before him. It is significant that neither of these ministers represented a rural constituency, which possibly limited their appreciation of the importance of the work of the Land Commission. In fact, in October 1948, McGilligan urged a radical redrawing of land settlement policy, including the postponement of land acquisition in non-congested areas in favour of preserving large commercial farms.[8] But his attempts to dictate policy to Lands were met with great opposition from Blowick who angrily rejected his proposals and in what was perhaps a fit of pique, as much as anything else, Blowick immediately lifted the 'close down order' on the acquisition of lands in the midlands and eastern areas of the country that had been in place since the Emergency. In Blowick's view, as David Seth Jones has pointed out, McGilligan was raising unnecessary fears about the costs and consequences of acquisition and division and he was having none of it.[9]

The following year, Blowick raised the standard size of holdings outside the main congested areas from 25 to 33 acres, largely in response to the changing economic and agricultural situation. In 1950, he introduced a land act to 'remove inequities from the existing law and to speed up the work of the Land Commission for the elimination of rural slums and the conversion of uneconomic farms throughout the country into workable economic holdings'.[10] But land for division was now a scarce commodity. It had been for a decade or more, so where was the Land Commission now to acquire it? Blowick estimated that around 200,000 acres of land came on to the open market for sale each year. He pointed out that

> this stream of land has never been tapped by the Land Commission although it is bound to contain a number of holdings which would be eminently suitable for the special purposes of migration and rearrangement. Many such holdings are purchasable from time to time as going concerns and I know they will prove to be as desirable if not more desirable propositions than the holdings which have to be carved out of acquired estates and fitted up with new dwellings, out-offices, fences and so on. Moreover, these holdings which are offered for sale are no longer required by the owners and no question of hardship to such owners could possibly arise, were the Land Commission to become the purchaser.[11]

Thus the 1950 Land Act gave the Land Commission the power to purchase for cash land that came on to the open market. Simultaneously, the ordinary processes of acquisition, resumption and purchase for land bonds were to continue.

The purchase of farms on the open market brought a critical response from some quarters, not least of all the Department of Finance. With rising values, the Land Commission was paying much more on the open market than had been the case in the past. A Department of Lands memorandum of October 1951 pointed out that 'the provision of holdings which will attract suitable migrants necessarily involves the purchase of high quality land' which, therefore, would mean higher prices and a greater cost to the state. Prior to 1940, the average price of land per acre was around £10–12. From the passing of the 1950 Land Act to October 1951, offers had been made by the Land Commission for 307 holdings totalling 35,716 acres for £629,677, an average of around £17.6 per acre. Only 74 of these were accepted and they were at £20.2 an acre. These rising costs were enough to heighten tensions between the Department of Lands and the Department of Finance once again. While McGilligan was willing to spend in order to intensify agricultural and turf production schemes, he considered it a most inopportune time to raise the Land Commission budget when the prices of lands and building materials were inflated and labour scarce. He felt that 'the energies of the Land Commission would be better directed towards disposing of the heavy arrears of revesting and remedying abuses in connection with users of distributed lands'.[12] Acidic correspondence continued to flow between both departments; Lands rebuked McGilligan's suggestions:

> The Minister [for Lands] feels that too narrow a view is taken in your department [Finance] of the benefits of land settlement. He desires to explain that cultivation and ownership cannot be divorced without detriment and that ownership provides an incentive which is absent when a man is putting his labour into land not his own.[13]

In the Senate, Senator Frank Loughman (Fianna Fáil) thought it was wrong for the government to compete with 'the industrious thrifty farmer' who had a number of sons and who should be allowed to purchase on the open market without having to compete with the Land Commission.[14] If anything, his comment merely recognised the fact that farmers formed their own tight-knit rural community and that they preferred to keep it that way.

The 1950 act also attempted to address the rundale problem, the evils of which Blowick had first-hand experience as it continued to operate in large parts of his own constituency. In 1951, the Land Commission admitted that the rearrangement of these communal strips of land to form compact viable holdings was 'extremely intricate and tedious and it requires much tact, discretion and skill to formulate proposals which will be practicable and, at the same time, will be acceptable to the tenants'.[15] There were many farmers who were holding up the process simply because they were not willing to give up their strips essentially holding their neighbours to ransom in an obvious attempt to secure a greater share of the better land for themselves. Such intransigence made it impossible for inspectors to draw up successful schemes.[16] Blowick himself elucidated this problem:

> Migration is inseparable from rearrangement but the natural reluctance of a family to leave the homestead, where they were born and bred, frequently constitutes a

major problem in the initial stages of preparing a rearrangement scheme. Sometimes when everything is settled a prospective key-migrant will change his mind at the last moment and everything is back in the melting pot once more, after all the trouble and arrangements. Very often acquisition proceedings for the lands, which are to provide the new holdings for the migrants, are vigorously contested and as a result the proceedings are long drawn out. In contrast, the successful rearrangements schemes must be based on the consent and cooperation of the participating tenants. Prolonged negotiations by the inspectorate are essential to secure the necessary goodwill of the landholders. Very often the more acute the congestion, and the intermixed condition of the holdings, the more difficult it is to secure general agreement for a satisfactory scheme.[17]

One of the aims of the 1950 act was to give senior inspectors the necessary legal authority to approve of rearrangement schemes and to push them through despite individual objections.

II THE IMPORTANCE OF REARRANGEMENT

Before moving on, it is necessary to expand upon the importance of rearrangement schemes and assess how they helped to alleviate at least some of the prevalent congestion problems in the west.

In 1953, the Land Commission in its annual report provided a case study of how a successful rearrangement scheme could benefit all involved. It chose as an example an area in the east (given the fictitious name of 'Ballyfarren') where it had recently acquired three estates (see Map 6.1a), with a total acreage of 681 acres for £24,300. The lands of Ballyfarren were described as being of mixed quality with good land predominating (246 acres were described as being of 'superior quality'; 269 acres were of 'good quality'; 105 acres were of 'medium quality'; 51 acres were of 'fair quality'; and ten were waste.) The only building on the lands was a herd's cottage and some outoffices that were almost all in ruins.

The first step in the preparation of the scheme of division was a thorough examination of the needs of locals. There was no local congestion. The inspectors decided to allot a standard holding to one ex-employee 'who was considered capable of working it', as well as a plot for a new school and playground and a plot for a local sports field (see D, J, M on map 6.1b.) An area of 637 acres remained, which could be divided into eighteen standard holdings of roughly equal size (A, B, C, E, F, G, H, K, L, N, O, P, Q, R, S, T, U, V on map 6.1b). Care had to be taken, as far as was practicable, to ensure that superior, good, medium and fair land was equally distributed. The average size of the holdings

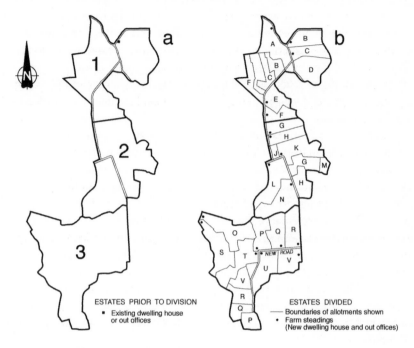

Map 6.1 a and b The division of 'Ballyfarren' estate, 1953
Source: ILC Report, 1953

created on estates 1 and 2 was 34 acres, while on estate 3, where the land was a little poorer in quality, the average size of holdings created was 37.5 acres. Each holding had also to have access to the water supplies for stock.

Each new holding was provided with a dwelling house comprising four rooms, a front and back porch, two outoffices (one for eight cows and the other a building comprising a barn, horse stable and shed for young stock). The ex-employee was provided only with new outoffices as he already had a house. A gravelled approach road was built to each new holding. One thousand three hundred and seven perches of new fences were erected and 2,609 perches of existing fences were repaired. Ten wells were sunk for domestic water supplies. The total cost of developing the farmsteads was £24,000 while the total cost of improvements was £3,800. (There was later expenditure of £2,300 on fuel, fodder and some farm implements required to get the families through their first year.)

Seventeen migrant families were then chosen (no criteria for selection was given). Six families were from one area in Galway and the other eleven from neighbouring areas in Mayo. Thirteen allottees were married men or widowers whose average age was fifty years, all of whom had young families; four were bachelors whose average age was 34, all of whom had elderly relatives. In total there were 77 persons of whom 52 were adults and 25 were children. Land Commission lorries and trailers transferred all their furniture, stock and goods (between all of the families they owned 32 cows, 47 young cattle, 27 calves, 239 sheep, one horse, two ponies, 13 donkeys, 19 pigs, 500 hens, eight horse carts, three donkey carts, five iron ploughs, five wooden harrows, five scufflers and a mowing machine).

The migrant families surrendered 310 acres and commonage shares of another 120 acres in the west leaving a total area of 430 acres for redistribution. (However, the poor law valuation of this entire acreage was only £66, or an average of £4 per surrendered holding.) According to the Commission, the 17 surrendered holdings formed 'strategically-placed reserves of vacated land which will be used to enlarge the remaining holdings and will act as an incentive to the tenants to join in re-arrangement schemes which will be designed to eliminate the widely-scattered type of holding and replace it with a compact conveniently-worked unit'.[18] In 1954, the Land Commission annual report illustrated how rearrangement had progressed in the Kilvine area of Mayo from where eleven of the families had left.[19] (This time for some reason or other the Land Commission did not find it necessary to camouflage the name of the area!)

The Kilvine district comprised the four townlands of Kilvine, Shanvallyboght, Levallyroe and Fallakeeran, about two miles north-east of Irishtown in the south of County Mayo and along the county's borders with Roscommon and Galway. There were 108 farmers on a total area of 1,078 acres holding an average of just less than ten acres each. Between them they owned 486 detached plots. There was another farm in the area of 270 acres. This large holding was resumed by the Land Commission but the existing rundale system meant that it was impossible to benefit from it until the other smallholders were moved.

Map 6.2a shows Kilvine townland prior to rearrangement. The grey areas were the holdings acquired by the Land Commission either through resumption or migration. The areas marked white and black were the holdings requiring rearrangement. To get an idea of how individuals owned intermixed plots see holdings marked 40, 40A, 40B, 40C, 40D, 40F, all of which belonged to one person. The main cluster of buildings in the townland was described as 'a rural slum' with 35 houses and adjoining outoffices located within a radius of ninety yards towards the centre of the townland. Housing conditions in the area were very poor (all houses were very old, thatched and structurally unsound).[20] The outbuildings were described as 'ramshackle' and manure heaps were close to the dwelling houses. It seems that living conditions had

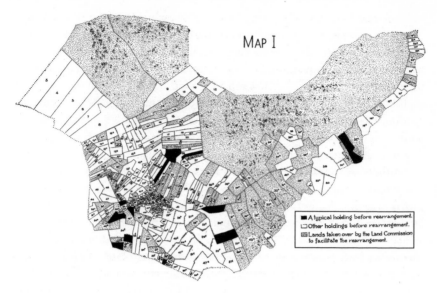

Map 6.2 a Kilvine townland prior to rearrangement
Source: ILC Report, 1954, p. 31

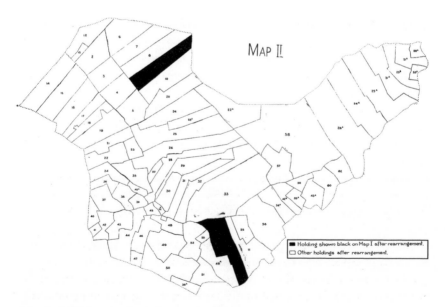

Map 6.2 b Kilvine townland after rearrangement
Source: ILC Report, 1954, p. 31

deteriorated in the previous few years as tenants, while awaiting the rearrangement of their holdings, had little incentive to undertake 'patchwork building improvements'. In other words, the rundale system had prevented men who were described as 'industrious and progressive' from working their holdings to the best advantage.[21] P. J. Sammon identified three inducements to entice such holders to co-operate with the inspectors: the prospects of a compact holding to replace a collection of tiny plots scattered over a large area; the addition of a few extra acres to make the new holding economic; the generous building allowances for dwelling houses and outoffices.

Initially, 20 acres were allotted to an ex-employee. While a general rearrangement scheme was still not possible, the Commission decided on the provisional distribution of the resumed land as an interim measure. Parcels of land of seven to 15 acres were let to suitable local congests. As holdings became available elsewhere, seven more tenants in the area were migrated. Again, their lands were temporarily let to their neighbours until such time as enough land had been freed to begin a systematic re-arrangement scheme. This scheme began in July 1952. By March 1953, the Land Commission inspectors carried through to a successful conclusion (at least from their point of view) the 'very involved and protracted negotiations which were necessary'. Thirty-three tenants were involved in the negotiations (see map 6.2b). The Land Commission report of 1953 pointed out that

> whilst they all agreed that their holdings should be 'striped' into a convenient and workable pattern, it was only natural that each tenant would bargain shrewdly for good terms for himself . . . All these rearrangement schemes have to be based largely on the consent and agreement of the tenants concerned.[22]

These schemes involved a great deal of patience and took a considerable amount of time. The average holding was increased to around 20 acres with an average valuation of £16. The Land Commission concluded that:

> The tenants and their families need no longer contend with the awkward and uneconomic pattern of intermixed plots but can settle down to improving their holdings, the boundaries of which have been finally settled on a rational basis.[23]

It was the problem of rearrangement that prompted the Land Commission once again to revive west to east migration schemes. But rather than colonies, groups were now moved from neighbourhoods.[24] Unfortunately, despite the fact that the Land Commission annual reports from 1950 onwards continually emphasised the importance of rearrangement programmes, nobody in the commission recorded precise statistics regarding what was happening in that respect. However, P. J. Sammon attempted to do so in his published memoirs when he calculated that over the 28-year period from 1950 to 1978, a total of 12,281 holdings on tenanted estates were rearranged and enlarged. The aggregate area of these holdings was almost 290,000 acres (roughly 23.5 acres each). Over the same period, an aggregate area of 322,172 acres of untenanted land was allotted in transactions involving migrants and rearrangements.[25]

During the tenure of the first Inter-Party government, there was also a return to the migration of large holders wherever practicable, as had been the policy of Cumann na nGaedheal, the argument being that in this way the maximum amount of land was made available for the relief of congestion with the minimum amount of disturbance. Of the 75 holdings provided for migrants during the year 1951–2, 21 were for migrants who had surrendered large holdings.[26]

The new government was rather unfairly criticised by Fianna Fáil for slowing down migration schemes. Michael Moran (Mayo, Fianna Fáil) told the Dáil in March 1948 that he was concerned 'that the policy of migrating congested tenants from the land slums of the west is now slowed up by the present Minister for Lands'.[27] Actually, during its three-year term, 430 families (an average of 143 per annum) had been allocated a total of 10,000 acres (an average of just over 23 acres each), whereas in the last three years of the Fianna Fáil administration, 372 families (an average of 124 per annum) had received an aggregated 8,724 acres (the same average). In total, for the three years roughly coinciding with the Inter-Party government's term of office, the Land Commission allotted 57,467 acres (a respectable average of 19,156 per annum). These figures were well up on the last three years of Fianna Fáil's administration when a total of 39,265 acres were allotted (or 13,088 per annum.) For the year ended 31 March 1950, 10,881 acres were used in enlargements, the largest annual figure since 1941. For the three years of the Inter-Party government, 1,897 allottees received 25,018 acres in enlargements (an average of just over 13 acres each); 69 ex-employees received 2,954 acres (a very high average of almost 43 acres each, perhaps reflecting the influence of Labour in the Inter-Party government); only 28 landless persons received a total of 896 acres (an average of 32 acres each); only one evicted tenant received seven acres.

III CHANGING GOVERNMENTS, 1951–7

There were four governments between the end of the Second World War in 1945 and 1957, an indication of electoral unease with policies that failed *inter alia* to effectively address the land question, stem rising unemployment and emigration flows or for that matter reinvigorate any aspect of Irish life. The stagnation of small farm life was too much for many, particularly along the western seaboard from where an incredible flight from the land of 100,000 people took place between 1948 and 1953.[28] As the Commission on Emigration found in the late 1940s, poor material standards of living in most of rural Ireland and total disillusionment with the drudgery of farm life were pushing young people off the land. As a Land Commission memorandum on land settlement concluded in 1952, they were 'becoming less willing to accept the relatively frugal standards of previous generations'.[29] Hundreds of smallholdings were literally abandoned – from 1946 to 1957, 24,000 people left Mayo alone (around 2,100 per annum) – as their owners emigrated or sought employment in urban centres, letting their lands on conacre to their neighbours.[30] More than half a million people were to emigrate from the end of the Emergency to 1960 and even more remarkable was the fact that four out of every five children born in the 1930s were to emigrate in the 1950s.[31]

In June 1951, the new Fianna Fáil government could come up with no better statement on land policy than the clichéd desire 'to expedite the work of land division for the relief of congestion'.[32] Thomas Derrig (Carlow–Kilkenny) became Minister for Lands. He was of the old school who believed that land division must be continued and that sufficient funds would have to be made available for that purpose. Even if the likes of Moylan and Lemass (and successive Ministers for Finance) might have wanted to move on in terms of land structural reform, there were others who had to be convinced, amongst them de Valera.[33] In 1950 (at which stage Fianna Fáil was in opposition), de Valera continued to remind the Dáil that the division of land and the provision for as many families as in the circumstances were practicable were still 'a fundamental national, social and economic question'.[34] Furthermore, the 1948 election defeat may very well have convinced even the likes of Lemass that land distribution remained, at least in the popular mind, 'a necessary form of welfare that helped to relieve poverty and unemployment in rural areas'.[35] Thus, Derrig's appointment was very much a throwback to traditional Fianna Fáil policy on land division.

Immediately, Derrig maintained that the budget allocation to Lands would have to be raised by 50 per cent in order to facilitate schemes to relieve congestion. But the Minister for Finance, Sean MacEntee,[36] continuing in the same vein as O'Kelly and McGilligan before him, was extremely reluctant to increase the costs of expenditure associated with acquisition and division. The Department of Finance was no longer willing to expend the huge sums on land division that had been necessary in the past. Losses on resale of lands to migrants amounted to almost £43,000 in 1950, £80,000 in 1951 and £46,600 in 1952.[37] The percentage loss on resale for these three years was almost 28 per cent compared with an average of four per cent for the years 1923 to 1949.

When MacEntee made it known that he was contemplating cutbacks instead of increases, the three most senior land commissioners wrote to him in October 1951:

> In our opinion the money expended on land resettlements, great though it be, is more than justified. It is gilt-edged investment from which the nation gets lucrative returns. Nothing worthwhile can be done without substantial capitalisation. If we are to complete our work in an efficient way the nation must be prepared to pay the price. That the price is well worth paying there can be no manner of doubt at all. Every penny of Land Commission expenditure is spent inside the country. It is an investment that, in a remarkably short time, will yield the nation a rich and abundant return in its outlay, not perhaps in cash dividends from investments in the Far East and other places nearer home, but in citizens, in stock and food supplied, to say nothing of increased internal markets. Each little rural homestead that the Land Commission creates is a permanent factory for producing human and animal stock, turning out its valuable quotas of the former every generation and of the latter every year.[38]

It could be argued that their concern with safeguarding jobs had blinded them to the paralysis in the Irish agricultural sector and to the fact that the human stock produced in 'each little rural homestead' was being largely produced for export.

At any rate, the early 1950s saw a change in emphasis in land reform policy that reverted to concentration upon the relief of congestion through migration and the rearrangement of holdings but on a much-reduced scale than before. For the three years 1951–2, 1952–3 and 1953–4, a total of 65,012 acres was divided amongst 4,096 allottees. Of this, 23,529 acres (36 per cent) went to 2,112 allottees as enlargements and 27,399 acres (42 per cent) went to 934 migrants.

There was no change of policy regarding the landless who had been relegated to the bottom of the hierarchy of allottees, largely as a result of the controversy over the perceived mismanagement of farms by a high proportion of landless allottees. During 1951–4, only 18 landless persons received a total of 730 acres (an average of 40.5 acres each.). It was a far cry from the period 1932–9 when hundreds of landless men received allotments aggregating thousands of acres in any given year. By 1960, Michael Moran, by then Fianna Fáil Minister for Lands, summed up this shift in attitude:

> In my view the suggestion of bringing in landless men and giving them farms and providing land for cottiers – up to ten acres as has been suggested – is unreal. Every new class that you include, merely cuts across the policy laid down by the State since its inception for the relief of congestion.[39]

In fact the period from 1948 to 1957 witnessed the virtual end of allotments to categories other than uneconomic holders and migrants. A total of only 183 ex-employees, 70 landless and two evicted tenants received allotments, totalling 8,293 acres (just over four per cent of the total land divided).

After years of criticising Sean Moylan for not expediting land division or spending more funds on it, Joseph Blowick found himself in no better position during his two tenures of office (1948–51, 1954–7). In his first year as Minister for Lands, he settled for a budget of around £1.5 million when a couple of years previously he had criticised Moylan for 'asking the House today for a sum that is slightly short of £1,500,000 for his department. In my opinion that sum is completely inadequate if any genuine effort is to be made to settle the land question'.[40] The leader of Clann na Talmhan as Minister for Lands could not live up to his party's pre-election promises of delivering to the congests and uneconomic holders of Ireland. Speeches that Blowick made in the past simply came back to haunt him.[41] By now there was the very real worry, as Commissioner Kevin O'Shiel pointed out, that 'a substantial proportion of all holdings . . . will be carried along to final vesting in their tenants without its having been possible to enlarge them'.[42] This was a major source of concern: enlargement was necessary for the needs and future economic independence of uneconomic farmers, while from the Land Commission's point of view it was also necessary because sub-economic holdings were perceived to be a 'dangerous and uncertain security for the advance in land bonds made by the state in respect of them'.[43]

Neither did there seem to be an answer to the rundale problem in the west. There still remained, at a conservative estimate, 9,000 holdings to be rearranged and it was estimated that it would take 12 to 15 years to complete this aspect of the Commission's work.[44] Scarcely any land was left for acquisition or resumption in the neighbourhood of the remaining congested areas and there was precious little untenanted land available elsewhere.

IV A COUNTRY OF SMALL FARMERS

In 1952 Eamon Mansfield was correct in suggesting that 'no rearrangement of parcels of poor mud . . . will change agricultural slums into anything else'.[45] By the mid-1950s there were some 100,000 small farms that did not offer a secure livelihood to a family. About ten per cent of these, in the western counties, were in extremely bad condition, still in rundale or intermixed plots, while a further ten per cent were situated on congested estates that were awaiting rearrangement. Financial stringency in the 1950s meant that only about 1,000 of these families per year could hope to be resettled. Land alone would never solve the problems associated with congestion. In 1952, an interdepartmental committee concluded that:

> further improvement in the economic conditions in the western counties can be effected by continued assistance to agriculture, forestry and fisheries, the development and expansion of rural industries, further expansion of industrial activities in the towns, the development of the tourist industry and mineral and peat development.[46]

While the economic viability of small farms was being questioned from the late 1950s, debate also centred on a number of socially related problems. In 1957, a Department of Lands memorandum lamented that in the past the low standard of education amongst the small farming class resulted from 'some inborn tradition that farming is a subsistence occupation, not a high grade commercial scientific industry of a vocational character'.[47] Progressive farming was, therefore, not seen as a characteristic of small-farm life.

The point has already been made that as attitudes began to change, a young generation was not willing to wait to inherit the drudgery of small-farm life but sought instead an immediate cash income abroad or in towns. The escalation in emigration levels in the 1950s[48] partly resulted in the disappearance of small farming communities, particularly in the west. Young women left in their thousands to seek employment in the cities of England, rather than settle down to a life of hardship on small, often isolated farms throughout rural Ireland. The natural consequence of this was that small farmers were left without wives. In 1958, the Department of Lands was concerned that younger, more energetic men were not inheriting farms early enough and that many elderly farmers were without heirs.[49] By the early 1970s, 25 per cent of the male farmers of less than fifty acres were over 65 years of age and 53 per cent were over 55. More than 33 per cent were over 45 and unmarried.[50]

In 1958, T. K. Whitaker, the highly influential secretary of the Department of Finance, produced his *Economic Development*, the first serious attempt at economic planning undertaken in independent Ireland.[51] Whitaker's conclusions recognised that there was a need to develop industry as an alternative to agricultural employment:

> The common talk among the people in the towns, as in rural Ireland, is of their children having to emigrate as soon as their education is completed in order to be sure of a reasonable livelihood. To the children themselves and to many already in employment the jobs available at home look unattractive by comparison to those obtained in such variety and so readily elsewhere. All this seems to be setting up a vicious circle – of increasing emigration, resulting in a smaller domestic market

depleted of initiative and skill, and a reduced incentive, whether for Irishmen or foreigners, to undertake and organise the productive enterprises which alone can provide increased employment opportunities and higher living standards.[52]

That year, when Lemass and Whitaker launched the *First Programme for Economic Expansion*, it had become obvious that it was futile attempting to create what Dunphy describes as 'an autonomous centre of capitalist development' in Ireland owing to the laws of international economics and the restricted size and potential of the home market.[53] The goal of self-sufficiency was abandoned and policy was dictated more by the drive to attract foreign capital to Ireland to promote new levels of industrialisation.[54]

Lemass and Whitaker's efforts have clouded much else of what was happening in Ireland at this time. A drive toward industrialisation did not mean that the land question suddenly disappeared. For one thing the attempts to attract foreign investors to Ireland sometimes led to a great deal of controversy when locals suspected that they were getting access to lands at their expense. More importantly, there remained a small farm problem to be sorted out and an agricultural industry badly in need of reinvigoration.

V ERSKINE CHILDERS AND THE LAND COMMISSION, MARCH 1957–JULY 1959

The year prior to the launch of the Programme for Economic Expansion, Erskine Childers[55] was appointed Minister for Lands in the latest Fianna Fáil government. His tenure in office was to be a short but controversial one.

Childers shared many of the views of Sean Moylan, believing, for example, that the Irish agricultural economy was seriously hampered by a predominance of small unviable farms and that what it needed to reinvigorate it were larger, more viable ones run by younger, more energetic farmers who needed access to a serious input of capital. In his first Lands estimate speech, he outlined his proposals for a reassessment of land policy. Childers pointed out that the Land Commission would have to set about 'conditioning itself, within its own sphere of activity, to grapple with our economic problems, particularly our inadequate agricultural production'. It was not continued division that was going to be important in the future but the careful monitoring of the use of allotments. He challenged his own party's orthodoxy that as many families as practicable should be established on the land by emphasising there must be an addendum that 'practicable' meant that 'the policy will result in the growth of high grade commercial farming, enabling families to remain in Ireland, providing more people with work in our towns'.[56] This was the first time that such a public pronouncement had been made by a minister when Fianna Fáil were in office.

But Childers was faced with the reality of tens of thousands of farms in the scheduled congested areas that had a valuation of £4 to £10, which the Department of Lands could not see being dealt with before 1975.[57] In fact, it was admitted in 1957 that it was 'far beyond the capacity of the Land Commission to deal with [them] under modern standards'.[58] And he also had to contend with continued opposition from the land commissioners which, it seems, was powerful enough to limit his range of movement.[59]

Childers, unlike the majority of his predecessors at Lands, did not represent a western constituency but he did represent Longford–Westmeath (1948–61), which possibly influenced him in July 1957 to have a survey carried out to inquire into the extent of congestion outside the designated areas. Its findings were startling. There were almost 97,600 holdings of under £15 valuation (defined as uneconomic) out of a total of just over 179,000 holdings in the 17 undesignated counties. In other words, 54.5 per cent of holdings in these counties were uneconomic. At least 49 per cent of the total holdings in each county were below the £15 valuation, with Longford (part of Childers's constituency) and Cavan at 64 per cent and 63 per cent respectively being the worst affected (see Appendix 1, table 6.1, p. 239). The findings convinced Childers that there was never going to be enough land to tackle land reform.[60]

Matters were further complicated by the fact that the standard size of holding of roughly 23 acres introduced in the 1920s had been revised a number of times since so that by the 1950s it stood at around 35 acres. As many as 80,000 previously enlarged farms and new farms could now be technically defined as uneconomic. By extension, this meant that there could be no solution to the problem of uneconomic holdings: as time passed one standard size would have to be replaced by another and the process of acquisition and division would have to commence all over again.

Childers was informed via another report that the increase in agricultural output since 1931 had been largely limited to farms in excess of 100 acres in size; there was 'virtual stagnancy' on farms under that acreage. This was obviously negating the results that had been expected to accrue from the creation of standard-sized farms.[61] Production from Irish land had risen at half the European rate since 1949 and was only 16 per cent above the 1911 level.[62] These statistics offered concrete evidence to Childers as to why emigration rates were so high – young people demanded a better standard of living, which Irish agriculture simply could not afford to provide.[63] Nowhere could he find evidence that would justify land division as a contribution to greater exports and more total employment, arguing in 1958 that 'a land division programme geared to about 25,000 acres a year and involving an annual improvements expenditure limited to about £600,000, can make little impact on the disturbing aspects of our economy'.[64]

Childers was adamant that only the 'very best allottees' should be selected in the future.[65] In April 1957, he told the Dáil:

> It is not too much to say that our entire economy will stand or fall by the use made of the land. An allottee should not regard his allotment an outright gift by the State to be used good, bad or indifferently as he sees fit. On the contrary, he should consider himself specially privileged in being allotted land acquired with public money and distributed in trust for the entire nation and on the definite under-standing that it will be worked to maximum capacity and so contribute to the general well-being.[66]

Future allottees would have to be agriculturists of proven ability, receptive to modern farming ideas and possessing the necessary energy and means to ensure increased production in the shortest possible time.[67] For Childers the future lay in large commercial farms. And now, it seems, there was greater cabinet consensus than at any time before.[68] In 1958, a cabinet committee comprising six ministers had been established to review land division policy. Its establishment coincided with the development of the *First Programme for Economic Expansion*, published as a government White Paper in November of that year. As Mary E. Daly points out, the *First Programme*, as a blueprint for Irish economic growth, assumed that agriculture would be the most dynamic sector.[69] By and large the committee agreed with Childers that there was a need to scale down land division and to concentrate on reforming land policy with the intention of modernising farming.[70] It proposed that the Land Commission should concentrate on 'identifying and popularising the good farmer' so that there was a renewed respect and national pride in progressive farming and a drive to expand markets in order to enable more families to stay on the land. Again, the great ambivalence to land division was exemplified in the opinions of James Ryan, Minister for Finance, who wanted the programme terminated in large areas of the country; ten years previously, as Minister for Agriculture, he had been a chief advocate of division. [71]

Childers virtually ruled out the future allotment of lands to the landless (not that they had been receiving very much since the Emergency) and issued a directive to the Commission that those who were to receive lands were to be carefully examined for their competence.[72] After 1958–9, no more than four landless people per annum received land in any given year and from that year to 1973, the landless received a total of only 1,376 acres (an average of 92 acres per annum).

Even more significantly, in June 1959, the Department of Agriculture, outlining the heads of agricultural policy, which came from the recommendations in the *First Programme*, emphasised that: 'Improvement in grassland is the most important objective in order to achieve a higher carrying capacity.'[73] Emphasis had shifted to cattle production and that meant the need to retain larger farms if the agricultural economy was to develop. There was going to be less land for division. Thus, in March 1958 the decision was taken that in congested districts outside East Galway, Clare, Roscommon, Sligo and East Donegal, existing holdings of £10 valuation and over would now be deemed to be of economic standard (despite the fact that the survey of the previous year had defined uneconomic holdings as those below £15 valuation) and ineligible for enlargement 'unless under exceptional circumstances'.[74]

Changing policies gave rise to reactionary agitation but Childers had little time for agitation or what he termed 'tough action groups', pointing out that 'the Land Commission will not be coerced by any kind of agitation whatever – peaceful or otherwise'.[75] In 1959, he resisted pressure from Lia Fáil, a rural protest movement that had its roots in Offaly and Galway, to break up certain large farms, arguing that the employment lost would far outweigh the social advantages of their acquisition.[76] He also had to resist pressure from farmers' groups such as the National Farmers' Association and Macra na Feirme whose members wanted their younger sons to have access to land. Childers's successors, Michael Moran, Padraig Faulkner and Sean Flanagan continued to ignore the claims of the landless. In October 1962, Moran told the Dáil:

> The claims of landless men, including cottiers, for allotments are fully considered by the Land Commission but, in present circumstances, I do not wish to be hopeful about their prospects. As I have pointed out on a number of occasions . . . the main emphasis of land policy must be directed towards uneconomic holders and migrants from congested areas with the objective of attaining for them family farms of the type enunciated by the Taoiseach [30–45 acres].[77]

In March 1971, Flanagan replying to John Bruton (Meath, Fine Gael) said:

> Landless men have always had a very low place in the priority list and if these are to be elevated to an equal status with existing holders the position will be chaotic. I cannot hold out any real hope that such a fundamental and radical change in Land Commision policy will take place. It would multiply the Land Commission's difficulties and make their situation impossible . . . Landless men must be accommodated in some other capacity.[78]

One other important policy change was made during the Childers administration. In the past the Land Commission had been reluctant to officially allow the letting of lands on the conacre system. Conacre was essential to the small farm economy, which had been sustained by the system for generations. It allowed farmers to increase the scale of their business, which they might not have otherwise been able to do as a result of capital shortage or the unavailability of land for sale on the open market.[79] As D. A. Gillmor has pointed out, it also had a very important social value: it allowed people to derive an income from land even if they were unable to work it themselves, at the same time allowing them to retain ownership.[80] As it stood, the owner of a holding that was still liable to annuities could not in theory let his land without Land Commission permission. Freeholders (those whose lands were not subject to Land Commission annuities) were excepted from leasing restrictions but it is also probable that as much land was let on the black market as was let legitimately. This was one of the great ambiguities of Irish rural life. While the Land Commission could technically acquire lands not being worked by their owners the conacre system still flourished and many of those who let their lands were annuitants. According to official statistics in 1950, an average of 5.4 per cent of lands in each of the 26 counties was let on conacre. The practice was most prevalent in the midland and northern counties of Louth, Monaghan, Donegal, Meath and Westmeath where between eight and 16 per cent of land was let.[81] By the late 1950s, around 730,000 acres were let each year. In 1958, the government was urged by the Department of Lands to encourage more lettings. Firstly, however, owners who agreed to lease their lands had to be assured that they would not be compulsorily acquired by the Commission as untenanted lands and so the department recommended that Land Commission policy should 'be changed and that widows and others who were unable to farm for a period should be encouraged to set their land to suitable farmers for a period of five, ten or fifteen years and be able to resume possession of the farm at the end of these periods'.[82]

The Land Commission agreed to long-term lettings provided that the arrangements did not interfere with land settlement operations or did not result in the concentration of a large acreage in the hands of a single person. The scheme applied only to the areas outside the congested districts.[83] By 1960, the average amount of land let on conacre in each of the 26 counties had risen to over seven per cent and by 1970 to a total of over one million acres (see map 6.3).[84] Lands were let by widows, elderly farmers unable to work them any more, 'lazy farmers' (who might not have got away with it in the past), men short of capital, emigrants who intended to return home some day, smallholders with alternative employment, religious orders and the Land Commission itself who let acquired estates that were awaiting division. Conacre was prevalent on the urban fringes in places such as Palmerstown Mulhuddart, Finglas and Castleknock where speculators had bought lands with no intention of farming them; they intended to sell them at profit in the future when they could be sold as potential development areas.[85]

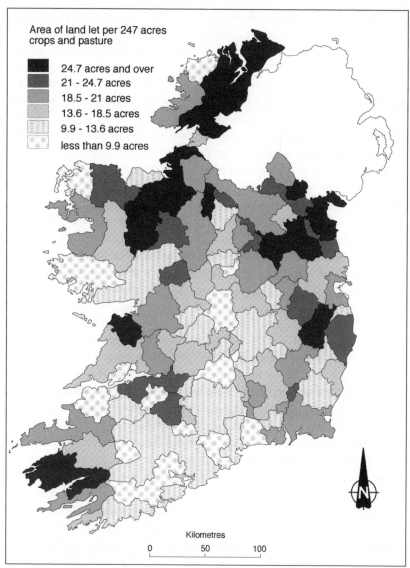

Map 6.3 Area of land let on conacre, *c.* 1970
Source: D. A. Gillmor, *Agriculture in the Republic of Ireland* (Budapest, 1977)

VI A RETURN TO TRADITIONAL POLICIES

During the year 1958–9, the Land Commission allotted almost 46,000 acres, the largest allotment since 1937–8. Six hundred and eighty-three migrants were given a total of 21,300 acres (an average of 32 acres each). This was the largest number of migrants in any given year since such statistics became available from 1937–8. The average number of migrants per year up to that date was 246 per annum.[86] Over 1,300 uneconomic holders received a total of 18,329 acres (or an average of just under 14 acres each). This was 10,000 acres more than the previous year, and more in any year since 1938–9. During the vote on Lands that year, Childers announced: 'the false rumours spread by half a dozen trouble makers regarding my attitude to land settlement should be dispelled by this very fine record'.[87] But it was not with acres acquired and divided that his detractors were concerned; it was with his attempts to reform land division policy that upset the senior Land Commission officials and also some of the senior members of Fianna Fáil, an issue to be dealt with in more detail in chapter 7.

Suffice it to say for now that when Sean Lemass became Taoiseach in 1959, rather than support Childers, he had him quickly changed to Transport and Power and replaced him at Lands with the far more traditional Michael Moran. Lemass's energies were much more firmly focused upon the development of industry and the attraction of foreign investment to Ireland, which, as we shall see below, conflicted in some ways with land division; but the removal of Childers does at least suggest that he was aware of the political implications of radically changing state social policy regarding land settlement. Moran's strategy was to be quite similar to Childers's, but his approach was a good deal more subtle and, therefore, more acceptable to the traditionalists within Fianna Fáil. Lemass's attitude may also have been conditioned by two significant developments during the following 18 months or so: the EEC's commitment to safeguard the family farm (at a time when Ireland was attempting to secure entry to the Community) and Pope John XXIII's 1961 encyclical, *Mater et Magistra*, which stated that governments had the responsibility to ensure that farming families had a comparable standard of living to other sections of the population.[88]

The perceived importance of continued acquisition and division for political as well as social reasons was clearly evident in Moran's appointment. Another western representative (Mayo South), he followed in a long line of Fianna Fáil traditionalists who were keen advocates of land division and who remained convinced that the agricultural economy was best served by the family farm, that the congested districts should receive primary consideration and that migration should continue.[89] He contended that the standard allotment should be based on the labour-quantum of one adult male who had 'full advantage of modern advisory services and allowing for a reasonable degree of mechanisation'.[90]

In April 1959, Moran instructed the Land Commission to undertake a survey of 'substantial holdings' (not specified but presumably in excess of 200 acres) still in existence, with particular reference to the east and midlands. The intention here was obviously to determine how many more estates could be earmarked for west to east migration. The survey found that there were 3,197 in Leinster including 424 in Kildare and 535 in Meath; 2,726 in Munster including 796 in Cork and 584 in Tipperary; 765 in Connaught including 358 in Galway; and 464 in the three Ulster counties, the vast majority of which, 379, were in Donegal (see Appendix I, table 6.2, p. 240). At that stage the Land Commission had initiated proceedings to acquire less than one per cent of these: 19 in Leinster, six in Munster, five in Connaught and one in the three Ulster counties.[91] These holdings had escaped possibly because of the loopholes in legislation that had allowed their owners to appeal continually against their acquisition and, just as likely, because of the changing post-Emergency attitudes towards the importance of large-scale commercial farming. The intention was now clear: these large farms were to be broken up and redistributed amongst migrants and uneconomic holders.

As we have already seen, the high point of land acquisition had been from 1935, when the terms of the 1933 Land Act effectively kicked into place, and 1939, the beginning of the Emergency, when almost 1,200 holdings had been acquired, an average of around 240 per year. The average size of these holdings was in excess of 200 acres. Throughout the 1940s, less than 50 holdings per year were acquired, although the average size remained much the same. From the late 1950s an explosion in acquisition took place once again, coinciding with Moran's efforts to target the substantial holdings. The number of holdings acquired in the period 1965–9 (almost 1,400) actually exceeded the number acquired in 1935–9, but the average size of holding had diminished greatly to around only 70 acres. It seems that many of the once very large holders were being targeted, for a second or perhaps even a third time, by the Land Commission. David Seth Jones points out that typical of these was Cornelius Garvin, a large grazier who occupied an unvested holding of 250 acres in Kells, County Meath. In 1936, the Land Commission compulsorily acquired 101 acres from him and then an additional 88 acres in 1959.[92]

In order to make additional land available, it was recommended that the Land Commission should be empowered to acquire any holding that had been let without the Land Commission's permission or left vacant for five years, and to acquire holdings offered for sale by elderly owners.[93] The problem of vacated holdings in the west had escalated by the 1960s with up to ten per cent of holdings falling into that category. Moran complained that up to then the compulsory acquisition of unused lands had been thwarted by bringing 'the nephew home from England' or selling the lands to 'a foreigner' or to anybody but the Land Commission. Some other owners who had emigrated transferred their lands to relatives living at home on a temporary basis, often through some unofficial arrangement.[94] Even when the Land Commission brought compulsory acquisition proceedings, it was usually two years before the case came to court during which time the person who had let the land for years had rehabilitated his holding so that he could argue in court that it was being used in a proper manner.[95]

In December 1962, at a meeting in Belturbet in County Cavan (the constituency of the Minister for Agriculture, Patrick Smith), Moran told his audience that because land was now such a scarce commodity in Ireland it was necessary for the government 'to take cognisance of derelict and un-worked land everywhere throughout the country' in order to deal with congestion.[96] The Land Commission had already been directed to compile a register of lands that had been let for five years or more. If a voluntary purchase agreement could not be reached with their owners, then the Land Commission would 'proceed with their full compulsory powers for the acquisition of these lands'. Not all were in agreement about state interference. But the Fianna Fáil mouth-organ, the *Irish Press*, argued:

> The plain fact is that too much of our land is abused by temporary tenants and neglected by careless, or even absent, owners . . . On the other side, we have badly congested districts where the holdings are too small to support a family. It is time that these differences were reconciled and a new move made towards social equality and more economic use of land launched.[97]

From 1 April 1958 to 1 April 1973, roughly coinciding with Fianna Fáil's second 16-year period in office, the Land Commission allotted 483,974 acres (a very respectable average of 30,248 per annum) to 27,204 allottees (1,700 per annum). Of these allottees, 7,159 were migrants who received a total of 194,315 acres (a total of just over 27 acres each), representing 40 per cent of the total divided. Another 15,431 holders received enlargements totalling 198,676 acres (an average of almost 13 acres each), representing 41 per cent of the total acreage allotted. The remaining 19 per cent went to 43 landless persons who received 1,504 acres (an average of 35 acres), 318 ex-employees who received 7,911 acres (an average of almost 25 acres each), one evicted tenant who received 50 acres and the remainder in accommodation plots, sports fields, forestry and turbary plots. Policy changes and the increase in the size of the standard holding in the early 1960s to around 45 acres obviously worked very much to the detriment of the landless, the representatives of evicted tenants and ex-employees all of whom had little hope of securing divisions of land. In 1962, Moran had suggested that 'the forty odd acres needed to establish just one landless person would be sufficient to advance three, or perhaps four, existing smallholders to economic level'.[98]

The bulk of inter-county migrations (individuals and groups) took place before the end of Moran's tenure as Minister for Lands in March 1968. His successor, Sean Flanagan, was not a proponent of such migration schemes. In 1972, he told the Dáil that:

> I still hold the view that as far as possible migration from one county to another should end and this for social rather than for other reasons, because I would simply like to have employment for our people in our own counties and obviate the necessity of their having to be shifted, and it is the view of the majority of the Deputies in my county [Mayo] that migration, except within counties, should as soon as possible be terminated.[99]

By 1975, at which time the Fine Gael-led Coalition was in office, Tom Fitzpatrick, the Minister for Lands admitted in the Dáil that 'migration generally from Connaught to Leinster has declined considerably in recent years' and cited County Mayo as an example from where 15 families migrated during 1968–9; nine in 1969–70; three in 1970–1; four in 1971–2; four in 1972–3 and only one in 1973–4. He emphasised that migration in the future would be 'very small':

> My information is that the number of offers from migrants with suitable holdings to surrender is very minimal and I am also told that where migrants have suitable holdings to surrender they have become in recent years much more difficult to satisfy and much more selective in their approach to the holding that they are going to take.[100]

A major contributory factor to this was, as we shall see below, the provision of social assistance payable to small farmers, which provided the incentive for them to stay on their own lands.

Inherent in all these developments was the need to develop Irish agriculture. Since the publication of the *First Programme for Economic Expansion* in 1958, agricultural development had not lived up to expectations. By 1963, net output in agriculture was only 15 per cent higher than in 1958 whereas industrial output was 44 per cent higher.[101] Mary E. Daly points to the fact that the stagnation in agricultural output could not be blamed on a lack of investment: by 1963, agriculture was absorbing 12.5 per cent of the current budget.[102] It had been anticipated in the *First Programme* that agriculture would remain the leading Irish industry. When it failed miserably to do so in comparison with the manufacturing industry, it was inevitable that the *Second Programme for Economic Expansion* in 1963 would recommend the promotion of the manufacturing industry over agriculture.

The *Second Programme* set out to ensure the more intensive use of land within the limits set by market possibilities so that the maximum number of people could be retained in agriculture consistent with social and economic progress; secondly to create viable family farm units with the minimum disturbance of the population; and thirdly, to ensure as far as practicable that those who left agricultural employment would be able to find employment in other sectors of the economy.[103]

In December 1963, Moran issued a directive that standard holdings should be brought up to 40 to 45 acres of good land in order to make farming 'effective and competitive'.[104] This obviously meant that all applicants for land, in any part of the country, whose holdings were less than the new standard size would be eligible for enlargements.[105] Moran pointed out that 'farming competence and evidence of the application of modern scientific methods of husbandry, under the guidance of the local advisory bodies, will inevitably become an increasing factor in the selection of allottees'.[106] Senior land commissioners feared that this stipulation would cause certain tensions in the localities. Thus, in October 1962, G. P. Campbell, chief inspector, issued instructions to his subordinates that while emphasis on farming competence should be progressively increased, it should be done only gradually as it was necessary to 'avoid precipitating acute opposition'. In drawing up divisional schemes, preference was to be given to applicants 'of progressive age and outlook' (meaning young, energetic farmers) who had experience of modern methods of farming such as grassland management, the use of fertilisers, a certain expertise in cattle-breeding, winter feeding and so on, whose present holdings exhibited evidence of the application of these farming methods and 'whose farmhouses have been improved in the interests of housewives'. The fitness of the applicant's wife to co-operate in making the allotment a success was to be taken into consideration. An allotment was to be given to an unmarried applicant only in exceptional cases. Campbell pointed out that:

> If strict adherence to these points would result in the elimination of a relatively few local applicants, who are not quite up to the desired level of suitability, and if their elimination could be regarded locally as seriously objectionable, then a special case may be made for the inclusion of such applicants exceptionally.[107]

VI THE 1965 LAND ACT

Another general election had to be fought in April 1965. One month before, the last significant land act of independent Ireland passed into law. Again, it was strategic timing as far as the government was concerned. The 1965 act empowered the Land Commission to purchase for cash, rather than bonds, lands that were required for any of its statutory purposes. It provided for loans to progressive farmers in congested areas to purchase viable farms of their choice on the open market, subject to making their existing lands available to the Land Commission for division amongst their congested neighbours. This was effectively a banking or credit service limited to £10,000 to each individual applicant.

The primary aim of this scheme was to augment existing land settlement schemes in the scheduled congested areas. Opposition deputies rather cynically taunted Moran as 'a westerner bringing in a western Bill for the sole benefit of the west of Ireland'.[108] Moran defended his stance: 'In so far as I am privileged . . . to undo the work of Cromwell we shall endeavour to make the best job of it we can and that is the purpose of this Bill'.[109] Up to December 1972, 158 applications for credit were received. Of these 155 had been investigated but in only 11 cases was agreement on price reached (most applications failed because the applicant's farm was not considered suitable for rearrangement or the relief of congestion). Of the 11, nine had taken possession of their new holdings, having surrendered a mere 343 acres in return for 980 acres and received advances and free grants to the sum of just over £40,000.[110] The scheme was not to be a success, which the then Fianna Fáil Minister for Lands, Sean Flanagan[111] (Mayo), was forced to admit in the Dáil in 1972.[112] Land prices had risen so dramatically that £10,000 simply would not buy a viable holding.

The 1965 act also introduced a voluntary-migration scheme whereby farmers in congested areas voluntarily agreed to give up their holdings and to move elsewhere. This scheme was to work independently of the migration schemes already in operation. Again, however, very few took advantage of it; by November 1972, only an average of around nine farmers per annum had done so.[113]

The act strengthened the acquisition powers of the Land Commission in regard to lands that were non-residential and/or offered for sale on the open market by their owners. It made provision for the strict control of subdivision and letting. It also attempted to tackle some of the socially related problems associated with farming by introducing a pension scheme that would allow the elderly and incapacitated to retire from farming if they offered their lands to the Land Commission for structural reform. This particular scheme had merits. It would have allowed ageing farmers to give up their land in the knowledge that their financial future was secure and it would have enabled young, energetic farmers to replace them.[114] But again, it was to have little impact: by 1972, only 35 farmers had availed themselves of it, emphasising once again the reluctance to relinquish land ownership.[115]

IX 'THE ALIEN INVASION'

The 1965 Land Act also attempted to address the increasing rural unrest related to the purchase of lands by foreigners. As land legislation stood, foreigners, in theory at least, could purchase land on the open market in the same way as Irish people. Section 3 of the Aliens Act 1935 provided that all foreigners could hold, acquire and dispose of real property in Ireland to the same extent as Irish nationals.[116] Alarmists looked to the fact that there were two international agreements made by the Irish government with other countries dealing with the rights of foreigners to acquire property in Ireland, namely the Treaty of Commerce and Navigation with Germany which had been ratified on 21 December 1931, and the Treaty of Friendship, Commerce and Navigation signed with the United States on 21 January 1950.[117]

As early as the mid-1940s, there had been growing concern about the number of foreigners/non-nationals/aliens (all interchangeable, popular contemporaneous terms) speculating in land in Ireland. This trend was facilitated by the relaxation of Fianna Fáil's traditional policy of protection. Foreign speculators began to purchase tracts of agricultural land as well as factory sites.[118] Criticism became so intense by 1947–8 that the government felt it might impact negatively upon its chances in the forthcoming general election of 1948 (and perhaps it did). Thus it decreed that from 1 April 1948, foreigners purchasing land in Ireland would have to pay 25 per cent stamp duty under section 13 of the Finance (no. 2) Act 1947. This offered little comfort to the cynics. For years afterwards, there were continuous accusations in the Dáil that 'an operation . . . of a quasi-secret character' had developed whereby foreigners had acquired companies established prior to 1947 and under the cover of these companies bought up Irish land. In this way they avoided the purchase tax of 25 per cent.[119]

There continued to be a widespread perception accompanied by a corresponding degree of resentment that certain foreign individuals were being accommodated. In 1950, Senator Frank Loughman referred to 'an English titled gentleman' who reportedly had bought two farms in Kerry with 'devalued English money' and was in negotiations for the purchase of a third. For Loughman, this was simply eviction of Irish farmers under a different guise:

> In the old days clearances were effected by the landlords with the RIC, the battering ram and the crowbar, but now if you have a banknote big enough you can buy three farms, clear out three Irish families and replace them by one English lord or perhaps by some of the new rich from that country.[120]

In May 1950, Bernard Commons (Mayo, Clann na Talmhan) asked his party leader, Joseph Blowick, the then Minister for Lands, if he was aware that an English army officer, Captain John Basil Brooke, son of Sir Basil Brooke, had just purchased an 800 farm near Rathangan in Kildare and whether he was going 'to take such steps as are necessary to have this non-national dispossessed and to have this land utilised for the settlement of Irish land problems'.[121] Blowick was unconcerned, for during the year he had instructed the Land Commission to carry out a survey of lands purchased by foreigners since 1939, which found that only 50,000 acres of land had been bought by 200 foreigners (it later transpired that some of these were actually returned emigrants) and at that rate, Blowick contended, it would take 2,400 years to reoccupy the country.[122]

The real point here is that the amount of land being purchased each year by foreigners was minuscule in the overall scheme of things, but land hunger remained such an integral part of rural life that the purchase of lands by foreigners could not be tolerated. Thus, when, during the 1950s, Germans and other foreigners bought up considerable tracts of lands in the midlands, it gave rise to such hostility that the German ambassador in Ireland is alleged to have told his fellow-countrymen

> to proceed with their industrial adventures in Ireland but warned that excessive purchases of agricultural land would certainly be misunderstood in this country [Ireland] and would give rise to sentiments which would do no service to the improvement of German–Irish relations.[123]

In the Dáil, James Dillon warned that

> It would be the greatest pity if the Germans or any other Continental people who feel the understandable need to 'get away from it all' were to parody the outworn slogan that 'England's difficulty is Ireland's opportunity' by acting on the basis that Ireland's economic difficulty was their opportunity.[124]

In areas of the midlands, land clubs were revived in opposition to foreign purchasers. One of the most vibrant of these was the Bennekerry Land Club in Carlow, which had originally been founded in the late 1930s by a local schoolteacher, Liam Hayes, 'in outrage at the failure of the Minister for Lands and the Land Commission to do their duty' by breaking up the large grazier farms that continued to exist in the county.[125] Grievances at the slow rate of acquisition and division in the county during the 1940s were compounded in the 1950s by the purchase of large ranch-type farms by foreign syndicates. For example, a British land speculating firm had bought the 2,000-acre Brown's

Hill farm on the outskirts of Carlow town. Then in 1957, the same syndicate bought the 1,600-acre Oak Park demesne for £50,000. The Land Commission had interfered in neither purchase. Erskine Childers explained in the Dáil that:

> In the case of . . . Oak Park, the statement was made by the purchasers that they intended to carry out a proper rotation as soon as they had cleaned the land by means of a tillage plan, that they were employing 57 persons and that, although they would only put cattle on the land in the autumn and winter to begin with, thereafter they would commence the raising of pedigree stock.[126]

Around the same time, he defended the purchase of Brown's Hill on similar grounds:

> We cannot play a full part in the modern world, cannot attract tourists, new technical skills or industrial capital, unless we take a sane commonsense view of landownership, particularly when it does not affect the general pattern of land tenure. Isolationism has no place in modern society and banging doors on people will achieve nothing.[127]

This was at a time when the survey carried out under Childers's instructions had found that 2,745 of the 4,958 holdings in Carlow were uneconomic (under £15 valuation, see Appendix 1, table 6.1, p. 239) and at a time when there were still 152 'substantial holdings' (not defined but probably in excess of 200 acres) in the county, of which only one had come to the attention of the Land Commission for acquisition (see Appendix 1, table 6.2, p. 240).

It was the sale of the Oak Park demesne that prompted the rejuvenation of the Bennekerry club. In August 1958, it organised a demonstration that attracted an estimated 10,000 people to Carlow Town, as well as a BBC news television crew. A resolution was passed demanding the Land Commission to acquire the demesne and divide it amongst local smallholders and landless men.[128] Another resolution deplored the fact that 'the right of Free Sale, for which the Land League contended in other days, now sanctions the sale of large tracts of Irish land to foreign syndicates'.[129] Again, the rhetoric here is very significant: it is not the rhetoric of 1916 or of the War of Independence but the rhetoric of the Land League that had very much come to the fore in politics (both inside and outside the Dáil) and society.

Interestingly, none of the five TDs for the Carlow–Kilkenny constituency (three Fianna Fáil and two Fine Gael) attended the Carlow meeting. Despite having offered their support the previous week, it seems as though the TDs were advised by their party whips to stay clear of land agitation, a fact resented by the Bennekerry Land Club, a member of which later wrote: 'The land clubs of Carlow found themselves the victims of a veritable political BOYCOTT. The land agitation had become too dangerous for a member of any party to be associated with.'[130] Particular anger was directed towards Fianna Fáil. Handbills were distributed throughout the county demanding the party to honour the fifth plank of its own constitution that as many people as practicable be placed on the land. In 1958–9, the Bennekerry Club made representations to Childers but were allegedly told that the minister did not care who owned the lands as long as they were well worked.[131]

When Childers moved from Lands a short time later, a representative of the Bennekerry Club proclaimed: 'No man ever brought the country nearer the brink of land war.'[132] (Perhaps significantly, Fianna Fáil lost one of its three seats in the Carlow–Kilkenny constituency in the 1961 General Election.) It may have been an exaggeration to claim that the whole of the country was threatened by land war, but Carlow certainly was. Some time after the Carlow Town demonstration, Dunleckny estate in the same county was put up for sale. The auction was held in North's auction rooms in Dublin, away from the centre of agitation. But members of the Carlow land clubs made their way to Dublin and picketed the auction rooms on the grounds that 'the entry of speculating syndicates with unlimited capital into the market against the small farmers did not constitute free purchase'.[133] The estate was withdrawn from sale that day although it was later sold (it seems by private treaty) to Keenan's Steel Working Company based in Muinebeag.

Throughout the remainder of the late 1950s, continued agitation took the form of the old Land War days of the 1880s. In October 1958 all the roads leading to the disputed farms (Browne's Hill, Oak Park and Dunleckny) were painted with slogans, and posters were found hanging from the gateposts to their entrances. Some of these posters were copies of the 1916 Proclamation with the section 'We declare the right of the people of Ireland to the owner-ship of Ireland' heavily underlined.[134] The agitation became so intense that the owners of Brown's Hill farm finally offered it for sale in 1959, which was regarded as a victory for the Bennekerry Club.

By the early 1960s the campaign against foreign speculators had assumed a much more national profile. In January 1961, a leading article in *The Irish Times* read:

> The tradition of Irish hospitality is a very proud and strong one; but we must draw the line somewhere. As the *Farmers' Journal* points out, we are the only country in Europe that allows the unrestricted purchase of land by foreigners. It would take the strongest evidence of an alien influx to disturb our liberal attitude towards the stranger, but one must ask whether the time has not come to call a halt to a move-ment that may eventually mean a social and economic upheaval of the first order.[135]

Statistics on how much land in total was purchased are unreliable, but the Minister for Lands, Michael Moran (Fianna Fáil), claimed in the Dáil that during the year 1960–1, 33 foreigners had all purchased in excess of 100 acres each, although he also claimed that 'the land consisted of snipe grass and stuff in which the Land Commission would have absolutely no interest'.[136] Jim Tully (Meath, Labour) later contended that nobody was buying the Fianna Fáil line that this was all 'bad land'.[137] By October 1963, over 14,000 acres had been purchased by foreigners since the register had come into operation in 1961. This was enough, the Opposition argued, to provide economic holdings to hundreds of families.[138] Around the same time, Oliver J. Flanagan (Laois–Offaly, Fine Gael) brought it to the attention of the Minister for Lands that there were 150 acres in the hands of foreigners in Trim, 250 in Edenderry, 500 in Naas, 160 in Straffan, 400 in Moyvalley, 100 in Ratoath, 100 in Slane and 100 in Ashbourne.[139] Similarly, John McQuillan (Roscommon, Independent Republican) had earlier argued that

> the problem is serious, particularly in Kildare, Meath, Westmeath and Longford. In those counties the purchase of good land by non-nationals has created a serious problem. A survey of the area within 15 miles of Mullingar would show how diffi-cult it is to find there an Irish citizen on a holding of reasonable size. The majority of the people who have large farms in that locality are non-nationals. On certain days of the week, listening to the conversation that takes place in some of the local taverns and hostels, one would imagine one was in the Kildare Street Club.[140]

On 13 April 1961, James Dillon (Fine Gael) was granted leave to introduce a Private Member's Bill, the Land (Regulation of Acquisition) Bill.[141] The bill proposed to establish within the Land Commission a register of all transfers of land to foreigners (either individuals or corporates) in an attempt, Dillon claimed, to avoid the 'very kind of social problems' related to the establishment of a landlord class that had dogged Irish society in the past.[142] The Minister for Lands, Michael Moran, assured the Dáil that such a register was unneces-sary; the revenue commissioners would in future keep a register and the Land Commission would be informed of purchases by non-national interests: 'In this way, the Land Commission will be in a position to assemble essential information about such transactions. This will be achieved without the irritating and superfluous machinery proposed in the Bill.'[143] The bill was defeated by 65 votes to 35.[144]

In July 1961, another attempt was made, this time by Clann na Talmhan, to introduce a similar Land (Control of Acquisition by Non-nationals) Bill.[145] The aim of this bill was to confine the acquisition of land by foreigners to worthless land, save under permit to be issued by the Minister for Lands. The

Department of Lands felt that the bill was objectionable for a number of reasons, *inter alia* that it could have a negative impact against the Irish abroad; that it could affect efforts to attract foreign capital and industry; that the bill did not cover land acquisition through companies and that it was in direct conflict with the 'the Right of Establishment' as set out under the Treaty of Rome.[146] As the Dáil was dissolved shortly after its introduction, the bill did not make it to the second stage. But questions continued to be asked in the Dáil regarding the purchase of lands by foreigners and the Opposition continued to highlight the issue as 'a very serious national problem'.[147] Once again, Jim Tully was forthright:

> The grants and other incentives made available by the government to attract industrialists should be sufficient in themselves, without also allowing those people to buy up all sporting and amenity rights as well as the best agricultural land in the country.[148]

After years of effectively refusing to do anything about the purchase of lands by foreigners, Fianna Fáil strategically introduced the 1965 Land Act[149] less than one month before the general election of 7 April. The new act legislated that subject to certain exceptions, foreigners could not acquire lands in rural Ireland save with the consent of the Land Commission. It seemed another cynical ploy to alleviate rural unrest prior to a general election; the terms of the act regarding foreign purchasers were not completely dissimilar to those of the Clann na Talmhan bill rejected out of hand by the government just four years before. Foreigners continued to have access to lands, although admittedly on a more reduced scale than in the early 1960s. In 1966, the Land Commission vested 3,900 acres in foreigners, pointing out that it 'consisted of the types of property which could hold no attraction for the ordinary Irish purchaser' and which the Minister for Lands claimed in the Dáil was 'either unsuitable or not required for land settlement purposes'.[150]

It seems surprising that the Land Commission had not intervened, regardless of the total acreage or the type of land, given that its policy was dictated by the settlement of as many families on the land as was practicable. There may in time, of course, be other stories to be told about corporate purchases of lands on urban fringes to which the Land Commission effectively turned a blind eye.[151] As Land Commission records become available, there may also be very many stories to be told about renewed agitation in the late 1960s and early 1970s associated with IRA involvement in the destruction of properties belonging to foreign investors. In 1969 allegations were made that the then Taoiseach, Jack Lynch, had met with editors of various national newspapers and asked them not to publicise statements from the IRA regarding their actions against foreign-owned property in the 26-county areas such as the burning of German-owned property in Meath and the attacks on foreign-owned landed estates at Dunleer in County Louth. Lynch, it has been alleged, feared that if the IRA became associated with land redistribution, it would add immeasurably to their credibility in rural areas, particularly those areas adjacent to the border.[152]

This IRA activity coincided with continued agrarian unrest in the midlands, now more concentrated in counties Westmeath and Longford, and in areas of north Leinster, particularly parts of Meath and Louth where small farmers continued to be dismayed by the slow progress of the Land Commission. (In the late 1950s, 64 per cent of Longford's 7,480 holdings were categorised as uneconomic; 60 per cent of Louth's 6,559 holdings; 51 per cent of Westmeath's 9,648 holdings and 49 per cent of Meath's 13,252 holdings. Furthermore, around the same time the Land Commission had initiated proceedings on only three of Meath's remaining 535 'substantial holdings'; on two of Westmeath's 309; on one of Louth's 117 and one of Longford's 76 (see Appendix 1, tables 6.1 and 6.2, pp. 239–40).

Despite the 1965 act, rural discontent eventually gave rise to the establishment of a new Land League organisation. The aim of the League was ostensibly to rectify what its members perceived to be 'a social injustice' that allowed foreign speculators to invest in Irish lands.[153] Its other objectives included the speeding up of land acquisition and division in areas of north Leinster and the midlands where farmers were aggrieved that the Land Commission efforts had been heavily concentrated in just a few counties, most notably Galway, Roscommon, Sligo, Kerry and Cork. By 1971, in the country as a whole, the Commission had 29,811 acres in its possession for over three years that it had not yet divided.[154] In Westmeath and Longford, where the new Land League flourished, the Commission had 2,709 acres and 1,132 acres respectively for over three years.[155] Thus, J. G. Esmonde (Wexford, Fine Gael) told the Dáil in 1974:

> Farmers have got the impression that the Land Commission are [sic] not with them . . . One gets the impression that the Land Commission feel [sic] that if they quickly allocate their land the Commission might become redundant.[156]

Perhaps! But there were others who speculated differently. One TD suggested that the Land Commission's dilatoriness was influenced by an unofficial policy of letting lands for a number of years at high rents, so that it could recoup some of its purchase costs.[157]

The agitation of the 1950s and 1960s bore witness once again to the intensity of feeling in rural Ireland regarding the land question. It was not until the early 1970s that it began to peter out, largely as a result of the wide-spread anticipation of agricultural prosperity, which, it was assumed, would follow upon Ireland gaining entry to the EEC.

X 'THE WRITING ON THE WALL': IRELAND'S ENTRY TO THE EEC, 1973

The rising price of land, which had increased by approximately 600 per cent between 1969 and 1973 in anticipation of Ireland's entry to the EEC, had a significant impact upon the operations of the Land Commission.[158] The final report of the Inter-Departmental Committee on Land Structure Reform stated in 1973:

> Rising land prices preclude access to land except by those with substantial resources and consequently greater access to credit. The problem has been aggravated by the inflation of recent years and entry into the land market of those anxious to invest in land as a hedge against inflation.[159]

The powers of the Land Commission were inadequate to meet this situation, as it had no control over what it termed 'the undesirable purchases by Irish citizens' other than acquiring the lands itself. And given the rising prices this was not always practicable. For example, for the four years 1976–9, the Commission issued land bonds to the value of £30.6 million for the purchase of 54,000 acres as against £20.8 million for the purchase of 168,000 acres over the previous ten years.[160]

The escalating price of land had equally severe implications for purchasing farmers because the annuities passed on to them were now substantially higher and many felt they would not be able to meet their annual repayments. There were cases of small farmers actually refusing new additions to their holdings, as some were afraid they would lose the Social Welfare benefits to which they were entitled.[161]

In January 1973, the Fianna Fáil government oversaw Ireland's entry into the EEC. (Within less than two months, Fianna Fáil were out of power, replaced by a Fine Gael–Labour coalition government that was to hold office for just over four years.) Ireland's membership of the EEC had a huge impact on Irish agriculture as a whole and because of this impact it also irrevocably changed land division policy, which was thereafter dictated to an increasing extent by EEC directives.[162]

By 1973, there were three existing directives concerned with agriculture.[163] Collectively, these directives were aimed at creating the largest number of farm units capable of yielding incomes comparable to levels secured in the non-farming sector. (Ireland was still unique among its European partners as regards the extent to which its economy was dependent upon agriculture. Over one fifth of the country's labour force was still engaged in farming and agriculture accounted for 20 per cent of gross domestic product and 40 per cent of total exports.[164] Ninety-two per cent of the agricultural area of the 26 counties was owner-occupied compared with 63 per cent in the EEC as a whole.[165]) The directives provided *inter alia* for the right of nationals of one member state to acquire farms in other member states which had been abandoned or left uncultivated for two or more years; the right of a national of a member state who had worked as a paid agricultural worker in another member state for at least two unbroken years to acquire a farm in that state; the right of access by a national of one member state who was established or who was establishing himself in farming in another member state to the rural lease system in that state; the right of a national of a member state who had been established as a farmer for two or more years in another state to sell his farm and buy an alternative farm' and the right of nationals self-employed in forestry to buy wooded land or forest soil in another member state.

The Minister for Lands (by then Tom Fitzpatrick, Fine Gael) saw none of these directives causing 'any significant problem for this country.'[166] But section 45 of the 1965 Land Act caused problems for the EEC, as the Land Commission continued to exercise statutory control over the purchase of rural lands by non-nationals and foreign companies. Despite the fact that from March 1965 to December 1976 the Land Commission had issued consents to 2,635 foreign persons/companies for the purchase of 148,500 acres,[167] the EEC Commission in 1979–80 issued a reasoned opinion that Ireland was in breach of the Treaty of Rome as state control of land purchase discriminated against nationals of other member states.[168]

In Ireland, directive 159, the Farm Modernisation Scheme, came into operation in 1974. The objective of modernisation was to increase productivity through the utilisation of new farming methods. Aid was to be provided on a selective basis to 'development farmers', those most likely to achieve income levels comparable with the non-farming sector in the short term. But farmers soon became critical of the fact that 'the degree of selectivity [was] much too great'.[169] The scheme effectively favoured those who already possessed 'reasonably large quantities of resources' and failed to provide sufficient support for those who had good managerial skills but who were limited by their land resources.[170]

Directive 160, the voluntary Farm Retirement Scheme, also came into operation in Ireland in 1974, superseding the Irish version already in operation. The new scheme was intended 'to enable farmers who wish to give up farming – particularly farmers over 55 years of age – to retire in dignity and financial security and to enable land thus made available to be used for structural reform'.[171] Applicants had to sell their holdings or lease them for a minimum of twelve years to 'a progressive farmer' whose development plans under the Farm Modernisation Scheme (which had come into operation on 1 February of that year bringing all Department of Agriculture schemes for farm improvement under its administration) provided for the acquisition of additional land. Alternatively the farmer could sell direct to the Land Commission. He had, of course, to undertake to retire from commercial farming, although he could continue to work in the agricultural sector. The owner could retain his house and two acres. He would receive a premium of 10 per cent of the purchase price if he was under 55 and the same premium plus a life annuity of £400–£600 (depending on whether he was married or widowed).[172] By 1978, only 396 farmers had taken part in the scheme through sales direct to the Land Commission of almost 13,400 acres. Twenty-two others had sold 870 acres to development farmers (whose income per labour unit was below that of non-farm workers) while 35 had agreed to lease a total of 1,300 acres.[173] A report by the IFA put this disappointing statistic down to:

> a combination of economic forces [that] tend to operate together to encourage farmers to remain on in farming despite very low standards of living in many cases. Amongst these factors are product price levels, the headage payments under the Disadvantaged Areas Directive, the smallholders assistance [the so-called farmers' dole] and the old age pension. These factors when combined appear to outweigh, at least in the farmer's mind, the benefits from retirement.[174]

As we have already seen, Irish farmers were traditionally loath to retire and even more loath to give up their land. As late as 1980, a government report on land policy emphasised that 'farmer retirement [has] not traditionally been a popular concept in rural Ireland'.[175] The escalation in land prices during the 1970s discouraged small farmers from disposing of their properties when they were rapidly increasing in value. (The corollary is, of course, also true: by 1978 land was making up to £2,000 per acre on the open market, a price which the small farmer could rarely afford to pay.) Furthermore, the Disadvantaged Areas Scheme that had been introduced by the EEC in 1975 was something of an anomaly because it now encouraged uneconomic holders to remain on their farms through a range of special incentives and grants. The fact of the matter was that the EEC's wider plan (the so-called Mansholt Plan) that had been originally intended to entice small farmers off the land into alternative employment had not been a success. The growing rates of unemployment throughout the EEC by the mid-1970s meant it was no longer practicable to encourage this scheme.[176] From 1961 to 1978, there was an increase of 71 per cent in the number of part-time farmers in Ireland. By the latter year, 25 per cent of all farmers with holdings in excess of five acres were working full time and farming part time.[177]

After 1973, Irish agricultural and land policy was largely (if at times not wholly) determined by the EEC's Common Agricultural Policy (CAP), regardless of what government was in office. As Mary E. Daly has concluded, the CAP 'was the framework within which farm policy and, in particular, price and market policy was conducted, and most of the funding for agriculture began to come from Community resources'.[178] Under the CAP, farm prices were broadly set at a level that maintained incomes on modern or efficient farms (defined as 'those which yield a labour income of between 80 per cent and 120 per cent of average non-agricultural earnings'[179]) in line with non-agricultural earnings. CAP aimed to increase productivity in the agricultural sector, to stabilise markets and to provide an adequate supply of reasonably priced products to the consumer. Irish farmers' representatives continued to argue that there was a need for a structural policy because price and market policy under the CAP could not by itself solve all the problems faced by farmers. The IFA, for example, argued: 'For the very large number of farms where the resources on the farm are inadequate to produce the volume of production necessary to yield a comparable income, the price and market policy needs to be supplemented by a programme for structural reform.'[180]

Arguably, the concept of reform had in the past implied a basic re-organisation of land structures in Ireland, aimed more at propping up a social order than increasing agricultural production. There was a long-standing popularly held perception that there was a moral need to break up grazing ranches, but was it, or had it ever been, economically justifiable? The grazier, although it had only ever been grudgingly recognised, was an indispensable middleman and a necessary economic link between the breeder and the fattener. Simply stated, the system worked as follows: the breeder, usually a small farmer, generally did not sell his young stock before they were a year old. These young cattle were bought by the grazier, who kept them for a period of six months to two years before selling them off to the fattener who lived mainly in the fertile regions of Kildare, Meath, Westmeath, parts of Roscommon, East Galway, Tipperary and Limerick and who, in turn, sold them on to an English market that was more than satisfied with the cattle that were by then ready and suitable for stall feeding.

The grazier with a large holding was therefore in a much better position to graze store cattle more effectively than 20 small farmers with 25 acres each. The break up of the grasslands in the decades after independence created a temporary dislocation of the course of trade while the small farmer was attempting to adapt himself to the new conditions. It was difficult for a small farmer to hold his stock longer before passing it on to the fattener. A poor hay crop, for example, left him with little winter fodder. The typical small farmer who had to diversify into tillage as well as grazing found himself at the mercy of an unpredictable Irish climate (something which had not affected the grazier to the same extent).

During the 1920s and the 1930s emphasis remained on the creation of the family farm as a basic unit of production and the desirability, enshrined in the constitution, of having as many people as possible on the land. In 1924 Conor Hogan (Clare, Farmers' Union) warned the Dáil: 'We are relieving congestion in this generation by dividing all the available lands, but we forget that we are intensifying congestion and that there will be no land then to go around.'[181] It was a very significant point but it was only as time passed that the desirability of a policy that divided land among the maximum number of eligible persons was increasingly questioned on the grounds that it was not conducive to improving agricultural production in Ireland.

The land reform programme from 1923 to the mid-1950s was not sufficiently extensive enough for the problem in hand: at least, that was the conclusion of the Commission on Emigration in 1954 which argued that had the programme been enlarged to provide annually for an extra few hundred new holdings and an extra one thousand enlargements, 'it would have gone a long way to half [*sic*] the decline [in population]' that had taken place in Ireland in less than a century.[182] This conclusion presumed that there should have been much more land division; the reality, of course, was that this was neither feasible nor possible. Not only had the amount of available land dwindled by then but the original standard holdings of 20 or so acres were now hopelessly uneconomic as, indeed, were the later standard holdings of up to 45 acres. While the Minister for Lands could argue in 1956 that were it not for 'the ever-present expectation of some alleviation in their conditions, to be brought about by the intervention of the Land Commission, many more thousands of these [congested] tenants would have emigrated',[183] the fact of the matter was that land acquisition and redistribution alone were never going to be the answer to the economic problems of these congested areas.

Very significantly, given its primary importance in the past, the relief of congestion was no longer regarded by the government as a priority by the 1970s. By then, agricultural and social commentators also considered farm restructuring (the consolidation of small farms to create larger commercial ones) to be much more important in order to ensure a comparable income for the agricultural sector with the industrial sector.[184] Des Maguire, news editor of the *Farmers' Journal*, one of the Land Commission's most outspoken critics, who exemplified the emergence of a public critique, wrote:

The Commission's present approach to the reorganisation of farms is faulty because the main objective is still the relief of rural congestion rather than the distribution of land among potential development farmers which would assure the country of a farm structure capable of utilising all agricultural resources. The role was inherited from the old Congested Districts Board and still clings like a hangover which has paralysed the thinking of the senior executives and seems to be impossible to shake off.[185]

In 1978, migration schemes were officially abandoned following the recommendation of the Inter-Departmental Committee on Land Structure Reform (that had been set up in 1976 'to review the existing policy and programme of land structural reform and to formulate proposals and options (with associated costs) which would best achieve the government's social and economic policy objectives', and which was chaired by H. J. Dowd of the Department of the Taoiseach.[186]) The purchase of land for migrants (at up to £3,000 per acre), the building of houses and outoffices and the general development of estates were too costly as far as the Department of Finance was concerned. And so ended a remarkable chapter in Irish social history.

XI A CHANGE IN EMPHASIS

The Land Structure Reform Committee's final report, published in 1978, recommended that mobility should be increased in favour of young, enterprising farmers by providing them with subsidised loans or tax concessions to purchase more land. These so-called 'development farmers' were to be given priority in all future land division schemes, as well as priority access to any lands that became available on the open market.[187]

The report's most significant conclusion was that Ireland's lack of agricultural progress was a result of the country's 'small farm problem'.[188] It was an interesting reversal: what was deemed a short time before to be the solution to the Irish land problem, that is the creation of a nation of small farmers, was now considered to have been a retrograde step. By the late 1970s, technological changes and income expectations were forcing upwards the economic size of holdings to such an extent that it was no longer possible for the Land Commission to keep pace.[189] As it then stood, one third of the farms in the Republic were still under 30 acres in size. In Connaught and the three Ulster counties this proportion was one half (see Appendix I, table 6.3, p. 241; also map 6.4) Studies in the late 1960s and the early 1970s had shown that the better operated farms in Ireland were those with more than fifty acres which gave employment to two or more people and that had 'good household structures', that is households with parents and children.[190]

The problem remained as to how to achieve a better matching of young development farmers with holdings of a reasonable size. There was still very little prospect of any dramatic change in land structures: for example, the smallholders' unemployment assistance, better known as the 'farmers' dole', simultaneously supplemented farm incomes and continued to retard the rate of transfer of lands. Coupled with the large-scale migration of young people that had characterised much of the 1950s and 1960s, this had 'resulted in a high proportion of smaller farms being occupied by an older and sometimes physically incapacitated farm population'.[191] This was further compounded by two other factors: firstly, many small farmers could take advantage of old-age non-contributory pensions while still retaining their holdings, and secondly fewer and fewer elderly farmers were participating in the farmers' retirement scheme with the numbers falling from 1,055 in 1974 to 106 in 1977.[192] Only 15,600 acres had become available under the scheme up to December 1977 of which only 1,600 had been allotted. And as we have already seen, the EEC retirement scheme was no more effective in this respect. All of which led to the continued retardation of Irish agriculture.[193]

The Land Reform Committee report recommended sweeping changes in land policy, chief amongst which was the complete abandonment of migration schemes: '*It is the view of the committee that the programme should be abandoned completely as expenditure of this order* [from £35,000 to £70,000] *could more effectively be applied to alternative measures designed to improve land structure*'.[194] Overall, the committee found that the existing policy of acquisition and division had outlived its usefulness. While, for obvious political reasons, it was careful to defend the work that the Land Commission had carried out in the past ('having regard to the particular historical circumstances from which it evolved, the owner-occupancy system was right and logical for its time'), it pointed out that there were now grounds to question the wisdom of the extent of owner-occupancy that had been conferred on Irish farmers by the various land acts.[195] Similarly, the Land Commission, according to the committee, had become 'an anachronism' and the whole policy of relieving rural congestion 'archaic'.[196] The report recommended that owing to the changing nature of Irish society, or more particularly in light of the cost and protracted time scale of operations, the Land Commission activities of acquisition and allocation should be discontinued:

in the future the land market should be conducted, as far as possible, without the state becoming involved in land acquisition and allocation. While we accept that such direct intervention (including in the last resort compulsory acquisition) cannot be avoided entirely, *we recommend that the land agency* [a proposed alternative to the Land Commission] *should limit the extent to which it might purchase land for subsequent distribution.*[197]

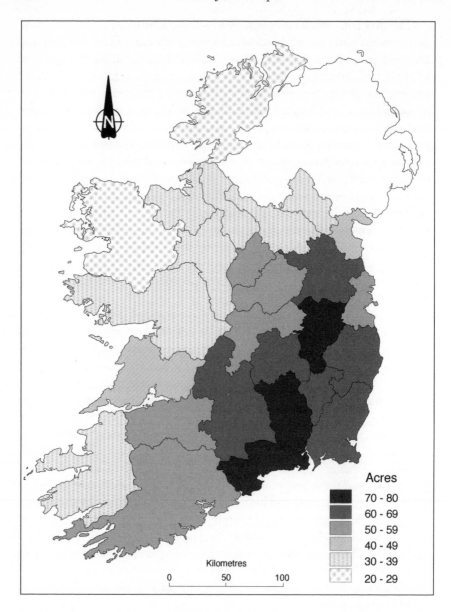

Map 6.4 Average size of farm holdings by counties, 1966
Source: T. W. Moody, F. X Martin, F. J. Byrne, *A New History of Ireland IX Maps, Geanealogies, Lists: A Companion to Irish History* (Oxford, 1984).

In December 1980, two years after the Committee on Land Structure Reform had reported, a White Paper on land policy was introduced.[198] It stated that the government was 'in broad agreement' with the recommendations of the 1978 report (although it opposed the introduction of a register of land applicants with priority entitlement).[199] The paper cleverly used the financial argument against continued acquisition and division to good effect, not by concentrating upon the cost to the state, as had been done in the past, but by highlighting the costs to future allottees by contending that the steep rise in land prices and high interest rates meant that a smallholder given an additional allotment would find it very difficult, if not impossible, to meet annuity payments. For example, by 1980 the annuity rate had risen to 16.75 per cent. On an allotment of seven acres, purchased at £2,000 per acre, the allottee would be required to make an annual repayment of £2,345. The White Paper argued:

> Outgoings of this magnitude could not continue to be met by a smallholder from any normal agricultural activity. As long as land prices and interest rates remain high, therefore, a policy of recovering the full cost of purchase of the lands plus improvements from the allottees is not a practical proposition.[200]

There was now a degree of moral justification for the abandonment of acquisition and division under the pretext that it was the smallholder who would suffer most. What the government was probably most concerned about was the fact that any further allocation of lands would involve substantial subvention by the exchequer.

Land policy had begun to be turned upside down. While the White Paper carefully acknowledged that any new departure from existing policy would have to concern itself with the national social position as enshrined in the constitution which dictated that as many families as practicable had to be established in economic security on the land, it contended that in an increasingly competitive agricultural climate it was no longer justifiable to limit a purchaser's total holding to a specific rateable valuation: 'the imposition of such a limitation would discourage initiative and would not be in the best interests of the agricultural economy as a whole'.[201] From the 1980s onwards, a more free and open market allowed large farmers to purchase more lands, so that by the turn of the twentieth century landownership was once again concentrated in fewer hands. It was impracticable to believe that a surcharge on non-EEC nationals (who could no longer be vetoed as purchasers by the state), non-farmers and farmers deriving substantial incomes from other sources other than farming would prove major stumbling blocks to those who had the capital to invest or speculate.[202] Nor was it likely that a special assistance scheme to allow development farmers, whose holdings were below £40 valuation, to purchase extra lands either through a direct grant or else on certain concessionary terms would meet with much success.[203]

What was of more benefit to the smallholders, at least in the short term, was the promotion of land leasing. Within the European Community, long-term leasing was widespread. In Holland, for example, 50 per cent of the land was let on long leases; in France 45 per cent; in Germany 22 per cent and in Belgium 20 per cent.[204] In Holland, a special Land Tribunal operated to control the system of leasing which, because of the widespread nature of the system, had been withdrawn from the civil code and incorporated into special legislation. The Land Commission had already facilitated leasing through the farmers' retirement scheme but only between a retiring farmer and a development farmer. There remained historical difficulties which had to be overcome and which were alluded to in the White Paper:

> For the past 100 years, land policy has aimed at eliminating 'landlordism' – a term which has been regarded as almost synonymous with expropriation and exploitation. Many would still see leasing as leading to the possible reintroduction of the more objectionable aspects of the landlord/tenant system.[205]

It is remarkable that almost a century and a quarter after it was active, part of the legacy of the Land League remained to influence land policy, and that the Land Commission feared tenants would be reluctant to give up occupancy at the end of a lease period despite legal obligations, thus reintroducing the odious bailiffs to the Irish countryside.[206] (There is perhaps also the consideration that the workload of the Land Commission's staff would be greatly increased and possibly made more complicated by asking them to become once again arbitrators of fair rents, as they had been during the previous century, and formulators of tenancy agreements to protect owner and tenant.) Thus, the White Paper, while acknowledging that hostility to 'landlordism', was understandable in the light of history, forcefully argued that it was no longer justifiable in an age when: 'for all practical purposes, the agricultural land of the country is owned and occupied by Irish citizens whose tenure would not be threatened in any way by a system of leasing which afforded full protection to the parties to the lease'.[207]

Finally, the White Paper did not recommend the dissolution of the Land Commission, as the 1978 report had done:[208]

> The government have considered whether the Land Commission as an institution should be abolished and they have decided that, on balance, the establishment of a second body to implement land policy would not be justified at this juncture. The intention is, therefore, that the Land Commission will be responsible for putting

the new policy measures into effect as well as operating the existing programme on whatever scale may be determined by the government from time to time.[209]

But the Commission continued to come under increasing pressure, not only from leading civil servants (outside the Land Commission) who had wanted it disbanded since the 1970s,[210] but also from agricultural commentators and others. In early 1983, a series of articles appeared in the *Farmers' Journal* that were highly critical of the Land Commission's cost effectiveness, lobbying the government to freeze the Land Commission's acquisition programme and to reassess the country's farm structural problems. The government acted accordingly. That same year, the Land Commission's policy of acquisition and redistribution was terminated and thus ended another significant chapter in the history of the land question in independent Ireland. After sixty years, politicians had finally moved away from land division; it was no longer the political vote catcher that it had been in the past.

The following year, 1984, the Fine Gael–Labour government introduced a land bill, largely aimed at promoting leasing as a more preferable system to letting lands on the eleven months', or conacre, system (which encouraged neither lessor nor lessee to carry out improvements). But because of the apprehension and trepidation in rural Ireland, much of which had been caused by Land Commission activity down through the years, it was necessary for the minister to give a concrete assurance that the Commission would make absolutely no attempt to acquire lands that were subject of a *bona fide* lease.[211] And a similar guarantee had to be given that the lessor would be able to resume possession without fuss or legal complication when the term of the lease had expired.

While the Fine Gael–Labour government contemplated the dissolution of the Land Commission and its replacement with an alternative land agency,[212] the Coalition's defeat in the 1989 general election meant it was somewhat ironically left to Fianna Fáil to take up the gauntlet to dismantle a state institution that had, arguably, more than anything else helped to cultivate the party's appeal in the imagination of the rural electorate back in the 1930s. Shortly after retaking office Fianna Fáil introduced a bill to dissolve the Commission and to transfer its functions to the Minister for Agriculture. However, it never completed the second stage because during a period of political uncertainty it was actually the Dáil that was dissolved.

It was not until 1992 that the Irish Land Commission (Dissolution) Act was finally passed but not signed into law until 11 November 1999.[213] Why the order was not signed for seven years remains a matter of conjecture. It is possible that the minister hesitated, realising the extent of work to be completed or even the repercussion its dissolution might have for the Commission's personnel. All functions of the Land Commission under the various land acts were passed to the Minister for Agriculture. Some branches of the Commission remained operational.[214] A Lands Division Branch, for example, continues to exist within the Department of Agriculture with offices in Castlebar and Cavan, and the collection of outstanding annuities amongst its responsibilities (in 2002, there were still almost 6,500 farmers with land purchase annuity commitments of €2.12 million to the Department of Agriculture).[215]

It was not until the 1980s, when land acquisition and division had finally begun to lose its political weight and Fianna Fáil had consolidated the support of the developing industrial and urban working classes, that there was enough confidence within a government of that party to dismantle the Commission. The government could argue the benefits of allowing progressive farmers access to lands on the open market in the name of agricultural progress, while small farmers could take advantage of the widening range of EC-backed schemes (such as agri-tourism, alternative enterprise schemes including grants for breeding goats, deer and horses) aimed at supplementing income levels. Grant aid under such programmes was running at £20 million in 1992. Headage payments totalling £100 million were made to farmers in disadvantaged areas in the same year.[216] At the same time, access to land was becoming less important in terms of social status as greater educational opportunities and alternative employment outlets expanded socio-economic horizons. In 1946, 575,000 – 40 per cent of the working population – had been involved in agriculture. By 1971, the number had dropped to 273,000 or by almost 50 per cent, despite the fact that the population remained relatively static over that 25-year period. By 1986, the number had dropped to 171,000 despite a population increase of around 15 per cent.

From the 1980s, the free market system that has operated has favoured those with capital resources, which has led to a much higher concentration of land in a decreasing number of landowners. Milk quotas, for example, dramatically increased the value of small farms which meant that when they were put up for sale, they were mainly out of the reach of neighbouring small farmers and were instead purchased by those with access to high finance. From the 1970s there was also the problem that the price of land was not so much determined by its productivity capacity as by the availability of finance or credit (and the friendly disposition of the local bank manager!) Many of the larger companies and corporations with surplus funds began to invest in lands from the 1980s.[217] Small farmers had no chance to compete. In 1989, one TD accurately predicted that 'a cheque book control of land distribution without any land agency' would develop.[218] Concern was no longer expressed that the return to the concentration of landownership in the hands of the few was contrary to the principles set out in the 1937 constitution.

SEVEN

LAND AND THE LOST POLITICS
OF INDEPENDENT IRELAND

As I grew up, I often heard stories from Fianna Fáil cumann meetings. Most of that period was Fianna Fáil dominated and at these meetings individual Ministers for Lands divided estates between members and he might forget about the Comhairle Ceanntar chairman who, at the end of the night, might say, 'You have not given me anything at all' and the whole lot would be scrubbed, they would start all over again and work out a new land division before ever a Land Commission inspector came near the place. . . . In dealing with small farmers, the division of estates was very important. It created a lot of bitterness and division but it also created unity amongst those who were going to get portions of the land. TDs at party meetings were faced with irate people who wanted to know how the other fellow could get the land, and the argument changed when a different government came into office.

ENDA KENNY

(Mayo, Fine Gael) *Dáil Debates*, vol. 389, 4 May 1989, 1384.

———

I INTRODUCTION

At various stages throughout this book, the continued importance of the land question to Irish politics in the post-independence period has been suggested. It is now time to elaborate further on the interrelationship between land and politics in independent Ireland.

It is no exaggeration to claim that the anticipated results of land acquisition and division as begun under the 1923 Land Act were economic prosperity for a much higher proportion of Irish farmers, as well as social and political stability. But, as S. J. Brandenburg, an American academic and economist, pointed out in 1932 when writing on Irish land transfers since independence: 'The wisest land legislation and the most effective land program can hardly yield all the blessings that men want and reformers promise.'[1] Yet most Irish politicians at this time and for decades after could hardly be accused of being as forthright as Brandenburg. Indeed what is remarkable about the Irish situation is that for well over fifty years there was an unspoken agreement between the major parties (adverted to in the Dáil in June 1959 by Erskine Childers: 'We disagree on many matters in this House but for many years there has been virtual unanimity on the fundamental principles of land settlement'[2]) that acknowledged that land acquisition and division, once begun, could not be abandoned without damaging political consequences.

Childers's was very much a public political statement. It did not mean that behind a façade of unity, there were no internal tensions within the major parties that manifested themselves in behind-the-scenes rows amongst cabinet members, or between politicians and senior civil servants (especially those attached to the Department of Finance). These tensions arose out of the complex ambivalence that existed towards land reform policy: the point has already been made that there were those politicians who supported the free market, commercialising approach to economic development as expounded by Patrick Hogan, Sean Moylan, Erskine Childers and Sean Lemass and those who remained loyal to the autarchic 'Sinn Féin' smallholding model that so appealed to Eamonn de Valera, Joseph Blowick, Michael Moran and others. Up to the 1960s, those in Fianna Fáil in particular who favoured the commercialising model did not or were not allowed to abandon land acquisition and division in favour of it; that would have been tantamount to political ruin.

Thus the intractable conflict between those who desired proprietorial security and those who wanted to bring acquisition to its natural conclusion, that is to the stage where all holdings in the country were small but economic, remained. Both sides could and did invoke the ideals of the Land League (which post 1923 really became a blanket term for the later National League and United Irish League as well) in their favour: one side could argue that from the 1880s the land movement had fought for security of tenure, while the other side could point to the prolonged struggle for the break up of the large grazier farms and untenanted estates.

Tensions were created by the false hope that prevailed, essentially because it had been manufactured by politicians in 1923, that there was possibly land for everybody when, of course, the reality was nothing of the sort. The great political debate was then to focus upon those to whom it was most politically expedient to give land. Who was to be relegated or simply ignored in the hierarchy of allottees at different times and why? I have already suggested that certain sections of rural society, namely the labourers and the landless, were disproportionately unrepresented in allotment schemes from the early 1940s because they did not have the socio-political clout of existing farmers.

Of course, it is notoriously difficult to prove political collusion in land acquisition and division schemes. Writing on this issue in 1989, J. J. Lee suggested that:

> The government was not . . . exposed to the temptation to manipulate land reform
> extensively for political purposes, which might have spawned massive corruption

and provoked widespread grievance. Such limited land re-distribution as occurred continued to be channelled through the safer conduits of the Land Commission. Communities were not generally rent asunder by rival claims to land.[3]

What follows in this chapter disputes Professor Lee's conclusions, arguing that governments were in fact desperately keen to manipulate land reform in order to make political gain. Some of the evidence that is presented below could be described as circumstantial (and will perforce remain so until the situation regarding the inaccessibility of the Land Commission's records is addressed), but there should also be a great significance attached to the fact that there were continued and explicit accusations of political impropriety with regard to land division schemes and – what is equally illuminating – very little denial. Appositely it could be argued that to be accused of manipulating a land division scheme was actually doing a politician a favour and for him to deny any act or part would lessen his popular appeal to the electorate!

II LAND DIVISION AND PARTY POLITICAL SUCCESS, 1932–48

It has been argued in chapter 2 that the 1923 Land Act passed by the Cumann na nGaedheal government made an important contribution to the return to more peaceful ways in the countryside. That government's 1931 Land Act failed, however, to capture the imagination of certain sectors of the rural electorate simply because it did not legislate for a more radical programme of acquisition and redistribution; its focus was more upon the completion of the transfer of unvested holdings from landlords to tenants. On the other hand, Fianna Fáil's 1933 Land Act helped to consolidate the party's success in the two previous general elections by removing many of the obstacles to a more radical acquisi-tion programme and legislating for a much greater redistribution that appealed to the landless and the labourers as well as to the uneconomic holders. There were considerable political points to be scored therefore by enacting legis-lation that would appeal to the mass of the rural electorate.

From the outset, both Cumann na nGaedheal/Fine Gael and – especially – Fianna Fáil expended considerable resources and energy on land reform policy in the knowledge that it would pay political dividends. It is significant that the Provisional Government decided in February 1922 that 'the issue of a statement of policy regarding the completion of land purchase should be deferred until an election campaign was opened'.[4] In December 1924, John Lyons (Longford–Westmeath, Independent Labour) was under no illusions as to why Cumann na nGaedheal introduced the 1923 Land Act: 'You had the Land Act introduced for the purpose of election propaganda.'[5]

There was much more than a grain of truth in Lyons's quip. During the election campaigns of 1922 and 1923, politicians promised sweeping changes in land reform policy: T. J. O'Connell (Galway, Labour) later claimed in the Dáil that 'we were told, practically from every platform, in 1923 and since, that it was only a matter of a short time until the people would be planted on the land'.[6] Following Cumann na nGaedheal's poor showing in Clare in the 1923 election – Professor Eoin MacNeill being the only member to secure one of the five seats there – a decision was taken in 1925 to send Patrick Hogan to the county on something of a propaganda tour. Because of his association with the 1923 Land Act, Cumann na nGaedheal posters announcing his impending arrival represented Hogan as a messiah-type figure sent to save smallholders from destitution:

> Cumann na nGaedheal [in County Clare] . . . has especially invited down the one man who can appreciate any losses sustained; who can promise the necessary aid and help, and, what is more important, who can redeem each and every promise he will make, not with empty, idle-sounding words but with something substantial and tangible, that will speak in louder and more eloquent fashion, to the poor distressed farmer than all the fanning tongues that ever voiced themselves in Babel. That man is the Minister for Agriculture. His Land Act is his credentials. There is a prairie of untenanted land in Clare; there are poor men in uneconomic holdings; there are bogs unevenly distributed; ranches in the hands of the very few. These must be partitioned and divided into lots, to make what was uneconomic economic.[7]

The argument could be made that the Cumann na nGaedhael government attempted to play both sides of the agricultural social divide: on the one hand the party had presented itself as being in favour of the break-up of estates and redistribution of lands; on the other hand, the terms of the 1923 Land Act protected large farmers, the party's main interest group. The fact that those who would support a much more radical distribution of land remained outside the Dáil until 1927 not only gave the Cosgrave government some breathing space but also possibly determined to some extent that land distribution would be slow and conservative in its approach until the 1930s.

Between 1923 and 1932 Cumann na nGaedheal did very little to attract the support of the small farming classes or the landless and still less to stem the tide of rising poverty in rural Ireland. By the early 1930s, small farm life was becoming more and more intolerable at a time when at least half of the country's farms remained below a viable economic standard.[8] Demands for the expediting of land acquisition and division had not been met. Credit was largely unavailable to either small farmers or agricultural labourers – they did not have the necessary collateral to secure loans, while large farmers benefited from the Agricultural Credit Corporation facilities. Small farmers could not hope to expand or even improve their holdings (no subsidies, for example, were available for pig farming, an integral part of the small farming economy[9]) and agricultural labourers, whose wages were actually declining during the 1920s, had obviously very little hope of purchasing lands on the open market.[10] Furthermore, the government had not done enough to stimulate the growth of industry to provide alternative employment opportunities to agriculture, with the result that there was an increase, even if rather moderate, in emigration levels during the 1920s.[11] By 1936, 644,000 persons continued to be engaged in agriculture (excluding farmers' wives) but only 14,000 of these were categorised as paid employees which meant that around 80 per cent of the agricultural labour force in Ireland was family labour. (To put this into context the corresponding percentage for Britain was only 33 per cent.[12]) Irish farmers were not renowned for their willingness to pay their own family members for a week's labour, all of which added to a great deal of rural frustration. Cumann na nGaedheal alienated the support of the small farming communities, the landless and the labourers (particularly in the west) who began to look for alternative representation.[13]

It is just as true that at an early stage Fianna Fáil recognised the importance of land division to its prospective electoral success. At the Fianna Fáil *ard-fheis* in October 1931, De Valera drew a revealing historical analogy:

> he remembered a great deal of argument as to whether the movement for Home Rule was being advanced or retarded by linking up with the fight for the land [in the 1880s]. There was [now] a certain linking up because it was thought that by doing so there would be brought to the national movement a support which it might not otherwise get.[14]

Fianna Fáil's socio-economic and cultural objectives were very much tied to a land reform policy that aimed to settle as many families as practicable on the land, keeping them there (as was to be laid down by Fianna Fáil in the 1937 Constitution) in economic security and free from privation, maintaining economic self-sufficiency through a tillage programme that was suited to a small-farm economy (which by extension meant getting rid of the graziers), resurrecting the Irish language and promoting the type of idyllic rural culture as espoused by de Valera.

In October 1933, the new Fianna Fáil government introduced its own extensive and complicated act, which provided the catalyst for record land acquisition and division statistics in 1934–5 and 1935–6 and was very much as Patrick Hogan contended, 'a purely political' act that pandered to the small farmer and labouring classes in an attempt to secure votes.[15] After the terms of the act became known, there was a rather dramatic growth in the number of Fianna Fáil *cumainn* from 1,265 in 1932 to 1,679 in 1933 (see Appendix I, table 7.1, p. 242). This growth was partly the result of more organised and sustained efforts by Fianna Fáil organisers in the rural constituencies but it also owed much to the stimulus provided by the 1933 act and the widely held belief that one would have to be a member of a *cumann* in order to benefit from division.

When acquisition and division records could not be matched after 1935–6 for reasons already discussed (see chapter 4), another bout of disillusionment, frustration and disappointment engulfed the small farmers of the west. Fianna Fáil attempted to maintain its growing momentum by introducing the 1936 Land Act[16] which empowered the Land Commission to compulsorily acquire holdings that had already been vested in purchasers under the previous land acts (provided a period of seven years had passed since vesting) where the condition and use of this land rendered this desirable. This was a deliberate assault on the large farmers and graziers who, in the main, supported Cumann na nGaedheal. It also empowered the Commission to sell off holdings repossessed from those who had defaulted in their annuity repayments. But still the figures for 1935–6 could not be matched. In the 1937 general election, Fianna Fáil support in the west fell by eight percentage points from its 1933 level. Similarly, when land acquisition and division were temporarily halted during the Emergency, Fianna Fáil support in the west plummeted to 43 per cent in the 1943 election, which represented a fall of 18 percentage points from 1933.[17] As far as the congests in the west were concerned, Fianna Fáil had not delivered upon its utopian promises.

More crucially, the 1933 Land Act should perhaps be viewed in light of the stimulus it gave to the growth of the Blueshirts. Historians are in agreement that the movement was dominated by large farmers and graziers who were determined to protect their interests from the full rigours of de Valera's tariff war with Britain.[18] The significance of the Economic War to the growth in the Blueshirt movement is accepted but it is also worth considering to what extent the threat to the proprietorial security of large farmers posed by the 1933 Land Act contributed to this growth. Mike Cronin, in his analysis of the socio-economic background of the Blueshirt movement, was surprised, for example, to find that 'counties such as Meath and Mayo where there was an absence of large landowners . . . saw big upturns in membership' in the early 1930s.[19] However, much of the land in these two counties was at that stage held by large landowners whose holdings were being targeted by Fianna Fáil after 1932 for acquisition and redistribution – in Mayo for local migrants, in Meath for those congests who would be migrated from the west. By 1982, when the Land Commission work of acquisition and division had effectively ended,

637 untenanted estates or purchased holdings had been acquired by the Land Commission in Meath (totalling 52,657 acres) and 1,573 in Mayo (totalling 48,828 acres). Mayo, therefore, had the highest number of holdings acquired/resumed in the country, while Meath was in fifth place. Meath had the second highest acreage acquired/resumed, while Mayo had the third highest (both behind Galway).[20] Is it then so surprising that there should be an influx of large farmers from these counties to the Blueshirts?

The majority of Cronin's sample Blueshirts came from families with under 60 acres who, he has argued, could not be classified as large farmers. However, in the early 1930s, 60-acre farms were actually almost three times the size of the standard Land Commission holding which means that in contemporaneous terms they were large farms and therefore legitimate targets for resumption and redistribution if they were deemed necessary for the relief of congestion. The largest influx of members to the Blueshirts occurred between 1932 and 1934 with recruits pouring into their ranks in 1933.[21] Was this because of the threat to the proprietorial rights of the large farmers posed by the land act of 1933? From 1 April 1934 to 31 March 1935 an unprecedented 102,000 acres were divided amongst 6,244 allottees.[22] The following year, the achievement was even greater, 104,000 acres amongst 7,712 allottees. For the first five-year period of Fianna Fáil's administration (ending 31 March 1937) almost 353,000 acres were divided amongst 25,802 allottees, over 100,000 acres more than in the preceding five-year period. Hardly surprisingly, Cumann na nGaedheal, defending the proprietorial rights of large farmers, argued that Fianna Fáil's radical land acquisition and redistribution policy was tantamount to 'the purest of communism'.[23]

Fianna Fáil, despite this initial success, failed to live up to its expectations in terms of its pre-1932 promises of land division, admittedly as much for logistical reasons as any others, in that not enough land could be acquired sufficiently quickly. This failure was perhaps one of the most important reasons for the post-Emergency shift away from Fianna Fáil and yet historians have given but little consideration to it.

Another consequence of this failure was the establishment of Clann na Talmhan in 1938. While the Clann claimed to have other agendas besides the land question, it was essentially upon this issue that its initial success was based.[24] In the 1943 General election Clann na Talmhan secured ten seats: one in Cavan (where the successful candidate polled 15 per cent of first preferences cast), one in Cork North (securing 15.4 per cent of first preferences), one in Cork West (securing 13.7 per cent of first preferences), one in Donegal East (securing 9.8 per cent of first preferences), one in Galway East (where the Clann's founder Michael Donnellan topped the poll securing 25.6 per cent of first preferences), one in Kerry North (securing 13.6 per cent of first preferences), two in Roscommon (where the two successful candidates between them secured 31 per cent of first preferences), one in Tipperary (securing 5.5 per cent of first preferences) and one in Wicklow (securing 18.7 pent of first preferences).[25] Arguably, Clann na Talmhan did best in areas where Fianna Fáil had failed to deliver upon its earlier election promises of more land acquisition and division. Even though this election was to mark the high point of the Clann's electoral success, it is still significant that the issues of land acquisition and division and their impact upon the small farming communities of the west had given rise to a new political party.

There is one further consideration. In June 1948, Bernard Commons (Mayo, Clann na Talmhan) claimed in the Dáil that Fianna Fáil's proposed land division policy in 1932 assured it of the support of every small farmer in the country and the hostility of every rancher. By 1948, that position had changed. According to Commons:

> in 1948, in the constituency which I represent, I found that 99.9 per cent of the ranchers of the locality were loyal and enthusiastic supporters of the Fianna Fáil Party and that 95 per cent of the uneconomic holders were up in arms against the Fianna Fáil Party because of their failure to provide them with what they wanted.[26]

Commons's statistics are certainly exaggerated, but the underlying claim is an important one that large farmers moved over to Fianna Fáil in an attempt to protect their holdings from acquisition or resumption. This being the case, the allegiance of large farmers was likely to shift again if a new government were elected to office. And so Commons claimed that shortly after the first Inter-Party government was elected in 1948, and his party leader Joseph Blowick (also Mayo) became Minister for Lands, he was allegedly approached by a number of ranchers who said to him: 'Now that you are a supporter of the government our cheque books will be available to you at the next election. Do not make any move in regard to our lands.'[27] It is hardly beyond the realm of credibility that people would want to protect their farms by 'twisting', to use a popular contemporary term, from one political party to another. The rise in the number of Fianna Fáil *cumainn* 1932–3, referred to above, may have been as much about protecting farm ownership as it was about securing land.

Finally, the 1948 general election was fought amidst huge controversy that surrounded the terms of the 1946 Land Act which had given powers to the Land Commission to resume holdings that had not been worked in a satisfactory fashion. Most of these holdings had been given to landless men in record numbers during the early years of Fianna Fáil's administration.[28] With little experience of running farms and even less capital, many of them floundered as farmers, having succumbed to the ravages of economic depression.

Fianna Fáil, by threatening to take lands back forcibly that it had allotted, was acting in a way that was tantamount to evicting tenants as had been done in the days of the Land War. Thus, during the course of the debate on the land bill, Oliver J. Flanagan (Leix-Offaly, Independent) exclaimed:

> I am going to oppose the Bill and my reason for doing so is that I am of opinion that the real title that the minister should have given to the Bill is the Vote Controlling Land Bill, 1945, because I believe the Bill is brought in for the purpose of dealing with ungrateful and disloyal Fianna Fáil supporters who secured land through the influence of the Fianna Fáil organization and who, for reasons of their own and probably because they have since gained intelligence, now see fit to support any political party. I am honestly of opinion that if this Bill is passed it will be used at every election by the Fianna Fáil Party as a threat over those holding land. They will be told that, unless they support the government, this Bill will be implemented against them.[29]

III POLITICIANS AND LAND REFORM PROMISES

Without any doubt, a promise of the division of a local estate by a prospective TD in the lead up to an election was a vote-catcher. In 1946, Senator J.J. Counihan announced in the Seanad that the daily debates on the land question in the Dáil '[are] one of the greatest vote-catching stunts for any government, Fianna Fáil, Fine Gael or Clann na Talmhan – this advocating the splitting up and division of land'.[30] Even as late as the 1960s, electioneering promises of more land division were seen to be the basis for a successful campaign. In an East Galway by-election in 1961, one candidate allegedly sent out 500 letters promising parcels of lands to each recipient from the forthcoming division of a 400-acre estate in the constituency.[31] In May 1965, a month after the general election, Oliver J. Flanagan (Leix–Offaly, and by then Fine Gael) sarcastically commented:

> I cannot help remarking on the extraordinary amount of disappointment that will be felt throughout the length and breadth of this country during the next few weeks. . . . I am given to understand that in practically every constituency in Ireland during the last general election campaign, practically more land was promised to the people than there is land in the country.[32]

As ever, Flanagan was somewhat over the top, but in truth such promises had been made during every general election campaign since independence. One could argue that it was a very gullible and naïve electorate that continued to be taken in by promises of inexhaustible land division but to do so would simply be to deny the hope and optimism that government land division policy held out to rural dwellers of a better way of life, and – as long as the Land Commission continued to exist – hope sprang eternal.

If politicians promised lands to constituents, could they or did they deliver on such promises? First of all, it was easiest for politicians to involve themselves in the acquisition of estates. As explained in chapter 3, uneconomic holders in an area could bring what might be considered appropriate lands for division to the attention of the Land Commission either directly or through representations made to their local TDs. These representations were often made formally at local party clinics or through the local Fianna Fáil *cumainn* or Cumann na nGaedheal/Fine Gael clubs that were growing in strength by the early 1930s, essentially because of the competition for votes. And Fianna Fáil, it seems, were much better at this type of organisation than Cumann na nGaedheal whose relationship with the electorate (at least some of the 40 per cent or so of it who had given their first preferences for the party in the 1922 and 1923 elections) had been soured by the slow progress of land acquisition and division. Its continued protection of the large farmer interest did not endear it to the more numerous smallholders. P. W. Shaw (Longford–Westmeath, Cumann na nGaedheal) alleged in the Dáil in 1927 that the Cumann na nGaedheal organisation had lost almost forty branches in County Westmeath as a result of the party not delivering on its land division policies there.[33] While Fianna Fáil could call upon 1,265 *cumainn* in 1932 and 1,679 in 1933, Cumann na nGaedheal or later Fine Gael never matched this type of organisational strength because, as Tom Garvin has argued,

> Cumann na nGaedheal suffered from a serious lack of organisation and strength at local level, in part because the leadership, which had never witnessed competitive party politics of a normal kind, was insensitive to the need for regular branch organisation in the late 1920s.[34]

At such *cumann* or club meetings politicians held themselves forth as agents for the acquisition and distribution of local lands. Thus grew the belief, and an understandable one, that using local TDs was a much more effective avenue towards acquisition. Many of them were also approached privately and informally at weddings, wakes and in public houses. TDs, in turn, made representations directly to the Land Commission (there were some deputies who acquired a reputation for 'haunting' the Land Commission offices, which invariably created 'a chain reaction of intrigue and suspicion'[35]); directly to the Minister for Lands; or, as seems to have been the most popular course of action, brought them to the attention of the minister during parliamentary question time. One can see in the *Dáil Debates* the extent to which parliamentary questions, particularly in the period from 1923 to 1948, are dominated by enquiries about when the minister is going to proceed with the acquisition of certain landed estates or seeking explanations for estates not being acquired. In the Dáil in 1925, Martin Roddy (Sligo–Leitrim) read a resolution passed at a meeting in his own constituency calling on him 'to bring pressure on the Minister for Lands to have the following ranches in our parish taken over and distributed amongst uneconomic landholders who are already starved for land to till for food for themselves and their families'. It was one of many that he received each week, some of which were of 'a much more violent character'.[36] The system was perhaps best summed up by John Browne (Wexford, Fianna Fáil) in 1991 when he told the Dáil that in the past 'there were queues at politicians' doors whenever Land Commission land became available' and that TDs 'got more hassle and abuse over the allocation of lands by the Land Commission than they did in regard to any other issue'.[37]

In the 1930s Sean MacEoin[38] (Longford, Cumann na nGaedheal/Fine Gael) kept records of those on whose behalf he had made representations with details of some of the outcomes. His 'success rate' was much more impressive when he was Minister for Defence in the first Inter-Party government, 1948–51.[39] Likewise, Frank Aiken's constituency correspondence shows that for a period spanning over forty years he concerned himself with land division issues in Louth. In March 1933, Aiken, then Minister for Defence, received a letter from one constituent who wanted a farm from an impending division who made sure to emphasise that he was chairman of the local Fianna Fáil *cumann*, while another man wrote of his annoyance that in 1933 the Redwood estate had been 'allotted by the essentially Cumann na Gael [*sic*] minded Mr. Goold'.[40] The probable implication was that Goold, the inspector in charge of the scheme, had spent too long dividing lands under the Cumann na nGaedheal government and was not taking cognisance of the fact that Fianna Fáil were now in power. As late as May 1970, a woman wrote to Aiken:

> I am terribly worried about my son. We had hoped all down the years that we might get a portion of land from or through the Land Commission and for more than thirty years they kept telling us from time to time that they were doing something in the matter. . . . [We] would never forget it if you could help us.[41]

Later that same year Aiken was approached at a Fianna Fáil meeting in the Ballymascanlon hotel in Dundalk where it was suggested to him that the Land Commission 'interest itself in the purchase of land in Cooley' from owners who were allegedly letting it on conacre rather than working it themselves.[42] Aiken made the recommendation to the Commission and the land was subsequently acquired and divided.[43]

It is only when local studies are carried out on land division schemes that we will see for certain if there was much truth in the claims that locally active members of the major parties were influential in having farms targeted for resumption that belonged to their political opponents. In September 1964, James O'Brien, a member of Westmeath County Council and a long time member of the Fianna Fáil National Executive, made the very bold statement that political favouritism played a major role in determining whose lands were to be acquired in that county.[44] There had already been many accusations made in the Dáil that the Cumann na nGaedheal government had compulsorily acquired lands belonging to Republicans (and by extension Fianna Fáil supporters) and later that Fianna Fáil supporters had used their *cumainn* to pressurise the Land Commission to send down inspectors to inspect lands of Fine Gael supporters.[45] Similarly, there were cases of landowners being persuaded to sell after witnessing large demonstrations in their area at which local politicians called for the break-up of their estates.[46] There were also cases of TDs threatening the Minister for Lands that unless a particular estate were divided, there would be trouble. In November 1926, for example, John Lyons (Longford–Westmeath, Independent Labour) warned Patrick Hogan that if the Gill estate at Glasson in Westmeath was not acquired and divided by the Land Commission: 'it will be taken some other way'.[47]

Recommending (or even demanding) what lands should be acquired was one thing but determining who should get them was quite another. The MacEoin papers and Aiken's correspondence certainly suggest that constituents believed their politicians to a large extent determined who got what land. Was this the case? In November 1946, Eamon de Valera wrote a most revealing letter to Patrick Moroney in Limerick who had just completed some valuable organisational work in his area on the party's behalf:

> I have yours of October 21st and am glad to note that you will have the local *cumann* registered as soon as possible. I have taken up the question of a further allotment for you with the Minister for Lands and you may be assured of my best efforts on your behalf.[48]

It is, however, extremely difficult to prove whether political collusion of this nature was widespread. Nevertheless, that should not prevent questions being asked. First of all, it is important to recall that according to statute the Minister for Lands had no control over what land was to be acquired, from whom it was to be acquired, to whom it was to be distributed and for how much. These were all excepted matters, the sole prerogative of the land commissioners. In theory, politicians could exert no political influence in determining land division schemes. Thus, Erskine Childers, while Minister for Lands, proclaimed in the Dáil in 1959:

The Land Commission is the organ of government exercising land settlement functions within the Republic. It is a statutory body, operating under the Constitution, pursuant to the Land Acts passed by the Oireachtas. The proceedings of the Land Commission are analogous to the judicial process, being based on the principle of a fair hearing for all interests, whether existing landowners or applicants for land. Neither the Government nor the Minister for Lands will intervene against the impartial decisions of the Land Commission in any of the excepted matters, including acquisition and land division.[49]

That was the official line but there was undoubtedly room for political manoeuvring. When inspectors arrived in an area, they invariably called on local politicians, clergymen, schoolteachers and other notables of the community for 'local direction', a practice that was generally widely accepted.[50] Local dignitaries felt justified in influencing schemes: when one inspector who was charged with dividing an estate near Birr in County Offaly in 1933, took a strictly independent stance, the local Catholic priest, Fr Dan Flynn, wrote to Frank Aiken:

> As Dev's supporters with this long past movement, we naturally ask what the hell is the reason for all this hurried and veratious [*sic*] allotment on the eve of the promised land act. We who have fought the fight for Fianna Fáil in two elections are supposed to look on quietly while the men we put in power allow this estate to be alloted [*sic*] to anyone but a Fianna Fáil serf.[51]

Thus when a community was organised into a Fianna Fáil *cumann*, as in the case above, it would be extremely difficult for an inspector coming into the area for the first time to ignore 'advice' given to him by the officers of the *cumann*. In 1937, the president of the Dunboyne Fianna Fáil *cumann* in Meath, referring to the recent division of a 600-acre estate in the area, explained the advantages of such an approach:

> If Fianna Fáil members got more land than people who were not members it was because the local *cumann* looked after the interests of its members. It saw that the claims were put forward in an intelligent way and submitted to the Land Commission in a proper manner.[52]

Land Commission officials, therefore despite their best intentions, did not have a totally independent hand in making out local schemes. There was invariably a certain amount of moral or physical intimidation from the local community and incessant pressure from local representatives. In July 1933, Frank Aiken admitted in the Dáil that 'the utter impossibility of satisfying the desires of all the people who wish to get possession of land sometimes is a nightmare to those who are immediately responsible for the division of land'.[53] In some instances local groups were accused of heavy-handed tactics. In 1938, James Fitzgerald-Kenney (Mayo, Fine Gael) claimed that when the Land Commission began a division scheme on the Hollymount estate in County Mayo, the local Fianna Fáil club 'by physical force' drove away the labourers involved in setting up the scheme and forced the inspectors to redraw their list of allottees.[54] Fianna Fáil TDs did not apologise for this aggressive approach. In fact in 1939, J. P. Kelly, Fianna Fáil TD for Meath, told the Dáil:

> A point made here this evening is that the Fianna Fáil clubs have been rather active in bringing cases before the Land Commission. It has been suggested that the Land Commission have been influenced to an unusual extent by the secretaries of clubs and by the deputies of the Fianna Fáil Party. I want to state publicly that, as far as Fianna Fáil clubs, the secretaries of such clubs and deputies of the Party are concerned, we only state the cases, the circumstances and the needs of our members. In doing that, if we do it very forcibly, and if we are able to place our cases in a better light before the Land Commission than the deputies and clubs of the Fine Gael Party, that is not our fault. Even if our activity is resented, I can assure the members of the Opposition that it will continue until we have placed the cases of all our members clearly before the Land Commission with the object of getting redress for their grievances.[55]

In 1945, Oliver J. Flanagan told the Dáil that some years previously he had been secretary of a Fianna Fáil *cumann* in Offaly when a local estate, known as Robinsons of the Rock, was being divided. A Land Commission inspector called to him and informed Flanagan that 'I was the first man in that district that he had received instructions for the Minister to come to because I was secretary of the Fianna Fáil club'. In the subsequent scheme of division, Flanagan claimed that 'on every occasion the applicant's political affiliations were investigated' and concluded:

> I would not be speaking with a clear conscience if I did not openly admit that, when I was secretary of a Fianna Fáil club, I saw the most corrupt and the most disgraceful things done to keep individuals out of land that I have ever known in all of my years of public life.[56]

Accusations of political patronage had played a dominant role in land-related debates in the Dáil since 1923. First Cumann na nGaedheal was accused of acting partially towards its supporters. In June 1926, Patrick Hogan (Clare, Labour – not to be confused with his namesake the Minister for Agriculture) objected in the Dáil to the way in which the Land Commission had divided an estate in his county: 'It is a matter of some concern and what is generally believed is that it is the sole survivor of the Cumann na nGaedheal organisation there who is responsible for the distribution of this land.'[57] During the same debate, James Everett (Wicklow, Labour) claimed to have definite proof that only members of the Cumann na nGaedheal party were allotted lands in his constituency.[58]

In 1927, Fianna Fáil took their seats in the Dáil for the first time and the government came under increasing criticism. P. J. Ruttledge (Mayo, Fianna Fáil) claimed that he could produce 'dozens of newspapers where at meeting after meeting of branches of Cumann na nGaedheal in North Mayo the people were told to join Cumann na nGaedheal as the lands were going to be divided'.[59] S. E. Holt (Leitrim–Sligo, Fianna Fáil) produced a document in the Dáil in April 1928 headed 'Irish Land Commission: division of farms at Cashel, Garristown and Deerpark' which requested applicants to furnish claims to J. J. Costello before 1 June 1925 'by order of the Land Commission'. But Holt pointed out: 'John J. Costello is not a land commissioner. He is not a resident commissioner. He is not an inspector. John J. Costello is secretary of the Cumann na nGaedheal organisation at Drumlion, County Roscommon' which meant to Holt that 'it is the Cumann na nGaedheal organisation that divides land'.[60]

Further accusations were made that the Cumann na nGaedheal government was facilitating their supporters in congested areas by giving them large tracts of land in the east. In the late 1920s, the government was accused of bringing a migrant from Kerry to Kilcock, giving him a holding of around 200 acres, the valuation of which was £80 higher than the one he had left, a house worth £2,000 plus 'the run of several hundred acres of land for a number of years' (on conacre).[61] In March 1928, Thomas Derrig (Fianna Fáil, Carlow–Kilkenny) claimed that when the Burton Hall estate was divided in Carlow

> people who never tilled an acre of soil in their lives, and who had forty acres of land – private gentlemen with private incomes – got parcels of land while 10 or 12 labourers who were living and working on the estate, through the operations of the Land Commission, have not alone lost their weekly wage of 30/- or whatever it was, but it is now proposed to throw them out without giving them a garden.[62]

The underlying accusation was that the large farmers who supported Cumann na nGaedheal in the area were being catered for with even more lands at the expense of the small farmers and agricultural labourers. From an early stage it was alleged by Cumann na nGaedheal's detractors that those with land, position, political influence (whether local or national) or a combination of all three were much more likely to secure farms or enlargements than those bereft of all three. In 1929 F. J. Carty (Leitrim–Sligo, Fianna Fáil) claimed that:

> When land is being divided in my constituency, it is not the most deserving applicants that secure allotments. The principal key-men and supporters of Cumann na nGaedheal invariably receive first preference. . . . Prominent followers of Cumann na nGaedheal were brought, some of them a distance of three or four miles, and given land at Raughly on the Gore Booth estate; while the claims of other small landholders and fishermen were ignored. Quite recently when land was being divided on the Mitchell estate near Dromore West, the local Cumann na nGaedheal secretary was brought in from an outside estate and given a section of these lands, to the exclusion of more deserving applicants including those who formerly obtained conacre tillage there.[63]

The same year, Richard Walsh (Mayo, Fianna Fáil) was incensed by the way the Browne estate in Castlebar had been divided. Those who had land, he argued, obtained more land, while those who needed it most received none. To compound the injustice, he said, 'The local secretary of Cumann na nGaedheal, who was in a very affluent position, also got land'.[64]

Of course, when Fianna Fáil took office in 1932, the tide of accusation merely turned. Patrick Hogan quickly criticised Fianna Fáil for building a mass of support at grass roots level by manipulating the land question and effectively promising land for votes:

> We all know that land is rather an acute political issue in Ireland. It is supposed to be good business politically. We all know that deputies on the benches opposite have been going round the country pointing out that all the land in Ireland would be divided in a year if only certain people got the power to do the right thing.[65]

There was uproar in the Dáil in December 1935 when Deputy John Fitzgerald-Kenney (Mayo, Fine Gael) announced that a local doctor and two schoolteachers had been sold plots of seven acres and two of five acres respectively by the Land Commission at an average of around £13 per acre on the division of a farm at Kilcommon in Mayo. This was land that had originally been acquired for the relief of local congestion. How then could it be sold to these individuals Fitzgerald-Kenney wondered.

> We know that the dispensary doctor was one of the very best canvassers that Fianna Fáil had at the last election in South Mayo. We know that every patient who came to that doctor's dispensary was canvassed on behalf of the Fianna Fáil Party. . . . Now he is getting his reward; he is getting his reward at the expense of

the state; he is getting his reward at the expense of the owners of congested holdings in the County Mayo. . . . I need hardly say, of course, that the schoolteachers
who received those plots are also staunch supporters of the present administration.[66]

The people of Kilcommon were understandably aggrieved by the fact and
were, according to M. M. Nally (Mayo, Cumann na nGaedheal), 'practically
unanimous in their condemnation of this highhanded action of the Land
Commission in selling land to professional people who enjoy substantial
salaries from the state'.[67]

There is little doubting the fact that those who established the Fianna Fáil
party on a solid local foundation were 'looked after'. The three professionals in
Kilcommon were treated in the same way as the Limerick man that de Valera
promised to secure land for in the letter quoted above. Similarly, in April 1950,
James Dillon, the Minister for Agriculture, could point out in the Dáil that of
eight allottees in a recent division scheme in Monaghan, seven had been
personating agents for the Fianna Fáil candidate at the last election.[68] These
were catered for in the same way as Free State soldiers had been during the
period of the Cumann na nGaedheal government. Dillon's claim with regard
to Monaghan illustrates the fact that a party did not have to be in office in
order to exert influence: much depended upon the strength at grass roots level
and that the establishment of *cumainn* or clubs gave a formal structure to the
lobbying process.[69] The point has already been made that an inspector coming
into an area would have to be of very strong character in order to ignore
pressure from locals banded together in a local *cumann* or club. It is important
to remember that it was in the locality that the allotment scheme was drawn
up. The inspector invariably depended upon the knowledge of local
dignitaries. He drew up an official list of applicants on which he noted who
recommended each of them. The Ministers for Lands were always keenly
interested in surveying the final list of allottees in each scheme and sometimes
were very annoyed by what they saw. One former executive officer who worked
in the Land Commission from 1947 to 1955 related a story about a very angry
Sean Moylan marching up and down the corridors of the Land Commission
offices in absolute rage, waving a list of allottees in the air, and shouting: 'Who
gave land to that hoor?'[70]

The Moylan story is much more revealing than might appear on the
surface. (It would be interesting to know what happened to the unfortunate
inspector after Moylan had identified him.) First of all, regardless of the
excepted matters, the Minister for Lands obviously kept himself well informed
with regard to final lists of allottees (and Moylan was certainly not the only
one in this respect). By the very nature of things, civil servants, no matter how
senior, were not immune to political influence and the point has already been

made that the appointment of two extra land commissioners by Fianna Fáil in 1933 was a deliberate political ploy to ensure the party had its own men in place at this strategic time. That one of them in particular, Eamonn Mansfield, was appointed with a particular agenda in mind is clear from P.J. Sammon's recollections of working with him:

> Right from his appointment as commissioner in 1933, Eamonn Mansfield displayed an unflagging zeal in performing his new duties. In particular, he showed a special interest in all those applicants for land who claimed to have pre-Truce IRA service. He frequently refused to sanction schemes until further local enquiries were pursued . . . I recall being called to Commissioner Mansfield's room one day in the late 1930s. It was a warm summer day and he was working away on a large scheme in my area. He had the scheme, applicants' files, file of applications for land and other papers spread out all over his room. He was in his shirt sleeves and was beavering away at some applicants who had claims for pre-truce IRA service. His trouble was that some of these did not figure amongst those selected for parcels. From his questions he seemed to be examining into how deeply I had delved into the claims of the rejected applicants in whom he was so interested.[71]

That politicians wanted to present themselves as brokers in land division schemes is undeniable; that they successfully acted as brokers in many, many cases is highly probable. Again, in his Land Commission memoirs, Sammon relates a revealing anecdote about a higher executive officer in the Commission who, around the mid-1950s, dared to criticise the 'highly convoluted' draft rules regarding compulsory acquisition prepared by the Commission's legal adviser. When the assistant secretary of the Commission read the criticism, he called Sammon and another official to his office and berated them:

> What sort of a dog's dinner have the pair of you dished up to me here? Don't you know that the Legal Adviser is a Fianna Fáil man and if he sets eyes on what you people have written here, he will go at once to complain to the Minister and get us all into serious trouble.[72]

In July 1957, a Department of Lands memorandum prepared for the government proclaimed: 'Allocation is fairly administered. In a sample survey one third of the land was allotted to persons who made no representations to TDs.'[73] Did 'fairly administered' mean that the two-thirds majority received lands because they had made representations to their local representatives? That year, the new Minister for Lands, Erskine Childers, decided to end the practice that had existed since 1923, in which the names of persons who were recommending prospective allottees appeared on the official list of applicants.

He argued ambiguously that the practice had not influenced the Land Commission in drawing up their final lists of allottees. If that was the case, why ban it? Furthermore, during the speech in which he advocated that the practice should cease, he attempted to draw attention to the ineffectiveness of the process:

> In one typical estate, 11 applicants who had not solicited recommendations were successful as compared with only five who had solicited recommendations. In another case, nine were successful without representations as compared with only two on whose behalf representations were made. In yet another case, six were successful without representations as compared with only three who had solicited recommendations.[74]

Surely a success rate of 38 per cent (and no doubt one grossly understated) amongst those who had representations made on their behalf speaks for itself, even if all other factors were taken into consideration.

At any rate, in his first Lands Estimate speech in 1957, Childers informed the Dáil that he would be sending a letter to all TDs to remind them that the selection of allottees was an excepted matter over which the Minister for Lands had no control. P. J. Sammon maintains that this new situation lasted only a matter of weeks because 'the Fianna Fáil TDs were up in arms' and following a party meeting, Childers was forced to drop his proposed approach.[75] At the very least, TDs did not want to surrender the perception that they were influential in determining the outcome of acquisition and division schemes. And as proof that old habits die hard, it is worth noting that as late as the 1980s agricultural commentators were highly critical of (and quite simply fed up with) politicians' vote-catching tactics that were of no benefit to the agricultural economy. Des Maguire, editor of the *Farmers' Journal*, summed up the rather ridiculous nature of this continued practice: 'Making land available to as many applicants as possible when estates are being divided may be good for votes, but does little to relieve congestion, unless recipients can reach the comparable income from enlargements.'[76]

It is perhaps understandable that Land Commission officials, because they were civil servants subordinate to the Minister for Lands and his department, were frequently apprehensive about drawing upon themselves the wrath of important politicians. In 1946, James Dillon accused Fianna Fáil of 'rotten, corrupt interference' in the work of the Land Commission since 1932. He conjectured that certain members of the Land Commission who had strenuously fought such interference had suffered as a result. And he was even more certain that files that would enlighten the public on such matters would never see the light of day.[77] They have not done so up to now!

IV DIVIDED LOCAL COMMUNITIES

While the Land Commission brought hope to certain sectors of local communities, it also brought a great deal of fear and apprehension to others. It generated suspicion and hostility amongst neighbours. During the 1920s, it alienated the small farmers and the landless by a tardy approach to acquisition and division. From the early 1930s, the hopes and fears generated by the 1933 Land Act politically polarised communities between those who supported land acquisition and division and who looked to Fianna Fáil to expedite the process and those large farmers and graziers who wanted to protect security of tenure who looked to Cumann na nGaedheal/Fine Gael.

The work of the Land Commission was, for obvious reasons, most resented by those whose estates and farms were compulsorily acquired. There was little justification in claims of discrimination on religious grounds – large Catholic owners were as likely to have their lands acquired as Protestants.[78] However, it is true that the class that initially suffered most was the old landlord class (which tended to be predominantly Protestant), the big house owners, who had sold the bulk of their estates under the pre-independence land acts. The grandees had received colossal sums of money from these sales and even after their debts and charges had been redeemed they were left with substantial sums to invest. Unfortunately for them events from the Russian Revolution in 1917 to the Wall Street Crash in 1929 completely devastated most of their share portfolios with the result that they really only had their remaining lands to support their houses and their lifestyles. When the Land Commission began to acquire these lands, there was no option for many owners other than to hand over their houses as well or simply to vacate them and let them fall into dereliction.[79]

From the 1880s at least, there had been very little sympathy for those who had retained untenanted lands or who were ranchers within local communities. During the revolutionary period the expropriation of lands from these classes by local agrarian radicals had been a regular occurrence. Cork IRA leader, Tom Barry, resented the fact that the rich fertile areas around Bandon, Clonakilty and Skibbereen were 'in the hands of a small minority, and the large majority of the people had a hard struggle for existence'. He despised the type of lifestyle that characterised big houses as well as 'the sycophants and lickspittles, happy in their master's benevolence [who] never thought to question how he had acquired his thousand acres, his cattle and his wealth, or thought of themselves as the descendants of the rightful owners of those robbed lands.'[80] 'Many a time', wrote Tipperary IRA leader, Dan Breen, reminiscing on his youth, 'I walked for three or four hours without meeting even one human being'. All that was to be seen in his area of Tipperary was a big house here and there, surrounded by expansive green fields in which no man was visible. He concluded: 'Landlordism, the willing instrument of British rule had wrought this desolation. I renewed my resolve to do my share in bringing about the change that must come sooner or later.'[81]

There was no more sympathy in the Dáil after independence. In early 1923, William Sears (Mayo, Cumann na nGaedheal) spoke of 'a die hard section' amongst landlords who refused to sell their estates: 'They did not care a straw for patriotic motives; they were stiff-necked and selfish, and because of that selfishness we have this legacy from the old Land War days to deal with in this parliament.' According to him, tenants had to be considered first and landlords second in the forthcoming act.[82] When Patrick Hogan set out the terms, Sears praised him for the 'courageous manner' in which he had dealt with landlords:

> the actions of these men in the past put them completely out of court with regard to any claim they would have on our consideration. I think most of the landlords should have accepted the terms of the Wyndham Act. An Act that was drafted by a British Tory government contained as much as they could reasonably expect. Terms arranged by the British House of Lords should have been good enough for landlords here. They did not accept those. . . . They held out . . . for their pound of flesh. . . . Perhaps it is fitting that they should have held out until a national parliament would dispose of the last remnant of Irish landlordism.[83]

While the 1923 Land Act was more conservative than Sears understood and fairer to landlords than he might have wished, there did remain a groundswell of opinion that traditional landlords should be relieved of their lands. When some estates escaped the acquisition net for one reason or another, local TDs lobbied determinedly to have them divided. In December 1950, for example, the Minister for Lands was asked if the Land Commission had 'considered the propriety of dividing the estate of Lord Decies' at Kinnity, County Offaly, 'amongst local deserving applicants'.[84] In March of the following year, the minister was asked what steps the Land Commission had taken for the acquisition of the Cox estate and the Abraham estate both in Laois.[85] The following month enquiries were made about the acquisition of the Louth Hall estate at Tallanstown.[86] In July, M. J. Keyes (Limerick, Labour) asked the minister when the Coll estate in Limerick was to be acquired and divided and Oliver J. Flanagan asked if the minister would receive a deputation from the local land committee with regard to the division of the Bennett estate at Clareen in Offaly.[87]

When the number of large untenanted estates began to dwindle (by the 1930s, the average size of the estate being acquired was down to around 290 acres and falling rapidly), and the 1936 Land Act proposed to acquire holdings worked in an unsatisfactory manner, local communities became rent with fear and suspicion. The role and nature of land hunger in this cannot be overstated. It was a hunger that was only too real to contemporaries. In 1938, William Davin (Leix–Offaly, Labour) told the Dáil that 'there is land hunger in almost every area in my constituency where estates are available for division'.[88] The Monaghan farmer–poet/author, Patrick Kavanagh, exposed his land-greedy neighbours of Inniskeen in his semi-autobiographical novel *Tarry Flynn* (1948) set in the late 1930s. In 1936, James Dillon, who was to become Fine Gael TD for Monaghan the following year, launched a stinging attack upon the Land Commission accusing it of

> creating through the country a belief that, if you are covetous of your neighbour's land, all you have to do is start a Fianna Fáil *cumann* and move a resolution asking the Land Commission to have the lands of so-and-so divided amongst the members.[89]

Dillon was of course extremely astute in his understanding of the Irish rural psyche and equally adept at describing it. He knew of the fear of the 'grabber', the one who would cast his greedy eye over the best holding and want it. He knew that 'the country people believe that representations . . . [for the acquisition or resumption of farms] carry great weight in the Land Commission'.[90] In 1936, Dillon addressed the Dáil on the threat that had been posed to security of tenure by the 1936 Land Act that empowered the Land Commission to sell holdings on which occupiers had defaulted in the payment of their annuities:

> I invite deputies who are living in the country to ask themselves this question: going about amongst their own neighbours, do their own neighbours living on the land feel that they have fixity of tenure? Do they not all live in a constant state of anxiety that they will get a notice from the Land Commission that inspectors are going down to inspect the land with a view to acquisition? . . . As a result of Fianna Fáil's policy since they took over the Land Commission, men are writing to them continually, asking them to send inspectors to inspect farms with a view to acquisition that ought never to have been inspected, and I say that the mental anguish and misery which is caused to small farmers by having these inspections carried out is an outrage on our people.[91]

As we saw in chapter 6, it was not so much the actual number of inspections that were carried out as the threat that they might be that sometimes retarded relationships in a community. Take the case of the farmer who wrote to Frank Aiken in 1969 about a neighbour who joined a Fianna Fáil cumann in Bellingam [sic] recently, not from any sense of loyalty to you or Mr. [Pádraig] Faulkner or the Fianna Fáil Party, but to enrich his own pocket in any way he can, including trying to get this little field of mine, now since he was so smart I will tell you something about him . . .[92]

In a way this letter epitomised the effect that the Land Commission had upon the psychology of rural Ireland. It captured the narrow-mindedness that grew out of suspicion and fear. It is reminiscent of the rural Ireland depicted so dolefully and caricatured so effectively by contemporaries such as Frank Hall in his *Pictorial Weekly* that ran on RTÉ television during the 1960s and early 1970s. But it also captured something much more important – the need of the individual to use whatever political wire-pulling was necessary in order to protect his land so that it would survive in the family name and on into the next generation at least. (If he was to destroy the character of his neighbour in order to achieve that, then so be it and the likelihood is that the Land Commission secretariat received thousands of similar letters every year during the course of its existence.) To underestimate the need to do that, or the lengths that people were prepared to go to maintain or gain access to land would be to underestimate the land question after independence which, perhaps more than anything else, shaped the political mind of rural Ireland.

V ATTITUDES TO THE LAND COMMISSION, 1923–73

Already it has been claimed in this book that the Irish Land Commission was the most controversial state body in existence in independent Ireland. Charged with the implementation of government land division policy, it was inevitable that it would attract criticism from every conceivable angle. During the 1920s and the 1930s, TDs frequently questioned the wisdom of passing a huge sum of money in the annual Department of Lands budget 'in order to allow the inefficiency of the Land Commission to continue'.[93] Even land commissioners themselves were not always entirely happy with the workings of the Commission. In 1943, Eamon Mansfield wrote: 'Personally I have no hesitation in saying that owing to a multiplicity of avoidable causes, mainly legal bungling, the huge and costly Irish Land Commission machine did not in the pre-war years justify its existence, much less will the suggested post-Emergency programme.'[94]

The attitude towards the Land Commission was perhaps most negative amongst the old landed class and the large farmers who had their lands compulsorily acquired or resumed. In 1989, Senator David Norris summed up his personal attitude to it, which admittedly was somewhat ambiguous:

I come from a background that did not always regard the Land Commission and its operations with unmixed admiration; I can think of family and friends who regarded it with a certain horror, like some rapacious wolf lying in wait until the proprietor became so feeble that they could be gobbled up but I have now come to the enlightened position where I regard it as a useful historical instrument in giving to people of no property, the men of no property, whom the great figures of the 19th century strove to represent, some degree of investment in their own country.[95]

In the old landed class circles, the contribution made by the Land Commission not only to their impoverishment but also to the destruction of country houses was widely condemned. In many cases where the Land Commission took over an estate on which there was a vacated country house, it simply demolished it. One country house owner told me that he had only one word to describe the Land Commission: 'Vandals'.[96] Yet it was not until the late 1950s that the Commission came in for any type of public criticism for its role in the demolition of country houses, the case of Shanbally Castle in Tipperary being one of the first.[97]

At various stages during the course of its existence, the Land Commission was accused *inter alia* of using draconian powers to acquire land; being discriminatory in regard to whose lands were acquired; criticised for its perceived pedestrian progress in dividing estates; accused of being politically manipulated by power elites in the various localities; being unfair in its allocation of lands; condemned for wasting valuable exchequer funds in the allocation of free grants and exorbitant expenditure on estate improvements prior to division and for then not maintaining the infrastructure that it had been responsible for creating; and of disturbing the peace of localities by bringing in migrants and giving them preference over deserving local applicants for land allotments. In 1945, after a very much-extended debate on the Lands budget, the Minister for Lands, Sean Moylan, summed up the old, jaded and oft-repeated speeches he had heard from the Opposition benches:

In the Land Commission, according to its critics in the Dáil, we are confronted with a miracle of human perversity – a department that is completely obsolete, ineffective, with a vested interest contempt for public opinion. We have the further miracle of the possibility of the continuance in being of a department which is completely unwanted by Deputies in the Dáil.[98]

But Moylan brushed aside these criticisms:

Long ago such a department should have succumbed to the accumulated consequences of its, more or less, catastrophic errors. However, it is still in existence and, in spite of all the criticisms, it is, in my belief, doing its job as well as any human organisation could do it in adverse circumstances.[99]

Admittedly, it was impossible for the Land Commission to please all of the people all of the time or even some of the people some of the time. Land Commission decisions and operations could never, in the nature of things, receive wholehearted public approval. As T. W. Enright (Laois–Offaly, Fine Gael) told the Dail in 1971: 'The Land Commission are [*sic*] a body who [*sic*] are criticised on all sides. I believe that even if Solomon were at their head, he, in his wisdom, would fail to satisfy the demands of everybody in regard to land division.'[100] Perhaps the real crux of the problem lay in the fact that government land division policy failed to take into account that farm viability was a constantly changing notion and that the 20-acre 'viable farm' of the 1920s, might not be viable some years down the road (which, of course, proved to be the case when it was raised at various stages up to 45 acres in the 1960s).[101]

If the Land Commission could be so bitterly criticised at times, why was it not dissolved? Quite simply, before the 1980s no government would dare contemplate doing so. As David Seth Jones has emphasised, successive governments gave a commitment to the people of independent Ireland that land-hunger, unemployment and poverty in the countryside would be eradicated through the distribution of land.[102] This, as we have seen, is what was promised by revolutionary Sinn Féin and despite the demise of that particular party in the post-Civil War period, it was widely held in Dáil circles that it was the duty of those who succeeded in power to see it through. For that purpose the Land Commission was reconstituted in 1923, and even if its progress was not to everybody's satisfaction, its continued existence was perceived to be much more important than its dissolution and this perception remained for as long as attitudes persisted that attributed social status and significance to land ownership. The result was that access to land was primarily through inheritance and only to a minor extent through purchase.[103] As we have seen, farmers persisted in holding on to land long after they were able to work it productively.[104]

While, by the 1930s, most European countries had experienced a movement away from the land, the then Irish Minister for Lands, Frank Aiken, was happy to inform the Dail that 'our people are still animated by the virile and healthy desire to till the soil'.[105] And, of course, political survival not only for individual TDs, but also for governments, depended largely upon their approach to land division. Small farmers, congests, migrants, labourers, representatives of evicted tenants and members of the pre-Truce IRA cumulatively accounted for a sizeable proportion of the electorate. From the 1940s, some cabinet members might have been sceptical about the future of land division, but they were slow to reflect this in their public speeches. It certainly was not reflected in any diminution of interest shown by back-benchers in estates to be acquired and divided in their constituencies.[106]

The social aspect of the Land Commission's work should also perhaps be highlighted. Its incidental work probably had a much more important bearing upon the reduction of local land feuds and disputes between neighbours than has been acknowledged; in other words, it did much to stabilise the fabric of rural society. Before purchase moneys were advanced and holdings vested in purchasers, a huge amount of work had to be done in fixing boundaries, settling rights-of-way and turbary rights, allocating liabilities for drainage and deciding the ownership of mineral and sporting rights. The purchaser subsequently had a well-defined title to his lands and its appurtenances, if any, which cleared the way of potential sources of friction, dispute and litigation. In 1959, Michael Moran, Fianna Fáil Minister for Lands, told the Agricultural Science Association that

> Occasionally . . . it will prove impossible to meet the demands of a local crank or bully, but, in general, the Land Commission has been instrumental in resolving many rural disputes, some of which have persisted for years and involved the disputants in costly litigation. . . . In this way the work of the Land Commission contributes towards the widespread harmony and good-neighbourly relations in rural parts, which make for a happy and contented countryside.[107]

It is arguable that the Land Commission contributed to a cleaner and tidier countryside, replacing rural slums with neat modern houses and outoffices. From 1923 to 1959, over 20,000 houses were built by the Land Commission. Extensive improvement works were carried out – roads were constructed, drainage was undertaken, fencing was erected and water supplies installed on farms (from 1923 to 1959, 300 wells were sunk for domestic water supplies). The social dimensions of the Land Commission's work were therefore considerable. Finally, the value of the Commission's regulatory function in regard to subdivision and control of access to land by non-qualified persons should not be underrated.

David Seth Jones also makes the very important link between land division and Catholic social thinking as enunciated in the papal encyclicals *Quadragesimo Anno* (1931) and *Mater et Magistra* (1961).[108] The latter, in particular, suggested the virtue of the family farm and with its references to land redistribution and the promotion of state intervention in the economy, it held certain appeal to the government of the time.[109] Thus in 1967, the then Minister for Lands, Michael Moran, could justify the continuation of land division as 'the practical application of Christian social principles as exemplified in the papal encyclicals'.[110]

One must also remember that if the Land Commission was the most controversial body, it was also one of the most powerful civil service bodies. By 1983, the Land Commission still employed up to 750 people despite the fact that it had only 48,000 acres on hand for rearrangement. In the early 1970s, at a time when there was almost £3 million being paid out per annum in Land Commission salaries alone, there were rumours that the operations of the Commission would be curtailed in the near future. When these rumours began to circulate, P. J. Sammon, on behalf of the higher officers (indoor and outdoor) of the Land Commission, wrote to the Minister for Lands, Sean Flanagan (Mayo, Fianna Fáil) and the government in January 1971. The memorandum expressed concern that the recent decision to suspend land acquisition indicated that the government intended to phase out the Commission. This, the memorandum argued, should not happen; too much remained to be done with regard to land structure reform, particularly in the scheduled congested areas and the Land Commission was the only body with 'the expertise, the knowledge and the trained manpower which could tackle the problem with any real hope of success'.[111] The memorandum was highly suggestive of what might happen if the Land Commission was dissolved:

> We live in an age of forceful agitation often culminating in actual violence. Land is a highly emotive factor in rural Ireland; we feel the existence of a revitalised Land Commission will constitute a bulwark against agrarian disturbances here in the decades ahead, especially when non-nationals of other member countries of EEC come to acquire land here, under the EEC's right of establishment and in face of pressures from our own people.[112]

EIGHT

CONCLUSION

The Irish Land Commission is the instrument by which the agriculturists of Ireland have been lifted from the misery and despair of a condition bordering on serfdom to the dignity of peasant proprietorship.
KEVIN O'SHIEL
'The work of the Land Commission' (1949), p. 59.

One could write the history of the last 100 years of this state by simply writing a history of the struggle for land. At the centre of this struggle is the Land Commission.
RUAIRÍ QUINN
(1991).

—

This book has focused on the interrelationship between land and politics in independent Ireland over a 50-year period from the passing of the influential Hogan Land Act and the reconstitution of the Irish Land Commission in 1923 to Ireland's entry to the EEC in 1973. Until now, the implications of this relationship had not been fully explored.

The book challenges the widely held orthodoxy that there was no land question in independent Ireland. Such orthodoxy has contended that after dominating Irish social and political life for generations, the land question somewhat mysteriously disappeared when the majority of tenant farmers became proprietors under the terms of the 1903 and 1909 Land Acts, thereby defusing the potential for agrarianism. This approach fails to consider the grievances which came to the surface during the ranch war of 1906–9, and which resurfaced in a possibly more virulent form from 1917. These grievances were part of the legacy of the pre-1922 Land Acts (1881–1909) that created a mass of peasant proprietors, while simultaneously failing to deal with the continued concentration of large tracts of land in the hands of landlords and graziers, except on a very limited basis in the designated congested areas. These grievances were easily exploited by militant nationalists during the early years of the Irish revolution (indeed, just as they had been by constitutional nationalists only a short time before).

Since the late 1970s, historians such as David Fitzpatrick, Paul Bew, Charles Townshend and Peter Hart have attempted to explain the the role of agrarianism in Irish nationalism and revolution. While work remains to be done in this area, this book has shown that the contribution of the 1923 Land Act to tempering agrarian radicalism by cutting off an important supply line of support to the anti-Treatyites during the Civil War, especially in the west, should not be underestimated. Agrarian radicals were warned that any further recalcitrant acts would automatically disqualify them from any grant of land and few were subsequently willing to present test cases to a government that had already shown its resolve to deal with agrarian disorder through the establishment of the controversial Special Infantry Corps.

When the achievement of peasant proprietorship had failed to provide the febrifuge to agrarian ills that had been anticipated, a weighty concern remained after independence that demanded an agrarian based social policy to relieve rural poverty, end emigration, tackle unemployment and dispose of the potentially explosive social problem of land hunger through land acquisition and redistribution. The relief of congestion was deemed a national imperative, particularly when it was realised that it was much more widespread than had been accepted by earlier land legislation that had established the Congested Districts Board, ostensibly to oversee the reform of land structures within the limited geographical area of the specifically designated areas of the west.

The interminable hunger for land was arguably heightened by the reconstitution of the Irish Land Commission in 1923 and the terms of the land act of the same year that offered hope to hundreds of thousands of smallholders and landless people in Ireland that there would be a revolutionary redistribution of lands resulting from the compulsory acquisition of sprawling untenanted estates and the break-up of the large grazing farms, for so long the targets of agrarian radicals. Such compulsory acquisition had been attempted on a limited scale in the past through the aegis of the Congested District Board. The 1923 act promised (or at least was perceived by large sectors of the rural community to promise) a much more complete redistribution of lands that would be carried out on a national scale, rather than being limited to the previously designated congested areas.

Acquisition and division, with all their threats and promises, ensured that after independence Irish society remained animated by land issues. Rural society remained in a state of continual flux where some people lived with the hope that the government, through the working of the Land Commission, would improve their social and economic situation by giving them more land, while others lived with the fear and the insecurity that the Commission might compulsorily acquire their land. The possibilities associated with land division quickly gripped the rural imagination in a way that no other rural policy had done in the past – because those who most desired land wanted to believe that the utopian ideal of 'the land for the people' was now attainable. Thus the land question remained possibly the most potent political issue in rural Ireland long after independence and one of the great determinants of political survival or decline.

By extension, the Land Commission became the most important state institution of the twentieth century – its impact on rural society matched only by the Catholic Church – and the most important vehicle of social engineering in modern Ireland. A key aspect in its social engineering policy was the migration of thousands of smallholders (and large farmers in the early years of Cumann na nGaedheal) from congested areas of the west to expansive grasslands of the east, broken up for the first time in generations in order to facilitate the creation of thousands of small tillage or mixed farms. In this way, an extremely costly land division programme was possibly the key component to Irish social policy for decades, something that has not been readily acknowledged.

Outwardly, the major parties supported policies that purported to promise land for almost everyone. No party could afford to stand against land division. Successive governments perceived land division to be the most logical means of overcoming unemployment, poverty, emigration and land hunger. While the majority went along with this, others were not so convinced. Within Fianna Fáil, for example, internal factions divided in their opinion on the merits of different approaches to economic development. There were those who saw the advantages of the free market, commercialising model (supported by senior members of Fianna Fáil such as Sean Moylan, Sean Lemass, Erskine Childers, Sean MacEntee) and those who clung to the autarchic Sinn Féin smallholding model whose traditionalist adherents included Eamon de Valera. At the end of the day, it was the traditionalists who tended to exert most influence.

Acquisition and division also became a notoriously divisive issue outside the Dáil. For example, it pitted the rights of the western migrants against local inhabitants in eastern counties leading to a great deal of local tension. Throughout the country, there was a ceaseless conflict between the landholders' desire for security and that of the smallholders and the landless for (more) land. Land reform policy all too often set neighbour against neighbour. As late as 1971, Jim Tully (Meath, Labour) contended:

> I . . . think it is wrong that too much emphasis is put on the information given to a
> Land Commission inspector by people other than the applicant. There is a
> tendency on the part of everybody whose job it is to get information to go to a
> neighbour for information about a particular person. This is wrong. The applicant
> should be allowed to make his own case and to stand or fall on that case. Let him
> look for recommendations if he wants to but let us not have the situation where

some of his neighbours who do not like him can put in a 'spoke' to try to prevent him from getting something to which he is morally entitled.[1]

Tully's remark epitomised what R. V. Comerford has referred to as 'the great constant of history', the fact that 'manoeuvring for survival and advancement of self and family through access to material resources and socio-political advantage is the great constant of history'.[2] In rural Ireland, nowhere was this more obvious than in the scramble for land. For most of the period under study here, no other social issue was as important to political survival – not only for individuals, but also for parties – as land division. No other socio-political issue dominated parliamentary debates and question times over such an extended period.

By the time the Land Commission published its final report in 1987, over 1.5 million acres had been acquired and redistributed under the various land acts from 1923, while another 840,000 acres acquired under previous land acts (for which the Commission became responsible after 1923) were also divided, giving an aggregated total of 2.34 million acres. Around 114,000 families benefited from having their holdings vested in them (or lost out because they were resumed by the Commission prior to vesting because they were required for the relief of congestion), while another 134,000 families (at least) benefited from enlargements, new holdings or accommodation plots. Again that represents a total of 248,000 families, a huge proportion of the total population of rural Ireland. Furthermore, between 1923 and 1974, Land Commission migration schemes moved up to 3,000 families in colonies, groups or singly.[3] Add to these figures the thousands of families who lost land through compulsory acquisition (not just landlords but many large farmers who had purchased their holdings under the pre-1922 Land Acts), and it becomes very clear that after 1923 the working of the Land Commission impacted positively or negatively on a significant percentage of families living in rural independent Ireland. Thus in 1992, Sean Dooney (a former employee of the Department of Agriculture) described, with some justification, events of the previous 70 years as 'a revolution without bloodshed that changed the whole structure of rural society and brought to it a great measure of peace'.[4]

Whether deliberate or not, Dooney's use of the phrase 'a great measure of peace' suggests that it was not total. It is accepted that agrarian crime of the type associated with the extended Land War of the late nineteenth and early twentieth centuries disappeared after independence (except for the odd sporadic outbreak). The achievement of political independence for the 26 counties and, therefore, the separation of the land struggle from the national struggle may be significant in this respect. But the principle enshrined in the 1937 constitution of settling as many families on the land as was practicable,

therefore creating a 'nation of small farmers', did not provide the dignified
future that had been previously imagined. In fact, for most of the period from
the 1920s to the 1970s it was overshadowed by the humiliation of drudgery that
was associated with small farm life during periods of economic depression. By
the mid-1960s, even the 45-acre standard allotted farms were not considered
large enough to be economically viable. It is arguable that it was not so much
land division as Ireland's entry into the EEC in the early 1970s (allied to growing
part-time employment opportunities) that gave the small farming class a
degree of social dignity.

Above all, land reform policy did not bring peace of mind. The trepidation
and fear that stalked rural Ireland of the Land Commission coming to acquire
estates or inspect farms with a view to their resumption certainly did not
engender social contentment. And this was probably quite easily matched by
the anxiety and frustration felt by those who waited for land or who were
ultimately disappointed not to get any.

Appendix I

Table 2.1 The number and size of holdings in Ireland in 1917 (32 counties).

	Leinster	Munster	Ulster	Connaught	Ireland
Less than 1 acre	39,131	33,261	32,022	8,373	112,787
More than 1 and less than 5 acres	13,085	9,678	16,387	8,469	47,619
More than 5 and less than 10 acres	10,645	8,076	27,920	19,421	66,062
More than 10 and less than 15 acres	8,211	7,062	25,072	19,411	59,756
More than 15 and less than 30 acres	18,009	20,221	48,593	36,306	123,129
More than 30 and less than 50 acres	13,268	20,494	24,555	14,071	72,388
More than 50 and less than 100 acres	13,055	22,406	15,427	6,588	57,476
More than 100 and less than 200 acres	6,889	9,789	4,112	2,369	23,159
More than 200 and less than 500 acres	2,966	2,901	1,153	1,211	8,231
More than 500 acres	666	481	310	510	1,967
TOTALS	125,925	134,369	195,551	116,729	572,574

Source: Agricultural Statistics for Ireland With Detailed Report for the Year 1917

[Cmd 1316], HC 1921, lxi. 135, p. xiv.

Table 2.2 The total number of agrarian crimes reported to the police for the periods 1 January 1919–31 December 1919 and 1 January 1920–31 December 1920.

Type of crime	1 Jan. 1919–31 Dec. 1919	1 Jan. 1920–31 Dec. 1920
Murder	1	7
Firing at person	20	43
Assault	1	9
Incendiary fire	54	106
Robbery	11	11
Injury to cattle	14	7
Threatening latter	184	349
Others	40	122
Injury to property	93	318
Firing into dwelling	48	120
TOTALS	481	1,114

Source: PRO, CO904, part iv, police reports 1914–21.

Table 3.1 The size and distribution of farms according to size in Ireland (26 counties) in 1930 (to the nearest 100).

County	More than 1, less than 5 acres	More than 5, less than 15 acres	More than 15, less than 30 acres	More than 30, less than 50 acres	More than 50, less than 100 acres	More than 100, less than 200 acres	Over 200, acres	Total number of holdings
Carlow	500	600	800	700	800	400	100	3,900
Dublin	1,400	1,000	600	500	500	300	200	4,500
Kildare	1,100	1,000	900	700	800	700	400	5,600
Kilkenny	900	1,100	1,400	1,700	2,000	1,000	300	8,400
Laois	1,000	1,400	1,600	1,300	1,300	700	300	7,600
Longford	400	1,800	2,500	1,300	700	200	100	7,000
Louth	900	1,800	1,200	600	500	200	100	5,300
Meath	1,300	1,900	2,200	1,500	1,100	800	600	9,400
Offaly	1,100	1,300	1,600	1,500	1,400	600	300	7,800
Westmeath	900	1,500	2,200	1,500	1,200	600	300	8,200
Wexford	1,300	1,500	1,800	1,900	2,400	1,100	300	10,300
Wicklow	600	800	900	900	1,200	700	300	5,400
LEINSTER TOTALS	11,400	15,700	17,700	14,100	13,900	7,300	3,300	83,400
Clare	1,100	2,100	4,000	3,700	3,000	1,000	400	15,300
Cork	2,500	3,300	4,700	5,800	7,700	3,800	900	28,700
Kerry	2,300	3,000	3,700	4,000	4,100	1,500	500	19,100
Limerick	1,400	1,800	2,400	2,800	3,000	1,200	200	12,800
Tipperary	1,500	2,300	3,100	3,400	3,800	1,700	600	16,400
Waterford	9,00	800	800	900	1,400	900	300	6,000
MUNSTER TOTALS	9,700	13,300	18,700	20,600	23,000	10,100	2,900	98,300
Galway	1,800	6,900	9,000	6,700	3,200	900	400	28,900
Leitrim	400	3,200	5,000	2,100	900	100	0	11,700
Mayo	2,200	10,900	11,600	4,600	1,700	400	300	31,700
Roscommon	1,000	4,800	7,200	3,300	1,300	400	100	18,100
Sligo	800	3,600	4,800	2,100	900	300	100	12,600
CONNAUGHT TOTALS	6,200	29,400	37,600	18,800	8,000	2,100	900	103,000
Cavan	700	4,100	6,200	2,900	1,200	300	100	15,500
Donegal	2,400	8,000	6,800	4,000	2,800	1,100	400	25,500
Monaghan	800	4,000	4,400	1,900	900	200	0	12,200
TOTALS ULSTER (3 counties)	3,900	16,100	17,400	8,800	4,900	1,600	500	53,200
TOTALS IRELAND	31,200	75,000	91,400	62,300	49,800	21,100	7,600	338,400

Table 4.1 The total of untenanted acres divided and number of allottees, 1933–9.

Year ending 31 March	Untenanted Acres divided	Number of allottees
1933	35,264	2,270
1934	39,354	3,595
1935	101,800	6,244
1936	103,872	7,712
1937	72,525	5,981
1938	60,907	4,959
1939	41,745	3,374
Totals	455,467	34,135

Source: Irish Land Commission Reports, 1933–40.

Table 4.2 The number of estates acquired, the area acquired and the average area of each estate, 1934–8.

Year	No. of estates acquired for division	Area acquired	Average area per estates
1934–5	415	101,903	246
1935–6	668	97,595	146
1936–7	612	70,196	115
1937–8	635	86,115	135

Source: NA, Dept. of Taoiseach files, S6490.

Table 4.3 Showing acreage divided and number of allottees, from year ending 31 March 1935 to year ending 31 March 1945.

Year ending 31 March	Acreage divided	Number of allottees
1935	101,800	6,244
1936	103,872	7,712
1937	72,525	5,981
1938	60,907	4,959
1939	41,745	3,374
1940	38,636	2,729
1941	25,678	1,804
1942	20,527	1,666
1943	20,520	1,288
1944	13,359	1,184
1945	14,229	861

Source: Irish Land Commission Reports, 1935–45

Table 4.4 Number of holdings repossessed by the Land Commission and re-allotted under the 1946 Land Act.

Year	Number of holdings recovered	Cases under review	Number of parcels re-allotted	Area re-allotted
1947–8	47	416	26	268
1948–9	48	503	29	488
1949–50	88	407	35	330
1950–1	86	205	45	539
1951–2	45	150	61	536
1952–3	36	117	36	513
1953–4	23	92	22	456
1954–5	20	63	20	311
1955–6	22	41	15	124
1956–7	17	48	5	70
1957–8	35	35	8	116
1958–9	27	29	12	169
1959–60	14	15	5	60
1960–1	17	10	5	46
1961–2	1	6	6	67
1962–3	2	1	1	26
1963–4	0	0	0	0
1964–5	0	0	0	0
1965–6	1	1	1	42
1966–7	0	0	0	0
1967–8	1	1	1	8
Totals	540	2,140	567	7,308

Source: *Irish Land Commission Reports, 1948–68.*

Table 5.1 Expenditure on Meath Gaeltacht colonies.

Colony	No. of holdings allocate	Average acreage per holding	Cost per holding: land	Average acreage per holding	Cost per holding: land	Cost per holding: equipment	Total cost for colony	Annuity per acre
Rathcarne	589	27		21.75	£431	£1010	£11,367	8s 8d
Gibbstown	1,142	50		21.75	£347	£866	£43,300	8s 8d
Kilbride	290	13		22.25	£305	£932	£12,116	6s 4d
Clongill	261	9		29	£317	Not available		4s 2d

Source: Dáil Debates, vol. 74, 8 Feb. 1939, 82–3.

Table 5.2 Gaeltacht colonies established in County Meath.

Year of migration	Number of families	Number of persons	County of origin	Townlands in Meath
1935	27	177	Galway	Rathcarne
1937	13	105	Galway	Kilbride
1937	18	133	Mayo	Gibbstown
	16	82	Kerry	Gibbstown
	14	95	Donegal	Gibbstown
	2	11	Cork	Gibbstown
1939	5	29	Kerry	Clongill
	4	23	Donegal	Clongill
1940	23	112	Galway	Allenstown
	122	767		

Source: Irish Land Commission Report, 1952, p. 30.

Table 6.1 Number of uneconomic holdings in each county outside the scheduled congested areas, 1957.

County	Total number of holdings	Number of holdings under £15 valuation	Percentage of uneconomic holdings
Carlow	4,958	2,745	55
Dublin	8,575	4,227	49
Kildare	8,329	4,939	59
Kilkenny	9,897	4,534	46
Laois	8,472	4,563	54
Longford	7,480	4,772	64
Louth	6,559	3,963	60
Meath	13,257	6,437	49
Offaly	8,661	4,552	53
Westmeath	9,648	4,783	51
Wexford	13,048	7,210	55
Wicklow	7,559	4,424	59
Limerick	17,431	9,835	56
Tipperary	20,295	9,987	49
Waterford	7,874	4,478	57
Cavan	15,569	9,878	63
Monaghan	11,628	6,233	54
Totals	17,906	97,560	54

Source: NA, DT S16265.

Table 6.2 Number of 'substantial holdings' in Ireland and number on which Land Commission proceedings had been initiated, 1958.

County	No. of holdings	Holdings on which proceedings initiated	County	No. of holdings	Holdings on which proceedings initiated
Carlow	152	1	Clare	356	
Dublin	152	0	Cork	796	
Kildare	424	1	Kerry	446	
Kilkenny	300	0	Limerick	239	
Laois	235	2	Tipperary	584	
Longford	76	1	Waterford	305	
Louth	117	1	Total	2,726	
Meath	535	3			
Offaly	298	5	Galway	358	4
Westmeath	309	2	Leitrim	22	0
Wexford	330	2	Mayo	209	1
Wicklow	269	1	Roscommon	90	0
Total	3,197	19	Sligo	86	0
			Total	765	5
Cavan	56	0			
Donegal	379	1			
Monaghan	29	0			
Total	464	1			

Source: NA, DT S16265

Table 6.3 Percentage distribution of farmers according to acreage farmed, 1971

Acreage farmed	Leinster	Munster	Connaught	Ulster (three counties)	Ireland (twenty-six counties)
Under 10	3	2.9	7.7	12.9	5.7
10–15	3.6	3.3	10.2	12.2	6.7
15–30	15.5	14.5	34.0	28.3	22.5
30–40	12.7	12.7	18.8	14.5	14.8
40–50	11.7	12.1	10.7	10.3	11.2
50–70	16.6	19.5	10.2	10.6	14.8
70–100	14.1	16.2	5.7	5.8	10.8
100–150	11.9	11.5	2.1	3.2	7.6
150–200	5	3.7	0.6	0.8	2.7
Over 200	5.4	3.1	0.6	0.9	2.6
Area not stated	1.1	0.6	0.4	0.8	0.7

Source: Census of population 1971, vol. iv.

Table 7.1 *The growth in Fianna Fáil cumainn, 1932–3 (counties are listed as they appear in the original source).*

County	1932	1933	County	1932	1933
Carlow	10	22	Louth	19	29
Kilkenny	41	53	Longford	19	30
Cavan	45	47	Westmeath	30	41
Clare	82	82	Mayo North	40	52
Cork East	46	43	Mayo South	66	94
Cork North	45	51	Meath	49	69
Cork West	32	60	Monaghan	25	39
Galway	128	137	Roscommon	65	89
Kerry	69	96	Tipperary	95	98
Kildare	29	45	Donegal	62	118
Leitrim	40	48	Waterford	33	57
Sligo	38	49	Wexford	41	45
Laois	33	48	Wicklow	16	31
Offaly	31	37			
Limerick	36	69			
			Total	1,265	1,679

Source: Fianna Fáil: Eighth Annual Ard-Fheis: Report of Proceedings, p. 4. (UCDA, Fianna Fáil papers, P176/747).

Appendix II

Return of untenanted land acquired and holdings resumed by the Land Commission in each county up to 31 December 1974.

County	Compulsory acquisition: number of estates	Area (acres)	Voluntary acquisition: number of estates	Area (acres)	Total number of estates and holdings resumed*	Area (acres)
Cavan	98	6,797	131	8,569	258	17,573
Donegal	124	64,661	74	14,794	292	81,763
Monaghan	69	5,671	86	6,918	171	14,000
Total	291	77,129	291	30,281	721	113,336
Carlow	42	8,116	42	7,959	103	20,794
Dublin	43	7,542	23	5,172	98	16,203
Kildare	163	50,312	109	19,623	310	76,196
Kilkenny	58	8,302	58	11,094	122	20,763
Laois	106	23,226	73	14,949	240	46,108
Longford	72	9,909	90	8,838	171	19,858
Louth	52	6,141	27	5,976	89	13,380
Meath	324	67,235	170	38,392	619	129,124
Offaly	120	28,459	137	25,728	303	64,674
Westmeath	119	27,921	165	30,378	332	69,570
Wexford	76	11,422	125	15,206	204	26,915
Wicklow	45	7,942	89	15,671	148	25,424
Total	1,220	256,527	1,108	198,986	2,739	529,009
Galway	612	125,748	375	50,338	1,156	201,519
Leitrim	152	15,760	198	13,834	371	30,920
Mayo	760	68,335	423	29,306	1,313	110,081
Roscommon	544	66,309	300	23,826	935	98,224
Sligo	293	28,790	152	15,946	501	47,858
Total	2,361	304,942	1,448	133,250	4,276	488,602

County	Compulsory acquisition: number of estates	Area (acres)	Voluntary acquisition: number of estates	Area (acres)	Total number of estates and holdings resumed*	Area (acres)
Clare	232	39,158	147	15,924	450	61,676
Cork	154	22,375	239	27,286	423	51,248
Kerry	146	15,011	121	11,511	290	27,672
Limerick	141	28,829	84	11,023	238	41,610
Tipperary	216	47,605	167	45,239	475	106,998
Waterford	47	6,104	45	5,988	113	13,515
Total	936	159,082	803	116,971	1,989	302,719
Totals	4,808	797,680	3,650	479,488	9,725	1,433,666

Source: Irish Land Commission Report, 1974, p. 48.

[* The total number includes estates purchased under section 24 of 1923 Land Act (compulsory acquisition); purchased under sections 35 and 36 of the 1923 act and section 27 of the 1950 Land Act (voluntary); holdings resumed under section 29 of the 1923 act and Land Bank estates under section 42 of 1927 Land Act. The figures are exclusive of 6,792 registered holdings (151,674 acres) transferred to the Land Commission under section 46 of 1923 Land Act; 4,920 unvested holdings (122,545 acres) surrendered to the Land Commission in exchange for new holdings; 3,008 holdings (40,578 acres) taken over by the Land Commission on provisional letting from the owners to expedite division; 152 holdings (14,269 acres) vested in the and Commission under section 37 of 1927 Land Act and 14 holdings (1,863 acres) vested in the Land Commission under section 30 of the 1950 Land Act.]

Appendix III

Lands acquired under the Land Acts 1923–65 and allotted to each category of allottees, 1938–73. *

Year ended March	Total acreage	Total allot-tees	Con-gests: acres	Con-gests: No.	Mi-grants: acres	Mi-grants: No.	Ex-employ-ees: acres	Ex-employ-ees: No.	Land-less acres	Land-less No.	Evic-ted Ten-ants: acres	Evic-ted Ten-ants: No.
1938	60,907	4,959	23,097	1,995	8,512	354	5,930	238	11,277	416	220	5
1939	41,745	3,374	18,870	1,760	5,114	286	3,556	134	6,821	226	150	3
1940	38,636	2,729	16,809	1,451	8,801	358	2,786	110	4,912	177	115	4
1941	25,678	1,804	11,240	1,020	5,842	237	1,403	59	1,563	49	36	1
1942	20,527	1,666	9,280	1,051	5,617	223	811	29	2,091	52	0	0
1943	20,520	1,288	9,852	776	4,500	218	523	30	1,405	38	96	3
1944	13,359	1,184	7,429	783	2,850	143	569	24	755	30	62	2
1945	14,229	861	6,725	581	3,591	166	1,113	24	545	16	0	0
1946	14,132	808	7,221	568	3,094	100	311	13	642	19	0	0
1947	14,240	1,018	8,366	642	2,737	127	995	26	417	12	0	0
1948	10,893	964	6,266	505	2,893	145	621	28	233	13	0	0
1949	16,031	1,126	7,205	494	2,382	138	568	17	83	10	0	0
1950	21,699	1,455	10,881	917	4,071	153	1,416	26	409	8	7	10
1951	19,737	874	6,932	486	3,550	139	970	26	404	10	0	0
1952	19,574	1,160	6,072	592	8,301	204	619	22	236	6	0	0
1953	21,048	1,279	7,989	680	7,735	283	899	29	130	5	0	0
1954	24,390	1,657	9,468	840	11,363	447	622	26	364	7	0	0
1955	23,324	1,436	8,931	722	11,925	374	451	15	199	9	0	0
1956	26,226	1,396	8,040	755	15,032	488	225	10	142	6	0	0
1957	23,650	1,081	5,376	543	13,875	356	257	12	234	9	58	1
1958	23,066	1,308	8,287	815	9,201	326	461	18	128	10	0	0
1959	45,840	2,456	18,329	1,335	21,265	682	999	46	184	4	0	0
1960	32,402	1,877	10,414	934	15,850	615	769	27	0	0	0	0
1961	32,703	1,800	8,582	798	16,941	558	631	27	179	3	50	1
1962	30,798	1,669	8,825	830	10,465	465	432	16	40	1	0	0

Year ended March	Total acreage	Total allot-tees	Con-gests: acres	Con-gests: No.	Mi-grants: acres	Mi-grants: No.	Ex-employ-ees: acres	Ex-employ-ees: No.	Land-less acres	Land-less No.	Evic-ted Ten-ants: acres	Evic-ted Ten-ants: No.
1963	27,967	1,563	10,090	792	13,193	500	308	13	63	2	0	0
1964	31,473	1,506	11,571	764	14,427	485	545	22	177	4	0	0
1965	31,697	1,677	9,670	825	16,428	533	323	13	0	0	0	0
1966	46,709	2,434	18,401	1,482	15,862	563	875	35	42	1	0	0
1967	28,262	1,595	13,557	960	9,370	377	483	14	74	2	0	0
1968	24,093	1,360	10,440	761	9,076	329	309	16	104	3	0	0
1969	24,813	1,486	13,188	961	7,154	309	381	14	9	2	0	0
1970	22,622	1,253	12,192	807	7,522	279	386	14	60	1	0	0
1971	26,091	1,662	16,152	1,134	6,772	296	559	17	122	2	0	0
1972	22,955	1,628	12,518	994	7,680	408	127	12	183	4	0	0
1973	32,483	1,930	16,460	1,239	13,107	434	323	14	139	4	0	0

*Lands allotted in accommodation plots, turbary plots, forestry plots or for sportsfields not included.
Source: ILC Reports 1937–1974; Sammon, In the Land Commission, pp. 260–1.

Notes

ONE: INTRODUCTION

1   R. V. Comerford, *Fenians in Context: Irish Politics and Society 1848–82* (Dublin, 1998 edn [1st edn 1985]), p. 115

2   R. V. Comerford, *Ireland* (London, 2003), pp. 9, 266.

3   Emmet Larkin, *The Historical Dimensions of Irish Catholicism* (New York, 1976), p. 96.

4   George O'Brien, 'Patrick Hogan: Minister for Agriculture, 1922–32', *Studies* (Sept. 1936), 356.

5   John A. O'Brien, *The Vanishing Irish* (London, 1954), p. 41; quoted in Louise Fuller, *Irish Catholicism Since 1950: The Undoing of a Culture* (Dublin, 2002), p. 47.

6   *Dáil Debates*, vol. 161, 24 Apr. 1957, 151ff.

7   Ibid., vol. 23, 18 Apr. 1927, 88.

8   Ibid., vol. 8, 24 July 1924, 2189.

9   As the terms conacre and eleven months' system are frequently used in this work, it is best to describe here what they mean. Originally conacre meant land rented by shopkeepers, labourers and small farmers for the planting of a single crop, usually potatoes. Plots of land that were to be let on conacre were auctioned each year, usually in November, and subsequently let to the highest bidder. The term also became associated with the letting of lands on the eleven months system. This practice became widespread during the late nineteenth century and developed as a result of the 1881 Land Act that established courts to fix fair rents between landlords and tenants who held their lands on an annual basis. To circumvent these terms landlords let significant tracts of untenanted lands to large tenants, often referred to as graziers, for eleven months instead of a year. Again, land to be let under this system was auctioned each year, usually in November, for a period of eleven months to the highest bidder. Thus, the terms eleven months' system and conacre eventually became interchangeable.

10   For more details see chapter 7.

11   Born Castlebar, County Mayo in 1912. First elected for Fianna Fáil in Mayo South in 1938 and returned in every subsequent election until his defeat in the newly formed constituency of Mayo West in 1973. He held a number of ministerial portfolios during this time: the Gaeltacht, 1957–9, Lands, 1959–68 (and Gaeltacht, 1961–8) and Justice 1968–70.

12   Quoted in *Irish Land Commission* [hereafter *ILC*] *Report*, 1962, p. 33.

13   Mary E. Daly, *The First Department: A History of the Department of Agriculture* (Dublin, 2002), p. 99.

14   Ibid.

15   See, for example, D. A. Gillmor, *Agriculture in the Republic of Ireland* (Budapest, 1977), p. 43.

16   Conrad Arensberg, *The Irish Countryman: An Anthropological Study* (Gloucester, Mass., 1959 edn [1st edn 1937]), p. 68.

17   *Dáil Debates*, vol. 275, 15 Nov. 1974, 1517.

18   Des Maguire, *The Land Problem: A Guide to Land Leasing* (Dublin, 1983), p. 5.

19 Arensberg, *The Irish Countryman*, p. 59.

20 See chapter 7.

21 Arensberg, *The Irish Countryman*, p. 76.

22 John B. Keane, *The Field* (Dublin, 1993 edn), p. 56.

23 Caitríona Clear, 'Women, work and memory in rural Ireland, 1921–61' in Carla King (ed.), *Famine, Land and Culture in Ireland* (Dublin, 2000), p. 183.

24 See chapter 7.

25 Clear, 'Women, work and memory', pp. 184–5; see also Pauric Travers, 'Emigration and gender: the case of Ireland, 1922–60' in Mary O'Dowd and Sabine Wichert (eds), *Chattel, Servant or Citizen? Women's Status in Church, State and Society* (Belfast, 1995), pp. 187–99; see also Caitríona Clear, *Women of the House: Women's Household Work in Ireland 1922–61* (Dublin, 2000).

26 Arensberg, *The Irish Countryman*, p. 15.

27 See *inter alia*, Paul Bew, *Land and the National Question in Ireland, 1858–82* (Dublin, 1978); Samuel Clarke, *Social Origins of the Irish Land War* (Princeton, 1979); J. S. Donnelly jr, *The Land and People of Nineteenth Century Cork* (London, 1975); Laurence Geary, *The Plan of Campaign 1886–91* (Cork, 1985); David Seth Jones, *Graziers, Land Reform and Political Conflict in Ireland* (Washington, 1995); T. W. Moody, *Davitt and the Irish Revolution 1846–82* (Oxford, 1981); B. L. Solow, *The Land Question and the Irish Economy 1870–1903* (Cambridge, Mass., 1971); W. E. Vaughan, *Landlords and Tenants in Mid-Victorian Ireland* (Oxford, 1994).

28 My thanks to Seamus MacGabhann and Jim King for bringing many of the following works to my attention and for so generously sharing their ideas with me; see *inter alia*, William Carleton, *Traits and Stories of the Irish Peasantry* (Dublin, 1833); Canon P. A. Sheehan, *The Graves of Kilmorna: A Story of '67* (New York, 1915); Anthony Trollope, *The Landleaguers*; C. J. Kickham, *Knocknagow or the Homes of Tipperary* (1873); Padraic Colum, *The Land* in id. *Three Plays* (Dublin, 1963 edn); Walter Macken, *The Bogman* (London, 1952); Tom McIntyre, *The Charolais* (London, 1969); Michael McLaverty, *Lost Fields* (New York, 1941); John McGahern, *That They May Face the Rising Sun* (London, 2002); id., *The Collected Stories* (London, 1992); see also Seamus MacGabhann, 'A people's art: the great songs of Meath and Oriel', *Riocht na Midhe* 9, 4 (1998): 103–19.

29 Daniel Corkery, *Synge and Anglo-Irish Literature: A Study* (Dublin, 1931), p. 19.

30 Peter Costello, 'Land and Liam O'Flaherty' in King (ed.), *Famine, Land and Culture*, p. 179.

31 Keane, *The Field*, p. 26.

32 Patrick Kavanagh remembered the fields around Inniskeen with names such as 'The field of the shop', 'The field of the well', 'The yellow meadow', 'The field of the musician' (all translated from their original Gaelic versions); Patrick Kavanagh, *The Green Fool* (London, 1971 edn [1st edn 1938]), p. 204.

33 Keane, *The Field*, p. 49.

34 Commander of the North Cork flying column during the War of Independence and IRA Director of Operations during the Civil War, he was a TD from 1921–2. Following the fallout from the Treaty split, he did not re-enter the Dáil until elected again in 1932. He lost his seat in 1957 but thereafter became a senator. Held the ministerial portfolio for Lands from 1943 to 1948. He was also Minister for Education 1951–4 and Minister for Agriculture (as a senator) from May 1957 to his death in November of that year.

35 *Dáil Debates*, vol. 118, 16 Nov. 1949, 914.

36 Ibid., vol. 95, 31 Jan. 1945, 1974.

37 *Report of the Irish Land Commissioners for the Period from 1 Apr. 1923 to 31 Mar. 1928 and for the Prior Period Ended 31 Mar. 1923*, p. 3.

38 R. V. Comerford, 'Land Commission' in S. J. Connolly (ed.), *The Oxford Companion to Irish History* (Oxford, 1998), p. 296.

39 Information gleaned from various *Irish Land Commission Reports.*

40 *The Land Act 1923: An Act to Amend the Law Relating to the Occupation and Ownership of Land and for Other Purposes Relating Thereto*, [9 Aug. 1923], no. 42/1923.

41 *Report of Estates Commissioners*, 1920–1, p. iv.

42 Ibid.

43 *Land Law (Commission) Act, 1923: An Act to Amend the Law Relating to the Irish Land Commission and to Dissolve the Congested Districts Board for Ireland and Transfer its Functions to the Irish Land Commission and for Other Purposes Connected Therewith* [24 July 1923], no. 27/1923.

44 *An Act to Amend Generally the Law, Finance and Practice Relating to Land Purchase, and in Particular to Make Further and Better Provision for the Execution of the Functions of the Judicial and Lay Commissioners of the Land Commission . . .* [13 Oct. 1933], No. 38/1933; see also H. J. Monahan, 'Administration of land acts' in F. C. King (ed.), *Public Administration in Ireland* (Dublin, n.d. [*c.*1944]), pp. 130–42.

45 *An Act to Amend the Law Relating to the Occupation and Ownership of Land and for Other Purposes Thereto* [9 Aug. 1923], no. 42/1923; *An Act to Make Provision for the Early Vesting of Holdings in the Purchasers Thereof Under the Land Purchase Acts and for that and Other Purposes . . .* [30 Apr. 1931], no. 11/1931.

46 From 1923, these included Kevin O'Shiel, Sam Waddell, M. J. Heavey and Michael Deegan. O'Shiel, as we shall see in the next chapter, had been a judge in the Sinn Féin land courts during the War of Independence. He served as a land commissioner from 1923 to his retirement in 1962. Waddell was chief inspector and land commissioner from the early 1930s to his retirement in 1950. He was also a playwright and actor. His play, *Bridge Head*, the central theme of which was the working of the Land Commission, was produced in the Abbey Theatre. P. J. Sammon writes of him: 'A most courteous man in his dealings with staff but I can guarantee that there was no non-sense such as an assistant secretary trying to fill the role of chief inspector while Sam Waddell was around'. P. J. Sammon, *In the Land Commission: A Memoir 1933–1978* (Dublin, 1997), p. 198.

47 These were Eamonn Mansfield, a former schoolteacher in Tipperary and Dan Browne a solicitor from Tralee; ibid., p. 9.

48 Ibid., p. 2; Richard Dunphy, *The Making of Fianna Fáil Power in Ireland* (Oxford, 1995), p. 71.

49 *An Act to Amend and Extend the Land Purchase Acts* [19 June 1950], no. 16/1950.

50 Born Balcarra, County Mayo. First elected for Clann na Talmhan in 1943 and returned in every election thereafter until 1965. He was leader of Clann na Talmhan from 1944 to 1958 and served as Minister for Lands for the duration of the first two coalition governments, 1948–51 and 1954–7.

51 *Seanad Debates*, vol. 43, 7 July 1954, 946.

52 *Commission of Enquiry into Banking, Currency and Credit, Memoranda and Minutes of Evidence*, vol. 11 (1938), p. 1129.

53 Ibid.

54 Ibid.

55 Ibid.

56 Sammon, *In the Land Commission*, p. 125.

57 See chapter 7.

58 *Dáil Debates*, vol. 118, 16 Nov. 1949, 901.

59 Department of Lands memo, 17 July 1948 (NA, DT S 2486).

60 Kevin O'Shiel, 'The work of the Land Commission' in King (ed.), *Public Administration in Ireland*, vol. 11, p. 70.

61 Ibid., p. 71.

62 *Dáil Debates*, vol. 70, 7 Apr. 1938, 1755.

63 *Meath Chronicle*, 27 Apr. 1935.

64 Migrants were those farmers who gave up their farms in congested areas to the Land Commission in exchange for a new holding elsewhere. Migrants and migration will be dealt with separately in chapter 4.

65 *ILC Report*, 1932–3, p. 11.

66 Rutherford Mayne [S. J. Waddell], *Bridge Head* (Dublin, n.d.), p. v.

67 Ibid., p. 3.

68 Ibid., p. 7.

69 Ibid., pp. 32–3.

70 Letter from Department of Lands to each member of the Executive Council regarding the appointment of Land Commission inspectors, 28 July 1934 (NA, DT S6664).

71 Memorandum prepared by the Department of Finance relating to Land Commission inspectorships, 2 Aug. 1934 (NA, DT S6664).

72 Born Kilmacowen, County Sligo in 1887. He was first elected as a Cumann na nGaedheal TD for Sligo–Leitrim in a by-election in 1925. He was defeated in the 1938 election but elected again in 1943 and 1944. He served as parliamentary secretary to the Minister for Fisheries 1927–30 and to the Minister for Lands and Fisheries 1930–2.

73 *Dáil Debates*, vol. 36, 27 Nov. 1930, 576.

74 Ibid., vol. 38, 14 May 1931, 1673.

75 Minister of Lands, 'Reply to parliamentary question no. 17: for private information', 27 Nov. 1930 (NA, DT S 6056A).

76 *Dáil Debates*, vol. 161, 24 Apr. 1957, 157.

77 Born south Armagh in 1898. He joined the Volunteers in 1913 and became Sinn Féin organiser for south Armagh in 1917. He played a prominent role in the War of Independence and Civil War, succeeding Liam Lynch as Chief of Staff of the anti-Treaty forces in 1923. He was elected Republican TD for Louth in 1923 and then Fianna Fáil TD in 1927. He was returned in every election until his retirement in 1973 during which time he was Minister for Defence 1932–45; Minister for Finance 1945–8; Minister for External Affairs 1951–4 and again 1957–69 and Tánaiste 1965–9. He was acting Minister for Lands for a short period.

78 Corrected typescript copies of a speech by Frank Aiken introducing the 1933 Land Bill to the Dáil, Aug. 1933 (UCD, Aiken papers, P104/3301).

79 *Dáil Debates*, vol. 13, 26 Nov. 1925, 977.

80 Ibid., vol. 3, 14 June 1923, 1969.

81 See note 27 above.

82 Charles Townshend, *Political Violence in Ireland* (Oxford, 1983), p. 339.

83 See Bew, 'Sinn Féin, agrarian radicalism and the War of Independence' in D. G. Boyce (ed.), *The Revolution in Ireland* (London, 1988), pp. 217–34.

84 See *inter alia* Erhardt Rumpf and A.C. Hepburn, *Nationalism and Socialism in Twentieth-century Ireland* (Dublin, 1977); David Fitzpatrick, *Politics and Irish Life, 1913–21* (Dublin, 1977); David Fitzpatrick, 'The geography of Irish nationalism, 1910–1921', *Past and Present* 77 (1978), 113–37; Tom Garvin, *The Evolution of Irish Nationalist Politics* (Dublin, 1981); Michael Hopkinson, *Green Against Green: The Irish Civil War* (Dublin, 1988); Joost Augusteijn, *From Public Defiance to Guerrilla Warfare: The Experience of Ordinary Volunteers in the Irish War of Independence 1916–21* (Dublin, 1996); Peter Hart, 'The geography of revolution in Ireland 1917–1923', *Past and Present* 155 (May 1997).

85 Patrick Lynch, 'The social revolution that never was' in Desmond Williams (ed.), *The Irish Struggle, 1916–1926* (London, 1966), p. 41.

86 J. M. Regan, *The Irish Counter-Revolution, 1921–36* (Dublin, 1999), p. 377.

87 Peter Hart, 'Defining the Irish revolution' in Augusteijn, *The Irish Revolution*, p. 27.

88 See J. T. Sheehan, 'Land purchase policy in Ireland, 1917–23: From the Irish Convention to the 1923 Land Act' (MA thesis, NUI Maynooth, 1993).

89 F. S. L. Lyons, *Ireland Since the Famine* (London, 1973 edn), p. 606; J. A. Murphy, *Ireland in the Twentieth Century* (Dublin, n.d.), p. 65; Ronan Fanning, *Independent Ireland* (Dublin, 1983), p. 73; David Fitzpatrick, *The Two Irelands 1912–1939* (Oxford, 1998), p. 240; Alvin Jackson, *Ireland, 1798–1998* (Oxford, 1999), p. 283.

90 See Eunan O'Halpin, *Defending Ireland: the Irish State and its Enemies Since 1922* (Oxford, 1999), pp. 33, 45. The absence of any type of detailed examination of the land question in independent Ireland in scholarly surveys such as Dermot Keogh's *Twentieth Century Ireland: Nation and State* (Dublin, 1994), Charles Townshend's *Ireland: The 20th Century* (Oxford, 1999), Cormac Ó Gráda's *Ireland: A New Economic History 1780–1939* (Oxford, 1994) and *A Rocky Road: The Irish Economy Since the 1920s* (Manchester, 1997) or in collections of essays such as Mike Cronin and J. M. Regan (eds), *Ireland: the Politics of Independence, 1922–49* (Basingstoke, 2000) is further testimony to this.

91 J. J. Lee, *Ireland 1912–1985: Politics and Society* (Cambridge, 1989), p. 71.

92 Valuable work in this area has already been begun by David Seth Jones in, 'Land reform legislation and security of tenure in Ireland after independence', *Eire-Ireland*, XXXII–XXXIII (1997–98): 116–43.

93 *Dáil Debates*, vol. 3, 28 May 1923, 1147.

94 Ibid., vol. 10, 26 Mar. 1925, 1544.

95 Ibid.

96 D. S. Jones, 'State financing of land division in the Irish Republic': paper presented to 'Land, politics and the state' conference, NUI Maynooth (9–10 May 2003), p. 24.

97 Memorandum prepared by Department of Lands regarding cabinet meeting on land division and economic planning [Feb. 1943] (NA, DT S12890).

98 Monahan, 'Administration of Land Acts', p. 141.

99 *Census of Population of Ireland 1946* (1949, P 9225), vol. 1, p. 18; vol. 11, pp. 10, 154–9.

100 *Statistical Abstract of Ireland 1962* (Pr. 6571), pp. 68–9.

101 *ILC Reports*, 1937–78; Sammon, *In the Land Commission*, pp. 260–1.

102 Department of Lands memorandum prepared for the government: review of Land Commission policy, July 1957 (NA, DT S16265).

103 One of P. J. Sammon's very interesting statistical appendices shows, for example, that 170 (former) landlords had almost 238,500 untenanted acres acquired between 1923 and 1936 alone; Sammon, *In the Land Commission*, pp. 264–78.

104 Born in 1891 at Kilrickle, Loughrea, County Galway. Elected Sinn Féin MP for Galway in 1918. As Minister for Agriculture 1922–32, he was responsible for the introduction of the 1923 Land Act. He was killed in a car crash in 1936.

105 The Ministers for Lands during the period under discussion in this book were: Patrick Hogan (Cumann na nGaedheal); P. J. Ruttledge (Fianna Fáil), Mar. 1932–Feb. 1933; Joseph Connolly (Fianna Fáil), Feb. 1933–June 1936; Frank Aiken (Fianna Fáil) June–Nov. 1936; Gerald Boland (Fianna Fáil), Nov. 1936–Aug. 1939; Thomas Derrig (Fianna Fáil), Sept. 1939–June 1943; Sean Moylan (Fianna Fáil), July 1943–Feb. 1948; Joseph Blowick (Clann na Talmhan), Feb. 1948 to June 1951; Thomas Derrig (Fianna Fáil), June 1951–June 1954; Joseph Blowick (Clann na Talmhan), June 1954–Mar. 1957; Erskine Childers, Mar. 1957–July 1959; Michael Moran (Fianna Fáil), July 1959–Mar. 1968; Padraig Faulkner (Fianna Fáil), Mar. 1968–July 1969; Sean Flanagan (Fianna Fáil), July 1969–Mar. 1973.

106 Patrick Commins, *The Impact of Re-distribution in Ireland 1923–1974: The Michael Dillon Memorial Lecture 1993* (Dublin, 1993), p. 1 (kindly supplied to this author by Dr Commins.)

107 *Dáil Debates*, vol. 106, 12 June 1947, 1666.

108 See bibliography for a listing of these.

109 Sammon, *In the Land Commission*.

110 For a general survey of records (particularly of the 1881–1923 period), see K. Buckley, 'The records of the Irish Land Commission as a source for historical evidence', *Irish Historical Studies* VIII (1952–3).

111 *Dáil Debates*, vol. 169, 3 July 1958, 1361; vol. 170, 8 July 1958, 22.

112 Ibid., vol. 170, 8 July 1958, 22.

113 *Seanad Debates*, vol. 134, 21 Oct. 1992, 348.

114 Ibid., vol. 134, 4 Nov. 1992, 973.

115 *Dáil Debates*, vol. 511, 30 Nov. 1999, 841.

116 Text of parliamentary question no. 84, ref. 4180/03, and reply of 13 Feb. 2003, forwarded to this author by Ms Deirdre Fennell, private secretary to Deputy John Bruton, 26 Aug. 2003.

TWO: CONTINUING THE LAND QUESTION

1   In the early days of the Board, congested districts were defined as 'those parts of the country which are unable, at least in their present state of development, to employ profitably in their cultivation, or to support by their own produce, the population at present inhabiting them'; E. O'Farrell, *The Congested Districts of Ireland and How to Deal With Them: A Paper Read Before the Statistical and Social Inquiry Society of Ireland, 14 Dec. 1886* (Dublin, 1887), p. 5.

2   *Twenty-Seventh Report of the Congested Districts Board for Ireland for the Period from 1 Apr. 1918 to 31 Mar. 1919* [cmd 759], HC 1920, vol. xix.889.

3   O'Shiel, 'The changes effected in recent Land Commission legislation' in King (ed.), *Public Administration in Ireland* vol. III, p. 302.

4   *Royal Commission on Congestion in Ireland: Final Report of the Commissioners* [Cd 4097], HC 1908, XLII.729, p. 5.

5   *Agricultural Statistics for Ireland With Detailed Report for the Year* 1917, [Cmd 1316], HC 1921, vol. LXI, p. xiv.

6   *Report of the Estates Commissioners for the Year from 1 Apr. 1920 to 31 Mar. 1921*, p. vi.

7   *ILC Report*, 1933, p. 9.

8   Ibid.; *Report of the Proceedings of the Irish Convention* [Cd 9019], HC 1918, vol. x. 697, p. 98.

9   *Report of Estates Commissioners for the Year from 1 Apr. 1919 to 31 Mar. 1920 and for the Period from 1 Nov. 1903 to 31 Mar. 1920* [Cmd 1150], HC 1921, vol. xiv, p. 661.

10   Jones, *Graziers*, pp. 184–208; see also Paul Bew, *Conflict and Conciliation in Ireland, 1898–1910: Parnellites and Agrarian Radicals* (Oxford, 1987); J. N. McEvoy, 'A study of the United Irish League in King's County, 1899–1918' (unpublished MA thesis, NUI, Maynooth, 1990).

11   For an insight to how landlords were affected during the revolutionary period, see Terence Dooley, *The Decline of the Big House in Ireland: A Study of Irish Landed Families, 1860–1960* (Dublin, 2001), pp. 127–31, 171–207.

12   Bew, *Conflict and Conciliation*; McEvoy, 'A study of the United Irish League'; Conal Thomas, *The Land for the People: The United Irish League and Land Reform in North Galway, 1898–1912* (Corrandulla, County Galway, 1999); Marie Coleman, *County Longford and the Irish Revolution, 1910–1923* (Dublin, 2003).

13   County Inspector's Confidential Monthly Reports [hereafter CICMR], County Monaghan, Jan.–Dec. 1907 (PRO, CO904, police reports).

14   Minutes of Monaghan County Council, 8 Jan. 1917 (Monaghan County Council Offices, Monaghan Town); see also Terence Dooley, *The Plight of Monaghan Protestants, 1911–26* (Dublin, 2000).

15   *Dundalk Democrat*, 13 Jan. 1917.

16   See M. J. Bonn, [translated by T. W. Rolleston], *Modern Ireland and Her Agrarian Problem* (London, 1906), p. 101.

17   Dan Breen, *My Fight for Irish Freedom* (Dublin, 1981 edn, [1st edn Dublin, 1924]), p. 8.

18   *Dáil Debates*, vol. 16, 24 June 1926, 1763.

19   *Report of Estates Commissioners*, 1920–1, p. v

20   *Dáil Debates*, vol. 2, 18 Jan. 1923, 967–8

21   *Twenty-Seventh Report of the Congested Districts Board*, p. 20.

22   For example, the price of wheat rose from 8s 8d per hundredweight in 1914 to £1 1s 6d by 1920 (the peak year for prices); oats rose from 7s 1d per cwt to 17s 3d; barley from 7s 3d to £1 2s 5d; potatoes from 3s 4d to 10s 2d and butter from £5 8s 6d to £16 0s 6d. The price of eggs rose from 9s 11d per ten dozen to £1 11s 2d. The price of beef per hundredweight rose from £3 3s 6d in 1914 to £7 18s 6d in 1920; mutton from £3 10s 6d to £9 3s 5d and pork from £2 19s 9d to £9 7s. The price of one- to two-year-old store cattle rose from £8 16s 9d in 1924 to £18 16s and 3d. The price of three year olds rose from £13 14s 3d per head to £35 2s 9d, while springers rose from £15 4s 3d to £39 6s 6d. The price of two-year-old sheep rose from 38s 6d to 108s 3d over the same period; *Return Showing to the Latest Year Available, for Ireland as a Whole, the Annual Average Prices for Each Year from 1881 . . .* HC 1921, vol. xli. 93.

23   Aodh De Blacam in foreword to Selina Sigerson, *Sinn Féin and Socialism* (Dublin, n.d.), p. 4; for Sigerson's similar views see ibid., p. 8.

24   Arthur Griffith, *Economic Salvation and the Means to Attain It* (Dublin, n.d.), p. 20.

25   Comerford, *Fenians in Context*, p. 115.

26   See Terence Dooley, *'The Greatest of the Fenians': John Devoy and Ireland* (Dublin, 2003).

27   John Devoy, *The Land of Eire* (New York, 1882), p. 20; see also J. S. Donnelly jr, 'The land question in nationalist politics' in T. E. Hachey and L. J. McCaffrey (eds), *Perspectives on Irish Nationalism* (Kentucky, 1989), pp. 90, 98; for the role of local Fenians in the Land League

of County Mayo, see Samuel Clarke, *Social Origins of the Irish Land War* (Princeton, 1979), pp. 272–5.

28 Bew, Hazelkorn and Patterson, *The Dynamics of Irish Politics*, p. 21.

29 Between 1916 and 1920, the area under wheat in Ireland increased by 34.3 per cent, the area under oats by 7.7 per cent and the area under barley by almost 40 per cent. At the same time the number of cattle in the country remained stable, so the cattle rearing industry was not unduly affected by increased tillage. *Agricultural Statistics of Ireland*, 1920 [Cmd 1317], HC 1921, vol. XLI, p. 99.

30 Minutes of Monaghan County Council, 8 Jan. 1917 (Monaghan County Council Offices, Monaghan Town).

31 IGCMR, Feb. 1917.

32 These commissioners, attached to the Land Commission as established in 1881, were appointed to carry through the sales of estates under the 1903 and amending land acts.

33 IGCMR, Jan. 1917.

34 Ibid.

35 Fergus Campbell, 'The hidden history of the Irish land war: a guide to local sources' in King (ed.), *Famine, Land and Culture*, p. 147.

36 See Patrick Maume, *The Long Gestation: Irish Nationalist Life, 1891–1918* (Dublin, 1999).

37 Labhras MacFhionghail, *The Land Question* (Dublin, n.d. [1917]), pp. 19–20.

38 Ibid., pp 18–19.

39 IGCMR, Jan. 1918.

40 See for example Rumpf and Hepburn, *Nationalism and Socialism in Twentieth-Century Ireland*; Fitzpatrick, *Politics and Irish Life*; Fitzpatrick, 'The geography of Irish nationalism'; Garvin, *The Evolution of Irish Nationalist Politics*; Hart, 'The geography of revolution in Ireland'.

41 See Terence Dooley, *Decline of the Big House in Ireland*.

42 Quoted in Michael Hopkinson, *Green Against Green: the Irish Civil War* (Dublin, 1988), p. 45.

43 Liam Deasy, *Towards Ireland Free: The West Cork Brigade in the War of Independence 1917–21* (Cork, 1973), p. 1.

44 Ibid., p. 162.

45 Ernie O'Malley, *On Another Man's Wound* (Dublin, 1979 edn, [first edn London, 1936]), p. 182.

46 Ibid., p. 150; *Dáil Debates*, vol. 99, 7 Feb. 1946, 594.

47 CICMR, County Galway ER, Feb. 1918.

48 De Valera at Elphin in County Roscommon; IGCMR, Feb. 1918.

49 CICMR, County Galway WR, Mar. 1918.

50 Ibid.

51 Quoted in *The Irish Times*, 4 June 1918.

52 Ibid.

53 Ibid.

54 *Irish Land (Provision for Soldiers and Sailors) Act* 1919 [9 & 10 Geo. V, ch. 82] (23 Dec. 1919).

55 *Report of Estates Commissioners for the Year from 1 Apr. 1920 to 31 Mar. 1921*, pp. x–xi; Minutes of meeting of Provisional Government, 1 Feb. 1922 (NA, A, G1/1).

56 *Minutes of the Proceedings of the First Parliament of the Republic of Ireland, 1919–21*, 4 Apr. 1919.

57 IGCMR, Mar. 1919.

58 *The Irish Times*, 11 Nov. 1966; see also O'Shiel's lengthy account in Bureau of Military History Archives (WS 1770).

59 All of these examples are taken from a précis of agrarian outrages reported from 19 May 1920 to 31 Dec. 1921 (PRO, CO904, part IV, police reports, 1914–21).

60 Memorandum by Patrick Hogan on the 1920 Land Bill, 14 Dec. 1922 (NA, DT S1995).

61 Dooley, *Decline of the Big House in Ireland*, pp. 171–207.

62 Duc De Stacpoole, *Irish and Other Memories*, (London, 1922), p. 255.

63 Mark Bence-Jones, *Twilight of the Ascendancy* (London, 1987), p. 193.

64 Art O'Connor, 'A brief survey of the work done by the Agricultural Department from April 1919 to August 1921' (UCD, Mulcahy papers, P7A/63).

65 Dooley, *Decline of the Big House in Ireland*, p. 130.

66 Ibid., pp. 130–1.

67 Provisional Government, minutes of meeting, 5 Apr. 1922 (NA, G1/2).

68 David Seth Jones, 'Land reform legislation and security of tenure in Ireland after independence' in *Eire-Ireland*, XXXII–XXXIII (1997–8), 117.

69 Tom Garvin, *1922: The Birth of Irish Democracy* (Dublin, 1996), pp. 44–5; see also Henry Patterson, *The Politics of Illusion: Republicanism and Socialism in Modern Ireland* (London, 1989), p. 24.

70 Maurice Moore to the Minister for Defence, 9 May 1922 (Military Archives, A/3126).

71 Copy memorandum on seizures of land [by Patrick Hogan], 22 Dec. 1922 (DT S1,943).

72 William Rochfort to secretary of Minister for Home Affairs, 7 Apr. 1923 (NA, DJ H5/56).

73 Raleigh Chichester Constable to Arthur Griffith, 31 Jan. 1922 (NA, DJ H5/128).

74 Statement in connection with the forcible ejection of Protestant tenants on the Luggacurren estate, Mar. and Apr. 1922 (NA, DJ H5/85).

75 Comerford, *Ireland*, p. 112.

76 For Cork, see Peter Hart, *The IRA and its Enemies: Violence and Community in Cork*, 1916–1923 (Oxford, 1998), pp. 273–92; see also Peter Hart, 'The Protestant experience of revolution in Ireland' in Richard English and Graham Walker (eds), *Unionism in Modern Ireland* (Dublin, 1996), pp. 81–98; Terence Dooley, 'Monaghan Protestants in a time of crisis, 1919–22' in R. V. Comerford et al. (eds), *Religion, Conflict and Coexistence in Ireland* (Dublin, 1990), pp. 235–51; Dooley, *Plight of Monaghan Protestants*.

77 For police reports on attacks on Protestants, see IGCMR, July, Aug. 1920; CICMR, County Leitrim, Apr. 1921; CICMR, County Leitrim, Apr. 1921; CICMR, Tipperary South Riding, Apr. 1921; CICMR, County Kerry, Apr., May 1921; IGCMR, May 1921

78 Joseph Johnston to Minister for Home Affairs, 6 Apr. 1922 (NA, DJ H5/85).

79 Report on land agitation in Queen's County [Laois], 1922 (NA, DT, S566).

80 Kathleen Harpur to Minister for Home Affairs, 1 May 1922 (NA, DJ H5/85).

81 Report on land agitation in Queen's County, 1922 (NA, DT S566).

82 Ibid.

83 Joseph Johnson to Minister for Home Affairs, 6 Apr. 1922 (NA, DJ H5/85).

84 Report on activity of Special Infantry Corps in County Cork from B. J. Geoghegan to Minister for Agriculture, 19 Apr. 1923 (Military Archives, A/8506); see also, report on O'Connell 'spy farm', 13 Nov. 1923 (Military Archives, A/613); for a comprehensive study of Cork at this time see Hart, *The IRA and its Enemies*.

85   Maurice Moore to Minister for Defence, 9 May 1922 (Military Archives, A/3121)

86   Ibid.; For further western experiences, see Michael Farry, *Sligo 1914–1921: A Chronicle of Conflict* (Trim 1992); id., *The Aftermath of Revolution: Sligo 1921–23* (Dublin, 2000).

87   CICMR, County Galway East Riding, May 1918.

88   *Minutes of Proceedings of Dáil Éireann*, 10 May 1922, p. 395.

89   William Mooney & Sons to J. E. Duggan, 16 Mar. 1922 (NA, DJ H5/12).

90   William Rochfort to Minister for Home Affairs, 28 Jan. 1924 (NA, DJ H5/56).

91   [Erskine Childers], *The Constructive Work of Dáil Éireann I* (Dublin, 1921), p. 10.

92   Ibid., p. 12.

93   Kevin O' Shiel in *The Irish Times*, 11 Nov. 1966.

94   *The Republican*, 26 July 1919.

95   Ibid., 23 Aug. 1919.

96   Childers, *The Constructive Work of Dáil Éireann II*, p. 7.

97   Quoted in Childers, *The Constructive Work of Dáil Éireann I*, p. 18.

98   Quoted in Sylvain Briollay, *Ireland in Rebellion* (London, 1922), p. 60.

99   Childers, *The Constructive Work of Dáil Éireann I*, p. 18; See Mary Kotsonouris, *Retreat From Revolution: The Dáil Courts 1920–24* (Dublin, 1994); Arthur Mitchell, *Revolutionary Government in Ireland: Dáil Éireann 1919–22* (Dublin, 1995), pp. 137–46.

100 *Minutes of Proceedings of Dáil Éireann*, 17 Aug. 1921, p. 58.

101 Ibid., p. 61.

102 Childers, *The Constructive Work of Dáil Éireann II*, pp 9–10.

103 Quoted in ibid., p. 12.

104 A newspaper published by the Friends of Irish Freedom in Washington.

105 *News Bulletin*, 10 June 1920.

106 Briollay, *Ireland in Rebellion*, pp. 56–7.

107 *Dáil Debates*, vol. 4, 6 July 1923, 357.

108 Ibid., 335–7.

109 Bew, 'Sinn Féin, agrarian radicalism and the War of Independence', p. 234.

110 Hogan to Minister for Defence, 7 June 1922; Colfer & Sons, New Ross: statement of facts relating to unlawful seizure of lands of Shambogh County Kilkenny for Minister for Home Affairs, 7 Apr. 1922 (NA, DJ H5/104).

111 Patrick Hogan to Minister for Defence, 7 June 1922 (Military Archives, A/613); See also R. B. McDowell, *Crisis and Decline: The Fate of Southern Unionists* (Dublin, 1997).

112 Quoted in Hopkinson, *Green Against Green*, p. 90.

113 Copy memo: land seizures [by Patrick Hogan].

114 Memorandum prepared for the Minister for Defence, 1 Feb. 1923 (Military Archives, A/7869); Patrick Hogan to Minister for Defence, 7 June 1923 (Military Archives, A/613).

115 B. Geoghegan to Minister for Agriculture, 19 Apr. 1923 (Military Archives, A/8506).

116 John Kelly to Sean Collins, 15 Mar. 1923 (NA, DJ H5/128).

117 *Dáil Debates*, vol. 3, 14 June 1923, 1956

118 See, for example, Military Archives files A/8506, A/7869, A/613 detailing activities of the Special Infantry Corps, resistance to the same in certain areas, its success in quelling agrarianism and so on.

119 *Enforcement of Law (Occasional Powers) Act, 1923*, [1 Mar. 1923], no. 4/1923; *District Justices (Temporary Provisions) Act, 1923*, [27 Mar. 1923], no. 6/1923.

120 Kevin O'Higgins, Minister for Home Affairs; *Dáil Debates*, vol. 2, 19 Jan. 1923, 971.

121 J. M. Duff to [?] McGann, 18 July 1922 (NA, DT S2981).

122 For earlier advice given to the government on this matter, see Lord Midleton to Michael Collins, 15 June 1922 (NA, DT S2981).

123 *Dáil Debates*, vol. 2, 5 Jan. 1923, 592,

124 Ibid., vol. 3, 28 May 1923, 1150–1.

125 Ibid., 1147–8.

126 Patrick Hogan, Report on the Land Purchase and Arrears Conference of 10–11 Apr. 1923, 17 Apr. 1923 (UCD, Blythe papers, P24/174).

127 Patrick Hogan to W. T. Cosgrave, 7 Apr. 1923 (NA, DT S3192).

128 Memorandum on 1923 Land Bill prepared by Patrick Hogan for W. T. Cosgrave, 18 Apr. 1923 (NA, DT S3192).

129 *Dáil Debates*, vol. 3, 28 May 1923, 1161–2.

130 Ibid., 1147–8, 1153.

131 *Constitution of the Irish Free State (Saorstát Éireann) Act, 1922*, no. 1/1922, Article 47.

132 *Dáil Debates*, vol. 1, 8 Aug. 1923, 1983–5.

133 *An Act to Provide for the Preservation of Public Safety and the Protection of Persons and Property and for Matters Connected Therewith or Arising Out of the Present Emergency* [1 Aug. 1923], no. 28/1923; *An Act to Make Provision for the Immediate Preservation of the Public Safety* [3 Aug. 1923], no. 29/1923.

134 Memo. on 1923 Land Bill prepared by Patrick Hogan for W. T. Cosgrave, 18 Apr. 1923 (NA, DT S3192).

135 *An Act to Amend the Law Relating to the Occupation and Ownership of Land and for Other Purposes Relating Thereto* [9 Aug. 1923], no. 42/1923.

136 This information is based on election results in B. M. Walker (ed.), *Parliamentary Election Results in Ireland*, 1918–92 (Dublin, 1992), pp. 108–15.

THREE: THE 1923 LAND ACT

1   *Dáil Debates*, vol. 10, 26 Mar. 1925, 1544.

2   S. J. Brandenburg, 'Progress of land transfers in the Irish Free State', *Journal of Land and Public Utility Economics* VIII, 3 (1932): 282.

3   *Dáil Debates*, vol. 1, 18 Oct. 1922, 1651–2; vol. 3, 28 May 1923, 1147.

4   Financial agreements between the Irish Free State government and the British government, 12 Feb. 1923 (NA, DT S3459).

5   Extracted from minutes of Executive Council meetings, 12 May 1923 (NA, DT S3192).

6   Memorandum on 1923 Land Bill prepared by Patrick Hogan for W. T. Cosgrave, 18 Apr. 1923 (NA, DT S3192); Financial agreements, 12 Feb. 1923, S3459.

7   *Hansard Parliamentary Debates*, vol. 127, 1920, 938.

8   *Report of the Proceedings of the Irish Convention* [Cd 9019], HC 1918, vol. x, 697.

9   Ibid., pp. 91–4.

10 Ibid., p. 89.

11 Memorandum on Land Bill of 1920 (NA, DT S1995A).

12   *The Land Act* 1923: *An Act to Amend the Law Relating to the Occupation and Ownership of Land and for Other Purposes Relating Thereto*, [9 Aug. 1923], no. 42/1923.

13   See for example, Lyons, *Ireland Since the Famine*, p. 606; Murphy, *Ireland in the Twentieth Century*, p. 65; Fanning, *Independent Ireland*, p. 73; Jackson, *Ireland, 1798–1998*, p. 283.

14   *Dáil Debates*, vol. 3, 28 May 1923, 1147.

15   See Jones, 'Land reform legislation', pp. 116–43.

16   *Dáil Debates*, vol. 3, 28 May 1923, 1152–3.

17   *Irish Land Act 1923*, 24.1

18   *Dáil Debates*, 28 May 1923, 1150

19   *Report of the Estates Commissioners for the Year from 1 Apr. 1920 to 31 Mar. 1921*, p. vi.

20   *Report of Estates Commissioners*, 1920–1, p. x; Report *of the Estates Commissioners for the Year from 1 Apr. 1918 to 31 Mar. 1919* [Cmd 577], HC 1919, xix, 965.

21   *Irish Land Act 1923*, 24.7.

22   F. F. MacCabe and T. E. Healey, 'Racing, steeplechasing and breeding in Ireland' in Charles Richardson (ed.), *British Steeplechasing* (London, 1927), pp. 294–6; Dooley, *Decline of the Big House*, pp. 267–8.

23   *Irish Land Act, 1923*, 24.4.

24   Ibid., 24.5.

25   Jones, 'Land reform legislation', pp. 125–6.

26   *Report of the Irish Land Commissioners, 1923–8*, p. 26.

27   *Dáil Debates*, vol. 49, 1 Aug. 1933, 967.

28   See Jones, 'Land reform legislation', pp. 116–43.

29   'Seizure of land' [by Patrick Hogan], 22 Dec. 1922 (S 1943).

30   *Royal Commission on Congestion in Ireland: Final Report*, pp. 47–8.

31   *Dáil Debates*, vol. 63, 15 July 1936, 1331.

32   Ibid., vol. 2, 5 Jan. 1923, 596.

33   Ibid., vol. 3, 28 May 1923, 1163.

34   *Report of Inter-Departmental Committee on Seasonal Migration to Great Britain 1937–1938* (Dublin, 1938), p. 25.

35   Ibid.

36   Ibid., p. 26.

37   See for example, *Dáil Debates*, vol. 4, 4 July 1923, 185–6.

38   Ibid., vol. 3, 14 June 1923, 1944.

39   Ibid., 6 July 1923, 333–4.

40   *Royal Commission on Congestion in Ireland: Final Report*, p. 48.

41   *Dáil Debates*, vol. 4, 4 July 1923, 183.

42   *Report of the Estates Commissioners for Year from 1 April 1918 to 31 March 1919*, [Cmd 577], HC 1919, xix, 965; *Report of Irish Estates Commissioners*, 1920–21, p. x.

43   *Dáil Debates*, vol. 3, 15 June 1923, 2110.

44   *An Act to Make Provision for the Early Vesting of Holdings in the Purchasers Thereof Under the Land Purchase Acts and for that and Other Purposes* . . . [30 Apr. 1931], no. 11/1931.

45   *An Act to Amend Generally the Law, Finance and Practice Relating to Land Purchase, and in Particular to Make Further and Better Provision for the Execution of the Functions of the Judicial and Lay Commissioners of the Land Commission* . . . [13 Oct. 1933], no. 38/1933

46   Report of Land Division Committee, 21 May 1936 (UCD, Aiken papers, P104/3338).

47 See for example, W. E. Wylie to Michael Deegan, 16 Mar. 1933 (UCD, Aiken papers, P104/3276).

48 Frank Aiken to the secretary of the Land Commission, n.d. [1933] (UCD, Aiken papers, P104/3298).

49 Ibid.

50 See, for example, Inspectorate notice no. 11/35, 4 May 1935 issued by S. J. Waddell, chief inspector and land commissioner (NA, DT S4690A).

51 Section 36 read: 'The Land Commission may purchase any untenanted land which they consider necessary for the purpose of providing parcels of land for any of the persons or bodies to whom advances may be made under the provisions of this Act, for such price, payable in 4 1/2 per cent Land Bonds of equal nominal value, as shall be agreed upon between the owner of such untenanted land and the Land Commission, and such land when vested in the Land Commission shall be subject to all the provisions of this Act relating to the providing of parcels of land for the persons or bodies aforesaid.'

52 See *ILC Report*, 1978.

53 These changes in policy will be discussed in later chapters.

54 Sammon, *In the Land Commission*, p. 240.

55 *Dáil Debates*, vol. 140, 7 July 1953, 598.

56 Ibid., vol. 118, 9 Nov. 1949, 562–5.

57 Ibid., vol. 112, 20 July 1948, 202.

58 Ibid., vol. 114, 16 Feb. 1949, 632.

59 See chapter 7.

60 Sammon, *In the Land Commission*, p. 241.

61 *An Act to Amend and Extend the Land Purchase Acts*, [19 June 1950], no. 16/1950.

62 1923 Land Act, section 35.

63 Sammon, *In the Land Commission*, p. 242.

64 Ibid.

65 *Dáil Debates*, vol. 235, 27 June 1968, 1943–4.

66 See chapter 7 for more details.

67 Sammon, *In the Land Commission*, pp. 243–4.

68 W. E. Wylie to Michael Deegan, 16 Mar. 1933 (UCD, Aiken papers, P104/3276).

69 Sammon, *In the Land Commission*, p. 242–8.

70 See Terence Dooley, 'IRA veterans and land division in independent Ireland, 1923–48' in Fearghal McGarry (ed.), *Republicanism in Modern Ireland* (Dublin, 2003), pp. 86–107.

71 *Dáil Debates*, vol. 140, 7 July 1953, 571.

72 Sammon, *In the Land Commission*, p. 244.

73 See chapter 5.

74 *Dáil Debates*, vol. 14, 4 Feb. 1926, 399.

75 Ibid., vol. 13, 2 Dec. 1925, 1127.

76 Ibid., vol. 29, 19 Apr. 1929, 718.

77 Ibid, vol. 13, 2 Dec. 1925, 1152.

78 Ibid., vol. 18, 24 Feb. 1927, 874–5.

79 Ibid., vol. 29, 11 July 1929, 821.

80 Ibid., vol. 14, 25 Mar. 1926, 1698–9.

81 Ibid., 1699.

82 Memorandum by Joseph Connolly on land division policy, 11 Oct. 1932 (NA, DT S6490A).

83 For an insight to the existence of the post-independence 'gombeenman' see, Liam Kennedy, 'A sceptical view on the reinacarnation of the Irish "Gombeenman"' in *Economic and Social Review* 8, 3 (1976–7): 213–21.

84 [D. P.] to the author, 6 May 2002.

85 *Dáil Debates*, vol. 22, 7 Mar. 1927, 843.

86 Quoted in ibid., vol. 23, 19 Apr. 1927, 151.

87 Ibid., 236.

88 *An Act to Facilitate the Provision of Land for Certain Evicted Tenants in Ireland and for Other Purposes Connected Therewith, and to Make Provision with Respect to the Tenure of Office by the Estates Commissioners* 7 Edw. 7, ch. 56 [26 Aug. 1907].

89 *Memo dated 10 May 1906 Issued by the Estates Commissioners for Guidance of Assistant Inspectors When Making Inquiries with Reference to Applications Received from Persons Seeking Reinstatement as Evicted Tenants or as the Representatives of Evicted Tenants* [Cd 3658], HC 1907, vol. LXX.1171.

90 *Report of Estates Commissioners for Year from 1 Apr. 1918 to 31 Mar. 1919* [Cmd. 577], HC 1919, vol. XIX. 965, p. xv; *Report of Estates Commissioners for the Year from 1 Apr. 1919 to 31 Mar. 1920 and for the Period from 1 Nov. 1903 to 31 Mar. 1920* [Cmd 1150], HC 1921, vol. XIV. 661. As examples of what happened on individual estates, 43 tenants who had been evicted during the Plan of Campaign had been reinstated on the Masserene and Ferrard estates in Meath and Louth by 1907; 82 on the Brooke estate in Wexford and 37 on the Lansdowne estate in Laois; *Return of Tenants (or Their Representatives) Who Had Been evicted from Three Plan of Campaign Estates Purchased or Proposed to be Purchased by the Estates Commissioners and Who Have Been Reinstated in their Former Holdings, or Provided with Other Holdings* [Cd 3664], HC 1907, vol. LXIX. 82.

91 Labhras MacFhionnghail [Laurence Ginnell], *The Land Question* (Dublin, n.d. [1917]), p. 5.

92 Ibid., pp. 4–5.

93 Ibid., p. 7.

94 PRO, CO904, part iv, police reports 1914–21.

95 Anonymous letter sent to Philip Houlihan, Apr. 1922 (N.A., DJ H5/118).

96 Report on land agitation in Queen's County [Laois], 1922 (NA, DT, S 566).

97 'Captain of local Volunteers' to OC 1st Midland Division IRA, 6 May 1922 (NA, DJ H5/15).

98 Patrick Hogan to W. T. Cosgrave, 7 Apr. 1923 (NA, DT S3192).

99 *Minutes of Proceedings of the First Dáil Eireann, 29 June 1920*, 178.

100 Ibid., 879.

101 *Dáil Debates*, vol. 3, 28 May 1923, 1167.

102 Ibid., vol. 9, 28 Oct. 1924, 289.

103 Ibid., vol. 4, 4 July 1923, 191.

104 W. E. Vaughan, *Sin, Sheep and Scotsmen: John George Adair and the Derryveagh Evictions, 1861* (Belfast, 1983).

105 *Dáil Debates*, vol. 21, 3 Nov. 1927, 737.

106 Ibid., vol. 57, 26 June 1935, 917–18.

107 In the years up to end of Dec. 1921, the county inspectors of the RIC estimated the numbers of these holdings in each county.

108 See Patrick Hogan in *Dáil Debates*, vol. 7, 29 May 1924, 1537.

109 *ILC Report*, 1933, p. 33.

110 *Dáil Debates*, vol. 7, 29 May 1924, 220.

111 Ibid., 248.

112 Ibid., vol. 6, 14 Feb. 1924, 1006.

113 It was later found that he was 72 with a daughter and granddaughters, but the decision was not reversed; *Dáil Debates*, vol. 10, 2 Apr. 1925, 1750–1; vol. 11, 7 May 1925, 1073–4.

114 Ibid., vol. 15, 3 June 1926, 269.

115 Ibid., vol. 19, 24 Mar. 1927, 248

116 Ibid., vol. 38, 29 Apr. 1931, 398–9.

117 Ibid., vol. 17, 8 Dec. 1926, 587.

118 *Freeman's Journal*, 23 Aug. 1923.

119 Ibid., 24 Aug. 1923.

120 John Flood to Frank Aiken, 27 Nov. 1927 (UCD, Aiken papers, P104/2241).

121 *Dáil Debates*, vol. 19, 24 Mar. 1927, 231.

122 Ibid., vol. 24, 13 June 1928, 414.

123 Quoted by James Cosgrave in Dáil Éireann, 24 Mar. 1927; in ibid., vol. 24, 13 June 1928, 238.

124 Ibid., vol. 19, 24 Mar. 1927, 225; ibid., vol. 19, 24 Mar. 1927, 229.

125 Ibid., vol. 22, 7 Mar. 1927, 866.

126 Ibid., vol. 29, 25 Apr. 1929, 1043.

127 *Seanad Debates*, vol. 1, 1 Aug. 1923, 1872.

128 *Report of Estates Commissioners for the Year from 1 Apr. 1919 to 31 Mar. 1920.*

129 *Dáil Éireann: Official Bulletin, Session 17–19 June 1919*, p. 19.

130 *Minutes of Proceedings of Second Dáil*, 23 Aug. 1921, p. 47.

131 Ibid., p. 48.

132 Ibid., 1 Mar. 1922, 144.

133 Public notice issued by Kyleavallagh and Kyleoughan Land Committee, Apr. 1922 (NA, DJ H5/123); Report compiled by Arthur Blennerhassett, Ballyseedy, County Kerry, 7 Mar. 1922 (NA, DJ H5/57).

134 *Dáil Debates*, vol. 12, 17 June 1925, 1359–60.

135 Ibid., vol. 69, 20 Oct. 1937, 403–4.

136 Ibid., vol. 4, 6 July 1923, 333–4.

137 Commission on Agriculture, *Final Report of the Commission on Agriculture* (Dublin, 1924), p. 35.

138 Ibid.

139 For an insight, see Brian Hanley, *The IRA, 1926–1936* (Dublin, 2002), pp. 56–9.

140 See also Dooley, 'IRA veterans and land division', pp. 86–107.

141 *Minutes of Proceedings of Dáil Éireann*, 1 Mar. 1922, p. 144.

142 Ibid., 11 Mar. 1922, p. 144.

143 Both Kent and de Markievicz were supported by Art O'Connor, former Director of Agriculture, on the point that if there was going to be land for the landless it should only be for those who had given 'good service to this country during the past two years'; *Minutes of Proceedings of Dáil Éireann*, 11 Mar. 1922 p. 160.

144 Ibid., pp. 160–1.

145 *Dáil Debates*, vol. 16, 17 June 1926.

146 O'Donnell, *There Will Be Another Day*, p. 48.

147 *Dáil Debates*, vol. 13, 2 Dec. 1925, 1109.

148 Ibid.

149 Ibid., 1151.

150 O'Halpin, *Defending Ireland*, p. 46.

151 At various stages there was the Reunited IRA Association or Reunited Irish Republican Pre-Truce Forces Association, as well as a host of other organisations at local and national level. In the late 1930s, the National Association of Old IRA was formed to reunite the factions and: 'to restore to the nation that unity of purpose and solidarity of organisation which, twenty years ago, brought forth the highest qualities of self-sacrificing patriotism in our people'. By the early 1940s the United Conference of Old IRA Organisations had taken under its wing among others the Old Cumann na mBan, the Association of Old Fianna Eireann, Association of Irish Citizen Army, National Association of the Old IRA, the 1916 Veterans' Association; Association of the Old Dublin Brigade. National Association of Old IRA, *Dublin Brigade Review* (Dublin, n.d.), p. 74; R. Muldoon, 'Report of IRA Old Comrades Association, All-Ireland Convention, 16 July 1933' (NA, DJ 8/718).

152 T. J. Keenan to Piaras Beaslai, 10 Mar. 1928 (NLI, Beaslai papers, MS 33,947(8)).

153 *An Phoblacht*, 27 Nov. 1925.

154 Ibid., 29 Jan. 1926; 14, 28 May 1926; 22 Apr. 1927.

155 List of landless Old IRA men suitable for holdings of land drawn up by West Limerick Old IRA Brigade, n.d., *c.*1934 (NLI, West Limerick Brigade papers, MS 27,607(2)).

156 *Dáil Debates*, vol. 29, 18 Apr. 1929.

157 Ibid., vol. 28, 7 Mar. 1929.

158 List of members in battalion areas deserving of land allotment with suggestions as to estates for acquisition in those areas, n.d. [*c.*1934?] (UCD, Aiken papers, P104/2886).

159 *The Irish Times* [property supplement], 9 Oct. 2003.

160 Fanning, *Independent Ireland*, p. 66.

161 For a record of untenanted lands held by landlords in 1906, see *Return of Untenanted Lands in Rural Districts, Distinguishing Demesnes on Which there is a Mansion, Showing Rural District and Electoral Divisions, Townland, Area in Statute Acres, Poor Law Valuation, Names of Occupiers as in Valuation Lists*, HC, 1906, c.177.

162 Dooley, *'The Greatest of the Fenians'*, p. 104.

163 John O'Donovan Rossa to Arthur Griffith, 31 Jan. 1922 (NA, DT S 561).

164 *Dáil Debates*, vol. 3, 28 May 1923, 1152–3.

165 Ibid., vol. 2, 5 Jan. 1923, 592.

166 *Dáil Debates*, vol. 3, 14 June 1923, 1965.

167 *Royal Commission on Congestion in Ireland: Final Report*, pp 58–9.

168 *Dáil Debates*, vol. 3, 28 May 1923, 1165.

169 Ibid., vol. 4, 3 July 1923, 32.

170 Information based on interviews with 25 surviving families carried out by this author, 2002–3; See also Terence Dooley, *A Future for Irish Historic Houses: A Study of Fifty Houses* (2003).

171 *Minutes of Proceedings of Dáil Éireann*, 17 Aug. 1921, p. 69.

172 Bew, Hazelkorn and Patterson, *The Dynamics of Irish Politics*, p. 18.

173 *Final Report of the Commission on Agriculture* (1924), p. 33.

174 *Dáil Debates*, vol. 29, 19 Apr. 1929, 718.

175 *Final Report of the Commission on Agriculture* (1924), p. 34.

176 Ibid., p. 35.

177 Ibid., p. 34.

178 Daly, *The First Department*, p. 101.

179 Ibid.

180 *Dáil Debates*, vol. 13, 25 Nov. 1925, 975.

181 Ibid.

182 Ibid., vol. 15, 27 May 1926, 2266.

183 Ibid., vol. 22,, 8 Mar. 1928, 978.

184 Ibid., vol. 22, 7 Mar. 1928, 871.

185 Ibid., vol. 17, 7 Dec. 1926, 466.

186 Ibid., vol. 18, 17 Feb. 1927, 622–3.

187 See for example, debate between Hugh Colohan (Kildare, Labour) and Martin Roddy in ibid., 16 Nov. 1927, 1383.

188 Ibid., vol. 19, 25 Mar. 1927, 1123–4.

189 Ibid., vol. 32, 23 Oct. 1929, 22.

190 Ibid., vol. 19, 25 Mar. 1927, 1019.

191 Ibid., vol. 21, 4 Nov. 1927, 854.

192 Ibid., vol. 40, 11, 25 Nov. 1931, 1201, 1998.

193 These figures have been culled from the annual reports of the Land Commission; also Sammon, *In the Land Commission*, pp. 256–7 (see also Sammon's note on these statistics, p. 257).

194 *ILC Report*, 1933, p. 13.

195 Jones, 'Land reform legislation', p. 135.

196 *Dáil Debates*, vol. 12, 4 June 1925, 344.

197 Ibid., vol. 13, 26 Nov. 1926, 1008.

198 Ibid., vol. 34, 21 May 1930, 2281.

199 *ILC Report*, 1923–8, p. 34.

200 Sammon, *In the Land Commission*, p. 288.

201 Monahan, 'Administration of land acts', p. 133.

202 Ibid.

203 Ibid., p. 133.

204 *Land Act, 1927: An Act to Amend the Law Relating to the Occupation and Ownership of Land and for Other Purposes Relating Thereto*, [21 May 1927], no. 19 of 1927.

205 *Land Act, 1923*.

206 *ILC Report*, 1923–8, p. 8.

207 *Dáil Debates*, vol. 38, 14 May 1931, 1327.

208 Ibid., vol. 22, 7 Mar. 1927, 846–7.

209 Ibid., vol. 48, 13 July 1933, 2381.

210 Typescript lists of motions put forward by Dáil deputies, 1934 (UCD, Aiken papers, P104/3353).

211 Quoted in Dunphy, *The Rise of Fianna Fáil*, p. 117.

FOUR: FIANNA FÁIL AND LAND REFORM POLICY

1   On the rise of Fianna Fáil see Richard Dunphy, *The Making of Fianna Fáil Power in Ireland 1923–1948* (Oxford, 1995), p. 8.

2   Taken from ibid., p. 83.

3   Fianna Fáil, *A Brief Outline of the Aims and Programme of Fianna Fáil* (Dublin, n.d.), p. 4; *Fianna Fáil: 1926–51: The Story of Twenty-Five Years of National Endeavour and Historic Achievement* (n.d. [1951]), p. 6.

4   Frank Aiken, for example, would later claim that 'one of the principle [*sic*] objects for which Fianna Fáil was founded was to establish on the land as many families as practicable. This was also one of the fundamental objects of the old Sinn Féin movement and of the First Dáil'; see *Dáil Debates*, vol. 48, 13 July 1933, 2381; also corrected typescript copies of a speech by Frank Aiken introducing the 1933 Land Bill to the Dáil, Aug. 1933 (UCD, Aiken papers, P104/3301).

5   Michael Laffan, *The Resurrection of Ireland: The Sinn Féin Party*, 1916–1923 (Cambridge, 1999), p. 457.

6   For statistical data, see Michael Gallagher (ed.), *Irish Elections 1922–44: Results and Analysis* (Shannon, 1993), pp. 56–90; see also Dunphy, *The Rise of Fianna Fáil*, p. 79.

7   Bew, Hazelkorn and Patterson, *The Dynamics of Irish Politics*, p. 30.

8   See chapter 8.

9   *Mayo News*, 6 Feb. 1932.

10   A. Orridge, 'The Blueshirts and the "Economic War": a study of Ireland in the context of dependency theory', *Political Studies* XXXI (1983): 358.

11   *A Brief Outline of the Aims and Programme of Fianna Fáil*, p. 6.

12   Bew, Hazelkorn and Patterson, *The Dynamics of Irish Politics*, p. 73.

13   *Fianna Fáil: Seventh Annual Ard-Fheis 1932: Report of Proceedings* (UCD, P176/746).

14   Aiken papers, UCD P104/3301.

15   Born Mayo in 1892, he was a member of Sinn Féin and the IRA and took an active part in the organisation of Sinn Féin courts in 1920–1 (he was a solicitor by profession.) He played an active role on the anti-Treaty side during the Civil War, becoming a member of the IRA Army Council 1923–6. A founding member and vice-president of Fianna Fáil, he was elected at every election for Fianna Fáil from 1927 to his death in 1952. He was Minister for Lands and Fisheries in 1932 and later held the ministerial portfolios for Justice and for Local Government and Public Health.

16   *Dáil Debates*, vol. 41, 11 May 1932, 1459.

17   J.A. Gaughan (ed.), *Memoirs of Senator Joseph Connolly (1885–1961): A Founder of Modern Ireland* (Dublin, 1996), p. 359.

18   Ibid., p. 361.

19   *Fianna Fáil Election Manifesto 1933: To the Electorate of Tipperary* (NLI).

20   *An Act to Amend Generally the Law, Finance and Practice Relating to Land Purchase, and in Particular to Make Further and Better Provision for the Execution of the Functions of the Judicial and Lay Commissioners of the Land Commission and to Provide for the Provisions of the Purchase Annuities and Certain Other Annual Payments and for the Funding of Arrears Thereof, and to Provide for Other Matters Connected with the Matters Aforesaid*, [13 Oct. 1933], no. 38/1933.

21   *Dáil Debates*, vol. 48, 13 July 1933, 2381; Land Bill 1933, government statement for the press, c.Aug. 1933 (UCD, Aiken papers, P104/3300).

22 Frank Aiken to secretary of the Land Commission, n.d. [1933] (UCD, Aiken papers, P104/3298).

23 *Seanad Debates*, vol. 17, 18 Aug. 1933, 1021–2.

24 Land Bill 1933, government statement for the press, *c.*Aug. 1933 (UCD, Aiken papers, P104/3300).

25 *Dáil Debates*, vol. 48, 13 July 1933, 2396.

26 G. C. Bennett (Limerick, Cumann na nGaedheal); *Dáil Debates*, vol. 60, 13 Feb. 1936, 724.

27 Born 1902 in Dublin, the fourth son of John Dillon, leader of the Irish Parliamnetary Party after the death of John Redmond. First elected as an Independent for Donegal in 1932, Dillon was one of the founders of the National Centre Party the same year which evolved into Fine Gael. In 1941, Dillon resigned from the Fine Gael party on the issue of Ireland's neutrality during the Second World War and did not rejoin for ten years. Nevertheless, he was Minister for Agriculture in the two coalition governments of 1948–51 and 1954–7. He became leader of Fine Gael in 1959. He resigned as leader in 1965 and from politics in 1969; see Maurice Manning, *James Dillon: A Biography* (Dublin, 1999).

28 *Dáil Debates*, vol. 60, 13 Feb. 1936, 715.

29 *Commission of Enquiry into Banking, Currency and Credit, Memoranda and Minutes of Evidence*, vol. 11, (1938), p. 1164.

30 Ibid., p. 1133.

31 Ibid.

32 Ibid., p. 1134.

33 Ibid., p. 1176.

34 Ibid., p. 1165.

35 *Dáil Debates*, vol. 48, 13 July 1933, 2410.

36 Government memo. on land policy prepared for the secretary of the Irish Land Commission [1933] (NA, DT S 6490 (A)).

37 According to Frank Aiken the Bill was intended to make provision for the landless men who could no longer emigrate; *Seanad Debates*, vol. 17, 18 Aug. 1933, 1033.

38 Frank Aiken to secretary of Land Commission, n.d. [1933] (UCD, Aiken papers, P104/3298).

39 *Dáil Debates*, vol. 48, 13 July 1933, 2400.

40 *An Act to Amend the Law Relating to Local Government Franchise and to the Registration of Local Government Electors*, [29 Mar. 1935], no. 9/1935.

41 *ILC Report* 1935, p. 5.

42 *Dáil Debates*, vol. 123, 6 Dec. 1951.

43 Dunphy, *The Making of Fianna Fáil*, p. 75.

44 Ibid.

45 These findings are based on the biographical notes of TDs in Vincent Browne (ed.), *The Magill Book of Irish Politics* (Dublin, 1981).

46 T. E. Duffy, 'Old Irish Republican Army Organisation: County of Meath and Environs: Report and schemes with appendices presented to president de valera and his government for consideration', May 1933 (UCD, Aiken papers, P104/2887). The president of the Fianna Fáil cumann in Navan, Henry O'Hagan was a member of the Old IRA; *Irish Press*, 17 Jan. 1933; for pledges of support from Meath, Roscommon and East Waterford Old IRA Associations, see *Irish Press*, 16, 18 Jan. 1933

47 Dunphy, *The Making of Fianna Fáil*, p. 82.

48 List of members in battalion areas deserving of land allotment with suggestions as to estates for acquisition in those areas (UCD, Aiken papers, P104/2886).

49 Report of Thurles conference of IRA, 2 Oct. 1932 (UCD, Twomey papers, P69/54 (37)).

50 P. J. Davern to Frank Aiken enclosing resolutions passed by United Republican Association of County Tipperary, 2 Apr. 1933 (UCD, Aiken papers, P104/2875).

51 *Meath Chronicle*, 19 Jan. 1935.

52 Enclosed in P. J. Davern to Frank Aiken enclosing resolutions passed by United Republican Association of County Tipperary, 2 Apr. 1933 (UCD, Aiken papers, P104/2875).

53 Sammon, *In the Land Commission*, p. 2.

54 Ibid., p.11.

55 Inspectorate notice no. 11/35: signed by S. J. Waddell, commissioner and chief inspector, 4 May 1935 (NA, DT S 6490 (A)).

56 Representations by County Clare Old IRA Association: administration of Military Service Pensions Act, 1934 (NA, DT 97/9/331).

57 Memorandum prepared by Minister for Lands for Executive Council on land division policy, 21 Aug. 1936 (NA, DT S 6490 (A)); Department of Lands: land division policy, 17 November 1936 (NA, DT S6490).

58 Draft letter from Maurice Moynihan to chairman of Old IRA Convention, *c.*21 Jan. 1937 (NA, DT S9240 (A)).

59 *Meath Chronicle*, 16 Mar. 1935.

60 Ibid., 16 Oct. 1937.

61 *Dáil Debates*, vol. 86, 24 Mar. 1942.

62 Report of Land Division Committee, 21 May 1936 (UCD, Aiken papers, P104/3388).

63 Gerald Boland was born in Manchester in 1885 but reared in Dublin. He fought in the 1916 Rebellion and played a prominent role in the War of Independence and as an anti-Treatyite in the Civil War. First elected as a Republican for Roscommon in 1932, he became a founding member of Fianna Fáil and was re-elected at every election as a Fianna Fáil candidate until his defeat in 1961. He held a number of ministerial portfolios including Lands 1936–9 (which included Fisheries 1936–7). He was a brother of Harry Boland.

64 *Dáil Debates*, vol. 66, 4 May 1937.

65 Ibid.

66 Born 1887. Moylan was one of the outstanding IRA leaders in County Cork during the War of Independence. He opposed the Treaty and became IRA Director of Operations during the Civil War. Represented Cork North from 1932 until his defeat in 1957, the year he died. He was Minister for Lands from 1943 to 1948, Minister for Education 1951–4 and briefly Minister for Agriculture in 1957 (as a senator).

67 Affiliated to this organisation were units such as Old Cumann na mBan, Association of Old Fianna Eireann, Association of Old Irish Citizen Army, National Association of the Old IRA, 1916 Veterans Association and Association of Old Dublin Brigade.

68 Memorandum prepared for the government: Old IRA preferential treatment, 12 Nov. 1942 (NA, DT S9240 (A)); Seosamh Ó Traithigh, secretary of United Conference of Old IRA, to Eamon De Valera, 8 Aug. 1942 (NA, DT S9240 (B)).

69 See, for example, John A. Costello to Sean Dowling, 14 Mar. 1957 (NA, DT S9240 (B)).

70 Seosamh Ó Cearnaigh [Joseph Kearney] to Eamon de Valera, 7 June 1957 (NA, DT S9240 (B)).

71 Typescript list of motions set down by TDs in 1934 (UCD, Aiken papers, 104/3354).

72 Copies of statements describing the contents and purposes of the 1936 Land Bill (UCD, Aiken papers, P104/3335).

73 O'Shiel, 'Changes effected in recent Land Commission legislation', pp. 298–9.

74 *Dáil Debates*, vol. 76, 6 June 1939, 589–90.

75 Ibid.

76 Confidential report by Eamon Mansfield, 'How laws in the legal machinery have held up Irish Land Commission work', 18 June 1943 (NA, DT S14399).

77 Ibid.

78 Ibid.

79 *ILC Report 1939*, p. 5.

80 Memorandum on land division policy prepared by Minister for Lands for Executive Council, 21 Aug. 1936 (NA, DT S6490 (A)).

81 Report of Land Division Committee, 21 May 1936 (UCD, Aiken papers, P104/3338); Department of Lands: memorandum on land division policy issued to each member of government, 13 Dec. 1938 (NA, DT S6490); Department of Lands: memo on land division policy issued to each member of government, 13 Dec. 1938 (NA, DT S6490)

82 *Dáil Debates*, vol. 75, 2 May 1939, 1484–5.

83 Memorandum prepared by S. J. Waddell for the Minister for Lands, Dec. 1936 (NA, DT S6490).

84 Ibid.

85 Department of Lands: land division policy, 9 Jan. 1937 (NA, DT S6490).

86 See Maurice Moynihan (ed.), *Speeches and Statements by Eamon de Valera, 1917–1973* (Dublin, 1980), pp. 466–9.

87 Memorandum by Kevin O'Shiel, 'Post-war policy and programme for the Land Commission', n.d. [*c*.Feb. 1945] (NA, DT, S 13101a).

88 Eamon Mansfield, 'Observations on memo. by Department of Lands', 21 June 1943 (NA, DT S14,399).

89 Minister of Lands [Sean Moylan] to the Taoiseach [Eamon de Valera] 1 Sept. 1943 (NA, DT S12890a).

90 Department of Lands memo. for the government on land division policy, Apr. 1947 (NA, DT S6490 B/1).

91 Ibid.

92 Department of Lands memo. for the government on land division policy, 6 June 1947 (NA, DT, S6490 B/1).

93 *Seanad Debates*, vol. 37, 4 May 1950, 1752.

94 *Dáil Debates*, vol. 100, 9 May 1946, 2639.

95 Memo. by Minister for Finance on land division policy, 29 Mar. 1945 (NA, DT S6490 B/1).

96 *ILC Report 1951*, p. 8.

97 *Dáil Debates*, vol. 146, 30 June 1954, 770–1.

98 *Commission of Enquiry into Banking*, 1938, p. 1182.

99 *Dáil Debates*, vol. 48, 13 July 1933, 2425.

100 *Dáil Debates*, vol. 114, 7 Apr. 1949, 2630–1.

101 Mary E. Daly, *Social and Economic History of Ireland Since 1800* (Dublin, 1981), p. 149.

102 Jones, 'Divisions within the Irish government', p. 87.

103 *Emergency Powers Act, 1939*, no. 28/1939.

104 Memorandum prepared by the Department of Lands for the government on the cost of acquisition and resumption of land, 14 Oct. 1851 (NA, DT S6490 B/2).

105 Ibid.

106 Memorandum prepared by the Department of Lands: work of the Land Commission as affected by the Emergency, 29 Mar. 1943 (NA, DT S11,465).

107 Thomas Derrig was the leading Fianna Fáil politician in Carlow–Kilkenny from his first election in 1927 until 1954. He was Minister for Lands 1951–4 and for shorter periods beforehand. He was also Minister for Education for most of the period 1932–48.

108 Townshend, *Ireland: The 20th Century*, p. 156.

109 Sean T. O'Kelly was born in Dublin in 1883. He was a founding member of Sinn Féin and general secretary of the Gaelic League in 1915. He was a founding member of the Irish Volunteers and fought in the 1916 Rebellion. In 1918 he was elected MP for Mid-Dublin and continued to hold one of the Dublin seats until his election as President of Ireland in 1945. He was a founding member of Fianna Fáil becoming vice-president of the party. He was appointed Minister for Finance in 1939.

110 See for example, Thomas Derrig to Sean T. O'Kelly, 29 Apr. 1941 (NA, DT S12890A).

111 Memorandum prepared by the Department of Finance for the government, 28 Apr. 1941 (NA, DT S11,465).

112 The Land Commission actually made the largest staff contribution to the Emergency services of all of the government departments. In 1942, four higher executive officers, twenty junior executive officers, two minor staff officers, four clerical officers and thirty 'writing assistants' were seconded to the Department of Supplies alone. Memorandum prepared by Department of Lands: work of the Land Commission as affected by the Emergency, 29 Mar. 1943 (NA, DT S11,465); Thomas Derrig to Sean T. O'Kelly, 29 Apr. 1941 (NA, DT S11465A); memorandum prepared by the government in regard to a proposal to transfer further staff from the Land Commission, 30 Jan. 1942 (NA, DT S11465A).

113 W. F. Nally to P. Ó Cinnéide, 16 May 1944 (NA, DT S12890).

114 Memorandum prepared by the Department of Lands for the government on the cost of acquisition and resumption of land, 14 Oct. 1851 (NA, DT S6490 B/2).

115 Land Commission memorandum on the relief of congestion, 26 June 1946 (NA, DT S6490A); Cabinet minutes, 2 Apr. 1948 (NA, GC/5/9).

116 *ILC Report* 1947, p. 6.

117 *The Irish Times*, 19 May 1976; quoted in Dunphy, *The Making of Fianna Fáil*, p. 236.

118 Memorandum from Sean Moylan to Eamon de Valera, 1 Sept. 1943 (NA, DT S 12890A).

119 Land Commission memorandum on the relief of congestion, 26 June 1946 (NA, DT S6490A); Memorandum for the Cabinet Committee on Economic Planning: land division policy, Apr. 1947 (NA, DT S6490 B/1).

120 Memorandum on land division policy, Apr. 1947.

121 Memorandum prepared by the Department of Finance for the Cabinet Committee on Economic Planning regarding land division policy, 29 Mar. 1945 (NA, DT S6490A).

122 Ibid.

123 Ibid.

124 Memorandum prepared for the Cabinet Committee on Economic Planning: land division policy, Apr. 1947 (NA, DT S6490 B/1).

125 *Dáil Debates*, vol. 96, 26 Apr. 1945, 2528.

126 Quoted in memorandum by Minister for Lands, 30 June 1956 (NA, DT S14249B).

127 Sean Moylan addressing the Seanad; *Seanad Debates*, vol. 31, 3 Apr. 1946, 1171–2.

128 *Dáil Debates*, vol. 99, 6 Feb. 1946, 526.

129 Ibid.

130 Jones, 'Land reform legislation', p. 142.

131 Ibid., vol. 96, 26 Apr. 1945, 2529–30.

132 Department of Lands, Industry and Commerce, 'Memo. on full employment policy', 17 Jan. 1945 (NA, DT S13101A).

133 Department of Lands, Industry and Commerce, 'Economic and social aspects of land policy', Apr. 1945 (NA, DT S6490).

134 Ibid.

135 Ibid.

136 Ibid.

137 Department of Lands memorandum prepared for the government on land division policy, Apr. 1947 (NA, DT S6490 B/1).

138 Comments by the Minister for Agriculture in response to memorandum by Minister for Industry and Commerce on full employment [1945] (NA, DT S13101(a)).

139 [P.D.] to author, 19 May 2001.

140 *Dáil Debates*, vol. 99, 31 Jan. 1946, 300.

141 Ibid., vol. 99, 7 Feb. 1946, 591.

142 *ILC Report*, 1947, p. 7.

143 Michael Moran, Minister for Lands 1959–68, claimed that this fear may have had the opposite effect 'of galvanizing many owners into greater activity, with consequent good results for the community as a whole'; quoted in *ILC Report*, 1960, p. 36

144 [J. B.] to this author, 12 Apr. 2002.

145 Patrick Kavanagh, *Tarry Flynn* (London, 1972 edn), p. 77

146 *Dáil Debates*, vol. 169, 3 July 1958, 1357, vol. 120, 27 Apr. 1950, 1367.

147 Ibid., vol. 120, 27 Apr. 1950, 1367.

148 Jones, 'Divisions within the Irish government', pp. 86–7.

149 Minister for Lands to Sean Lemass, 5 May 1944; quoted in W. F. Nally to Padraig Ó Cinnéide, 16 May 1944 (NA, DT S12890).

150 Commissioner Michael Deegan, 'The work and policy of the Land Commission and the need for economy in the existing Emergency', 15 Apr. 1940 (NA, DT S)

151 *Committee of Enquiry on Post-Emergency Agricultural Policy: Reports on Agricultural Policy*, 1945 (P. 7175), p. 6.

152 Ibid., pp. 84–5.

153 Department of Lands memorandum for the government on land division policy, Apr. 1947 (NA, DT S6490 B/1).

154 Ibid.

155 Memorandum prepared for the government by the Department of Finance on land division policy, 28 Nov. 1948 (NA, DT S6490 B/1).

156 Ibid.

157 Ibid..

158 Department of Lands memorandum prepared for the government on land division policy, Apr. 1947 (NA, DT S6490 B/1).

159 *Dáil Debates*, vol. 92, 16 Dec. 1943, 939–40.

FIVE: REVERSING CROMWELL'S POLICY

1 See William Nolan, 'New farms and fields: migration policies of state land agencies 1891–1980' in W. J. Smyth and Kevin Whelan (eds), *Common Ground: Essays on the Historical Geography of Ireland* (Cork, 1988); Commins, *The Impact of Re-distribution in Ireland*; Micheal Ó Conghaile (ed.), *Gaeltach Ráthcairn: Leachtaí Comórtha* (Galway, 1986).

2 *An Act to Further Amend the Law Relating to the Occupation and Ownership of Land in Ireland and for Other Purposes Relating Thereto* [22 Aug. 1881], ch. 49, 44 & 45 Vict.

3 *Reports and Papers Relating to the Proceedings of the Committee of 'Mr. Tuke's Fund' During the Years 1882, 1883 and 1884: Collected for the Private use of the Committee* (privately published, n.d. [*c.*1885]), pp. 4, 5, 26, 34, 43.

4 Comerford, *Ireland*, p. 38.

5 Ibid.

6 *Royal Commission on Congestion in Ireland: Final Report*, p. 47.

7 Congested Districts Board, *Inspectors Local Reports* (Dublin, 1898), pp. 421–8; *Twenty-Seventh Report of the Congested Districts Board for Ireland for the Period from 1 Apr. 1918 to 31 Mar. 1919* [Cmd 759], HC 1920, vol. XIX. 889, p. 19.

8 See for example, Congested Districts Board, *Inspectors Local Reports*, pp. 2, 380, 386, 403.

9 *Congested Districts Board Annual Report*, 1902, p. 23.

10 Horace Plunkett, *Ireland in the New Century* (London, 1904), p. 49.

11 E. O'Farrell, *The Congested Districts of Ireland and How to Deal With Them: a Paper Read Before the Statistical and Social Inquiry Society of Ireland, 14 Dec. 1886* (Dublin, 1887), p. 5.

12 Plunkett, *Ireland in the New Century*, p. 54.

13 Enda Delaney, *Demography, State and Society: Irish Migration to Britain, 1912–1971* (Liverpool, 2000), pp. 10–11.

14 J. G. Hughes and B. M. Walsh, *Internal Migration Flows in Ireland and their Determinants: ESRI Paper no. 90* (Dublin, 1980), pp. 16, 75.

15 Plunkett, *Ireland in the New Century*, p. 56.

16 *Coimisiún na Gaeltachta: Minutes of Evidence*, vol. VI, p. 1.

17 *Commission on Emigration and Other Population Problems, 1948–54: Reports* (PR. 2541), p.137.

18 Plunkett, *Ireland in the New Century*, p. 48.

19 *Royal Commission on Congestion in Ireland: Final Report*, pp. 13–14; *Report of the Irish Landowners' Convention, 1908–9*, pp. 55–6.

20 Mary E. Daly, 'Social structure of the Dublin working class, 1871–1911' in *Irish Historical Studies* XXIII, 90 (Nov. 1982): 129.

21 CICMR, County Galway ER, May 1918.

22 Rutherford Mayne, *Bridge Head* (Dublin, n.d.), p. v.

23 *ILC Report*, 1929, p. 7.

24 Plunkett, *Ireland in the New Century*, p. 49.

25 *Congested Districts Board Annual Report*, 1905, p. 19.

26 *ILC Report*, 1933, p. 12.

27 *Dáil Debates*, vol. 2, 5 Jan. 1923, 598.

28 Ibid., vol. 38, 14 May 1931, 1334–5.

29 Ibid., vol. 2, 5 Jan. 1923, 596.

30 Quoted in Townshend, *Ireland: the 20th Century*, p. 43.

31 Comerford, *Ireland*, p. 141; see also Townshend, *Ireland: The 20th Century*, pp. 123–4.

32 See, for example, O'Malley, *On Another Man's Wound*, pp. 53, 57–8; Sean Ó Lúing, *I Die in a Good Cause: A Study of Thomas Ashe, Idealist and Revolutionary* (Tralee, 1970); Townshend, *Ireland: The 20th Century*, pp. 40–3; Hopkinson, *The War of Independence*, p. 15; Harte, *IRA and its Enemies*, pp. 24, 206, 232; Fitzpatrick, *Two Irelands*, pp. 16–17.

33 *Dáil Debates*, vol. 8, 24 July 1924, 2175.

34 *Report of Coimisiún na Gaeltachta* (Dublin, 1926), p. 40.

35 See evidence of Patrick Conroy, *Coimisiún na Gaeltachta: Minutes of Evidence*, vol. XVIII, p. 14.

36 *Coimisiún na Gaeltachta: Statements of Evidence Furnished by Persons Who Were Not Examined Before the Commission* (SO, 1926), p. 22.

37 *Coimisiun na Gaeltachta: Minutes of Evidence*, vol. XV, pp. 19, 27.

38 *Report of Coimisiun na Gaeltachta* (Dublin, 1926), p. 45.

39 Ibid., p. 42.

40 Quoted in Gearoid Ó Tuathaigh, 'Aistriú Pobail Ghaeltachta go hÁiteanna Eile in Éirinn: Culrá an Pholaisí' in Mícheál Ó Conghaile (ed.), *Gaeltach Ráthcairn: Leachtaí Comórtha* (Galway, 1986), p. 22.

41 *Coimisiún na Gaeltachta: Persons Who Were Not Examined Before the Commission*, p. 23.

42 Ibid.

43 *ILC Report*, 1930, p. 7.

44 Lee, *Ireland 1912–85*, p. 134; Commins, *The Impact of Re-distribution in Ireland*, p. 6.

45 W. T. Cosgrave, *Policy of the Cumann na nGaedheal Party* (Dublin, 1927), p. 14.

46 *Dáil Debates*, vol. 23, 3 May 1928, 941.

47 Ibid., vol. 31, 14 May 1931, 1160–1.

48 Ibid.

49 The Land Commission only began to publish such statistics in 1938.

50 *Dáil Debates*, vol. 34, 26 Mar. 1930,

51 Ibid., vol. 15, 1 June 1926, 10.

52 Ibid., vol. 15, 2 June 1926, 140–1.

53 Ibid., vol. 21, 4 Nov. 1927, 853.

54 Ibid., vol. 19, 22 Mar. 1927, 111–12.

55 Ibid., vol. 25, 19 July 1928.

56 Ibid., vol. 8, 24 July 1924, 2156.

57 Ibid., vol. 18, 17 Feb. 1927, 619.

58 Ibid., vol. 20, 23 June 1927, 46–51.

59 Ibid., vol. 38, 14 May 1932, 1375.

60 Ibid., vol. 20, 12 Aug. 1927, 1635.

61 Ibid., vol. 21, 4 Nov. 1927, 963–4.

62 Ibid., vol. 39, 15 July 1931.

63 Quoted in ibid., vol. 34, 22 May 1930, 2323.

64 Ibid., vol. 23, 4 May 1928, 1032.

65 Ibid., vol. 66, 7 Apr. 1937, 323.

66 Commins, *The Impact of Re-distribution in Ireland*, p. 7.

67 Padraig Mac Donncha, 'Ráthcairn: 50 Bliain ar Aghaidh' in *Comhar* 4 (Apr. 1985): 8.

68 *Irish Press*, 15 Nov. 1934.

69 Townshend, *Ireland: The 20th Century*, p. 156.

70 Outline of career of John C. Gamble, 4 Sept. 1905–6 Mar. 1948 (NA, DT S2487C).

71 *Meath Chronicle*, 26 Jan. 1935; in the same edition, the editor of the *Meath Chronicle* contended that there was enough land for everybody in the county and that the new migrants were 'hard-working God-fearing people. They are honest and clean. They speak the language of our forefathers and are proud to speak it'.

72 Quoted in *Meath Chronicle*, 26 Jan. 1935.

73 Commins, *The Impact of Re-distribution in Ireland*, p. 9.

74 Vincent Browne (ed.), *The Magill Book of Irish Politics* (Dublin, 1981), p. 293.

75 *Meath Chronicle*, 8 May 1937.

76 Ibid., 9 Jan. 1937.

77 Ibid., 19 June 1937.

78 Resolution of Dunderry Fianna Fáil *cumann*, quoted in ibid., 24 July 1937.

79 Ibid., 16 Oct. 1937.

80 Bew, Hazelkorn and Patterson, *The Dynamics of Irish Politics*, p. 77.

81 *Dáil Debates*, vol. 79, 5 Mar. 1940, 18.

82 Ibid., vol. 82, 6 Mar. 1941, 173

83 Ibid., vol. 120, 25 Apr. 1950, 953.

84 Ibid., vol. 129, 14 Feb. 1952, 552.

85 *ILC Report*, 1935, p. 6.

86 Summaries of Evidence: Land Commission (TCD, Arnold Marsh papers, MS 8301).

87 Report by S. J. Waddell, senior land commissioner, 4 Dec. 1942 (NA, DT, S12890A).

88 *Dáil Debates*, vol. 161, 24 Apr. 1957, 249.

89 *ILC Report*, 1936, p. 6.

90 Senator Connolly later pointed out that the Rathcarne colonists were 'all married men with families and picked for their ability to work their new farms'; Gaughan (ed.), *Memoirs of Senator Joseph Connolly*, p. 369; Information supplied by the Irish Land Commission, Records Branch, Bishop Street, Dublin.

91 *Irish Press*, 13 Apr. 1935.

92 *Connaught Tribune*, 19 Apr. 1935.

93 Ó Conghaile, 'An Imirce agus na Teaghliagh', p. 59.

94 *Meath Chronicle*, 3 Apr. 1937.

95 *ILC Report*, 1952, p. 30.

96 Ibid.

97 Quoted in Ó Conghaile, 'An Imirce agus na Teaghliagh', p. 60.

98 *Dáil Debates*, vol. 77, 8 Nov. 1939, 938.

99 Ibid.

100 Ibid., vol. 99, 31 Jan. 1946.

101 [C.M.] to author, 16 Apr. 2001.

102 See for example, Commins, *The Impact of Re-distribution in Ireland*, p. 9.

103 *Meath Chronicle*, 23 Oct. 1937.

104 Ibid., 10 Apr. 1937.

105 See Meath County Council, *Local Plan for Rathcairn Gaeltacht* (n.d. [c.1979]).

106 Quoted in *Meath Chronicle*, 10 Apr. 1937.

107 Quoted in *Labour News*, 3 Apr. 1937.

108 *Dáil Debates*, vol. 67, 11 May 1937, 26–7.

109 Quoted in *Labour News*, 3 Apr. 1937.

110 *Dáil Debates*, vol. 63, 15 July 1936, 1374.

111 *Meath Chronicle*, 10 Apr. 1937.

112 *Meath* Chronicle, 10 Apr. 1937; see also *Dáil Debates*, vol. 63, 15 July 1936, 1373.

113 *Meath Chronicle*, 10 Apr. 1937.

114 *ILC report*, 1939, p. 6.

115 *Labour News*, 3 Apr. 1937; see also *Meath Chronicle*, 6 Feb. 1937

116 Quoted in *Labour News*, 3 Apr. 1937.

117 Memorandum prepared by S. J. Waddell to Minister for Lands, Dec. 1936 (NA, DT, S6490).

118 *Meath Chronicle Special Issue*.

119 Micheál Seoighe,'Rathcairn, 1939–67' in Ó Conghaile, *Gaeltacht Ráthcairn*, pp. 93–94.

120 *Dáil Debates*, vol. 185, 1 Dec. 1960, 592–3.

121 Ibid., vol. 254, 26 May 1971, 245.

122 Meath County Council, *Local Plan for Rathcairn Gaeltacht*, p. 12

123 *The Irish Times*, 10 June 1964.

124 Quoted in *Irish Press*, 1 Feb. 1969.

125 *ILC Report*, 1939, p. 6.

126 O'Shiel, Changes effected in recent Land Commission legislation', p. 304.

127 Meath County Council, *Local Plan for Rathcairn Gaeltacht* (n.d. [c. 1979]), p. 7.

128 D. F. Hannon and Patrick Commins, 'The significance of small-scale landholders in Ireland's socio-economic transformation' in J. H. Goldthorpe and C. T. Whelan (eds), *The Development of Industrial Society in Ireland* (Oxford, 1992), pp. 79–104.

129 *Report of Inter-Departmental Committee on Seasonal Migration to Great Britain 1937–1938* (Dublin, 1938), p. 29.

130 Ibid., pp. 30–1.

131 Memorandum for the government on land settlement, 14 Nov. 1952 (NA, DT, S6490 B/2).

132 Recommendations for the provision of holdings for migrants from the congested districts, 19 Aug. 1939 (NA, DT S6490).

133 Ibid.

134 Memorandum on migrants from congested districts: provision of holdings, 30 Aug. 1939 (NA, DT S6490).

135 *Dáil Debates*, vol. 151, 26 May 1955, 267.

136 Eamon Mansfield, 'Observations on memorandum by Department of Lands', 21 June 1943 (NA, DT S14,399); see also Report by Professor T. A. Smiddy on land division and enlargement of holdings, Apr. 1942 (NA, DT S6490A).

SIX: AMBIVALENT ATTITUDES AND CHANGING POLICIES

1 Paul Bew and Henry Patterson, *Sean Lemass and the Making of Modern Ireland* (Dublin, 1978), p. 24.

2 See, for example, J. A. Murphy, 'The Irish party system, 1938–51', in K. B. Nowlan and T. D. Williams (eds), *Ireland in the War Years and After* (Dublin 1969), p. 158; Townshend, *Ireland: The 20th Century*, p. 159.

3 Walker, *Parliamentary Results*, 1918–92, pp. 154–61.

4   Ibid., pp. 168–76.

5   *Dáil Debates*, vol. 110, 26 May 1948, 2258.

6   Ibid., 2259.

7   Born in County Derry in 1889. McGilligan was a TD from 1923 to 1965. He was Minister for Industry and Commerce from March 1924 until 1927 when External Affairs was also added to his portfolio. He was the minister responsible for the Shannon Scheme. He was Minister for Finance, 1948–51 and Attorney-General in the Second Coalition 1954–7. He died in 1979.

8   Memorandum from Minister for Finance to government: land division policy, 28 Oct. 1948 (NA, DT S6490B).

9   Jones, 'Divisions within the Irish government', p. 102.

10 *Seanad Debates*, vol. 37, 4 May 1950, 1739.

11 Ibid., 1738–9.

12 Copy of letter from O. J. Redmond to secretary of Department of Lands, 19 Feb. 1951 (NA, DT S6490 B/2).

13 W. F. Nally to secretary of Department of Finance, 15 Mar. 1951(NA, DT S6490 B/2).

14 *Seanad Debates*, vol. 37, 4 May 1950, 1764.

15 *ILC Report*, 1951, p. 6.

16 See for example, *ILC Report*, 1953, p. 31; *ILC Report*, 1955, p. 4.

17 *Dáil Debates*, vol. 157, 6 June 1956, 1489–90.

18 *ILC Report*, 1953, p. 35.

19 This rearrangement was described by P. J. Sammon as 'one of the largest and most important rearrangements carried out by the Land Commission in Co. Mayo'; Sammon, *In the Land Commission*, p. 37.

20 *ILC Report*, 1954, p. 31.

21 Ibid., p. 32.

22 Ibid., p. 33.

23 Ibid., p. 34.

24 Sammon, *In the Land Commission*, p. 33.

25 Ibid., p. 282.

26 Land Commission Memorandum for the government on land settlement, 14 Nov. 1952 (NA, DT S6490 B/2).

27 *Dáil Debates*, vol. 110, 10 Mar. 1948, 478.

28 Department of Lands Memorandum for the government: review of Land Commission policy, July 1957 (NA, DT S16265); See also Hugh Brody, *Innishkillane: Change and Decline in the West of Ireland* (London, 1973), p. 71.

29 Land Commission Memorandum, 14 Nov. 1952.

30 *Dáil Debates*, vol.161, 24 Apr. 1957, 161; vol. 182, 15 June 1960, 1345 ff.

31 Townshend, *Ireland: The 20th Century*, p. 168.

32 Land Commission Memorandum, 14 Nov. 1952.

33 See Moynihan, *Speeches and Statements of Eamon de Valera*, pp. 466–9.

34 *Dáil Debates*, vol. 120, 27 Apr. 1950, 1348.

35 Jones, 'Divisions within the Irish government', p. 89.

36 Born in Belfast in 1889. He was sentenced to death for his role in the 1916 Rising but the sentence was later commuted to penal servitude for life. He was released under the general amnesty of 1917. He took part in the War of Independence and Civil War. He was elected MP

for South Monaghan in 1918. He was elected to the Dáil in 1922 and thereafter at every general election until 1969. During his career he was Fianna Fáil Minister for Finance in 1932 and again from 1951 to 1954. At various times he was also Minister for Industry and Commerce, Local Government, Public Health, and Tanaiste from 1959 to 1965.

37 *Dáil Debates*, vol. 141, 5 Aug. 1953, 1363.

38 The opinion of the three land commissioners as contained in a Memorandum prepared by the Department of Lands for the government, 22 Oct. 1951 (NA, DT S6490 B/2).

39 *Dáil Debates*, vol. 182, 15 June 1960, 1372.

40 *Dáil Debates*, vol. 105, 7 May 1947, 2143.

41 See ibid., vol. 114, 6 Apr. 1949, 2468–71.

42 O'Shiel, 'Changes effected in recent land commission legislation', p. 295.

43 Ibid.

44 Memorandum from the Minister for Lands, 30 June 1956 (NA, DT S14249B); *ILC Report*, 1955, p.4.

45 Land Commission Memorandum, 14 Nov. 1952.

46 Ibid.

47 Department of Lands Memorandum: review of Land Commission activities, 5 July 1957 (NA, DT S16265).

48 See Delaney, *Demography, State and Society*, pp. 226–8.

49 Department of Lands Memorandum: review of Land Commission policy, n.d. [July 1958] (NA, DT S16265).

50 Irish Farmers' Association, *Low Farm Incomes in Western Counties: the Problems and the Policies* (n.d.), p. 5.

51 Department of Finance, *Economic Development* (Dublin, 1958), p. 5.

52 Ibid.

53 Dunphy, *The Making of Fianna Fáil*, p. 26.

54 T. K. Whitaker, 'Economic development 1958–1985' in K. A. Kennedy (ed.), *Ireland in Transition: Economic and Social Change Since 1960* (Dublin, 1986), p. 11.

55 Born in London in 1905. His father was executed during the Civil War. Erskine Childers became TD for Athlone–Longford in 1938 and held his seat until 1974 (TD for Longford–Westmeath, 1948–57 and Monaghan 1961–74), when he resigned his seat after his election as President of Ireland. His ministerial portfolios included Posts and Telegraphs, Lands and Fisheries, Transport and Power, and Health. He was also Tanaiste from 1969 to 1973.

56 *Dáil Debates*, vol. 161, 24 Apr. 1957, 161.

57 Department of Lands Memorandum: review of Land Commission policy, July 1958.

58 Department of Lands Memorandum, 5 July 1957.

59 Report of private meeting of land commissioners, 20 June 1958 (NA, DT S 16265); Jones, 'Divisions within the Irish government', p. 95; Sammon, *In the Land Commission*, pp. 56–7.

60 *Dáil Debates*, vol. 170, 8 July 1958, 15–16.

61 Department of Lands Memorandum, 5 July 1957.

62 *Dáil Debates*, vol. 161, 24 Apr. 1957, 160.

63 Ibid.

64 Land Commission Memorandum: review of policy: proposals adopted by the government, 2 May 1958 (NA, DT S16265).

65 *Dáil Debates*, vol. 161, 24 Apr. 1957, 155.

66 Ibid., 155–6.

67 Ibid.

68 Jones, 'Divisions within the Irish government', p. 94.

69 Daly, *The First Department*, p. 343.

70 Quoted in Department of Lands Memorandum [July 1958].

71 Ibid.

72 See *Dáil Debates*, vol. 170, 8 July 1958, 16.

73 Quoted in Daly, *The First Department*, p. 345.

74 Draft decision in relation to paragraph 40 (a) of Memorandum to government, 14 Mar. 1958 (NA, DT S16265).

75 Ibid., vol. 175, 9 June 1959, 1113.

76 Jones, 'Divisions within the Irish government', p. 94; see B. S. Murphy, '"The land for the people, the road for the bullock": Lia Fáil, the smallholders crisis and public policy in Ireland, 1957–60' in William Nolan and T. P. O'Neill (eds), *Offaly History and Society* (Dublin, 1998), pp. 855–88.

77 Ibid., vol. 197, 31 Oct. 1962, 346.

78 Ibid., vol. 252, 24 Mar. 1971, 1300.

79 D. A. Gillmor, *Agriculture in the Republic of Ireland* (Budapest, 1977), p. 59.

80 Ibid.

81 Breandán S. MacAodha, *Conacre in Ireland: the Distribution of Conacre in the Twenty-six Counties* (Dublin, 1967), p. 7.

82 Department of Lands Memorandum, 5 July 1957.

83 Memorandum on letting of lands, *c.*20 June 1958 (NA, DT S16265).

84 *Inter-Departmental Committee on Land Structure Reform: Final Report*, May 1978 (Pr. 7176), p. 34; MacAodha, *Conacre in Ireland*, pp. 3–7; Gillmor, *Agriculture in the Republic of Ireland*, pp. 56–9.

85 MacAodha, *Conacre in Ireland*, p. 7.

86 *Dáil Debates*, vol. 175, 9 June 1959, 1109–10.

87 Ibid.; Childers's figures given here differ to the official Land Commission statistics as his totals include other lands divided which had not been acquired through the Land Commission under the 1923 and later acts.

88 Daly, *The First Department*, pp. 373–4.

89 Jones, 'Divisions within the Irish government', p. 95.

90 *ILC Report*, 1961, p. 31.

91 Land Commission statistics, 14 Apr. 1958 (NA, DT S16265).

92 Jones, 'Land reform legislation', p. 139.

93 Department of Agriculture, *Agriculture in the Second Programme for Economic Expansion* (SO (Pr.7697) (Dublin, 1969), p. 49.

94 *Dáil Debates*, vol. 206, 4 Dec. 1963, 572.

95 Ibid., 587.

96 *Irish Press*, 3 Dec. 1962.

97 Editorial in ibid., 7 Dec. 1962.

98 *ILC Report*, 1962, p. 34.

99 Ibid., vol. 279, 1 Mar. 1972, 764.

100 Ibid., 345.

101 Daly, *The First Department*, p. 385.

102 Ibid.

103 Department of Agriculture, *Agriculture in the Second Programme*, p. 188.

104 Ibid., vol. 206, 4 Dec. 1963, 572; this move had already been recommended in the *Report of the Inter-Departmental Committee on the Problems of Small Western Farms*, 1962 (Pr. 6540) (Dublin, 1969), p. 11

105 *ILC Report*, 1962, p. 34.

106 Ibid..

107 G. P. Campbell, Land settlement policy: instructions to divisional inspectors, inspectors in charge and resale inspectors, 28 Oct. 1962 (NA, DT 17378A/62); see also *ILC Report*, 1962, p. 34.

108 *Dáil Debates*, vol. 206, 4 Dec. 1963, 572.

109 Ibid.

110 Ibid., vol. 264, 5 Dec. 1972, 1045.

111 Born Ballyhaunis, County Mayo in 1922. A solicitor by profession, Flanagan captained the Mayo senior football team to successive All-Ireland titles in 1950 and 1951. In the latter year, he was elected Fianna Fáil TD for South Mayo. He was defeated in the 1977 election but was elected a Member of the European Parliament in 1979. He was Minister for Health 1966–9 and Minister for Lands 1969–73.

112 *Dáil Debates*, vol. 264, 5 Dec. 1972, 1045–6.

113 Ibid., vol. 263, 23 Nov. 1972, 239.

114 *Report of the Inter-Departmental Committee on the Problems of Small Western Farms*, 1962 (Pr. 6540) (Dublin, 1969), p. 12.

115 *Dáil Debates*, vol. 264, 5 Dec. 1972, 1044.

116 *An Act to Provide for the Control of Aliens and for Other Matters Relating to Aliens*, no. 14 1935, 10 Apr. 1935.

117 *Dáil Debates*, vol. 121, 31 May 1950, 904.

118 Ibid., vol. 188, 4 May 1961, 1680 ff.

119 Ibid., 1681.

120 *Seanad Debates*, vol. 37, 4 May 1950, 1764.

121 *Dáil Debates*, vol. 121, 24 May 1950, 456.

122 Childers in ibid., vol. 175, 9 June 1959, 1113.

123 Ibid., vol. 188, 4 May 1961, 1683.

124 Ibid., 1682.

125 *The Crusade for a Better Ireland*, Aug. 1959 [newspaper produced by Bennekerry Land Club].

126 *Dáil Debates*, vol. 170, 8 July 1958, 23–4.

127 Ibid., vol. 175, 9 June 1959, 1113–14.

128 *The Crusade for a Better Ireland*, Aug. 1959.

129 Ibid.

130 Ibid.

131 Ibid.

132 Ibid.

133 Ibid.

134 Ibid.

135 *The Irish Times*, 14 Jan. 1961.

136 *Dáil Debates*, vol. 188, 4 May 1961, 1698.

137 Ibid, vol. 205, 29 Oct. 1963, 440.

138 Ibid., vol. 205, 29 Oct. 1963, 438.

139 Ibid., vol. 206, 27 Nov. 1963, 95.

140 Ibid., vol. 188, 4 May 1961, 1710.

141 Land (Regulation of Acquisitions) Bill, 1961; *Dáil Debates*, vol. 188, 13 Apr. 1961.

142 Ibid., vol. 188, 4 May 1961, 1686–7.

143 Ibid., 1696.

144 Ibid., vol. 188, 4 May 1961, 1736.

145 Ibid., vol. 191, 12 July 1961, 706.

146 Department of Lands Memorandum on Land (Control of Acquisitions by Non-nationals) Bill, 1961 (NA, DT 17097/61)

147 *Dáil Debates*, vol. 205, 29 Oct. 1963, 443.

148 Ibid., vol. 205, 29 Oct. 1963, 438.

149 *An Act to Amend and Extend the Land Purchase Acts,*[9 Mar. 1965], no. 2/1965.

150 *ILC Report*, 1962, p. 28; *Dáil Debates*, vol. 223, 7 June 1966, 30.

151 *Dáil Debates*, vol. 210, 10 June 1964, 984.

152 Anon, *Fianna Fáil: the IRA Connection* (n.d. [?1969]).

153 *Dáil Debates*, vol. 264, 13 Dec. 1972, 1475.

154 Ibid., vol. 252, 11 Mar. 1971, 53.

155 Ibid., vol. 253, 18 May 1971, 149.

156 Ibid., vol. 275, 15 Nov. 1974, 1519.

157 Ibid., 1527.

158 *Dáil Debates*, vol. 279, 16 Apr. 1975, 1712.

159 *Inter-Departmental Committee on Land Structure Reform: Final Report, May* 1978 (Pr. 7176), p. 24.

160 *Land Policy: Laid by the Government Before Each House of the Oireachtas, Dec.* 1980 (SO, 1980, Pr. 9372), p. 9.

161 *Dáil Debates*, vol. 309, 9 Nov. 1978, 643.

162 See Daly, *The First Department*, pp. 504 ff.

163 Directive 72/159/EEC on the modernisation of farms; Directive 72/160/EEC on measures to ensure the cessation of farming and the reallocation of land released for structural improvement; Directive 72/161/EEC on the provision of socio-economic guidance and training for farmers.

164 *Inter-Departmental Committee on Land Structure Reform: Final Report, May 1978*, p. 21.

165 Ibid., p. 23.

166 *Dáil Debates*, vol. 266, 27 June 1973, 1374.

167 Ibid., vol. 296, 25 Jan. 1977, 21.

168 *Land policy, Dec. 1980*, p. 13.

169 Irish Farmers' Association, *Low Farm Incomes*, p. 14.

170 J. A. Walsh, 'Agricultural change and development' (paper presented to conference on 'Change and development in rural Ireland', 20 Oct. 1984), p. 27.

171 *ILC Report*, 1974, p. 7.

172 Ibid., pp. 8–10.

173 *ILC Report*, 1978, p. 24.

174 Irish Farmers' Association, *Low Farm Incomes*, p. 15.

175 *Land policy, Dec. 1980*, p. 12.

176 Daly, *The First Department*, pp. 516–17.

177 J. Higgins, *A Study of Part-time Farmers in the Republic of Ireland: Socio-Economic Research Series*, no. 3 (Dublin, 1983), pp. 1–2

178 Daly, *The First Department*, p. 504.

179 Irish Farmers' Association, *Low Farm Incomes*, p. 8.

180 Ibid., p. 13.

181 *Dáil Debates*, vol. 8, 24 July 1924, 2173.

182 Memorandum by Minister for Lands, 30 June 1956 (NA, DT S14249B).

183 Ibid.

184 Maguire, *The Land Commission*, p. 8.

185 Ibid.

186 *Inter-Departmental Committee on Land Structure Reform: Final Report, May 1978*, p. 5.

187 Irish Farmers Association, *Low Farm Incomes*, p. 20.

188 *Inter-Departmental Committee on Land Structure Reform: Final Report, May 1978*, p. 27.

189 Ibid., p. 38.

190 R. G. Johnson and A. G. Conway, 'Factors associated with growth in farm output', paper presented to the Agricultural Economics Society of Ireland, Dublin, June 1976; *Inter-Departmental Committee on Land Structure Reform: Final Report, May 1978*, p. 31.

191 *Inter-Departmental Committee on Land Structure Reform: Final Report*, p. 34.

192 Ibid., p. 37.

193 Ibid., p. 32.

194 Ibid.

195 Ibid., p. 34.

196 Ibid., pp. 80–1.

197 Ibid., pp. 56–7.

198 *Land Policy: Laid by the Government Before Each House of the Oireachtas, December, 1980* (SO, 1980, Pr. 9372).

199 Ibid., p. 16.

200 Ibid., p. 11.

201 Ibid., pp. 2, 16.

202 For these three categories the surcharge was to be 60 per cent. For farmers (and their sons and daughters) this surcharge would be applied on a progressively scaled basis as the size of the holding increased, subject to a threshold below which the surcharge would not operate, and ranging from 50 per cent on portions of purchase that brought the total holding above £200 rateable valuation to 0 per cent in cases on which the portion of purchase would not bring the total holding above £70 valuation. This surcharge would encourage vendors of large farms to sell in lots so as to attract farmer-purchasers who would either be exempt from the surcharge or subject only to a low rate; ibid., p. 19.

203 For details of this scheme, see ibid., pp. 20–1.

204 Maguire, *The Land Commission*, p. 11.

205 *Land policy, Dec. 1980*, p. 28.

206 Maguire, *The Land Commission*, p. 9.

207 *Land policy, Dec. 1980*, p. 28.

208 Ibid., p. 18.

209 Ibid., p. 29.

210 Former senior member of Land Commission staff in conversation with this author, June 2003.

211 *Seanad Debates*, vol. 103, 4 Apr. 1984, 772.

212 See *Dáil Debates*, vol. 389, 4 May 1989, 1365.

213 Ibid., vol. 511, 30 Nov. 1999, 444.

214 Ibid., 179.

215 *Irish Independent*, 2 Apr. 2002.

216 Ibid., vol. 418, 2 Apr. 1992, 408.

217 *Dáil Debates*, vol. 389, 4 May 1989, 1385.

218 Ibid., vol. 392, 26 Oct. 1989, 854.

SEVEN: LAND AND THE LOST POLITICS
OF INDEPENDENT IRELAND

1   Brandenburg, 'Progress of land transfers', pp. 275, 286.

2   *Dáil Debates*, vol. 175, 9 June 1959, 1112.

3   Lee, *Ireland 1912–1985*, p. 71

4   Provisional Government minutes of meeting, 10 Feb. 1922 (NA, G1/1).

5   *Dáil Debates*, vol. 9, 12 Dec. 1924, 2591.

6   *Dáil Debates*, vol. 12, 17 June 1925, 1126.

7   *Sunday Record*, 23 May 1925; quoted in *Dáil Debates*, vol. 12, 17 June 1925, 1155–6

8   By then, it was widely held by agricultural experts that under the economic conditions of the time, a farm of 30 acres was required to provide a reasonable standard of living. Around 25 per cent of holdings in Ireland were still less than 15 acres in size and 25 per cent more were over 15 acres and less than 30 acres in size. A. W. Menzias-Kitchin and J. R. Raeburn, *Report on Eire Food Production and Export Possibilities* (n.d.), p. 6.

9   Dunphy, *The Rise of Fianna Fáil*, p. 95.

10   Ibid.

11   Delaney, *Demography, State and Society*, p. 60.

12   Menzias-Kitchin and Raeburn, *Report on Eire Food Production*, p. 5.

13   Dunphy, *The Rise of Fianna Fáil*, pp. 94–6; see also Michael Gallagher, *Electoral Support for Irish Political Parties, 1927–73* (London, 1976).

14   *Irish Press*, 29 Oct. 1931.

15   *Dáil Debates*, vol. 48, 13 July 1933, 2396.

16   *An Act to Amend and Extend the Land Purchase Acts in Divers Respects*, [14 Aug. 1936], no. 41/1936.

17   *Fianna Fáil Seventh Annual Ard-Fheis, 1932: Report of Proceedings* (UCD, Fianna Fáil papers, P176/746).

18   See Mike Cronin, 'The socio-economic background and membership of the Blueshirt movement, 1932–35', *Irish Historical Studies* XXIX (Nov. 1994): 239; Bew, Hazelkorn and Patterson, *The Dynamics of Irish Politics*, p. 52.

19   Cronin, 'The Blueshirt movement', p. 239.

20   *ILC. Report*, 1981–82, pp. 10–11.

21   Cronin, 'The Blueshirt movement', pp. 237–8.

22 *ILC Report*, 1934–5, p. 5.

23 *Dáil Debates*, vol. 49, 1 Aug. 1933, 937.

24 See Tony Varley, 'Farmers against nationalists: the rise and fall of Clann na Talmhan in Galway' in Gerard Moran (ed.), *Galway: History and Society* (Dublin, 1996), pp. 580–622.

25 Walker, *Parliamentary Election Results*, 1918–92, pp. 154–61.

26 *Dáil Debates.*, vol. III, 3 June 1948, 352–3.

27 Ibid.

28 Sean Moylan to Eamon de Valera 1 Sept. 1943 (NA, DT S12890a); Sean Moylan to Sean Lemass, 5 May 1944, quoted in W. F. Nally to Padraig Ó Cinnéide, 16 May 1944 (NA DT, S12890).

29 *Dáil Debates*, vol. 99, 1 Feb. 1946, 355.

30 *Seanad Debates*, vol. 31, 3 Apr. 1946, 1183.

31 Ibid., vol. 58, 20 Jan. 1965, vol. 210.

32 *Dáil Debates*, vol. 215, 4 May 1965, 528.

33 *Dáil Debates*, vol. 22, 7 Mar. 1927, 889.

34 Tom Garvin, *The Evolution of Irish Nationalist Politics* (Dublin, 1981), p. 146.

35 Ibid., vol. 161, 24 Apr. 1957, 157.

36 *Dáil Debates*, vol. 13, 26 Nov. 1925, 979.

37 *Dáil Debates*, vol. 164, 10 Dec. 1991, 609.

38 Born in Longford in 1894. He was commandant of the 1st Battalion of the Longford Brigade of the IRA during the War of Independence and one of the most prominent leaders in the country. He was GOC of the Western Command of the Free State forces during the Civil War and Chief of Staff in 1923. He rose to the rank of army general before concentrating on a political career. He was Cumann na nGaedheal TD for Leitrim–Sligo in 1929 and for Longford–Westmeath in 1932. He contested the presidential elections of 1945 and 1959. He held the ministerial portfolios for Justice (1948–51) and Defence (1951, 1954–7).

39 Representations on behalf of constituents, 1922–57 (UCD, MacEoin papers, P151/416, 441, 443).

40 Fr Dan Flynn to Sean [?], 28 Mar. 1933; ibid., P104/2247.

41 [D. F.] to Frank Aiken, 21 May 1970; ibid., P104/2299 (61).

42 [J. J. M.] to Frank Aiken, 13 Dec. 1970; ibid., P104/2299 (63).

43 Frank Aiken to [E. McA], 13 July 1971; ibid., P104/2299 (67).

44 *Westmeath Examiner*, 12 Sept. 1964.

45 See for example, *Dáil Debates*, vol. 63, 22 July 1936, 1645; vol. III, 2 June 1948, 230.

46 *Dáil Debates*, vol. 106, 13 May 1947, 127–8.

47 Ibid., vol. 17, 16 Nov. 1926, 13.

48 'Ard runaí' to Patrick Moroney 25 Nov. 1946 (UCD, Fianna Fáil papers, P176/62 (67)); when I made enquiries to the Fianna Fáil research office, they informed me that Eamon de Valera held that position within the party at this time and that the letter undoubtedly was sent by him.

49 Ibid., vol. 175, 9 June 1959, 1112; In Apr. 1951, Joseph Blowick, Minister for Lands in the Inter-Party government, had made a similar statement: 'Deputies are not allowed, by the laws they make themselves in this House, to divide land. The sooner deputies realise that the sooner they will save themselves a lot of trouble.' Ibid., vol. 125, 11 Apr. 1951, 491.

50 *Dáil Debates*, vol. III, 3 June 1948, 339–40.

51 Fr Dan Flynn to Frank Aiken, 6 Apr. 1933 (UCD, Aikens papers, P104/3277).

52 *Meath Chronicle*, 16 Oct. 1937.

53 *Dáil Debates*, vol. 48, 13 July 1933, 2379.

54 Ibid., vol. 70, 7 Apr. 1938, 1720–1.

55 Ibid., vol. 75, 26 Apr. 1939, 1125.

56 Ibid., vol. 96, 25 Apr. 1945, 2456.

57 Ibid., vol. 16, 17 June 1926, 1351–2.

58 Ibid., 1354.

59 Ibid., vol. 22, 7 Mar. 1927, 886–7.

60 Ibid., vol. 23, 19 Apr. 1928, 181.

61 Ibid., vol. 29, 18 Apr. 1929, 639.

62 Ibid., vol. 22, 7 Mar. 1928, 843.

63 Ibid., vol. 29, 18 Apr. 1929, 665–6.

64 Ibid., vol. 29, 11 July 1929, 827.

65 Ibid., vol. 22, 7 Mar. 1928, 857.

66 Ibid., vol. 59, 10 Dec. 1935, 2338.

67 Ibid., 2340.

68 Ibid., vol. 120, 27 Apr. 1950, 1375.

69 See *Fianna Fáil: Second Annual Ard-Fheis 1927: Report of Proceedings*, p. 5 (UCD, Fianna Fáil records, P176/741).

70 [EO 1947–55], in conversation with this author, 11 Nov. 2003.

71 Sammon, *In the Land Commission*, p. 11

72 Ibid., p. 45.

73 Department. of Lands memorandum for the government: review of Land Commission activities, 5 July 1957 (NA, DT S16265).

74 Ibid., 158.

75 Sammon, *In the Land Commission*, p. 126.

76 Maguire, *The Land Problem*, p. 25.

77 *Dáil Debates*, vol. 99, 31 Jan. 1946, 315.

78 For one such accusation see Bryan Cooper's speech in ibid., vol. 14, 25 Feb. 1926, 1163–5.

79 See Dooley, *Decline of the Big House*.

80 Tom Barry, *Guerilla Days in Ireland* (Dublin, 1991 edn, [1st edn Cork, 1949]), pp. 6–7.

81 Breen, *My Fight for Irish Freedom*, p. 100.

82 *Dáil Debates*, vol. 2, 5 Jan. 1923, 592.

83 Ibid., vol. 3, 28 May 1923, 1152–3.

84 Ibid., vol. 123, 14 Dec. 1950, 2234.

85 Ibid., 8 Mar. 1951, 864.

86 Ibid., 15 Mar. 1951, 2017.

87 Ibid., 19 July 1951, 2111

88 *Dáil Debates*, vol. 70, 7 Apr. 1938, 1696.

89 Ibid., vol. 60, 13 Feb. 1936, 716.

90 Ibid., 717.

91 Ibid., vol. 63, 22 July 1936, 1636–7.

92 Both Aiken and Faulkner represented Louth in the 1960s and when Aiken was Minister for External Affairs, he was approached on numerous occasions to intercede with Faulkner as Minister for Lands. [S. D. B.] to Frank Aiken, 6 May 1969 (UCD, Aiken papers, P104/2296(5)).

93 *Dáil Debates*, vol. 22, 7 Mar. 1926, 837.

94 Eamon Mansfield, 'Observations on a memo. of the Department of Lands', 21 June 1943 (NA, DT S14399).

95 *Seanad Debates*, vol. 134, 21 Oct. 1989, 349–50.

96 Sir John Nugent in conversation with the author.

97 Sammon, *In the Land Commission*, p. 45.

98 *Dáil Debates*, vol. 96, 26 Apr. 1945, 2517.

99 Ibid., 2517–18.

100 Ibid., vol. 252, 24 Mar. 1971, 1288.

101 Maguire, *The Land Problem*, p. 25.

102 Jones, 'Divisions within the Irish government', p. 105.

103 *Inter-Departmental Committee on Land Structure Reform: Final Report, May 1978* (Pr. 7176), p. 34.

104 *Seanad Debates*, vol. 103, 4 Apr. 1984, 771.

105 Corrected typescript copies of a speech by Frank Aiken introducing the 1933 Land Bill to the Dáil, Aug. 1933 (UCD, Aiken papers, P104/3301).

106 Seth Jones, 'Divisions within the Irish government', p. 108.

107 Quoted in *ILC Report*, 1960, p. 34.

108 Jones, 'Divisions within the Irish government', p. 105.

109 Ibid., p. 105; Fuller, *Irish Catholicism*, p. 214.

110 Quoted in Jones, 'Divisions within the Irish government', p. 105.

111 Sammon, *In the Land Commission*, p. 216.

112 Quoted in ibid.

EIGHT: CONCLUSION

1 *Dáil Debates*, vol. 256, 28 Oct. 1971, 509.

2 Comerford, *Ireland*, p. 266.

3 Department. of Lands memo for the Government: Review of Land Commission Policy, July 1957 (NA, DT S16265).

4 Quoted in *The Irish Times*, 23 Oct. 1992.

Bibliography

MANUSCRIPT SOURCES

National Archives of Ireland
Dáil Éireann files (DE 2, 3, 4, and 5)
Dáil Éireann: Land Settlement Commission papers
Department of Agriculture files
Department of the Environment files
Department of Finance files
Department of Home Affairs files
Department of Industry and Commerce files
Department of Justice files
Department of the Taoiseach files
Minutes of Provisional Government, 1922 (A, G1/1)
Minutes of the Executive Council, 1923–32 (G2/1–8)
Papers Relating to the Irish Convention, 1917–18
Sinn Féin Standing Committee, Minutes 5 June 1919–23 Mar. 1922

National Library of Ireland
Piaras Béaslaí papers
George Gavan Duffy papers
Murray papers
Art Ó Briain papers

Public Records Office, London
Colonial Office papers, CO 904 (Dublin Castle records):
Part i: Anti-government Organisations, 1882–1921.
Part ii: Police Reports, Jan. 1892–Dec. 1897.
Part iii: Police Reports, Feb. 1898–Dec. 1913.
Part iv: Police Reports, 1914–21.
Part vi: Judicial Proceedings, Enquiries and Miscellaneous Records, 1872–1926.
(Consulted on microfilm, National Library of Ireland)

University College, Dublin, Archives Department
Frank Aiken papers
Ernest Blythe papers
Cumann na nGaedheal/Fine Gael papers
Fianna Fáil papers
Sean MacEntee papers
Sean MacEoin papers

Patrick MacGilligan papers
Richard Mulcahy papers
Ernie O'Malley papers
Kevin O'Shiel papers
Moss Twomey papers

Trinity College, Dublin, Manuscripts Department
Arnold Marsh papers

Military Archives, Cathal Brugha Barracks, Dublin
Files relating to the Special Infantry Corps
Statement of Kevin O'Shiel (WS/1770).

PRINTED PARLIAMENTARY DEBATES

Minutes of Proceedings of Dáil Éireann, 1919–22.
Dáil Éireann Debates
Seanad Éireann Debates

IRISH GOVERNMENT PUBLICATIONS

Census reports
Department of Industry and Commerce, *Census of Population of Ireland, 1926*
Department of Industry and Commerce, *Census of Population of Ireland, 1936*
Central Statistics Office, *Census of Population of Ireland, 1946*
Central Statistics Office, *Census of Population of Ireland, 1951*
Central Statistics Office, *Census of Population of Ireland, 1956*
Central Statistics Office, *Census of Population of Ireland, 1961*
Central Statistics Office, *Census of Population of Ireland, 1966*
Central Statistics Office, *Census of Population of Ireland, 1971*

Annual reports of government departments
Irish Land Commission, Annual Reports, 1923–84.
Annual Reports of the Department of Agriculture and Technical Instruction, 1921–31
Annual Reports of the Minister for Agriculture, 1931–65
Annual Reports of the Minister for Agriculture and Fisheries, 1966–73

Other reports (in chronological order)
Commission on Agriculture, *Final Report of the Commission on Agriculture, 1923–4* (Dublin,
    1924).
Gaeltacht Commission, *Report of the Commission of Inquiry into the Preservation of the
    Gaeltacht,* 1926, R23/27.

Coimisiún na Gaeltachta: Statements of Evidence Furnished by Persons Who Were Not Examined Before the Commission (1926)

Department of Lands and Agriculture, *Interim Report of the Tribunal to Inquire into the Marketing of Butter*, 1930, A 18/1.

Report on the Inter-Departmental Committee on Seasonal Migration to Great Britain, 1937–8, 1938, P. 3403.

Commission of Inquiry into Banking, Currency and Credit, 1938, Reports, 1938, P. 2628.

Committee of Enquiry on Post-Emergency Agricultural Policy: Reports on Agricultural Policy, 1945, 1945, P.7175.

Department of Agriculture, *Policy in Regard to Crops, Pastures, Fertilisers and Feeding Stuffs*, 1946, A.36.

Department of Agriculture (G. A. Holmes), *Report on the Present State and Methods for Improvement of Irish Grasslands*, 1949, A.38.

Commission on Emigration and Other Population Problems, 1948–54, Reports, 1955, Pr. 2541

Report of the Commission on Youth Unemployment, 1951, Pr. 709.

Economic Development, 1958, Pr. 4803.

Programme for Economic Expansion, 1958, Pr. 4976.

Report by the Inter-Departmental Committee on the Problem of Small Western Farms, 1962, Pr. 6540.

National Farm Survey 1955/6–1957/8, Final Report, 1962, I.110.

Statistical Abstract of Ireland 1962, 1962, Pr. 6571.

Second Programme for Economic Expansion, Parts I and II, 1963–4, Pr. 7239, Pr. 7670.

Report on Pilot Area Development by the Inter-Departmental Committee on the Problem of Small Western Farms, 1964, Pr. 7616.

Department of Agriculture, *Agriculture and the Second Programme for Economic Expansion*, 1964, A.55.

Second Programme of Economic Expansion, Review of Progress 1964–7, 1968, F. 57/6.

Presentation and Summary of the Report of the Commission on Higher Education, 1960–7, 1967, E.59/1–2.

Third Programme for Economic and Social Development, 1969–72: Laid by the Government Before Each House of the Oireachtas, March 1969, 1969, Prl. 431.

Department of Agriculture, *Agriculture in the Second Programme for Economic Expansion*, 1969, Pr.7697.

Report of the Committee on the Review of State Expenditure in Relation to Agriculture, 1970, A. 65.

J. J. Scully, *Agriculture in the West of Ireland: A Study of the Low Farm Income Problem*, 1971, Pr.l. 2017.

Inter-Departmental Committee on Land Structure Reform: Final Report, 1978, Pr. 7176.

Land Policy: Laid by the Government Before Each House of the Oireachtas, December 1980, 1980, Pr. 9372.

ACTS PASSED BY THE IRISH GOVERNMENT

Constitution of the Irish Free State (Saorstát Éireann) Act, 1922, no. 1/1922.

Enforcement of Law (Occasional Powers) Act, 1923, [1 Mar. 1923], no. 4/1923. *District Justices (Temporary Provisions) Act, 1923*, [27 Mar. 1923], no. 6/1923.

An Act to Provide for the Preservation of Public Safety and the Protection of Persons and Property and for Matters Connected Therewith or Arising Out of the Present Emergency [1 Aug. 1923], no. 28/1923.

An Act to Make Provision for the Immediate Preservation of the Public Safety [3 Aug. 1923], no. 29/1923.

The Land Act 1923: An Act to Amend the Law Relating to the Occupation and Ownership of Land and for Other Purposes Relating Thereto, [9 Aug. 1923], no. 42/1923.

Land Law (Commission) Act, 1923: An Act to Amend the Law Relating to the Irish Land Commission and to Dissolve the Congested Districts Board for Ireland and Transfer its Functions to the Irish Land Commission and for Other Purposes Connected Therewith, [24 July 1923], no. 27/1923.

Land Act, 1927: An Act to Amend the Law Relating to the Occupation and Ownership of Land and for Other Purposes Relating Thereto, [21 May 1927], no. 19/ 1927.

An Act to Make Provision for the Early Vesting of Holdings in the Purchasers Thereof Under the Land Purchase Acts and for that and Other Purposes . . . [30 Apr. 1931], no. 11/1931.

An Act to Amend Generally the Law, Finance and Practice Relating to Land Purchase, and in Particular to Make Further and Better Provision for the Execution of the Functions of the Judicial and Lay Commissioners of the Land Commission . . . [13 Oct. 1933], no. 38/1933

An Act to Amend the Law Relating to Local Government Franchise and to the Registration of Local Government Electors, [29 Mar. 1935], no. 9/1935.

An Act to Provide for the Control of Aliens and for Other Matters Relating to Aliens, [10 Apr. 1935], no. 14/1935.

An Act to Amend and Extend the Land Purchase Acts in Divers Respects, [14 Aug. 1936], no. 41/1936.

An Act to Amend and Extend the Land Purchase Acts in Divers Respects and to Amend the Law in Relation to the Application of the Increase of Rent and Mortgage Interest (Restrictions) Acts, 1923 to 1930, to Dwellinghouses of Which the Land Commission is the Landlord, [8 Aug. 1939], no. 26/1939.

An Act to Amend and Extend the Land Purchase Acts, [11 June 1946], no. 12/1946.

An Act to Amend and Extend the Land Purchase Acts, [19 June 1950], no. 16/1950.

An Act to Amend and Extend the Land Purchase Acts, [7 July 1953], no. 18/1953.

An Act to Amend Section 15 of the Land Act 1950, [13 July 1954], no. 21/1954.

An Act to Amend and Extend the Land Purchase Acts, [9 Mar. 1965], no. 2 /1965.

ACTS PASSED BY THE BRITISH GOVERNMENT

An Act to Further Amend the Law Relating to the Occupation and Ownership of Land in Ireland and for Other Purposes Relating Thereto [22 Aug. 1881], ch.49, 44 & 45 Vict.

An Act to Facilitate the Provision of Land for Certain Evicted Tenants in Ireland and for Other Purposes Connected Therewith, and to Make Provision with Respect to the Tenure of Office by the Estates Commissioners [26 Aug. 1907] ch.56, 7 Edw.7.

Irish Land (Provision for Soldiers and Sailors) Act [23 Dec. 1919] ch. 82, 9 & 10 Geo. V.

BRITISH PARLIAMENTARY PAPERS (IN CHRONOLOGICAL ORDER)

Return Showing to the Latest Year Available, for Ireland as a Whole, the Annual Average Prices for Each Year from 1881 . . . HC 1921, vol. XLI. 93.

Annual Reports of the Congested Districts Board for Ireland, 1893–1921.

Return of Untenanted Lands in Rural Districts, Distinguishing Demesnes on Which there is a Mansion, Showing Rural District and Electoral Divisions, Townland, Area in Statute Acres, Poor Law Valuation, Names of Occupiers as in Valuation Lists, HC, 1906, c.177.

Memo dated 10 May 1906 Issued by the Estates Commissioners for Guidance of Assistant Inspectors When Making Inquiries with Reference to Applications Received from Persons Seeking Reinstatement as Evicted Tenants or as the Representatives of Evicted Tenants [Cd 3658], HC 1907, vol. LXX. 1171.

Return of Tenants (or Their Representatives) Who Had Been evicted from Three Plan of Campaign Estates Purchased or Proposed to be Purchased by the Estates Commissioners and Who Have Been Reinstated in their Former Holdings, or Provided with Other Holdings [Cd 3664], HC 1907, vol. LXIX. 82.

Royal Commission on Congestion in Ireland: Final Report of the Commissioners [Cd 4097], HC 1908, XLII. 729.

Agricultural Statistics for Ireland With Detailed Report for the Year 1917, [Cmd 1316], HC 1921, vol LXI, p. xiv.

Report of the Proceedings of the Irish Convention [Cd 9019], HC 1918, vol. X. 697

Report of Estates Commissioners for the Year from 1 April 1919 to 31 March 1920 and for the Period from 1 November 1903 to 31 March 1920 [Cmd 1150], HC 1921, vol. XIV. 661.

Twenty-Seventh Report of the Congested Districts Board for Ireland for the Period from 1 April 1918 to 31 March 1919 [Cmd 759], HC 1920, XIX, 889.

Report *of the Estates Commissioners for the Year from 1 April 1918 to 31 March 1919,* [Cmd 577], HC 1919, XIX, 965.

Twenty-Eight Report of the Congested Districts Board for Ireland for the Period from 1 April 1919 to 31 March 1920, [Cmd 1409], HC 1921, XIV, 613.

Agricultural Statistics for Ireland with Detailed Report for the Year 1920 [Cmd 1317], HC 1921, vol. XLI. 99.

GUIDES AND WORKS OF REFERENCE

Browne, Vincent (ed.), *The Magill Book of Irish Politics* (Dublin, 1981).

Connolly, S. J. (ed.), *The Oxford Companion to Irish History* (Oxford, 1998)

Dooley, Terence, *Sources for the History of Irish Landed Estates,* (Dublin, 2000)

Finnegan, R. B., and Wiles, J. L., *Irish Government Publications: A Select List 1972–92* (Dublin, 1995).

Ford, Percy, and Ford, Grace, *A Breviate of Parliamentary Papers, 1917–39* (Oxford, 1951).

Ford, Percy, and Ford, Grace, *A Select List of Reports and Inquiries of the Irish Dáil and Senate, 1922–1974* (Shannon, 1974)

Gallagher, Michael (ed.), *Irish Elections 1922–44: Results and Analysis* (Shannon, 1993).

Maltby, Arthur, and McKenna, Brian, *Irish Official Publications: A Guide to the Republic of Ireland Papers, with a Breviate of Reports, 1922–70* (Oxford, 1980).

Walker, B. M. (ed.), *Parliamentary Election Results in Ireland, 1918-92* (Dublin, 1992).

NEWSPAPERS AND JOURNALS

Anglo-Celt
An Phoblacht
An tOglach
Capuchin Annual
Connaught Tribune
Dundalk Democrat
Farmers Gazette
Farmers' Journal
Freeman's Journal
Galway Express
Irish Independent
Irish Press
Kerryman
Labour News

Landmark
Mayo News
Meath Chronicle
News Bulletin
Northern Standard
Notes From Ireland (Irish Unionist Alliance), 1918–21.
The Crusade for a Better Ireland, Aug. 1959 [newspaper produced by Bennekerry Land Club.]
The Irish Times
The Republican
Western People
Westmeath Examiner

CONTEMPORARY PUBLICATIONS AND MEMOIRS

A Brief Outline of the Aims and Programme of Fianna Fáil (Dublin, n.d.)

Barry, Tom, *Guerilla Days in Ireland* (Dublin, 1991 edn).

Bonn, M. J. [translated by T. W. Rolleston], *Modern Ireland and Her Agrarian Problem* (London, 1906).

Breen, Dan, *My Fight for Irish Freedom* (Dublin, 1981 edn, [first edn Dublin, 1924]).

Briollay, Sylvain, *Ireland in Rebellion* (London, 1922).

[Childers, Erskine], *The Constructive Work of Dáil Éireann: I and II* (Dublin, 1921).

Congested Districts Board, *Inspectors Local Reports* (Dublin, 1898).

Connolly, James, *Labour in Ireland* (Dublin, 1917).

Cosgrave, W. T., *Policy of the Cumann na nGaedheal Party* (Dublin, 1927).

Costello, John A., *Land Purchase Annuities* (Dublin, 1931).

Cumann na nGaedheal, *To the Electorate of the Irish Free State,* (Dublin, n.d. [1932]).

Deasy, Liam, *Towards Ireland Free: the West Cork Brigade in the War of Independence 1917–21* (Cork, 1973).

Department of Finance, *Economic Development* (Dublin, 1958).

De Stacpoole, Duc, *Irish and Other Memories,* (London, 1922).

Devoy, John, *The Land of Éire* (New York, 1882).

Enright, S., *The Life of a Cattle Dealer* (Galway, 1986).

Fianna Fáil, *A National Policy Outlined by Eamon de Valera Delivered at the Inaugural Meeting of Fianna Fáil at La Scala Theatre, Dublin, May 1926* (Dublin, n.d. [1927]).

Fianna Fáil, *Fianna Fáil: 1926–51: The Story of Twenty-Five Years of National Endeavour and Historic Achievement* (n.d. [1951])

Fianna Fáil National Executive, *The Land Annuities* (Dublin, 1932).

Fighting Points for the Cumann na nGaedheal Speakers and Workers, General Election 1932 (Dublin, 1932).

FitzGerald, Garret, *All in a Life* (Dublin, 1992).

Gaughan, J. A. (ed.), *Memoirs of Senator Joseph Connolly (1885–1961): A Founder of Modern Ireland* (Dublin, 1996).

Griffith, Arthur, *Economic Salvation and the Means to Attain It* (Dublin, n.d.).

Harrison, Henry, *The Strange Case of the Irish Land Purchase Annuities* (Dublin, 1932).

Hughes, Hector, *The Land Acts 1923 to 1927* (Dublin, 1928).

King, F. C. (ed.), *Public Administration in Ireland* (Dublin, 1944).

McCarthy, M. J. F., *Irish Land and Irish Liberty: A Study of the New Lords of the Soil* (London, 1911).

MacFhionghail, Labhras, *The Land Question* (Dublin, n.d. [1917]).

MacNeill, Eoin, 'Ten years of the Irish Free State', *Foreign Affairs* x (1932).

Marsh, Arnold, *Full Employment in Ireland* (Dublin, 1945).

Menzias-Kitchin, A. W. and Raeburn, J. R., *Report on Eire Food Production and Export Possibilities* (n.d.).

Monahan, H. J., 'Administration of Land Acts' in F. C. King (ed.), *Public Administration in Ireland* (Dublin, n.d. [c.1944]), pp. 130–42.

Moore, Maurice, *British Plunder and Irish Blunder or the Story of the Land Purchase Annuities* (Dublin, n.d.).

Moynihan, Maurice (ed.), *Speeches and Statements by Eamon de Valera, 1917–73* (Dublin, 1980).

O'Donnell, Peadar, *There Will be Another Day* (Dublin, 1963).

O'Duffy, Eoin, *An Outline of the Political, Social and Economic Policy of Fine Gael* (Dublin, 1934).

O'Farrell, E., *The Congested Districts of Ireland and How to Deal With Them: A Paper Read Before the Statistical and Social Inquiry Society of Ireland, 14 December 1886* (Dublin, 1887).

O'Malley, Ernie, *On Another Man's Wound* (Dublin, 1979 edn, [1st edn London, 1936]).

O'Neill, Brian, *The War for the Land in Ireland* (London, 1933).

O'Shiel, Kevin, 'Some recent phases of the land question in Ireland', *Manchester Guardian,* 10 May 1926.

O'Shiel, Kevin, 'The Work of the Land Commission' in F. C. King (ed.), *Public Administration in Ireland,* vol. 11 (Dublin, 1949).

O'Shiel, Kevin, and O'Brien, T., *The Land Problem in Ireland and its Settlement* (Dublin, n.d. [1954?]).

O'Shiel, Kevin, 'Memories of my lifetime', *The Irish Times*, 11–22 Nov. 1966.

O'Sullivan, D. J., *The Free State and its Senate: A Study in Contemporary Politics* (London, 1940).

Phillips, A. W., *The Revolution in Ireland, 1906–23* (London, 1923).

Plunkett, Horace, *Ireland in the New Century* (London, 1904)

Reports and Papers Relating to the Proceedings of the Committee of 'Mr. Tuke's Fund' During the Years 1882, 1883 and 1884: Collected for the Private use of the Committee (privately published, n.d. [c.1885]).

Sammon, P. J., *In the Land Commission: A Memoir 1933–1978* (Dublin, 1997)

Sigerson, Selina, *Sinn Féin and Socialism* (Dublin, n.d.)

Whitaker, T. K., 'Economic Development 1958-1985' in K. A. Kennedy (ed.), *Ireland in Transition: Economic and Social Change Since 1960* (Dublin, 1986).

SECONDARY WORKS

Allen, Kieran, *Fianna Fáil and Labour* (London, 1997).

Attwood, E. A., 'Agriculture and economic growth in western Ireland', *Journal of the Statistical and Social Enquiry of Ireland* xx, 5 (1961–2): 172–95.

Augusteijn, Joost, *From Public Defiance to Guerrilla Warfare: The Experience of Ordinary Volunteers in the Irish War of Independence 1916–21* (Dublin, 1996).

Baillie, I. F. and Sheehy, S. J., *Irish Agriculture in a Changing World* (Edinburgh, 1971).

Bence-Jones, Mark, *Twilight of the Ascendancy* (London, 1987).

Bew, Paul, *Land and the National Question in Ireland, 1858–82* (Dublin, 1978).

Bew, Paul, *Charles Stewart Parnell* (Dublin, 1980).

Bew, Paul, and Patterson, Henry, *Sean Lemass and the Making of Modern Ireland, 1945–66* (Dublin, 1982).

Bew, Paul, *Conflict and Conciliation in Ireland. 1898–1910: Parnellites and Agrarian Radicals* (Oxford, 1987).

Bew, Paul, Patterson, Henry, and Hazelkorn, Ellen, *The Dynamics of Irish Politics* (London, 1989).

Boland, Kevin, *The Rise and Decline of Fianna Fáil* (Dublin, 1982).

Boyce, D. G. (ed.), *The Revolution in Ireland 1879–1923* (London, 1988).

Brandenburg, S. J., 'Progress of land transfers in the Irish Free State', *Journal of Land and Public Utility Economics* viii, 3 (1932): 275–85.

Breen, Richard, 'Farm servanthood in Ireland 1900–40', *Economic History Review* xxxvi (1983): 87–102.

Brody, Hugh, *Innishkillane: Change and Decline in the West of Ireland* (London, 1973).

Brown, Terence, *Ireland: A Social and Cultural History* (London, 1981).

Bull, Philip, *Land, Politics and Nationalism: A Study of the Irish Land Question* (Dublin, 1996).

Campbell, Fergus, 'The hidden history of the Irish land war: a guide to local sources' in Carla King (ed.), *Famine, Land and Culture in Ireland* (Dublin, 2000), pp. 140–52.

Chubb, Basil, *The Government and Politics of Ireland* (Oxford, 1974).

Clarke, Samuel, *Social Origins of the Irish Land War* (Princeton, 1979).

Coleman, Marie, *County Longford and the Irish Revolution 1910–1923* (Dublin, 2003).

Colum, Padraic, *The Land* in Padraic Colum, *Three Plays* (Dublin, 1963 edn).

Comerford, R. V., *Fenians in Context: Irish Politics and Society 1848–82* (Dublin, 1998 edn [1st edn, 1985]).

Comerford, R. V., *Ireland* (London, 2003).

Commins, Patrick, *The Impact of Re-Distribution in Ireland 1923–1974: The Michael Dillon Memorial Lecture 1993* (Dublin, 1993).

Corkery, Daniel, *Synge and Anglo-Irish Literature: A Study* (Dublin, 1931).

Costello, Peter, 'Land and Liam O'Flaherty' in Carla King (ed.), *Famine, Land and Culture in Ireland* (Dublin, 2000), pp. 169–79.

Cronin, Mike, 'The socio-economic background and membership of the Blueshirt movement, 1932–35', *Irish Historical Studies* XXIX, 114 (Nov. 1994), pp. 234–49.

Cronin, Mike, *The Blueshirts and Irish Politics* (Dublin, 1997).

Cronin, Mike and Regan, J. M. (eds), *Ireland: The Politics of Independence, 1922–49* (Basingstoke, 2000).

Crotty, Raymond, *Irish Agricultural Production: its Volume and Structure* (Cork, 1966).

Daly, Mary E., *Social and Economic History of Ireland Since 1800* (Dublin, 1981).

Daly, Mary E., 'Social structure of the Dublin working class, 1871–1911', *Irish Historical Studies* XXIII, 90 (Nov. 1982).

Daly, Mary E., *The First Department: A History of the Department of Agriculture* (Dublin, 2002).

Daniel, T. K., 'Griffith on his noble head: the determinants of Cumann na nGaedheal economic policy, 1922–32', *Irish Economic and Social History* III (1976): 55–65.

Delaney, Enda, *Demography, State and Society: Irish Migration to Britain, 1912–1971* (Liverpool, 2000).

Donnelly, J. S. jr, *The Land and People of Nineteenth Century Cork* (London, 1975).

Donnelly, J. S. jr, 'The land question in nationalist politics' in T. E. Hachey and L.J. McCaffrey (eds), *Perspectives on Irish Nationalism* (Kentucky, 1989), pp. 79–98.

Dooley, Terence, 'Monaghan Protestants in a time of crisis, 1919–22' in R. V. Comerford et al. (eds), *Religion, Conflict and Coexistence in Ireland* (Dublin, 1990), pp. 235–51.

Dooley, Terence, *The Plight of Monaghan Protestants, 1911–26* (Dublin, 2000).

Dooley, Terence, *The Decline of the Big House in Ireland: A Study of Irish Landed Families, 1860–1960* (Dublin, 2001).

Dooley, Terence, 'IRA veterans and land division in independent Ireland, 1923–48' in Fearghal McGarry (ed.), *Republicanism in Modern Ireland* (Dublin, 2003), pp. 86–107.

Dooley, Terence, 'The Greatest of the Fenians': John Devoy and Ireland* (Dublin, 2003).

Dooley, Terence, *A Future for Irish Historic Houses: A Study of Fifty Houses* (Dublin, 2003).

Drudy, P. J. (ed.), *Ireland: Land, Politics and People* (Cambridge, 1982).

Dunphy, Richard, *The Making of Fianna Fáil Power in Ireland* (Oxford, 1995)

Fanning, Ronan, *The Irish Department of Finance 1922–58* (Dublin, 1979).

Fanning, Ronan, *Independent Ireland* (Dublin, 1983)

Farry, Michael, *Sligo 1914–1921: A Chronicle of Conflict* (Trim, 1992).

Farry, Michael, *The Aftermath of Revolution: Sligo 1921–23* (Dublin, 2000).

Fennell, Rosemary, *Industrialisation and Agricultural Development in the Congested Districts* (Dublin, 1962).

Fitzpatrick, David, *Politics and Irish Life, 1913–21* (Dublin, 1977)

Fitzpatrick, David, 'The geography of Irish nationalism', *Past and Present* 77 (1978): 113–37

Fitzpatrick, David, *The Two Irelands 1912–1939* (Oxford, 1998)

Foster, R. F., *Modern Ireland 1600–1972* (London, 1989 edn).

Gallagher, Michael, *Electoral Support for Irish Political Parties, 1927–73* (London, 1976).

Garvin, Tom, *The Evolution of Irish Nationalist Politics* (Dublin, 1981).

Garvin, Tom, *1922: the Birth of Irish Democracy* (Dublin, 1996).

Geary, Laurence, *The Plan of Campaign 1886–91* (Cork, 1985),

Geary, R. C. and Hughes, J. G., *Internal Migration in Ireland*, ESRI paper no. 54 (Dublin, 1970).

Gillmor, D. A., *Agriculture in the Republic of Ireland* (Budapest, 1977).

Hanley, Brian *The IRA, 1926–1936* (Dublin, 2002).

Hannan, D. F. and Commins, Patrick 'The significance of small-scale landholders in Ireland's socio-economic transformation' in J. H. Goldthorpe and C. T. Whelan (eds), *The Development of Industrial Society in Ireland* (Oxford, 1992), pp. 79–104.

Hannan, D. F., and Katsiaouni, Louise, *Traditional Families? From Culturally Prescribed to Negotiated Roles in Farm Families*, ESRI paper no. 87 (Dublin, 1977).

Hart, Peter, 'The Protestant experience of revolution in Ireland' in Richard English and Graham Walker (eds), *Unionism in Modern Ireland* (Dublin, 1996), pp. 81–98.

Hart, Peter, 'The geography of revolution in Ireland 1917–1923', *Past and Present* 155 (May 1997), pp. 142–76.

Hart, Peter, *The IRA and its Enemies: Violence and Community in Cork, 1916–1923* (Oxford, 1998)

Hart, Peter, 'Defining the Irish revolution' in Joost Augusteijn (ed.), *The Irish Revolution* (Basingstoke, 2003), pp. 17–33.

Higgins, J., *A Study of Part-time Farmers in the Republic of Ireland: Socio-Economic Research Series, no. 3* (Dublin, 1983).

Hoctor, Daniel, *The Department's Story: A History of the Department of Agriculture* (Dublin, 1971).

Hooker, E. R., *Readjustments of Agricultural Tenure in Ireland* (Chapel Hill, 1938).

Hopkinson, Michael, *Green Against Green: The Irish Civil War* (Dublin, 1988).

Horgan, John, *Seán Lemass: The Enigmatic Patriot* (Dublin, 1997).

Hughes J. G., and Walsh, B. M., *Internal Migration Flows in Ireland and their Determinants: ESRI Paper no. 90* (Dublin, 1980).

Irish Farmers' Association, *Low Farm Incomes in Western Counties: The Problems and the Policies* (n.d.).

Jackson, Alvin, *Ireland, 1798–1998* (Oxford, 1999)

Johnson, D. S., *The Inter-War Economy in Ireland* (Dundalk, 1985).

Jones, David Seth, *Graziers, Land Reform and Political Conflict in Ireland* (Washington, 1995)

Jones, David Seth, 'Land reform legislation and security of tenure in Ireland after independence', *Eire-Ireland* XXXII–XXXIII (1997–8): 116–43.

Jones, David Seth, 'Divisions within the Irish government over land-distribution policy, 1940–70', *Eire-Ireland* XXXVI (Fall/Winter 2001): 83–109.

Kavanagh, Patrick, *The Green Fool* (London, 1971 edn).

Kavanagh, Patrick, *Tarry Flynn* (London, 1972 edn).

Keane, John B., *The Field* (Dublin, 1993 edn).

Kennedy, Kieran, and Dowling, Brendan, *Economic Growth in Ireland: The Experience since 1947* (Dublin, 1975).

Kennedy, Liam, 'A sceptical view on the reinacarnation of the Irish "gombeenman"', *Economic and Social Review* 8, 3 (1976–7): 213–21.

Keogh, Dermot, *Twentieth Century Ireland: Nation and State* (Dublin, 1994)

Kickham, C. J., *Knocknagow or the Homes of Tipperary* (1873).

King, Carla (ed.), *Famine, Land and Culture in Ireland* (Dublin, 2000).

Kotsonouris, Mary, *Retreat From Revolution: the Dáil Courts 1920–24* (Dublin, 1994).

Laffan, Michael, *The Resurrection of Ireland: The Sinn Féin Party, 1916–1923* (Cambridge, 1999).

Lee, J. J., *Ireland 1912–1985: Politics and Society* (Cambridge, 1989)

Lynch, Patrick, 'The social revolution that never was' in Desmond Williams (ed.), *The Irish Struggle, 1916–1926* (London, 1966), pp. 41–54.

Lyons, F. S. L., *Ireland Since the Famine* (London, 1973 edn)

MacAodha, B. S., *Conacre in Ireland: the Distribution of Conacre in the Twenty-six Counties* (Dublin, 1967).

MacCabe. F. F. and Healey, T. E., 'Racing, steeplechasing and breeding in Ireland' in Charles Richardson (ed.), *British Steeplechasing* (London, 1927).

McCarthy, J. F., (ed.), *Planning Ireland's Future: The Legacy of T. K. Whitaker* (Dublin, 1990).

McCullough, David, *A Makeshift Majority: The First Inter-Party Government 1948–51* (Dublin, 1998).

McDermott, Eithne, *Clan na Poblachta* (Cork, 1998).

Mac Donncha, Padraig, 'Ráthcairn: 50 Bliain ar Aghaidh', *Comhar* (Apr. 1985).

McDowell, R. B., *Crisis and Decline: The Fate of Southern Unionists* (Dublin, 1997).

MacGabhann, Seamus, 'A people's art: the great songs of Meath and Oriel', *Riocht na Midhe* 9, 4 (1998): 103–19.

McGahern, John, *That They May Face the Rising Sun* (London, 2002)

McGahern, John, *The Collected Stories* (London, 1992).

McLaverty, Michael, *Lost Fields* (New York, 1941).

Macken, Walter, *The Bogman* (London, 1952).

Maguire, Des, *The Land Commission* (Bray, n.d.).

Maguire, Des, *The Land Problem: A Guide to Land Leasing* (Dublin, 1983).

Manning, Maurice, *The Blueshirts* (Dublin, 1987).

Manning, Maurice, *James Dillon: A Biography* (Dublin, 1999).

Maume, Patrick, *The Long Gestation: Irish Nationalist Life, 1891–1918* (Dublin, 1999).

Mayne, Rutherford [S. J. Waddell], *Bridge Head* (Dublin, n.d.).

Meath County Council, *Local Plan for Rathcairn Gaeltacht* (n.d. [c.1979]).

Meenan, James, *The Irish Economy since 1922* (Liverpool, 1970).

Micks, W. L., *The History of the Congested Districts Board* (Dublin, 1925).

Mitchell, Arthur, *Revolutionary Government in Ireland: Dáil Éireann 1919–22* (Dublin, 1995).

Moody, T. W., *Davitt and Irish Revolution 1846–82* (Oxford, 1981)

Murphy, B. S., "The land for the people, the road for the bullock": Lia Fáil, the smallholders crisis and public policy in Ireland, 1957–60' in William Nolan and T. P. O'Neill (eds), *Offaly History and Society* (Dublin, 1998), pp. 855–88.

Murphy, J. A. 'The Irish party system, 1948–51' in K. B. Nowlan and T. D. Williams (eds), *Ireland in the War Years and After* (Dublin, 1969), pp. 147–66.

Murphy, J. A., *Ireland in the Twentieth Century* (Dublin, n.d.).

Neary, J. P., and Ó Gráda, Cormac, *Protection, Economic War and Structural Change: The 1930s in Ireland* (London, 1986).

Nolan, William, 'New farms and fields: migration policies of state land agencies 1891–1980' in W. J. Smyth and Kevin Whelan (eds), *Common Ground: Essays on the Historical Geography of Ireland* (Cork, 1988).

Nowlan, K. B. and Williams, T. D. (eds), *Ireland in the War Years and After, 1939–1951* (Dublin, 1969).

O'Brien, George, 'Patrick Hogan', *Studies* xxv (Sept. 1936): 353–68.

O'Connor, Emmet, 'Agrarian unrest and the labour movement in County Waterford, 1917–1923', *Saothar* vi (1980): 40–58.

O'Connor, Emmet, *A Labour History of Ireland 1824–1960* (Dublin, 1992).

Ó Gráda, Cormac, *Ireland: A New Economic History 1780–1939* (Oxford, 1994)

Ó Gráda, Cormac, *A Rocky Road: The Irish Economy Since the 1920s* (Manchester, 1997)

O'Halpin, Eunan, *Defending Ireland: The Irish State and its Enemies Since 1922* (Oxford, 1999)

Ó Tuathaigh, Gearoid, 'Aistriú Pobail Ghaeltachta go hÁiteanna Eile in Éirinn: Culrá an Pholaisí' in Michéal Ó Conghaile (ed.), *Gaeltach Ráthcairn: Leachtaí Comórtha* (Galway, 1986), pp. 13–31.

Orridge, A., 'The Blueshirts and the "Economic War": a study of Ireland in the context of dependency theory', *Political Studies* xxxi (1983).

Patterson, Henry, *The Politics of Illusion: Republicanism and Socialism in Modern Ireland* (London, 1989).

Pomfret, J. E., *The Struggle for Land in Ireland 1800–1923* (Princeton, NJ, 1930).

Regan, J. M., *The Irish Counter-Revolution, 1921–36* (Dublin, 1999).

Rumpf, Erhardt and Hepburn, A. C., *Nationalism and Socialism in Twentieth- Century Ireland* (Dublin, 1977)

Sheehan, P. A., *The Graves of Kilmorna: A Story of '67* (New York, 1915)

Solow, B. L., *The Land Question and the Irish Economy 1870–1903* (Cambridge, Mass., 1971).

Thomas, Conal, *The Land for the People: The United Irish League and Land Reform in North Galway, 1898–1912* (Corrandulla Co. Galway, 1999).

Townshend, Charles, *Political Violence in Ireland* (Oxford, 1983).

Townshend, Charles, *Ireland: The 20th Century* (Oxford, 1999)

Travers, Pauric, 'Emigration and gender: the case of Ireland, 1922–60' in Mary O'Dowd and Sabine Wichert (eds.), *Chattel, Servant or Citizen? Women's Status in Church, State and Society* (Belfast, 1995), pp. 187–99.

Varley, Tony, 'Farmers against nationalists: the rise and fall of Clann na Talmhan in Galway' in Gerard Moran (ed.), *Galway: History and Society* (Dublin, 1996), pp. 580–622.

Vaughan, W. E., *Sin, Sheep and Scotsmen: John George Adair and the Derryveagh Evictions, 1861* (Belfast, 1983).

Vaughan, W. E., *Landlords and Tenants in Mid-Victorian Ireland* (Oxford, 1994).

UNPUBLISHED THESES

McEvoy, J. N., 'A study of the United Irish League in King's County, 1899–1918' (MA thesis, NUI, Maynooth, 1990).

Sheehan, J. T., 'Land purchase policy in Ireland, 1917–23: From the Irish Convention to the 1923 Land Act' (MA thesis, NUI, Maynooth, 1993).

Index